The Dressing Station

Jonathan Kaplan

The Dressing Station

a surgeon's chronicle
of war and medicine

GROVE PRESS
New York

First published in 2001 in Great Britain by Picador, London, England

Published simultaneously in Canada
Printed in the United States of America

FIRST AMERICAN EDITION

Library of Congress Cataloging-in-Publication Data

Kaplan, Jonathan, 1954–
The dressing station : a surgeon's chronicle of war and medicine / Jonathan Kaplan.
p. cm.
ISBN 0-8021-1707-4
1. Kaplan, Jonathan, 1954– 2. Surgeons—Biography. 3. Medicine, Military—History.

R134 .K35 2002
617'.092—dc21
[B] 2001051241

Grove Press
841 Broadway
New York, NY 10003

02 03 04 05 10 9 8 7 6 5 4 3 2 1

This book is dedicated to my parents,
Dr Cyril Kaplan and Dr Sylvia Kisner,
and to colleagues, teachers, friends and
comrades, both living and dead.
It is they who have revealed to me
all that I have learned within and beyond
the practice of medicine.

Contents

Prologue

I am a surgeon, some of the time. In certain clinical situations – penetrating wounds, massive bleeding – there remains no treatment but the knife. I have been fortunate, at times, to have saved the lives of patients who reached me on the threshold of death. Much of my work has dealt with trauma; among people changed abruptly from wholeness to injury, with all the fear of sudden mortality. Some of it has taken place in extreme circumstances – with only the most basic of resources – against a backdrop of dislocation and despair. I have seen people die, of wounds or disease or deprivation, and been unable to help.

All doctors have their ghosts. Sometimes they jostle me: the ones I couldn't save, the ones I killed. For all of us – even the most dedicated and skilled – the dead pile up, the results of decisions swayed by fatigue or hubris or blind bad luck. And there are those who are simply the inexorable casualties of the system, for medicine is not always benign or balanced, or even practised necessarily to the benefit of the suffering. Every loss diminishes us, yet with clinical detachment – and with exhilaration, fear and fatalism – we continue, always in the hope of redemption.

I have practised medicine in diverse fields: as a hospital surgeon, a flying doctor, a ship's medical officer. I have operated on wounded straight off the battlefield, treated people with rich strains of tropical disease raging in their bloodstreams, and tried to help those afflicted by occupational illness from industrial toxins or work-place stress. I have run research programmes funded by corporate finance – that met the needs of shareholders before they benefited any patients – and I've cared for children wasted by the diseases of famine and war. Like most doctors, I have seen my craft used and abused; been a part of its successes and witnessed its failings. It is by the terms of this unforgiving arena that we struggle to define ourselves.

No clinician can give an objective account of that work: the interaction between doctor and patient is mutual and intimate, and in the end comes down to something between us that is a fragile thing, as fragile as life. All we can do is the best we can in the war against death and against despair, including our own. For at its extremes the practice of medicine is a succession of front lines, and each victory is only a temporary respite. Perhaps you wonder what it's like to stand at that intense interface. Perhaps you believe in the existence of some profound morality, some metaphysical awareness that is vouchsafed by contact with the texture of suffering and the aura of pain. I guarantee nothing; you will have to find out for yourself. Come and see.

1

South Africa

I grew up with the expectation that I would serve. One of my mother's brothers went through the Somalia campaign as a regimental surgeon in the King's African Rifles; he'd been commended for bravery. The other had been an army engineer, clearing German minefields under fire in the Western Desert. My father spent five years in uniform, in Africa and Europe, treating casualties in tented field hospitals. His medical colleagues – our family friends – had been there too. His anaesthetist received a medal for diving off the deck of a hospital ship in the shark-thick Mozambique Channel to rescue an African soldier, maddened from a head-wound, who had thrown himself overboard. Even my dentist had a covert fame, from the time when he had worked in an army hospital in North Africa and replaced his uniform badges with ones cast in gold ('Fillings, Officers, for the use of'), easily convertible to cash during abandoned weekends in Cairo's brothels and bars.

We were a medical family: my father the orthopaedic surgeon, his brother the virologist; my mother the pathologist, her brother the urologist. In Durban, as we walked along the beachfront, we got respect. People would approach my father, expecting that he should instantly remember the history of their pain and survival. He used the trick (I have since used it myself) of asking to see their scars, and from the track of the knife he would recall first the operation, then the problem, and often, finally, their names. Among these erstwhile patients, as well as among the nurses and doctors I met as I trailed my father on his rounds through the hospital wards, the assumption was clear: I too would become a doctor, and serve. Exactly what form that service would take was uncertain: with the prospect of political change in South Africa apparently remote, there seemed no great, impending conflict in which I would be tested.

I was accepted by the School of Medicine at Cape Town University and, beneath the loom of Table Mountain, found a new burden of tradition. The university library contained the same leather-bound volumes by Wells and Kipling that my father had read. In the chemical reek of the dissecting rooms I studied the same intricate anatomy texts, and laughed at the old practical jokes involving cadaver fingers slipped into the lunch boxes of the unsuspecting. The senior anatomist – an elderly rake who wore a linen suit and sported the Panama hat, white goatee and moustache that a brand of fried chicken was later to make famous – had been there for four decades, and talked wistfully of the 'gentlemen' he had taught before the war. He would hold tea parties in his office for groups of old ladies, trying to coax them into leaving their bodies to science. Afterwards he led them on a tour of the dissecting rooms, warning us in advance to be on our best behaviour.

'Think of yourselves resting here, girls,' he would say, patting the enamel tables, 'in the hands of these young men,' and the ladies would giggle and gasp, and, presumably, be seduced.

These first years of study were basic blood and bones: anatomy, physiology, pathology and bacteriology, pharmacology. Some took their studies seriously, attending every lecture and reading textbooks into the night, but for myself and my friends there were too many diversions to learn any more than we needed to get through the examinations. The sun shone for nine months a year and white beaches surrounded us, washed on one side by green Indian Ocean breakers and on the other by the cold swell of the Atlantic. There was surfing and diving and cinemas and parties and pinball bars, and the all-night clubs near the harbour frequented by prostitutes and drunken sailors. On weekends we would leave the city to stay on farms in the wine lands or in beach cottages along the striking coastline.

It was extraordinary how frivolously we lived: in student paradise. Cape Town was a cosmopolitan outpost at the continent's tip, created by the first European settlers. Africa began beyond the city, on the bleak sand-plain known as the Cape Flats. This was the site of racially classified townships that supplied labour for the factories, and the domestic servants who maintained white homes to a standard envied by overseas visitors. Few white South Africans – apart from policemen and officials – ever ventured inside the townships, where garbage burned on the streets and the silhouette of Table Mountain shimmered in the summer's heat.

We weren't really callous, or blind to the iniquities of a political system that denied the basic freedoms of most of the country's people. It dictated the identities of our classmates: the university's intake was controlled by government quotas that limited 'non-white' students to ten per cent, few of whom could surmount the deficiencies of their segregated schooling to meet the entrance requirements for medical studies. There were groups trying to raise political awareness on campus, meeting with underground black trade union organizers and discussing revolutionary theory, but such activities seemed of little value in the face of the state's pervasive grip.

Politics had been a significant issue when my father was a medical student. In 1937 he and a friend had decided to go to Spain as volunteers to join the International Brigades fighting for the Republic. They went to tell a much-respected professor of their decision. The man had served in the Great War, and knew something of the impatience of youth. He too had been watching events unfold in Europe.

'This is just the first round in the war against fascism,' he told them. 'It will go on for years, right across the world. You want to go and help the people of Spain. As soldiers [he had the kindness not to call them cannon-fodder] you may kill some of the enemy, or be killed. But, if you really wish to help, you can do much more as trained doctors. There are going to be many sick and wounded who'll need your care.' Persuaded, they had finished their studies, graduating at the end of 1940 and going directly into uniform.

For us the equivalent might have been to leave the country and join the ANC in exile, but few of us had that sort of commitment. I don't think we had much comprehension of being useful in any worthwhile way; we hadn't even seen a patient yet, and would only do so when we started our clinical training a year later. So the first time I got blood on my hands had little to do with my studies. It began, improbably, in the middle of a dull basic-sciences lecture.

A small group of students had marched through the centre of Cape Town that morning, carrying banners calling for an end to apartheid. By lunchtime they were ranged on the steps of the Anglican cathedral near the Parliament buildings, their banners aloft, when the police arrived. A stand-off ensued in the warm sunshine, with motorists steering carefully along the road between the opposing groups. Though the police seemed uncertain about taking action against the students in such a public place, riot squad reinforcements were gathering in the sidestreets, and student messengers were sent to the campus to ask for help.

I was drowsing over my lecture notes when there was a bustle in the corridor outside, and the sound of running feet.

The door to the lecture hall opened with a crash. A face peered in and addressed us, ignoring the man at the podium.

'There's going to be trouble at St George's Cathedral; hundreds of cops and riot trucks. We need lots of people there; they can't arrest everyone.'

'Young man!' shouted the lecturer, but the messenger had already left to spread the word. A few of my friends stood up. I joined them. Perhaps ten, in that class of a hundred, made for the door. Some of our classmates hissed at us. The lecturer glowered, and a Catholic girl crossed herself. Outside it was clear that there had been a much better response from the liberal arts faculties, for all over campus students streamed out of the buildings and jostled for lifts, piling into cars and pickups and VW buses that roared off down to the highway that led to town.

We approached the cathedral from the rear, through public gardens unusually empty of sweepers and gardeners and nannies with their charges. From ahead came a thready chanting and a thumping sound that I couldn't identify. Rounding the building, we came to where the battle lines were drawn. A host of students, men and women, occupied the stone steps of the cathedral and the pavement in front of it. Across the street, drawn up in solid rows, stood a phalanx of riot police. Steady as a heartbeat, they struck their batons against the Perspex shields they carried. The crowd flinched at each resounding blow, shrinking back towards the cathedral steps. Then a police colonel stepped to the front of the line, sunlight blinking off the braid on his cap. In one hand he held a yellow megaphone.

'This is a prohibited gathering.' The metallic warp cut through the sudden silence. 'You have thirty seconds to disperse.'

He stood there in his dark uniform, the bright yellow cone raised to his mouth.

'It's Daffy Duck!' yelled a wag in the crowd, and a roar of laughter drowned out the colonel's next words. He turned to the police lines, raising an arm. There was a cracking sound and tear-gas canisters lofted skyward, trailing arcs of haze. They struck the street, squirting smoke as they rolled towards us. A student scooped one up and flung it back into the police ranks, where it fumed under their feet. Gagging and swearing, the riot cops reeled, then charged in a body, their long batons raised. The banner-holders in the front went down under a storm of blows and were dragged across the roadway to the waiting trucks. The rest of us fled up the cathedral steps, gas canisters churning white clouds under our feet. We kicked them off the top step and stared, horrified, at the melee below, where people screamed and choked in the rising smoke and knots of students cowered under flailing clubs.

Men and women leapt up the steps, their arms outstretched towards us, while red-faced cops grabbed at their clothes and hurled them down, kicking them as they fell. In front of me a grisly tugging match ensued as we dragged at the hands of a girl while a policeman continued to rain blows on her back and legs. There was a shouted command and she fell, sobbing, into our arms. The police line retreated, stair by stair, exposing a wasteland of blood-splashed stone and lost shoes. We stood at the top of the stairs between the open cathedral doors. My eyes streamed; the gas stung my lips and smarted where it found moisture on my sweating face. People retched and coughed. Some helped to pass our injured to the rear, and carry them inside the nave. Others screamed insults at the police, calling them slime and filth and Boer baboons.

A breeze turned the scraps of paper in the street, thinning the tear-gas haze. The noise of the city returned, and I could hear the voices of office workers watching us from the windows of the buildings opposite. Then the colonel's megaphone screeched again.

'You are all under arrest!'

From our step came ragged laughter and shouts of defiance.

'Come and get us, you fuckers!' screamed a girl in a torn coat, then fell silent. Fresh police files were wheeling into line in the street below and lock-up trucks were backing up, their mesh doors open. The colonel waved his swagger-stick; the cops charged and the students recoiled. Those who could fled back into the church, the press of bodies carrying me with it. Over their heads I could see the flash of falling batons and hear the crack as they made contact. A tear-gas canister was bowled through the opening and then the doors shut with a crash on the daylight outside. Some students sprinted down the aisles to escape through the transepts, but those doors too were slammed shut before they reached them. We were sealed inside. From the street came cries, and the sounds of beatings.

The gloomy nave seemed filled with people. Some sobbed, or dashed about frantically, their chests heaving. Others staggered where they stood, their hair matted from bleeding scalp wounds. The shock of confrontation had revealed us for what we were: a bunch of self-styled rebels without cohesion. Someone had clapped a cleaner's bucket over the tear-gas canister, but trails of smoke leaked along the floor around its edge. It was not only the gas that made our eyes burn. I collapsed on a pew and lit a cigarette, my hands trembling.

'Not a fastidious churchgoer, I see,' said a voice beside me. I looked up and recognized the speaker, a medical student in the year ahead of me. Stefan gazed around at the defeated mob and shook his head. 'Looks like Casualty on a Saturday night,' he said. 'Smoke up, and we'll do something constructive.'

This was my first taste of trauma, but Stefan seemed to know what to do. He stood on a pew and addressed the refugees, his voice cutting through the moans and whimpers.

'Let's get the injured seen to,' he said. 'Anyone got some clean cloth?'

A girl pulled a blouse from her bag and held it up. Someone else produced a white lab-coat, and a couple of handkerchiefs were handed forward.

'Bring all those who've been hurt here to the front,' said Stefan, and he began, with the help of a penknife, to tear the fabric into strips. A cavalcade of wounded were assisted from the shadows; limping, shoeless, with bloodied faces and lacerated heads. I looked at their ragged cuts and thought I might faint. I set to work nervously, folding the cloth into pads and holding them against gashed scalps to staunch the bleeding. Other volunteers came forward to help. Stefan appeared at my side.

'Reassure them,' he said softly. 'Tell them head wounds always bleed a lot, but they soon stop. Tell them it's going to be OK.'

Stefan had gathered the worst tear-gas victims at the font. Some, their faces scorched by the irritant gas, could hardly see between their swollen eyelids. He spoke to them gently as he bathed the blistered skin. 'Don't worry, it burns at first when the water reacts with the chemicals. It'll stop after a few seconds.' His voice worked like a tranquillizer, and I began to understand a little of what healing involved.

✪

I had treated my first casualties, however minor, and embraced my first cause. 'The Siege of St George's' they called it in the papers the next morning, and those of us who had been there gained a brief notoriety. A few went on to make names for themselves as political activists. One of them was my friend Stefan. For a while I occupied a student squat with him and Neil and Nils; the Marxist-Lentilists, who shared an admiration for Albanian communism and a conviction that meat or fruit, or anything but the most rigorous of subsistence diets signified bourgeois softness and a betrayal of the oppressed masses. They shared their spartan meals with some coloured children who slept rough in the cemetery behind the house, and laughed when our possessions were regularly stolen – 'redistributed' – by the most enterprising among them.

I didn't really mind the absence of luxuries. I was short of money and augmenting my living allowance by working as a mechanic, rebuilding the engines of the VW buses and Beetles that were the most popular student transport. And my social life had improved. Our kitchen was always full of people talking socialism through the night. A number of them were young women, attracted to the aura of revolutionary virility that hung around the house. With a few gallon jugs of proletarian wine the gatherings became parties. Though I didn't pretend to be an activist, some of the girls would try to expand my political consciousness through slippery sex, augmented by potent buds of marijuana.

But I was becoming aware of the political aspects of studying medicine in South Africa, as one of the select minority who qualified. The ironies of this privilege became apparent when we started our clinical training. Our professors adhered to the exacting standards of the English medical schools from which most of them had graduated. They had been drawn to the University of Cape Town's Groote Schuur Hospital because it was an international centre of excellence; it was here that the world's first heart transplant had been performed in 1967, and overseas doctors considered themselves honoured to work in the department of cardiac surgery and other specialities. One day we too would enter that elect society of healers, and begin to make a difference to humanity. Our medical training was rigorous and complete, for what we had in abundant supply was 'clinical material': the disinherited and oppressed from the townships and bleak rural homelands.

We would see pathology that had all but disappeared in the developed West. TB patients coughed up bloody sputum, their heaving chests resonant from cavities where the disease had corroded their lungs. On the neurology ward a patient, asked to stand, would reel when he closed his eyes, and walk with stamping, uncertain feet. 'Come now,' our tutor challenged, 'are we looking at Beriberi or General Paresis of the Insane?' and we would strain our diagnostic faculties to try to distinguish vitamin-deficient dementia from delusions of grandeur, and to identify the vacant face and irregular pupils of advanced syphilis. Schizophrenics would be admitted to the psychiatric wards with florid catatonia, holding for hours the positions in which their ductile limbs were placed. By the time some cancer patients reached us from the rural areas their tumours would be huge and ulcerating and beyond hope: graphic opportunities for the surgeons to demonstrate to us their cutting skills.

There was also exposure to more acute surgical crises. Violence seemed to be the main export of the Cape Flats townships. Those of us who wished could spend nights working in the accident and emergency department, clamping arteries and stitching wounds. An excitable camaraderie embraced us all – nurses, orderlies, students and casualty officers – facing that steady tide of perforated bodies, as we worked together to stop bleeding and stabilize vital signs. I began to gain a little more confidence in my skills and judgement, but remained in awe of the registrars and consultants who stood solid in that workshop of pain, making life-saving decisions. It was terrifying to imagine that I might ever have to shoulder such responsibilities myself.

Other experiences invoked a vertiginous awareness of our own mortality. We saw patients pass through the terminal stages of illness, and followed the hospital cardiac arrest teams to hover at the fringes of unsuccessful resuscitations. Learning clinical pathology, we crowded around the autopsy tables to see the face of victorious disease. Probably for the first time, I truly realized that one day I would die. It was disturbingly easy to imagine myself on the slab, sliced and gutted, with the pathologist opening my chest with a buzzsaw and his assistant sluicing away the blood clots. Most graphic were the sights in the police mortuary, where, during our study of forensic medicine, we would see every permutation of unnatural death.

The white bodies tended to be tidier. There was a regular attrition among young men in that society, who went scuba diving and hang-gliding and rock climbing, or drove too fast on winding mountain roads. A few, beaten down by loneliness or the fear of failure, would hang themselves or take fatal overdoses. In the 'non-white' mortuary (here too the principle of racial segregation was observed) the corpses were less reposeful: dead from spear-thrust, gunshot and axe. Bodies were disembowelled, bled dry from multiple chop-wounds, or contracted and charred by fire. They came from a place beyond the frontier of our known lives, where other rules of death appeared to prevail.

What we felt about that place was a sort of horror. People slaughtered each other there in a malevolent frenzy. One day, on the autopsy table, lay the body of a young woman. She was exquisitely beautiful. Even the coarse line of undertaker's stitches that ran from her neck down between her breasts to her pubic hair could not diminish her perfection. She had bled to death; gang-raped and then despatched with a bottle kicked up her vagina that had shattered, slashing the arteries in her pelvis. The social theorists would explain such incidents as the product of economic despair, or rage at the impotence that apartheid had produced among the dispossessed. I felt dizzy, terrified at the thought of such contemptuous destruction. The only way to deal with that fear was to keep it at bay through clinical detachment, clinical study.

So we lay on the beach and studied, slept and studied, fell in love and studied. A number of my classmates were pairing off, getting married, setting up medical partnerships for the future. Others were planning to specialize, dreaming of a secure future of private practice and social standing. When I visited Durban my parent's friends smiled at me, and nodded their approval.

'You'll do orthopaedics, like your father,' they suggested. 'You can join his practice. One day he'll need someone to carry on his work.'

The idea seemed quite improbable. The charm of the city's avenues of jacaranda trees, the genteel respect of my father's patients, even his worthy work at the black leper hospital up the coast, appeared irrelevant and transitory. Something apocalyptic was about to happen.

⊕

In 1975 the South African army invaded Angola. Late the previous year there had been a coup in Portugal, led by junior officers against a senile military government. The officers objected to the slaughter of so many young conscripts in the Portuguese colonies of Angola and Mozambique, where they were fighting an unwinnable conflict against black independence movements. Their first move on taking power was to divest Portugal of its overseas possessions. Suddenly the colonial authorities were gone, along with many of the white settlers. Units of the main Angolan independence force, the MPLA (Popular Movement for the Liberation of Angola) entered the capital. Shortly afterwards there was heavy fighting to the south of the city, and a column of tanks and troops rolled in; white men speaking Afrikaans. The South African army was operating outside its country's borders for the first time since the Second World War.

I expected, like all white males in South Africa, to do National Service. Call-up came directly on leaving school at sixteen or seventeen to spend a year in desolate base towns in the Karoo or the Highveld, being bullied through drill and inspections by Permanent Force sergeants. For farm kids it represented a chance to experience the sophisticated delights of tinned food and a daily change of socks. City boys aimed for the navy, where they might have a chance to polish their surfing skills in Cape Town or Durban. You could apply for deferment to go to university, at the end of which you were called up anyway, to apply your tertiary education in mysterious ways: accountants would be sent to repair tanks, engineers to army intelligence, linguists to the quartermaster's arm. For most young men, service in the South African Defence force offered the prospect of a long period of dullness, enlivened only by the opportunity for some gratuitous damage to government property such as rolling a Bedford truck. The army had a high rate of serious motor accidents. Only graduating doctors could find any merit in this; drafted into the medical corps once you'd finished your year of hospital internship, you might see some vehicle trauma between treating conscripts' athlete's foot.

Now all that was changed. The Angolan invasion had been repelled by Cuban troops airlifted in to help the MPLA. Driven back to South West Africa, the army dug in along the Angolan border. The 'operational zone' extended from the Atlantic coast in the west to Rhodesia, where Ian Smith's government was losing its own war against black guerrilla forces. It was in the operational zone that you now did your service, which was extended to two years. From the border district of Ovamboland the army launched regular attacks into Angola. Even Ovamboland was enemy territory: the populace were supporters of SWAPO, the South West African Peoples' Organization, whose military wing was waging its own struggle against the South African occupiers.

The next year things got worse. In 1976 the Pretoria government decided that all black schoolchildren across South Africa should be taught in Afrikaans. There was enormous resentment against the decree. It was pointed out that few children, or their teachers, knew the language. Petitions were submitted, school deputations sent to the government. All were ignored. The children poured out of their schools onto the streets of Soweto, waving rough placards. The police opened fire, killing some kids and wounding many others. The accumulated pressures of almost thirty years of apartheid could no longer be contained. Pupils, parents and workers marched on every symbol of the hated system – schools, administration offices, government beerhalls – and burned them to the ground. Roads were blocked with flaming tyres. For two days the police couldn't enter Soweto, until they came in armoured cars. It took months to crush the uprising in the townships around Johannesburg, by which time it had spread across the country.

Many hundreds of blacks died, and a few whites; killed by mobs as they drove too near to the townships and were caught in the conflagration. Suddenly all those atavistic fears of ravening black hordes seemed about to become reality. As unrest became endemic, the tacticians of apartheid declared that the 'Total Onslaught' was upon us, and a 'Total Strategy' was needed to counter it. The army, already aggressively committed along the borders, would now also serve in the townships. The war was everywhere, but it hadn't yet touched me directly. In the temporary stillness of the storm's centre I concentrated on learning my art.

2

South Africa

There is a unique thrill to operating. Opening a belly, for example, and knowing how the layers of the abdominal wall will cleave under the line of the knife. The skin, bronzed by the coat of sterilizing iodine, must be opened in a single sweep, for its elastic tension pulls the wound-ends apart, and later extensions to the cut will look dog-eared and ragged. Under the skin lies fat; creamy or a rich yellow, dense or semi-liquid, according to body type and diet. As it parts, the first drops of red are starting from the cut surfaces. They are promptly sealed by cautery forceps, and a wisp of blue smoke and a brief smell of barbecue rise under the theatre lights.

Then comes the muscle layer, easiest to split along its fibrous junction in the midline. This must be divided with care, for immediately beneath it lie delicate structures: the sliding contents of the abdominal cavity and the delicate film of the peritoneum that sheaths them. A small hole is made with scissors. The cut gapes like a buttonhole. You slide your fingers behind the muscle sheath – the first intimate contact with the patient – and the scissors advance, clipping through fibres that grit faintly between the steel jaws.

The peritoneum itself is cut next, its milky blue membrane retracting like an anemone. Retractors are hooked into the wound edges and the frame cranked apart, and a wonderland is revealed. Loops of neatly layered bowel pulsate in slow waves like wind over a cornfield. The edge of the liver, a rich brown, forms a notched line below the ribcage, and nuggets of fat gleam among the fine vessels that fan out between the translucent layers of the mesentery. A faint odour, fresh yet slightly sour, rises from the exposed tissue.

Not every abdomen looks like this inside. Sometimes the fine architecture has been blasted and torn. Such bellies might carry a warning: the blue hole of a bullet wound or the pout of a stab. Sometimes there is only the sullen crescent of a bruise beneath the ribs that tells of a blow sufficient to rupture the delicate organs within. A common factor is rigidity of the abdominal muscles – 'board-like', as the textbooks call it – fixed in an involuntary spasm that attempts to guard against the pain of movement. The patient may be in shock, with a high pulse and falling blood pressure, and getting him to surgery will be a priority. As soon as he is stable enough to endure the hazards of an anaesthetic – and sometimes before, while resuscitation is still underway – the abdomen is opened.

The first thing that will strike you is the smell, the reek of an abattoir. A swill of blood, bile and faeces obscures the clean structures, signifying ruptured viscera and torn vessels. Bowel can wait a while for patching; bleeding can't, and while the anaesthetist pumps transfusions into neck or arm veins, the surgeon looks for where it leaks, and he sweats. Even old hands, veteran operators, feel the fear as dark blood wells from down where the great vessels lie. Sometimes I still dream about that feeling of helplessness, when my knowledge seems useless against the implacable approach of death. It began when I opened my first patient, in a hospital near the edge of Cape Town.

⊕

Conradie was an old army hospital, now converted to civilian use. It included a spinal unit, general medical and surgical wards, a paediatric department and a small neurosurgery unit. Long barrack wards with wide verandas lay among a grid of paths, along which raced the wheelchairs of the paraplegics. Khaki-clad convicts from a local jail mowed the grass and dressed the regimented flower-beds, while prison officers supervised the work from the shade, pointing with their thermos flasks. As a district hospital with a reputation for roughness, it was avoided by the academic high-flyers, who preferred the ambience of the university teaching hospital. It was here that I came to take up the post of surgical house-officer, shortly after graduating from medical school.

Conradie Hospital lay in an unusual position. On one side stretched the expansive avenues and bungalow homes of Pinelands, a white suburb of watered lawns where civil servants retired to bully their servants. The Cape Flats began on the other, a mosaic of concrete cube-houses and potholed roads that zoned the grey beach-sand into 'townships' – Mitchell's Plain for 'coloureds'; Nyanga, Langa and Gugulethu for blacks – and between them stunted jungles of scrub willow that hid the tracks and shanties of squatter settlements thrown up by migrants from the hinterland. The hospital served all races, after a fashion, with its patients delivered in racially specific ambulances to its segregated casualty departments.

It was often busy. The odd solid citizen from Pinelands, with diabetes or an asthma attack, would arrive in 'white' Casualty, expecting instant service from the single medical officer on night duty. Across the hall, on the 'black' side, victims of assaults, traffic accidents and incomplete abortions would turn up through the evening, filling the benches in the waiting room. Now and then a turf-fight would rage between coloured gangs, and the corridor would be flanked with trolleys from which slashed Gypsy Jokers and Manhattans, their jail-tattoos smeared with blood, screamed threats at one another while the walking wounded grappled in the reception area, feet sliding on the blood-slick floor. Those too embattled to have their injuries tended would be separated by the cops, cruel but impartial, who would club the casualties back into line. 'Listen to the doctor,' they'd order. 'You cunts can carry on killing each other outside when he's finished.' On my second night on duty a big-bellied sergeant, mug of tea at his elbow, showed me how to put a drain into the chest of a stab-victim with a collapsed lung. He liked to hang around the department chatting up the nursing sisters and sometimes pitched in as an extra medic, cobbling together ragged machete wounds with big, efficient sutures.

In South Africa that passed for normal hospital life. Its even tenor was about to be disrupted. Unrest had been simmering in the black townships around Cape Town, and the authorities now decided to suppress it with vigour. One morning I drove to work past convoys of police trucks on their way to Langa, Nyanga and Gugulethu, their windscreens blanked with steel mesh. They were led by a file of Casspirs: armoured vehicles, high and long and almost sleek, like racing coffins, their great lugged tyres raising the occupants above their surroundings. The cabs were framed by slabs of bullet-proof glass that also formed slits above a row of gunports along each side. They looked capable of driving right through township shacks, but over the course of that baking, windless day the confrontation which they portended seemed to have fizzled out. A contingent of riot police lounging at the hospital gates announced that the 'troublemakers' had been dispersed, a few arrested. Nevertheless the hospital staff remained on edge, and by 4 p.m. all those who could had left to make sure 'that everything was all right at home'. I stayed because I was the medical officer on duty that night.

By sunset the Casualty department would usually be

starting to fill with the evening's harvest. It remained empty. I stood outside in the dusk, feeling the overheated stillness of the day give way to a wind blowing steadily from the east. With it came a smell of woodsmoke and the crackle of shots, rising and falling like an approaching brushfire. A helicopter clattered overhead, and then another, heading for the townships. A column of smoke rose against the darkening sky. From the distance came the sound of sirens. I thought I knew what was coming. I recalled the stories of war service I had been hearing since I was a child.

The first ambulance swung onto the tarmac outside Casualty. Another was just behind it, and another, and a snake of flashing lights that stretched back down the road. It was suddenly clear that those stories – and my training – hadn't prepared me for anything on this scale. I fled into the building from which startled nurses were beginning to emerge, pushing bed-trolleys.

'Call the switchboard!' I yelled to the receptionist. 'Tell them to page every doctor they can. We're going to be flooded!'

The Casualty staff were already mobilizing. Orderlies were opening crates of intravenous fluid, bottles being hung in jingling bunches from the drip stands. Hastily arranged stacks of dressing packs and chest drain kits spilled across the floor. Outside, under the arc-lights, each ambulance disgorged its load of six or eight bodies directly onto the ground, their limbs tangled. We pulled them apart, sorting the dead from the living, and lifted those who still breathed onto the trolleys. Then we ran with our limp cargoes into the treatment area.

The bodies were full of holes. Dark blood welled from punctured skin or jetted red from open arteries. I dashed from wound to wound with a tray of instruments, clamping bleeding points, while the senior sister slid a drip-line into the arm of each patient who required one. A group of boys in football gear had been shot down from above. (I heard later that a police helicopter had circled above their playing field, spraying it with automatic fire.) We had left all but one outside among the dead; from my forensic studies I recognized the effects of high-velocity bullets that exploded in muscle and bone, leaving cavities of shattered flesh. The sole survivor was rushed into the Casualty operating theatre. He was unconscious, and an entrance wound at the base of his neck bubbled and sucked. I stitched it hastily, then stuck a drain into his chest. Blood flooded through the tube, filling the drain bottle, as his last breath gurgled in his throat.

Many casualties had been hit by shotgun fire on their legs and backs, and were peppered with pellets that made hard mounds under the skin. These could wait till later. Some had lost great ragged bites of tissue from the blasts. We packed their wounds with dressings and moved on. Others had been struck by pistol bullets – I could tell by the neat blue holes – but some of these wounds showed the scorched edges of close-range shots. An ambulance driver told me why.

'The cops go through, shooting from the Casspirs. If they see someone at the end of the street they blaze away, because they're frightened that the kids will get them with petrol bombs if they let them get too close. Then they call us in to pick up the bodies. When we reach the wounded their friends sometimes try to pull them away or attack us, and we've got to defend ourselves.' The ambulance driver patted his side, where a revolver hung. 'Most of the crews carry guns. The ones we shoot we throw in the back and bring them here, with all the rest.'

By now some doctors had arrived, drawn by their pagers, and were taking over treatment and resuscitation. An anaesthetist had also appeared, and he and I checked the patients who needed urgent surgery. My job as duty doctor – as soon as I was relieved in Casualty – was to get the most acute case into theatre and prepared for operating while the surgical registrar was on his way. I had dealt almost mechanically with the carnage in Casualty, but now, as I tried to make a clinical judgement, I was intensely aware of my lack of experience. I pointed uncertainly at a youth on a nearby trolley. Although we had been pouring fluid into his veins his blood pressure was barely recordable. Two holes in his abdomen indicated the path of the bullets that had struck him down.

'We've got six units of blood on the way for him,' I told the anaesthetist. 'It looks like the upper round might have hit his liver. There's also an exit wound in his back, near his left kidney. I'd say his condition is the most critical.'

'I think you're right,' said the gas-man. 'He's first for the chop.'

We shunted the trolley through the theatre doors. By the time I'd changed and found a cap and mask, the orderlies had the patient on the table with his clothes cut away, and the anaesthetist had begun his work. I scrubbed my hands and forearms, watching through the theatre window as he slid a tube into the unconscious boy's throat. The ventilator started its steady sighing. Gowned and gloved, I wiped the rigid belly down with iodine and framed it in green drapes. The anaesthetist flung an empty blood-bag on the floor and connected up a new one, pumping at a pressure cuff to squirt it through the drip as fast as possible. He turned to me.

'He's sliding. You may save him if you get him open quick.'

'But the registrar isn't here yet.'

The theatre sister looked at me across the sterile drapes. 'If you wait any longer it'll be too late,' she said. 'You may as well do the best you can.'

I took the knife from her, and held it uncertainly. I had made a few small incisions before, removing minor skin lumps. I had assisted surgeons at operation, but I had never opened a belly myself. Taking a great breath, I placed two fingers at the lower end of the patient's sternum, and poised the blade just below them. Then, tentatively, I drew the scalpel down to the umbilicus. A faint line, fine as a cat-scratch, showed my failure.

'Harder,' said the sister, 'as though you're slicing steak.'

I cut again, more strongly, and the skin opened reluctantly, fighting the blade. The youth's spare body carried almost no fat, and I found my way through the layer of lean muscle. Revealed, the pale translucency of the peritoneum was dulled by an underlying blue-black shadow.

'Blood,' said the sister. 'His belly's full of blood. I've got the suction ready.'

I lifted a fold of the membrane between two artery clips and snipped the raised edge. The sister plunged the suction nozzle into the gap and it slurped and hiccuped, swallowing fluid and dark clots that rushed away down the plastic hose.

'Quickly,' called the anaesthetist, fussing over his readings, 'get in there and find the bleeding.'

I glanced at the window into the scrub room, hoping desperately to see the registrar. I thought I might faint. Trembling, I opened the peritoneum and laid it back. Blood lapped at the wound edges and overflowed on to the floor while the suction line choked, and cleared. For an instant I saw a pit of lacerated liver and leaking bile. Then blood welled up again, from some deep recess of the wound. Shreds of yellow shit floated in the mess. I felt entirely alone. Time seemed to be rushing by, measured by the rapid tick of blood hitting the floor. I had to stop the flow, long enough to think.

'Give me the biggest swab, no, three of them.'

I balled the big gauze compresses and thrust them into the depths beneath the liver's edge. I wrapped another round a piece of punctured bowel and sluiced out the abdomen with fresh saline. Slowly and then faster the debris cleared, hoovered up by the voracious suction-line. I began to recognize some anatomy.

One of the bullets had struck beside the umbilicus, punching through some loops of small bowel before exiting through the back, close to the edge of the left kidney. I looked below the drapes to the catheter bag hooked onto the operating table's edge. The urine in it was pale and clear; the kidney hadn't been hit. It was the other shot that had done most damage. It had struck the liver, shattering part of it, and evidently damaging the biliary system. Then it had travelled on to unknown, mortal regions, where the portal and hepatic veins run into the liver and the great vena cava drains the lower body, carrying blood back to the labouring heart. The wad of gauze I had packed in there was sodden with blood and leaked a sullen, rising pool. I didn't want to move it, but I had to.

I found the gall bladder where it lay beneath the liver. It had been perforated, and I clamped the hole with a forceps to stop more bile leaking out. Then, lifting the clamp gently forwards, I traced the bile duct back into the mess below. It seemed undamaged, and for the first time I began to hope; perhaps the bile leak was from the hole in the gall bladder, and the delicate biliary ducts themselves were still intact. I peeled back the sodden compress bit by bit. Blood oozed from a star-shaped fissure in the under-surface of the liver. It coursed thickly from one edge of the crater, where it appeared that a branch of a vein had been torn. I tried to clamp it, but the jelly-like liver crumbled under the steel jaws. Hoping that I was doing the right thing, I placed a couple of wide catgut stitches across the area, tightening the knot with caution so that it wouldn't cut through the tissue. The bleeding dwindled as the surface of the laceration began to clot. I straightened up, realizing that my theatre boots were squelching with sweat. I looked towards the anaesthetist, who lifted his thumb and nodded. I nodded too, wildly, because I could see behind him that the registrar was coming through the theatre doors, snapping on his gloves.

It took almost another hour to trace each source of bleeding and explore the bullet tracks. We lifted every inch of intestine, inspecting it for holes. Some small punctures could be closed with sutures, but other sections looked bruised and torn. Gut heals poorly if the blood supply is compromised, and we cut out these sections between clamps and rejoined the ends with close, neat stitches. Fortunately the large bowel appeared intact, for an injury there would have needed to be a colostomy to rest the damaged area while it healed. Finally we flushed out the abdominal cavity, washing clots and flecks of bowel content from between its folds. A couple of drainage tubes were placed – behind the liver and under the repaired bowel, where leakage or infection might occur – and I carefully joined the layers of the abdomen. The last line of sutures closed the skin. I lifted off the drapes and looked at this small battlefield. Skin-stitches ran like a zipper down the midline. Red rubber tube drains jutted to the right and left, and neat oval wounds marked the trimmed bullet holes. Inside this arena I had been lost, and then restored. I had learned that I could cope.

⊕

Surgery, it seemed, was what I wanted to do, to feel that rush of confidence as my hands negotiated the intricate demands of operating. If I was to stay in South Africa, I could assume that I would be doing a lot more trauma work. In the evening I would drive back from the hospital and up through the steep Constantia valley, to park on a farm track under the oaks. A scramble up a rutted path brought me to the house, a bungalow dressed in flowering creeper that gazed out across the Cape Flats to the sawtooth range of the Hottentots

Holland mountains lit by the sunset. Each morning I would leave the calm of that charmed place and plunge back into hospital life: challenging and exhilarating. That was the way I lived then, and it seemed unlikely that I would find another country like it.

But there was the army, waiting to pounce on me as soon as I finished my year of internship; to draft me, short-back-and-sides, into military service. Despite the prospect of two years in uniform, plus a further three months a year thereafter at the army's whim, it was hard to contemplate exile. I could go to work in England, where my medical degree would be recognized, or to join my family in the United States where my father had taken up a professorship at a medical school in New York. But the truth was, I wanted to stay.

We young doctors discussed the issue exhaustively. My radical friends said change was inevitable, even if it was to be through bloody revolution, and they wanted to see it happen. To do so they would have to remain in South Africa, which meant going into the army. Others took an ethical standpoint: a doctor was a doctor, in uniform or out, and doing National Service one was still trying to heal people. My friend Stefan had been a strong contender of this view. Called up several months before, he was now stationed somewhere on the Angolan border. As yet I hadn't heard from him, but I knew he'd be due for leave before the year's end. I was looking forward to seeing him and laughing at his haircut, and finding out whether he was managing to survive the army with his principles intact.

One day I received a message that Stefan was in Cape Town, and wished to see me. I was surprised that he hadn't called me himself to let me know he was back, but that evening I went to the address I'd been given; a flat near the seafront where I'd been told he was staying. The man who answered the door seemed suspicious of me, but a voice from behind him – high and unfamiliar – told him to let me in. Stefan sat in the lounge. His face looked hollow, as though something vital had been squeezed from it. His embrace was perfunctory.

'How was basic training?' I wanted to know. 'How was the border? How did you manage to get leave so soon? I wasn't expecting you for another couple of months.'

'Have a drink,' he answered, pouring me a brimming glass of neat vodka. He took a swallow from his own glass then topped it up, placing the bottle beside the leg of his chair.

'Let me tell you what it's like,' he said, lighting a cigarette. I'd never seen him smoke before.

Stefan had been sent first to Oshakati in the north of South West Africa, forty miles from the Angolan border. It was a town of around ten thousand white civilians with bomb shelters at their front doors, and a huge army camp. He'd been put to work in the main hospital. It was busy. South African army units were in Angola, and every now and then a patrol would get ambushed and be brought in by helicopter. 'We'd also get black civilians,' Stefan said. 'Sometimes a busload who'd hit a mine, and we'd look after them; trying to win their hearts and minds even if they lost their arms and legs. Those cases were the most upsetting.' The mines had been laid by their own people – SWAPO guerrillas – trying to kill the occupiers, the South Africans. 'If we hadn't been there, neither would the mines. All these people wanted was for us to leave, yet there I was, an army doctor, trying to help them. The result was incomprehensible confusion, for them and me.'

Then he'd been sent to the forward base at Oshikango to relieve an army doctor who was down with malaria. It was right on the border, surrounded by minefields: tents and sandbagged bunkers and a look-out tower inside a bulldozed wall of red earth. Late one night, after he had been there for about a month, Stefan was woken and told to report to the hospital tent. A group of men in camouflage uniform were standing around a stretcher. On it lay a black man shot through the thigh, gasping in pain.

'I examined him. I got a drip running and prepared some antibiotics. The captain in charge checked the ampoules. He had a full beard, he looked like a pirate.'

'I don't want you giving him any painkillers, doc,' he ordered. 'He's a fokkin terrorist. We need him to talk.'

Stefan objected that the man's thigh-bone was fractured: it would need to be stabilized, otherwise he could bleed to death.

'Do what you like, doc. Put it in a splint,' the officer said. 'You can have him back when we've finished with him.'

Stefan described how the wounded man had watched him as he strapped his leg into the frame. He protested again that the man needed proper care, but the captain ignored him. Four black troopers picked up the stretcher and took him away.

'Over the sound of the generator I thought I could hear screaming,' Stefan continued. 'I went to find the senior duty officer and told him they were questioning a prisoner and denying him proper medical treatment. He said there was nothing he could do; the others were a police counter-insurgency unit, not under army control, and I should go back to sleep. I couldn't. I sat in the dispensary trying to read. The screaming went on, sometimes blocked out by the roar of a truck engine. I covered my ears.'

Then a police trooper came running in and told Stefan to bring his bag. He sprinted across to their camp. Between a pair of Casspir armoured vehicles an arc-light was strung, and a group of men stood beneath it around a figure on the ground.

'He's passed out, doc, just when we were getting somewhere,' the officer said. 'You have to bring him round.'

There was a terrible smell, like burning meat. The skin on the man's legs and back was scorched off, hanging in long strips. He was unconscious. The splint had been discarded, and the end of his fractured femur stuck through the flesh. Stefan asked what had happened to him, how he'd got burned. The bearded policeman had laughed. 'We had a barbecue. We put him on the hot exhaust pipe of the Casspir, let him cook. It always works. Plus we gave his leg a twist, to help him concentrate.'

Stefan said the man needed to go to hospital or he would die.

'He'll die anyway,' said the captain. 'We don't take prisoners. Just give him an injection or something to wake him up for a while before he goes.'

Stefan fumbled in his medical bag. He found his stethoscope and listened to the man's heart. It beat fast and strong. He pulled out an ampoule of potassium solution and cracked it open.

'No painkillers, doc,' warned the officer.

'No painkillers,' Stefan had said, injecting the potassium into the drip site. 'He's in shock. I'll try to jolt his heart a bit, to bring him round.'

The man opened his eyes, and took a deep, racking breath. The policemen began to pull him upright. His mouth opened, then he arched his back convulsively and slumped back.

'Shit,' said the captain, 'he was starting to talk. I suppose he was just too far gone, hey, doc?'

'Too far gone,' Stefan had agreed.

'I went back to my cot,' he went on. 'I lay down, but at once the horror of what I had done overwhelmed me. Everything was swept away, all the principles that had guided my life. I had just murdered someone. I hung onto the edge of the bed, shuddering with fear.'

Then he'd opened his medical bag and brought out the pethidine that he'd been forbidden to give the wounded man. He'd drawn it into a syringe, and injected it into his arm.

Stefan subsided into his chair. His thin hands vibrated where they clasped the armrests.

'I managed to last another three weeks, stealing pethidine from the dispensary and shooting up every night. When I tried to sleep I couldn't bear the solitude. I came down with malaria, and was sent back to Oshakati. I knew one of the doctors there, and he had me transferred to the military hospital here in Cape Town. Ten days ago I bribed an orderly to get me twenty ampoules. Then I walked out of the place and came here.'

He pulled up his sleeve, and I saw that his arm was a mesh of bruises. Stefan explained that Michael, the owner of the flat where we were talking, was a psychiatrist and trying to help him. 'In the meantime I'm trying to avoid the drugs, by using this.' Stefan sucked deeply from his glass of vodka. He gagged, then drank again. 'You won't see me again for a while. Tomorrow I'm being moved from here, to somewhere safer. Michael's making plans to get me out of the country.'

'What about your family? Your friends?'

Stefan shook his head.

'They'll hear from me once I've made it overseas. Don't tell anyone you've seen me. And don't believe that bullshit I used to tell you about being able to keep your humanity by being a doctor. It isn't true. There are situations where that option simply doesn't exist.'

3

England

Precipitously, six days before I was due to report for duty in the South African army, I jumped on a plane and left. Cowardice was a factor in helping me decide to pursue my medical career somewhere else, where the moral alternatives weren't so extreme. England drew me as a place to begin my exile. It was where my father had made his new start after being demobilized at the war's end. With food rationing still in force and swathes of central London just bombed-out ruins, he'd found a hospital post, bought the thickest overcoat he could find, and applied himself to studying for the examination of Fellowship of the Royal College of Surgeons. Victory beer had been vile stuff, he'd said, and that first winter of peace was one of the coldest recorded. For me, thirty-five years later and on the run from military service, England did its atmospheric best to repeat that combination of historic discomforts.

The East End hospital has since closed, and only ghosts now wander the gothic chapel, or hang themselves from light fittings in the old psychiatric emergency unit. When I worked there, however, it provided all the medical services in this part of London's grimy fringe, where brickwork enclosed the horizon and a low grey sky sat over stepped rooftops. The hospital had once been a Victorian poorhouse, a barracks for the indigent. An air of deprivation still hung around its spike-topped walls. Ward-blocks enclosed quadrangles, unvisited by sunlight, where grey snow lay till late spring. All year round the radiators raged, blasting out a desiccating heat that crumbled the linoleum floors, yet it was always cold. A faulty firebell rang nightly in the passage of the doctors' quarters unless the clapper was jammed with towels. The food in the hospital canteen was stiff, a frozen landscape of roast beef plains and resilient potato cliffs, which had to be decorated with the contents of little packets of sauce – red, yellow and brown – to counterpoint its intense blandness. The rewards lay in the job.

I was working there as a Casualty Officer. All night, drunks, misfits and violent men came through the door of the Accident and Emergency Unit, along with their victims. Of course the violence was relative – there were no gunshot wounds or firebombs, and a significant fracas might involve the use of pint beer mugs, flung wildly in a swirling pub fight – but in its time the hospital was considered a pretty rough manor by those that worked there. Sometimes there'd be a shouting match in Casualty and a few slack punches, but the iron-busted matron quelled the drunkards with withering words. The serious injuries were a product of the drug wars that erupted now and then on the gritty streets. The young black gang members took pain seriously; they inflicted and endured their injuries with deliberation. Clench-jawed, they'd refuse local anaesthetic while their wounds were stitched.

'Do you know who did this?' I'd ask as I closed a knife wound.

'I know.'

'You should tell the cops.'

They would make that sucking sound between their teeth that denotes disgust.

'Just get me fix, doc. It me own business.'

One midday a local warlord was brought in by his henchmen. His hair was razored into lightning bolts, his body powerfully muscled, and he had cut the arteries in his wrists because his woman had left him. His dark skin concealed his pallor but his gums were the palest blue. He refused all treatment.

'You have to have a transfusion immediately,' I warned him, checking his blood pressure. 'You've lost a lot of blood.'

He tucked his bleeding arms behind his back so that I couldn't place a drip.

'That bitch,' he said, and began to convulse as his heart arrested. A few minutes later, still fighting the attentions of the resuscitation team, he died.

These hard cases, irredeemably tragic, were nonetheless an echo of Cape Town, where most patients only arrived in hospital as a final resort. All too often the Casualty department here was simply a refuge for the desolate and bereft, those with no one to care about them. In the small hours it hosted the sad teenage girls with their token overdoses of vodka and ten of mum's Valium, their mascara smeared; a whimper for help. They were guaranteed, at least, our professional concern, as they sobbed and puked around the thick rubber stomach tube. Despite the indignity some returned again and again, jilted by a succession of housing estate bad-boys. Afterwards, sucking on a cigarette, they would share the benches with those further down the pile; the frankly mad.

One regular crazy was Bernard. His file of Casualty cards was solid as a brick, emblazoned with red 'REPEATER' stickers and studded with staples like a tribal fetish. His idiosyncrasy, the sister informed me, was eating jewellery; nothing costly, just the trinkets that those in that poor part of the city adorned themselves with. He'd required surgery once, after a tangle of metal showed up on an X-ray of his gut. The surgeon removed a great knot of cheap gold chains. Bernard had been a fan of the hospital ever since. The psychiatrists had decided that his affliction was pretty mild – by local standards – so refused to see him. Bernard didn't mind. He lay on the treatment couch with a look of contentment; he had 'done something again', he told me coyly. A prod of his belly was unrevealing, but an X-ray revealed the ghostly outline of a plastic Swiss watch, face-on in his stomach. It also showed some metallic links low in his abdomen. With Bernard's puzzled compliance, I donned a glove and stuck a finger up his bottom. I deposited my find, a shit-encrusted bracelet, in a steel bowl and held it out for him to see.

'Ah,' he said, his brow clearing, 'I wondered where that had got to,' and, scooping it from the dish, swallowed it with a gulp.

⊕

Put-upon patients of the local GPs would also wash up there, propped awkwardly on the trolleys as they waited for a bed on the ward. The little old ladies, frail and tremulous, chattered like starlings.

'Are you from New Zealand?' they would ask me. 'Only our Maisie used to go with a boy from Auckland, in the airforce he was. Ever such a nice man.'

'I'm really sorry about the delay,' I'd say, tucking crocheted blankets (brought from home by doting, middle-aged daughters) up to their chins. 'We should have a bed for you any minute.'

'Ooh, doctor,' they'd quaver, 'we don't mind waiting. It was much worse in the Blitz.'

That very same survivalist spirit had formed the NHS. The government proposal for a National Health Service had been written in 1944, while German buzz-bombs droned over the roofs of London and everything, from toothbrushes to time itself, was rationed in the service of the war effort. The service in which I now worked wasn't exactly the 'healthcare system fit for heroes' that had originally been visualized as the victory reward for the nation's sacrifice. It carried the imprint of its make-do wartime origins; a mixture of improvisation and inspired bureaucracy. But, in its sometimes cumbersome way, the NHS met the purpose it was designed for: the needs of the people, whoever they might be. In its many niches could even be found a welcome for a refugee like me, who believed in its socialist tenets of free medical care and equal treatment for all.

What made the system function was the camaraderie among the staff. Nurses, orderlies, doctors and cleaners all seemed to feel their work was valued. The consultants were dedicated individuals, though leavened with a scattering of hyper-achievers, time-servers and incompetents who could complicate life for we senior house-officers. Some of us were graduates from the Commonwealth – New Zealanders, Australians, South Africans – places where the medical education system still turned out graduates taught along traditional British lines. Often we had had a bit more clinical experience and responsibility than the English house-officers, and we used to tease them about the 'superiority' of our training; an Australian once joked to the doctors' mess that he and his fellow-countrymen had come to England for a spot of 'P. O. P.': Practice on the Poms. But his commitment was real enough – I think most of us were fairly dedicated – for life as a junior doctor in the National Health Service was distinctly short on comfort. There were however a few rewards.

One of mine was that I worked for a highly entertaining consultant. I'd decided to stay on at the hospital after my Casualty job to gain a further six months of orthopaedic experience. My chief was a trencherman, a big-bellied epicure with a deft hand and a surgeon's sense of humour. Orthopaedic specialists need to be strong – considerable physical power is needed to wrench an arthritic hip-joint from its socket so that it can be sawed off and a replacement fitted – and inured to gore – the power-drills hurl pink bone-froth against the face-masks of those around the operating table – but he affected a dainty disgust against the barbarity of his trade.

'What's all this blood?' he'd demand as he sliced through muscle and the wound filled with red. 'How can I be expected to operate with all this blood?'

'It'll stop when the patient's lost a bit more and his pressure falls,' the anaesthetist would murmur, chuckling behind his mask. The senior registrar, a dignified Asian with soulful eyes, would set to work with the cautery forceps while I mopped at the operating field and wondered whether I should have had the foresight to cross-match some extra units of blood. Tissue structures would reappear. My boss was unmollified.

'Christ,' he'd grumble, 'what's all this anatomy doing here? Orthopaedics is supposed to be simple, that's why I took it up. I'll lose my way amidst all these complicated bits. You're trying to get me sued.'

His rough charm had earned him a rich private practice that took up his evenings and weekends. Once, in the early hours of the morning, I admitted a woman with a smashed elbow. She informed me that she wished to 'go private', and I suggested, helpfully, that there was no point; she would be seen earlier, and treated by the same specialist, if she remained a National Health Service patient. She was duly added to my consultant's morning list, operated on, and expressed her thanks at his ward-round the next day.

'Do you know, doctor,' she told him, 'if it hadn't been for this young man I might have paid a fortune for private care. Instead he persuaded me to be treated under the NHS, and it's been just wonderful.'

'Good, good, pleased to hear it,' said my boss-man. 'Would you excuse us for a moment?'

He led me from the bedside, down to the far end of the ward. 'You've got a lot to learn,' he began gravely, though I noticed he was smiling. 'You're a good senior house-officer, conscientious. But you don't understand an essential principle of surgery.'

That, I'd decided, was what I was here to learn. Not how to build a private practice, but the skill itself. I faced a stringent apprenticeship. The first step was the Primary Examination of the Royal College of Surgeons; three months of lectures in gloomy halls, ploughing through the minutiae of human anatomy and physiology at a level of detail far more comprehensive than I'd known at medical school. Then there was the practical experience, which required a particular sequence of senior house-officer posts. My Casualty and orthopaedic posts were the start of a series of these six-month jobs, and I'd no sooner started each one than I would be scanning the advertisements in the *British Medical Journal* for the next opening, visiting other surgical departments and trying to catch the eye and attention of a potential new boss.

The British system of surgical training depended on a sort of feudal patronage. The idea, tried and trusted, was to find backing from a powerful man. (Less than one in twenty surgical consultant posts in Britain were held by women; surgery was very much a male preserve.) Under his paternal eye your progress up the ladder into desirable jobs might be eased through his influence on the interview committee. If you were already well-connected that vital start-off post would be arranged almost from birth through family favours; in some medical schools seventy per cent of the students were the children of previous graduates, whose genealogical links formed a mutual network of support. If, however, you were an outsider, you put together your own career plan, and tried to find a patron to notice you by taking a job at a London teaching hospital.

Teaching hospitals were hierarchical mazes where young doctors wept. I served time at one of them, another Victorian pile lying alongside one of Her Majesty's more notorious prisons. The department chiefs were dedicated academics; most of them preoccupied with building empires of prestige or money. My new boss was a professor who, each Tuesday, would fly into pale-faced rage if any of his retinue – surgical consultants, senior registrars, registrars, senior house-officers and assorted matrons, sisters, physiotherapists and nutritionists – were not at his 'grand round', to hear him declaim his successes to a series of visiting specialists. Apparently without family or home-life, he would materialize on the wards in the small hours to insist that his senior house-officers join him in protracted rounds. Those roused from snatched sleep would stumble behind him from bed to bed, hoping not to be the target of his scorn. This was almost impossible to avoid: he would demand to know a set of obscure blood results, and how those values differed from previous ones, and woe was the lot of the doctor that didn't have these figures committed to memory for every patient. His most potent weapon was the threat – not to be taken lightly – that he would withhold a reference from a junior, who would struggle, and probably fail, to find his next post without it.

⊕

I became a connoisseur of the architecture and ambience of hospitals in and around London. There were nineteen-thirties Deco edifices of rounded line and monstrous dimensions; the main corridor of one – nicknamed 'The Burma Road' – was three-quarters of a mile long. Beneath the older establishments ran a network of tunnels where water dripped from asbestos-lagged pipes and caged lights cast a dim, red glow on the walls like the bowels of a battleship. One place was famous for its morgue, three levels below ground, that could only be reached by a creaking goods-lift. The story ran that the lift had once broken down, and the mortuary technician had been forced to escape by crawling through a service conduit when, after eight hours of incarceration, he'd become convinced that he could hear voices behind the refrigerated doors.

There were cold, concrete tower-blocks, over-engineered; with automatic doors that stuck and 'intelligent' elevators that took ages to arrive and then delivered you to whatever floor they fancied. I served in rustic cottage hospitals, with rose-beds and croquet lawns and elegant trays of crustless sandwiches at teatime. One place I worked in resembled a Bavarian schloss: weighty with heraldic emblems and steep-pitched roofs around a cobbled courtyard, its raftered attics were a perfect place for erotic assignations. However varied the layout of individual hospitals the atmosphere on the wards was always the same; an after-smell of disinfectant, a miasma of steam-heated food, and the pervasive clatter of drip-stands and cleaners' buckets and cutlery that formed a counterpoint to the drone of TV sets. At night there would be flurries of activity in the pool of light about the nurses' station, the moan of disturbed patients. The hospitals never slept.

I too became inured to tiredness. I could emerge from profoundest sleep at the first bleat of my pager, pick up the phone and make rational decisions about clinical management. I could place a drip at four in the morning into veins collapsed by shock or scarred into string, or slip a catheter into a clot-obstructed bladder with a conjurer's wrist-flick. I had worked for general surgeons, orthopaedic surgeons, urologists, arterial surgeons and an ear, nose and throat specialist. Keen to learn all I could – within the limited opportunities allowed a junior to actually operate – I had picked up surgical crumbs from the theatre tables of generous seniors. I could set fractures, strip out varicose veins, scoop tonsils from little throats and whip out an inflamed appendix in sixteen minutes from the first incision to the final skin-stitch. After three years as a senior house-officer I was ready to become a registrar and start my training in earnest.

⊕

The actual quality of surgical training could be a haphazard business. It depended substantially on the consultant on whose 'firm' you worked, whose attentiveness might range from active interest in your career to an apparent failure even to remember your name. A good boss would teach as he operated, demonstrating the best approach to a problem and deftly revealing the hidden nerve or vessel waiting to be damaged by the unwary. A bad one would rush through the procedure, using his registrar only as a retractor-holder, limiting his communication to instructions to 'get out of the way', or 'move the light'.

Often the best surgical teacher would be a colleague, a registrar one rung higher up the ladder, who'd show some trick of knot-tying or sleight of access to a difficult corner of the abdomen. It would be he who revealed the existence of rules so basic that they are never stated – 'don't cut a tubular structure unless you know exactly where it goes'; 'never close the jaws of your scissors if you can't see their tips' – and demonstrate patiently the best way to perform a bowel anastomosis by joining up the gut in two clean layers so that it would not leak. It was with these committed comrades, often in the small hours of the night, that you formed real bonds; or with your house-officer, whose confidence in his registrar would carry you through a difficult emergency operation while he flipped the pages of the surgical textbook and held anatomy diagrams up to the theatre light.

In the end surgery is instinct, and has much to do with an inherent feeling for the handling of tissues. Those with the gift know intuitively how structures will separate with the least damage, how to stroke them apart along tissue planes using the minimal pressure of the tips of a pair of dissecting scissors, even in areas of the body that are being explored for the first time. Some will never learn this touch; hacking instead across natural lines of cleavage, destroying the anatomy and laying waste to its delicate structures. But, if you're good, the resistance of muscle, gut and vessel will speak back to you through your fingers. Guided by these elemental instincts, you can do whatever you are called upon to do. After seeing an operation for the first time you can usually perform the next one yourself. And having done it once, you are qualified to show a colleague how it's done. This three-step is summed up in the adage: see one, do one, teach one. By this concise process is the art of surgery passed on.

✪

And as I learned, I worked. Morning rounds would commence before eight, to assess the patients on the ward and correct any problems before the consultant's look-in at half-past. Then there'd be the morning operating list or outpatients session, with a quick re-check of the wards before a snatched lunch. The last hour of the afternoon might be spent teaching medical students, or collating discharge figures for the past month, or seeing in the new admissions for the next day's list, after another outpatients stint. Twice a week there would be a full day's operating from nine to six, with a toxic cup of coffee and a desiccated sandwich at midday if there was time between cases. After the day's work, a final ward round – instructions to the nurses about post-operative monitoring – and visits to in-hospital referrals, might get you out of the place by seven-thirty or eight in the evening. Except if there was night duty.

The usual registrar post was a 'one-in-three', indicating that every third day, night and weekend your consultant's firm was 'on-call'. During on-call – besides the routine work of rounds, outpatients, admissions and operating lists – you were responsible for all acute surgical cases arriving via the Casualty department, and any emergency surgery that might be required. The registrar was the person on the line – the consultant's representative in the hospital – to be called down to Casualty to make the first assessment of a patient, to recognize a life-threatening situation and initiate treatment, and to be responsible for its outcome. He had to know when his skills were insufficient to deal with a situation and to call in the consultant from home; something to avoid doing unnecessarily, or too often.

On-call weekends were particularly onerous, beginning at nine in the morning on a Friday and ending seventy-two hours later at the same time on Monday, when you grabbed a quick shave and began another normal working day. The hallucinatory fatigue that came at midnight on a Sunday – after a total of perhaps four hours of interrupted sleep accumulated since the weekend duty had commenced – made judgement difficult. Exhaustion caused disorientation and simple decisions became insurmountable; the familiar inside of an abdomen could resemble suddenly a monstrous maze where tiny vessels seemed huge and haemorrhage occurred from unexpected places, and you laboured to reach an end to this desperate, unravelling venture of blood and knots in order to sleep. It was actually remarkable how seldom patient care suffered, but the risks were justified thus by the profession: we were training to be the surgeons of the future, and the harder we worked, the better we would become.

Older consultants would point out – rightly – that their training days had been far worse. I remembered my father's accounts of his time as a military surgeon, on duty day and night for weeks on end. Battles happened in the distance; the only realities were the ambulance convoys bringing waves of wounded. All had to be treated – rest was simply not possible until this had been done – and often another attack would fill the reception tents with new casualties before the last load had been completed. Those who'd experienced such ordeals were altered. They displayed a calmness – confident, from the experience of past crises, that each new one could be handled – and had earned the responsibility and respect with which they were invested. Through our exhaustion we believed that we too were being annealed by clinical pressure into better instruments. Gradually we acquired the arrogance of the elect, and scorned the easy lives of ordinary doctors. I became accustomed to working up to a hundred hours a week, absorbing the principles of general surgery, theoretical and practical. My free time I spent studying for the Surgical Fellowship.

The Royal College of Surgeons of England lies on the south side of Lincoln's Inn Fields, in a corner of central London known as the Inns of Court where black-draped barristers dash to the nearby Law Courts, clutching at their Elizabethan wigs. The college started life as the Company of Barber-Surgeons, established by Henry VIII in 1540. The flesh-cutters elected to distinguish themselves from the face-shavers, and by 1800 the Royal College of Surgeons of England was established. Its columned frontage, while not quite so imposing as the black granite of its Edinburgh equivalent (founded in 1505, becoming the Royal College of Surgeons of Edinburgh in 1778), was nevertheless far more daunting to the young trainee surgeon because of the difficulty of passing the English Fellowship examination.

This protracted trial (written, oral and practical sections spread over several weeks) had a scant fifteen per cent success rate and only four attempts were allowed; worse than that, the English College of Surgeons had a reputation for elitism, and candidates claimed that a commensurately harder time was given to those whose accent, ethnicity or gender set them at variance with the image to which Harley Street aspired. By comparison, the Edinburgh College was a sort of Commonwealth of surgery, training practitioners from all over the world. On a corner opposite the entrance was a sweet shop that made a type of toffee called Edinburgh hard-bake. The appearance of the spleen when infiltrated with leukaemia was said to resemble this confection, and the 'hard-bake spleen' was a descriptive pathological term understood by surgeons from Calcutta through Cairo to the Caribbean.

The skills required to obtain the Fellowship qualifications of these institutions were themselves valuable professional techniques. Surgeons, it is said, are permitted to be sometimes wrong but never in doubt, and the examiners expected of us the art of instant verisimilitude; the ability to speak confidently on any matter, even on a topic whose existence had never been suspected until the moment we were asked a question about it. A story is told of a candidate in the clinical section who was asked to examine a patient's testicles. After rolling, palpating and weighing the orbs – and finding nothing obviously wrong with them – the doctor whipped out his stethoscope, clapped it to the scrotum and listened intently.

'Er . . . what do you hear?' asked the curious College examiner.

'Oh, normal scrotal sounds,' said the candidate airily, and passed with flying colours.

✪

Now, with the peculiar inverted snobbery granted by Fellowship of both these institutions, I was pleased to call myself by the honorific 'Mister' instead of 'Doctor'. However, as I advanced up the career ladder it became clear that surgery, in London at least, was a field where connections could count more than competence. At job interviews I generally found myself being selected – my relative surgical confidence, established early on in South Africa, was important to a consultant who wanted a registrar who would not call him from his bed inappropriately in the middle of the night – but a couple of times I lost a post to someone apparently with less experience and qualifications than I had.

These tended to be the products of a couple of prestigious London medical schools that occupied sites near one another just south of the Thames. Their student bodies contained relatively few women, and the lads seemed to be groomed for private practice. Graduates of one of them, it was said, avoided excessive contact with their NHS patients by examining them with one hand in a pocket. Chaps from the other were allegedly even more fastidious, keeping both hands in their pockets. There were rumours of Masonic networks governing appointments within and beyond these august institutions. Sometimes at a job interview there would be an obvious 'ringer' whose father had been a classmate of the appointing consultant, with the rest of us there to create a semblance of impartiality. 'What it comes down to,' I was once told by a public-school-accented fellow lolling confidently on the bench as we waited for the interviewers' decision, 'is not whom you know, but whom I know.'

And I didn't know the right people. The consultants I worked for tended to be competent, undramatic individuals, apart perhaps for the one who suffered from that rare (though much popularized) condition known as Gilles de la Tourette's syndrome. It is characterized by muscular spasms that affect the head and body, accompanied by involuntary noises which might include grunting and barking: an experience likely to disconcert even the most stoical patient. In around sixty per cent of cases, according to clinical data, the noises are replaced by single-syllabled swear words. Picture, then, Mrs Smith, mid-fifties; tucked up in bed awaiting her pre-anaesthetic injection, being greeted by the surgeon who is soon to operate on her.

'Mrs Smith,' he says warmly, 'we'll have you up in theatre in no time, and then we'll–'

'Yes, doctor?' she says, but the consultant's hands have suddenly gripped the bedclothes and begun to wring them convulsively.

'We'll get you up to theatre–' His head thrusts sideways and an anguished expression crosses his face. 'We'll – we'll– Ahhh, shit. F-f-f-fuck! Piss, fuck!' and he runs from the ward to collect himself.

'Don't worry, Mrs Smith,' we would tell the stunned patient, 'it's just a tic he has. He's really a very good surgeon.' And so it would prove, for the symptoms of Tourette's syndrome disappear when the subject's concentration is fixed upon a demanding task.

A measure of professional autonomy gave consultants the freedom to organize their hospital surgical practice as they wished – even when they were a little quirky – any excesses or faults ostensibly being overseen and corrected by pressure from their vigilant peers. But the system didn't always work, especially in district hospitals outside the big towns where there might be little oversight and no controls, and one such failing of the self-regulating mechanism provided me with the worst post of my life.

My registrar training rotation had taken me to a hospital well outside London, where I was to spend a year working for the senior consultant. The place had been constructed during the war as a military burns unit, and the wards and operating theatres were still housed in the original prefab blocks. Something of the suffering of those tortured bodies seemed to have permeated the fibre-board walls. It was a miserable place, with a wind that sighed down the corridors. The doctors' quarters lay a half-mile away across boggy fields, where roaming cows would loom out of the darkness as you stumbled through puddles on the way to Casualty. Such hard-time postings were difficult to fill, and many of the London hospitals would include a year of this type of clinical isolation in their registrar training programmes to keep these district outposts staffed.

The senior surgeon, my new boss, was a man unburdened by charisma. He mistrusted one of his two consultant colleagues, pronouncing him 'too young'. Against the other – a surgeon named McOboe, who had once questioned his management of a patient – he waged a relentless vendetta. The registrar I was replacing had alluded to this at a pre-appointment visit when I came to look around the hospital. After describing the job with a gushing cheerfulness – that I recognized only later as desperation; if I had refused to take the post he would have been stuck there until a replacement was found – he uttered, in an undertone, the curious statement: 'You'll love it here, if you follow the rules. And the main one is this: never, ever consult Mr McOboe about any of the boss's patients. Don't even be seen talking to him, or you could be fired on the spot.'

Starting the job, I forgot my predecessor's parting comment in trying to adjust to another of my new consultant's diktats: the surgery department's uniquely gruelling on-call system. It involved the usual one-in-three duty rota, but instead of being in the hospital every third night, on-call duty lasted the entire length of every third week. I would drive to work on Monday morning, knowing that I wouldn't see my

London flat again until the following Monday evening; an unrelieved vista of draughty duty rooms, stale canteen food and the singed smell of electric heaters stretched ahead.

Some of those seven days would be dull, but an unpredictable percentage were surprisingly busy. There was the usual surgical fare of a district general hospital serving a moderate-sized population – appendicitis, perforated or bleeding ulcers, strangulated bowel, head injuries. The odd cluster of major trauma cases might be delivered from a pile-up on a nearby highway. Variety came from the agricultural sector, as farmers periodically lost their hats into threshing machines or the whirling blades of harvesters and dove incontinently after them, arriving diced – sometimes dead – in Casualty. And the local youth, disaffected by existence in the dreary town, would stage bruising fights outside the burger bar and stick each other with whatever came to hand, including, on one occasion, a plastic fork that jutted from the neck of a terrified boy, and pulsated with the carotid artery against which its prongs were jammed.

My boss used my on-call weeks to cover any post-operative problems that might arise with his private cases. Vasectomies – from which he could collect forty pounds from the Family Planning Services on top of his private fee – were his speciality. This simple procedure involves injecting local anaesthetic under the skin on either side of the top of the scrotum, then gently advancing the needle to infiltrate the lignocaine around the spermatic cord and its attendant vessels. Through a half-inch cut over the desensitized area, the cord is gently delivered through the wound, its structures separated by the fluid of the injected anaesthetic. It is easy to sweep the leash of small veins and the testicular artery off the robust cord, which is then divided between clamps and its ends tied off. These ends are looped back against themselves and tied again, and the stumps tucked beneath different tissue planes to prevent them rejoining. A single stitch suffices to re-close the scrotal skin.

In my consultant's hands this uncomplicated operation achieved a spectacular complication rate. The phone beside my bed would ring at 2 a.m., and his dyspeptic voice would ask me to 'pop down to Casualty' and take a look at a private case who had disturbed him at home to complain about post-operative discomfort. I would arrive to find a pale-faced patient with a scrotum swollen to melon dimensions, purple with trapped blood from oozing testicular veins, and have to take him to theatre. My boss would be more than happy to leave such messy patch-up operations to me; 'for the experience, old chap'.

Even off-duty nights were not my own. Because of his deep loathing for his fellow surgeon, any nocturnal problems arising with one of my boss's patients during McOboe's on-call week could not be dealt with by the hated man's registrar or his junior doctors: instead, the nursing staff would be instructed to call me. Asleep at home in London, I would be woken by the apologetic tones of a ward sister, who would request that I make the hour-long journey back to the hospital to unblock a bladder catheter or re-site a drip. Normal life became an improbable memory. The plants in my flat had given up the ghost. My girlfriend, whom I scarcely saw, was involved in a passionate relationship with someone else, and I hadn't even noticed. It was then, at that hospital, that I killed my first patient.

My consultant was away on holiday. I'd admitted an elderly woman, a diabetic, who had been treated for constipation by her GP with the administration of vigorous enemas. These had been unproductive; her abdomen had become painful and distended, and when she reached me it was apparent from her collapsed state that she was suffering from life-threatening peritonitis. In the operating theatre I opened her belly. Her gut was indeed loaded with faeces, but that wasn't the cause of her problem. Years of refined Western diet had caused diverticular disease; a condition attributed to the muscular pressure needed to push a low-fibre residue through the colon. This pressure results in the developments of out-pouchings – diverticuli – from the large bowel, as the gut-lining balloons through weak points in its muscle wall. These pockets, like the appendix, can become inflamed, and sometimes rupture.

I found a diverticulum that had burst. The inflammatory reaction that would normally have caused the omentum – the curtain of peritoneal membrane draping the abdominal organs – to seal the site, had failed – diabetics have a poor inflammatory response – and there had been a free release of colonic bacteria into the abdomen. Fluid in the abdominal cavity had acted as a culture medium for the proliferating microbes, whose toxins had been absorbed freely by the peritoneal lining. Endotoxic shock had ensued: the circulating poisons had caused the walls of her capillaries to leak serum into the tissues, causing a catastrophic fall in blood pressure that started a cascade of problems involving liver, lungs and kidneys.

While antibiotics and fluids were poured into the woman's veins I did the quickest operation I could, bringing the leaking bowel to the surface of her abdomen as a colostomy. Then I washed out the foetid liquid from her belly, placed a drainage tube behind the colon in the area where further pus could form, and closed her up. Afterwards she lay in her Intensive Care bed, moored to the life-support systems. A ventilator pushed air through a tube in her trachea. A gastric tube ran through her nose down into her stomach, sucking out the secretions until her bowel would start working again. A central line in her neck vein monitored blood pressure, a drip entered her arm, there was a catheter in her bladder and the abdominal drain came out near her flank.

There is a crude assessment tool that surgeons use, called the 'rule of five'. It states, simply, that any patient with five or more drips, lines, drains, tubes and catheters entering and leaving the body is probably going to die, however optimistic the forecast of the Intensive Care consultant. My patient's arithmetic did not look favourable. Initially she seemed to rally and the ventilator became unnecessary, but she remained semi-conscious. Within a couple of days there appeared the signs of a dreaded complication: disseminated intravascular coagulopathy. The bacterial toxins had activated the woman's blood-clotting system, filling her circulation with clusters of thrombosis that had threatened to block vessels in brain and kidneys. Though these clots had since dissolved, the result had been utter depletion of the bloodstream's clotting ability. She now began to bleed; from intravenous sites, her operation wound and the edge of her colostomy, and from her nose and mouth. Most worrying, the nasogastric tube in her stomach brought up large quantities of uncoagulated blood.

The metabolic ordeal of major surgery can cause shedding of areas of the stomach lining – a 'stress ulcer' – a complication to which diabetics are particularly prone. In this case, a look down an endoscope revealed that the lower third of the woman's stomach was a raw erosion, from which at least one sizeable vessel was spurting. She was running out of blood faster than it could be pumped into her veins. In a relatively fit patient this situation is fraught enough. Here it was pretty much terminal, and left me with a stark choice – to watch her bleed, inevitably, to death, or to subject her to further, desperate surgery in an attempt to stop the source of bleeding by performing a partial removal of her stomach. Although I had performed gastrectomies before, I was skewered by doubt. The anaesthetic consultant running the Intensive Care

Unit suggested that I should consult my boss. I explained that he was away, and that the only surgeon in the hospital at that time, as I had already established, was his elected enemy. The consultant nodded; he knew all about the implacable prohibition. Feeling very unsupported, I took the woman back to the operating theatre.

For major surgery to succeed on someone in so unstable a condition, the procedure should be quick. It became clear at once that speed would be impossible. As I cut the sutures with which I had recently closed the abdomen, the wound edges wept a steady flow of blood that refused to stop, despite the packs of clotting factor that the anaesthetist was pouring into her veins. Any touch to the tissues – bowel, omentum, the surface of the stomach – produced the same unquenchable ooze. Resection of the stomach requires the clamping and division of a ladder of individual vessels, branches of the main gastro-epiploic artery running along its lower curve. The large right gastric artery has to be divided along the stomach's upper edge. Under a constant tide of blood, that filled the operating field as fast as it could be sucked and swabbed away, these procedures had to be performed by feel alone. Somewhere in the inaccessible reaches behind the beginning of the duodenum, a misplaced clamp slipped before a vessel could be tied, and the tide became a flood. I was, quite literally, out of my depth.

While my house-officer leaned on a bundle of swabs packed into the wound, I called the man to whom I was never to speak, and explained the crisis. McOboe arrived in theatre a few minutes later, scrubbed and joined me. Together we tried to control the geyser that I had unleashed. His expertise saved me from the ultimate fear of every surgeon – that of a patient dying on the operating table – and finally we closed her belly and got the woman back to Intensive Care. She lasted another few hours, while I sat beside her bed and watched her die. Shortly before the end, McOboe brought in the woman's husband and explained to him that the prognosis was hopeless. Then he beckoned me out of the cubicle. 'Situation should never have arisen,' he muttered, shaking his head. 'Poor bastard.' I wasn't sure which of us he was talking about.

I might have given up surgery there and then. Despite the odds against her survival, the circumstances of that woman's death weighed heavily on me. It seemed suddenly that all the major, life-balancing decisions that I had been making since my first surgical experience as a house-officer in Cape Town had succeeded purely through chance. I had always believed that my knowledge and my good intentions were what counted, but now I saw that sound motives were no guard against mistakes, and in my work some of those mistakes, inevitably, could have fatal consequences. Yet all surgeons in training have horror stories. I told mine to a group of registrar colleagues when we sat in a pub after an evening clinical meeting. Some shivered with superstitious dread; others, it turned out, had similarly frightening tales. Only one, a ginger-haired Yorkshireman, offered a comment that verged on the philosophical. 'Every now and then I go back to the Royal College of Surgeons,' he said. 'I have a stroll around the Hunterian Museum and remember why I chose this field in the first place.'

I recalled a previous visit to the museum; a monument to the eclectic interests of John Hunter, Father of the College. There was the skeleton of a giant, an Irishman nearly eight feet tall, displayed beside that of a famous midget with her tiny shoes. Natural history specimens stood with paintings of exotic animals in allegorical landscapes. Human heads in formalin, intricately dissected, exposed the thread-like branches of the cranial nerves, and giant tumours bulged against the lids of the jars containing them. Hunter had also been a pioneer of transplantation, implanting freshly extracted human teeth into the combs of cocks, where they'd taken root and flourished on the rich blood supply. Tooth-fringed rooster-heads, like mutant dentures, stared glassily from their preserving fluids. There were rows of antique scalpels; bone-handled, folding lancets that had once nestled in the waistcoat pockets of surgeons for ready use on abscesses and bladder stones. Trepanning knives for cracking skulls, and brass-bound amputation saws, shone on beds of velvet.

Alongside Hunter's original collection were newer, more utilitarian items: tight arrays of steel scissors, clamps and retractors; the tools of modern surgery. There seemed to be a fundamental truth embodied in their sharp perfection that derided my loss of faith. Yet my training had been a constant process of eroding certainties. First to go had been security: life was tremblingly insecure; death, easy and close. Love was readily found but hard to sustain in the intensity of nights on hospital duty, and rarely more than 'skin-to-skin', the phrase used to define the time taken for a surgical procedure from first incision to last stitch. Repose had gone too, lost in the stress of advising patients on the risks of surgery and explaining afterwards the finding at operation; of having foreknowledge of a person's death. That, finally, was the responsibility invested in me; my years of surgical training had granted me an intimacy with death, against which my patients expected me to intercede on their behalf. There seemed nothing else I could do but grow up, and go on. And there was a senior registrar post waiting for me.

Surgical senior registrars are consultant understudies. They learn to wear suits, and to cultivate that air of inner wisdom and outward efficiency – part butcher, part priest – that will lead patients to trust them with their lives. I had worked for serene surgeons whose mistakes would have filled a small cemetery, whose patients continued to love them even while enduring wound infections and other complications. Though my recent crisis had shaken my composure, my surgical skills still seemed fairly durable, and I decided to trust in them to carry me through the next career stage, however long it might take.

Senior registrar posts typically lasted for years and years, time needed for the vigorous networking required to progress eventually into a consultantship. Part of the process involved socializing with the bosses at unrelaxing evenings at the Royal Society of Medicine – the notorious 'trial by sherry' – as the consultants replaced their worktime autocracy with a brittle evening bonhomie. The bulk of it was just hard clinical work. Now the process is a little shorter and more structured (though not much more fair; it is still the case that less than five per cent of British surgical consultants are women), but at the time that I was training it could not be rushed, and fourteen or fifteen years would normally pass from medical school graduation to achieving the final goal: one hoped to become a consultant surgeon around one's fortieth birthday.

At the same time, changes were underway in the National Health Service itself, begun by Margaret Thatcher and compounded by every British government since. New tiers of administration were being created – purchase managers, finance managers, clinical managers and strategy managers – tasked with applying market forces to the provision of health services. Overheads were reduced by closing wards and hospitals, putting unsustainable pressure on remaining beds. Competition – which was supposed to increase efficiency – set department against department, with doctors fighting one another to retain some share of dwindling resources with which to treat their patients. Consultants began retiring as early as they could, or transferring their skills to private practice. I held my first senior registrar post in the autumn of the old National Health Service, at a time when it was impossible to foresee the extent of that sad pillage, or the pervasive cynicism that has been its lasting legacy.

I worked at a hospital in London, not far from where I lived. My responsibilities included supervising a registrar and two house-officers, and teaching surgery to the students that arrived in batches from an affiliated medical school. At night I had the mature responsibility of being on call from home, ready to drive at once to the hospital when a situation arose that my registrar couldn't deal with. Above me were two consultants; a wise professor of intestinal surgery and a fast-thinking ex-naval officer whose surgical field was arteries and veins.

Together they refined my skills and introduced me to new areas of specialist knowledge. I became interested in vascular surgery, learning how to perform the tiny, regular stitches that are used to join vessels, and to operate on aortic aneurysms – bulging distensions of the biggest artery in the body – that can burst abruptly with often fatal consequences. I had access to an excellent reference library and an archive of treatment records, and saw my first clinical papers appear in learned professional journals.

I hadn't made it, quite. Before I could apply for a consultant post I needed a Master's Degree in Surgery, but outside the quiet cloisters of my hospital the cost-cutters had been busy, with research budgets an easy target. When a subsequent job took me back to a teaching hospital, I became aware of the way power had shifted from the hands of the doctors. My new professor was fighting to survive. His office and parking space had been requisitioned by management, and he operated from a laboratory in a shabby prefab. He asked me for a research proposal that he would submit to medical grant foundations, to fund an academic post for me in his previously bustling department.

Having been working for a gastro-enterology surgeon, I

wrote an outline on assessing the role of a cellular defence mechanism against bowel cancer. Through my interest in vascular surgery I drafted another proposal, for research into the use of lasers for angioplasty: opening blocked arteries. When both projects were rejected for funding, the professor took me aside.

'They were both good projects,' he said, 'and I'm sorry we weren't successful. It may be a long time before the quality of clinical research in this country recovers from the loss of finance. Meantime, perhaps you should consider the value of another qualification, one becoming increasingly popular among young surgeons nowadays. It's called BTA: Been to America.'

4

America

The lecture auditorium was far grander than anything I had seen in a British medical school. Its banks of seats stepped vertiginously down to the stage at the front, a setting for a symphony orchestra. A thousand could be seated amidst the affluent dazzle of blond wood and acoustic panels, though today it was only a mere two hundred: the new intake of medical students, on the momentous day of their induction into the professional world that would shape their futures. I didn't remember such speechifying on my first day at Cape Town University, but this was the American way of marking a portentous event, and all these young faces, impressionable academic fodder, were buying into it with full commitment.

They were about to be addressed by the Commander. He was the medical school's Emeritus Professor of Surgery, and the obvious person to open these commencement ceremonials. It was in his department that I was working for my Master of Surgery degree. The Commander was in his middle seventies, an imposing, patrician figure with the sort of waved grey hair that makes for social distinction. And, yes, he was a senior officer on the Military Reserve List, with the rosette of a high decoration in the buttonhole of his excellent suit for services rendered to the United States Navy during the Vietnam war. He was a leader, a man to take us places. An expectant hush fell as he approached the podium.

'Ladies and gentlemen; scholars of science; future

members of the healing profession,' he began, in that kindly, unmilitary tone that I had nonetheless heard used to flay the foolish, 'this moment is perhaps the most important in your lives, for today you commence on that great journey, the study of medicine. Medicine includes those vital components that make up life: the human body, and the human soul. You have just finished that part of your studies that deal with the soul. From now on you will be concerned only with the human body.'

I knew the Commander's sly humour by now, and I watched while he paused for some recognition that he was being ironic, or cynical, or just irreverent. There was nothing. These aspirant American doctors were a solemn bunch. Some were already taking notes in this, their introductory lecture, and I saw how attentively they sat, waiting for the next word. The Commander tried to defuse their tension.

'I was told that by the Dean of my Medical School in 1946,' he said, 'when I was sitting where you are now. Things have moved on a long way since then, and doctors are perhaps less dogmatic about the boundary between the physical and the metaphysical.'

A few of his audience scratched out what they had already written, but most, now, simply sat. After school, college, and a couple of years of pre-med studies, they were astute enough to realize that discussion about these intangibles would surely not form the basis for an examination question.

⊕

I was a member of the Commander's Club, one of those obscure, intimate fraternities, informal yet ritual-bound, wherein lie the real power of academic medicine in America. Within this hospital, at others in the city and dotted around the New England states, most of the senior practitioners of vascular surgery were the Commander's protégés. They sat together on examining boards, collaborated on research, and came to garden parties on the wide lawns of the Commander's colonial mansion, where they plotted ways to confound the power of the monolithic HMOs; the Health Management Organizations dictating the terms of surgical and medical practice throughout the USA.

I had a great deal of respect for the Commander. He had worked under the legendary De Bakey, pioneer of the modern science of arterial surgery, so his cutting credentials were impeccable. His re-organization of vascular services in the American military had probably saved thousands of lives – and limbs – in the war in Vietnam. He had a flair for identifying opportunities, and the means to exploit them. I had met him while sitting in a lobby in his hospital, having arrived early for an appointment with another doctor to discuss possible research posts. The Commander, passing by on his way to lunch, asked for whom I was waiting. I explained that I was looking for a means to help me to produce a Master's thesis.

'Come in to my office,' he said, 'let's chat for a while until it's time for your meeting.'

Such genial courtesy was something I was unused to from my seniors in England. So was his exceptional power to make things happen.

'I've just been approached with a very interesting proposition,' he said, opening a folder on his desk. 'Do you know anything about the use of electrical fields to generate heat in arteries?'

A school-friend who'd built metal detectors had once taught me how they used electrical fields to search through solid earth. I had recently learned something of the effects of heat on vessel tissue while preparing my research proposal on laser treatment of arterial disease. Combining these shards of knowledge, I produced for the Commander an apparently plausible summary of how such a system might work, and its possible effects. American surgical training has no equivalent of the Royal College of Surgeons examinations, which require a skill in logical confabulation to get the candidate through impossible questions. The Commander appeared impressed.

'We can create a research post for you, in the vascular laboratory,' he said. 'You'll be able to write your thesis, and the company that's developing this idea will get its device tested for therapeutic use.'

With the Commander's invitation in hand I'd gone back to London, renounced my hospital post and dumped my possessions in storage. Then I'd returned with a single suitcase, knowing not a soul in the city apart from my patron. But after you've been exiled, each subsequent change of country is less heartbreaking. Staying my first week in a colleague's spare room, I walked the city in search of somewhere to live. I found a place in a creaking clapboard mansion – its garage adorned with hubcaps and old railway signs – in a leafy suburb. I shared the house with an artist and a photographer and their dogs. It felt a little like a version of the bohemian life I'd known in Cape Town, heightened by the presence – a block beyond the house – of the beginning of the ghetto. Men loitered on the corners. Shops were fortified, and service came from behind a steel grill. Crack cocaine was easier to buy there than beer; places closed before nightfall to reduce the risk of hold-ups, and gunshots were commonplace.

A similar contrast was apparent at the hospital. With its schools of medicine, dentistry and veterinary science, it stretched over several city blocks, a collection of glass cubes and masonry towers and monumental brownstones. The complex lay in a mean area of the city and glass bridges soared between the buildings, keeping staff and students insulated from the streets below. Squad cars patrolled the multi-level parking garage, their roof-lights flashing. A police post operated in the hospital's emergency room, with its own reception area where felons were handcuffed to the benches while they awaited medical attention.

Away from these utilitarian areas, the hospital was rather plush. The main lobby was high and dark-panelled and hung with tapestries, though it was possible to leave it via a wrong turning and find oneself entering a mysterious annex where sensitive research was being carried out for the US Government, and the security guards wore guns and X-rayed every briefcase. Each building carried on flank or pediment the name of the philanthropist who'd endowed it. Original artworks, bought for their investment value, brightened offices and waiting areas and the consulting rooms of the senior specialists in each department.

The department of vascular surgery was one of the hospital's best-appointed and most influential divisions. Its power was predicated by its ability to bring in capital: from the patients – surgery on blood vessels is a high-tech, high-yield business – and much more from the revenue generated by medical research. The vascular laboratory, in which I was now an overseas research fellow, existed to push forward the boundaries of knowledge in this specialized field. Also, it was a gold mine. Surgical appliance manufacturers, instrument designers, drug developers and inventors of arterial balloons, springs, lasers and grafts would come to meetings with the department's scientists and lawyers. Tenders would be prepared to compete with other hospitals for the business of testing these ideas. Experimental and clinical trials would be designed to assess their effectiveness, with the additional aim of showing a profit for the hospital group.

This was a world away from the rigours of British academic medical research, with its gritty sub-subsistence despair. The hospital operated as an industry, whose senior staff – its directors – benefited through salaries, bonuses and shares. In such a fervent anthill of therapeutic investment, they could do very well. There were the benefits of inside knowledge. The vascular department, spotting a likely product under development in its laboratory, might invest in it itself, forming a partnership with the company that owned it. The post of chief of the department (half managing director, half professor) had a special aura, because a share of the potential profits – a tiny part of a percentage point, it was true, but one that could be worth a fortune – could become his personal gain.

The result was a delicate tight-rope act between scientific rigour and financial imperatives. It was vital to have many papers published in the professional journals, for active research departments attract business. Favourable results would be used by medical companies as press releases, extolling the market potential of their product to boost their share price. A thriving company would invest more in research, and that meant more money coming in to the hospital. Of course the benefits of these transactions didn't generally filter down to the scientists doing the work, which engendered a certain cynicism among them.

'What, for example, is the definition of a medical advance?' asked Steve – research professor and head of the laboratory – on my first day at work. 'Well, in this business, a medical advance is something which, if applied to a rat, will produce a paper. A medical breakthrough is when the rat survives.'

Steve was foremost a scientist, a dedicated man. He had a PhD in some abstruse field of cell wall physiology, and appreciated the exquisite awkwardness of the interface between medicine and money.

A favourite story was his account of the afternoon the New York stock-market crashed. Some surgeons had been at work in the vascular surgery operating room, implanting a new type of arterial graft in the first human recipient. Steve, having overseen the development project in his laboratory, was there to watch. The calm silence of professionals at work – overlaid by the music chosen by the senior surgeon to operate by; some easy-listening stuff, Steve recalled – was interrupted by a young doctor hurrying in. 'Excuse me, everyone,' he said, with the solemnity of a bearer of big news, 'I think you ought to know. There's something weird happening to the Dow Jones Average.'

'Can't you see we're busy here?' boomed the senior, looking up in annoyance through his special operating spectacles. The new arrival conferred in whispers with the anaesthesiologist.

'I really think you ought to hear this,' said the gas-man. 'I'm getting the TV set brought in from the surgeons' room.'

The box was set up on a shelf and the muzak turned down, and the doctors listened while an announcer recorded, in shocked tones, Wall Street's inexorable plunge. The operation faltered. One by one the surgeons turned from the table and stood gazing at the screen, their gloved hands clasped, as the financial figures reeled downwards.

'They were keeping their hands together to stop them touching anything that wasn't sterile,' explained Steve, 'but it sure as hell looked like they were praying.'

He noticed that the senior surgeon's eyes, enlarged by his magnifying lenses, were swimming with tears. They began to drip off the edge of his spectacles and splash to the floor.

'The guy was actually sobbing,' said Steve, 'he couldn't go on; his tears would have flooded the wound. The operation had to be finished by one of the others with less stock-market exposure.'

✪

The medical development company for whom I was doing my research work had their offices in a restored textile mill beside the river. The old factory buildings along the waterfront had been gentrified with tinted glass and cobbled sidewalks and planted birch trees, and were now the corporate headquarters of America's new industries. Their products – computer software, bio-genetics technology, micro-electronics – were conceptualized on these pristine premises, but the real work of development took place in the unadorned surroundings of research laboratories such as the one I worked in at the hospital. My company specialized in the development of medical devices. Its owners were sharp young men in designer suits who looked like media executives, and who tossed out phrases – 'boundary-pushing', 'consumer-responsiveness' – that stressed more than anything their distance from the task of making people better.

For the first time in my career I was involved with the commercial face of medicine, and I didn't feel entirely comfortable. Steve was, I think, slightly puzzled by my qualms. 'You need the research post, the company needs the science done properly,' he said. 'By helping them you help yourself. You come out of it more qualified. In the end, your patients benefit.'

So I stuck to looking at the clinical issues. Apart from blood-vessel injuries, almost all arterial surgery is performed for arteriosclerosis; narrowing of the arteries. This can occur in mid-sized vessels such as the carotid and femoral arteries, but the commonest and most significant site is in the coronary arteries supplying the heart. The disease is associated with fat-rich diets, high cholesterol, obesity, smoking, lack of exercise: not a general problem in the developing world, but in the USA, cardiac vessels often start furring up at thirty. Treatment can be surgical – by inserting a bypass graft to bridge the narrowed area – but over the past twenty years the technique of balloon angioplasty has become increasingly common. A small balloon, at the end of a fine, flexible tube, is passed through a needle in the groin and up the arterial system to the narrowed area. The balloon is inflated, stretching the coronary vessel to its original diameter, and then removed, allowing normal blood flow to resume.

Over half a million Coronary Artery Balloon Angioplasties are performed a year in the USA. Though much simpler than artery bypass surgery, it can be less successful. When the balloon has forced open the narrow area, layers of arterial wall can split away, blocking the vessel like a flap. Blood clots can form in the splits and on the raw surface left behind when the balloon is removed. Healthy artery alongside the treated section can close in a reflex spasm. In about five per cent of cases, these problems will cause the treated vessel to block shortly after the procedure. My research was directed at reducing these causes of failure. If successful, one result would in fact be less work for practitioners of my speciality – surgeons were called in to operate when balloon angioplasty failed – but an improved outcome for patients.

The theory I was testing was that localized heat could improve the success of balloon angioplasty. A medical engineer had designed a method of creating accurately controlled electrical heating in tissues, and this technology had been built into a modified angioplasty balloon. We hoped that when it was inflated at a point of arterial narrowing, the balloon would stretch the vessel while the combination of heat and pressure would seal together split layers in the arterial wall, preventing flaps and leaving a smoother surface that would result in less blood-clot formation. The heating system had been shown to have this sealing effect on pieces of artery tested in the lab. It was my job to design and perform a programme of experiments that would show its effectiveness in living vessels. Many of these steps related to safety, for such a device could have unexpected side-effects.

I would have to show that the heated balloon didn't actually worsen blood-clotting, or have effects outside the wall of the artery that would cook adjacent tissue. The correct temperature had to be found for best effect. It would have to be proved that the heat-treated section of artery didn't develop scarring and accelerated re-narrowing, or be weakened and form an aneurysm; an abnormal dilatation. Finally, the device had to show results at least as good as standard balloon angioplasty, before anyone would consider putting it to use in human trials. These goals, then, formed the body of my thesis.

The work also had to meet the needs of the company that had developed the concept, who would use these results in its submission to have the heat system licensed by the Food and Drug Administration. In the United States, the FDA is the regulatory body that decides whether a new device, drug or treatment may be tried on humans. Its standards are rigorous, for FDA approval indicates that all reasonable steps have been taken to ensure that the new concept is as safe as accepted methods of treatment. Once approved, the invention can go into commercial use, hopefully to recoup the millions spent on research and development – and the even larger amount poured into product marketing – and eventually to show a profit for its creators.

Although the heating mechanism was based on established medical technology, it had never been applied in this exacting manner. Its effects on all aspects of vessel structure and cellular function would have to be assessed; areas of scientific detail that lay outside my training. Fortunately I had expert support from Tim, a company scientist who had initiated basic research on the device. We could take advice from specialists working in diverse hospital departments – pathologists, haematologists, histologists, cell biologists and medical engineers – as well as the other doctors and scientists in the laboratory, and from Steve himself, a veteran of many successful FDA submissions.

While I read the latest publications on arterial disease, heat effects and vessel healing, we began our experiments. We immersed heated balloons in radioactive-isotope-labelled blood and used gamma-counters to show that the amount of clot that formed on them was the same as that found on standard angioplasty balloons. We created splits between the layers of artery walls, fused them with heat, then injected saline through the join to show that they resisted four or five times normal arterial blood pressure before breaking apart. With sensitive thermal sensors, we worked out how far the heat effect extended into the surrounding tissue. Having calculated the effective settings for the device, we applied the heated balloon treatment to arteries, and monitored the vessels at intervals to assess the effects.

Other vascular laboratories were working with technology that used lasers to burn through arterial narrowings. A competing research group was trying out a system in which a laser, shining through an inflated angioplasty balloon, tried to vaporize the narrowed area in the artery wall while the vessel was being stretched. The medical laser manufacturers were funding a lot of research, and pushing their products hard. It was all part of the therapeutics business; lasers used for arterial treatment cost around a hundred thousand dollars each, but if the companies could carve themselves a slice of the two hundred billion dollars spent annually in the USA on the treatment of coronary artery disease, their financial success would be assured.

Keeping our ears attuned to scientific rumours about the progress of our competitors – we'd heard they were finding that laser-heat was absorbed unevenly by normal and diseased parts of the artery wall, and that vessel perforations could occur unpredictably – we concentrated on our painstaking work. An experiment could take days to design, a week to set up, and a month to show results, at which point it might become clear that we'd neglected some factor whose absence nullified the outcome. But as we began to accumulate dependable data, our elation grew: our device caused only moderate heating of tissue lying against the balloon, and did not appear to produce arterial perforation.

The heated balloons appeared to have a number of other favourable effects. We could see on angiography – filling the vessel at the end of each procedure with a liquid that outlined it on X-ray – that comparison artery sites stretched with an ordinary balloon sometimes went into spasm, while the areas treated by the heated balloon remained expanded to the size of the balloon. We postulated that the heat had inactivated the muscle cells in the arterial wall responsible for the spasm reflex. On repeating the angiogram at two-weekly intervals after the procedure, the expanded area persisted. The most interesting results were noted when we looked at the treated areas under a microscope.

A major problem of ordinary coronary balloon angioplasty is that around a third of treated heart arteries will undergo re-narrowing within six months, sometimes to the point of blocking the vessel completely. This does not seem to be just a recurrence of the original disease, but due to an apparent overgrowth of the muscle cells normally found in the vessel wall. It is thought that this is the effect of growth factors – chemical stimulants of cell proliferation – released as a result of damage to the vessel when the balloon has stretched it. The type of arteries we were studying were particularly prone to developing muscle cell overgrowth when they were injured, and by eight weeks after angioplasty this effect could be plainly seen in the comparison vessels treated by ordinary balloons: whorls of new muscle cells had forced their way between the layers of the arterial wall, causing it to thicken and bulge.

By contrast, the heat-treated areas were smooth. Tissue samples taken within an hour of the procedure had shown that all the muscle cells had disappeared, leaving the structural fibres of the arterial wall intact. Two weeks later a few cells were beginning to reappear between the preserved supporting fibres. There were more at four weeks, and by eight weeks the arterial wall appeared to have been entirely repopulated by normal-looking muscle cells, without any sign of cell overgrowth. It seemed that the heat treatment might work in part by inactivating and removing the muscle cells – the source of the overgrowth – which then grew back slowly when the growth factors were no longer being released. We still needed to discover whether this new treatment technique might have long-term side-effects.

⊕

In the meantime, I was greatly enjoying my new life. I made friends among those working at the hospital, and hung out in the city's cocktail lounges and student bars, where I was entertained by the invigorating directness of the women. I discovered how the city was stratified into ethnic districts – Italian, Irish, Polish, Vietnamese – each preserving its odd exclusivity. On summer weekends my friends and I would lie on the beach, or drive to Vermont or New Hampshire and stay in a farmhouse. We'd wander the country back-roads in an old Ford pick-up, drinking beer at roadside bars and swimming in the rivers while the wild boys blasted derelict cars with pump-action shotguns. I was delighted by the cinematic quality of life in America.

What I found most exciting was the innovative atmosphere of the laboratory, and the opportunities to collaborate on other research. I ran a project assessing potential side-effects of a synthetic blood substitute, that could avoid incompatible transfusions and transmission of infections; it might also appeal to Jehovah's Witnesses. A colleague and I collated the outcome of five years' surgery on aortic aneurysms performed in our hospital, and presented the results at a vascular surgery symposium in Canada. I even made a study of that most humble of surgical procedures, the treatment of piles. Haemorrhoids are blown-up vessels – effectively, varicose veins of the anal canal – but their treatment is usually the province of the rectal specialist rather than the vascular surgeon. I had done a fair amount of haemorrhoid surgery during my surgical training, and when I was asked to make a research assessment of a new therapy for the condition, I started by reviewing the outcome of the standard treatments currently in use.

The results were unexpected. Piles, in English surgical practice, were considered to merit operation only if they were severe. Here, however, these criteria seemed less stringent; often minor piles that might have responded to injection of an irritant to shrink the vein, were going under the knife. I was puzzled by this difference in approach – the results of surgery on small haemorrhoids are generally unimpressive – until I found the payment invoices in each patient's folder. These were met by the health insurers, who paid out a lot more for an operation than injections. In the medical school library I read a US Senate investigation which suggested that two and a half million unnecessary operations were performed a year in the United States. I wondered to what extent market forces dictated treatment decisions. The logic of a for-profit medical system appeared to lead to expensive solutions and spiralling costs, in the same way that expensive equipment – such as arterial lasers – produced pressure for the investment to be used to show returns.

But medicine here was business, as I discovered when I presented aspects of my heated-balloon research at medical conferences across the country. These galas – in Chicago or Indianapolis or Washington DC – were sumptuous affairs, where issues of treatment-cost relative to benefit seldom arose. The biggest symposium I attended was the national American Heart Association meeting in California, next to Disneyland. It was very popular. Delegates brought along their partners and kids, ate at groaning buffets of rich food provided by the heart-drug manufacturers, and joined ten thousand other doctors at the acres of indoor conference space to take their pick of the three hundred lectures and presentations available daily. The commercial might of high-technology medicine was on display.

At the stands of the various therapeutics companies – amidst the free promotional briefcases, coffee mugs and mouse-pads – I met the doyens of vascular research whose names I knew from learned journals. In the evenings these eminences would be guests at company cocktail parties where million-dollar funding would be discussed for future collaborations; in the corners their research staff, fuelled by bottomless Margueritas, would discuss academic scandals that lay behind well-publicized breakthroughs. Many grumbled at the practice of padding scientific publications with extra authors, so that those who did the actual work might find themselves sharing recognition with assorted individuals to whom their professor might owe favours. A simple paper, therefore, might appear to have been written by twelve people, ten of whom would now be able to claim the publication on their résumés without having been involved in – or even necessarily understood – a jot of the painstaking work that had gone into it. Even company chief executives might appear as co-authors, a bit of harmless flattery that could generate another massive research contract.

These conferences provided opportunities to meet other overseas research fellows; bemused, like myself, at the way this cornucopia of wealth affected the basic philosophy of American medicine. Our research fellowships generally included the teaching of medical students, and all of us were struck by the different emphasis of their training. Prospective physicians in the US – groomed for practice using technological diagnostic aids – tended to receive relatively less teaching in basic clinical skills. Also, unlike the British system where all newly qualified doctors spend an internship year in general hospital medicine and surgery, American doctors tended to enter their chosen area of specialization immediately on graduation. One research fellow, a man from Glasgow, described a recent bed-side tutorial he'd held with a group of final-year medical students at the university where he worked.

'I want you to examine this man's abdomen,' he instructed one of them. 'Tell me what you find.'

'I'm not sure what I'm looking for,' said the student. 'Can I see his laboratory results?'

'Imagine there aren't any lab results,' said the Glaswegian, knowing that every test report includes a computer-generated list of possible diagnoses. 'Imagine you're in the middle of the jungle.'

'In the jungle?' queried the student. 'Some sort of tropical disease? I wouldn't know about those. I'm going to be a child allergist.'

'OK, forget the jungle. Let's just say he's just arrived in the emergency room, unconscious, and you have to work out what's wrong with him.'

'If he's unconscious then I definitely wouldn't be seeing him,' said the student smugly. 'He'd go straight to the neurologists for a brain scan.'

✪

With tuition fees an important source of university revenue, American medical schools vied with one another to attract students, by advertising special features in the academic syllabus. I visited another overseas research fellow at the university where he worked and saw one such Unique Selling Point in action. Thomas and I had been taught surgery in much the same way at our respective medical schools – his in Australia, mine South African – both operated along British lines. After a couple of years of academic studies we had started our first clinical year, during which we had been attached to a surgical firm: to follow the consultant around the wards, to sit in at out-patient consultations, and to stand at the back of the operating theatre trying not to faint. As the theory we'd learned began to make sense, our involvement had increased. By the third and final clinical year we would be helping the surgical house-officers in the wards and Casualty, and might assist at operations ourselves.

Thomas wished to show me how training differed at his American university. He took me to the surgical laboratory and introduced me to the professor. A group of medical students were sitting in a lecture room, where they had just finished a tutorial on surgical procedures. Thomas told me that they were in their first year of clinical studies, but I noticed that they were all dressed in operating greens, like baby doctors. I looked among their solemn ranks for anarchists and long-hairs – the types who'd been my student friends, who had provided diversity in my medical class – but no such elements were present.

'Most of these kids go into medicine as a business decision,' observed Thomas. 'They have to be serious because at the end of their studies they'll each have average debts of forty thousand dollars to work off. They're too busy thinking about their prospects to relax much. We get a new bunch like this every month.'

The professor led his students into the large surgical lab. I peered through the doors. Ranged around the floor were half a dozen operating tables, each surmounted by the still form of an anaesthetized pig. Laboratory technicians fussed around, checking airways and gas-lines and shrouding parts of each animal with green drapes. Stretched out on their backs, the animals looked disturbingly human; an impression reinforced by the pink areas of exposed pig-skin.

'Let's go and change,' said Thomas. 'You can lend a hand as an extra tutor.'

By the time we returned, the students had been divided into groups around each animal. One pair took up station at the neck, another couple at the abdomen and a third pair at the flanks. At the table nearest to me there was much discussion, and a nervous flourishing of scalpels. I introduced myself and asked how I could help.

'Well,' said a lad standing at the animal's neck, 'we've had the lecture on how to take out the thyroid, but my partner and I can't work out where to make the cut.' He gestured at the square of skin before him.

'We're supposed to remove the spleen,' said the pair at the top of the abdomen.

'We're going to cut and rejoin some gut,' chimed in the couple at the lower end.

I showed them how to identify the anatomical landmarks necessary to place their incisions, and they began. At first the pace was hesitant, with much consultation of text-books, but once they got through the skin and the blood started running, they made up for their lack of skill with a braggadocio enthusiasm. Across the room some paled at the bleeding and went to sit down, while their hardier classmates exchanged glances under their eyebrows: not surgical material.

The operations that the students had been set were delicate procedures, requiring careful dissection. Each had potential complications. A large vein – a branch of the internal jugular – runs into the edge of the thyroid. This, along with the arteries that supply the top and bottom of the gland on either side, can be a source of troublesome bleeding. All these vessels must be carefully tied and cut to prevent bleeding into the tissues of the neck and later respiratory obstruction, while avoiding damage to the recurrent laryngeal nerve lying behind them. Major arteries run into the spleen and from it into the stomach, and these need to be divided between clamps and tied securely before the organ can be removed. A gut anastomosis is a demanding procedure that must be done gently so that the blood supply to the gut-ends is not damaged, or the join will break down and leak.

These techniques take years to learn thoroughly, so I concentrated on showing them some obvious pitfalls, and tidying up the worst mistakes myself as a teaching demonstration. The poor pigs had to survive at least another twenty-four hours, so that a further set of procedures – a tracheostomy, removal of a kidney, and opening and patching of a femoral artery in the groin – could be performed, before they were sacrificed on the altar of scientific learning. By the end of the afternoon my students could handle tissues after a fashion, and were at least tying competent surgical knots that would not slip and result in the animal bleeding to death. I showed them how to close the skin wounds evenly, without tension. After the students left, now swaggering like surgical matadors, Thomas came over to me.

'Hard work, isn't it?' he said. 'Tonight they'll be at the surgical textbooks, and tomorrow they'll be rapping out acronyms and fancying themselves as their favourite television-doctor characters. This practical surgery class is really popular, the students love it. Many of them are Jewish – good kosher kids who won't eat at the hospital canteen – but when it comes to pig surgery you can't keep them away.' It would be three years before these students graduated and came to do any actual operating, continued Thomas, and that was only the minority who chose a career in surgery. I rather agreed with his suspicion that such a slaughter of animals – for the training of first-year surgical students – wouldn't be approved by a British medical research ethics committee.

Back at our laboratory I was soon to experience another unexpected aspect of the US medical system. A research colleague and I, both trained in vascular surgery, had been implanting a range of experimental arterial grafts. The vital part of vessel surgery is the anastomosis: joining the ends with meticulous, tiny sutures. As we laboured together, we wondered whether this repetitious exercise could be carried out by mechanical means. Such methods already existed for bowel surgery; a clean seal can be made between two ends of gut by a special device that joins the edges together with a ring of tiny steel staples. Indeed, Russian technicians had made an arterial stapling device for joining the ends of medium-sized vessels, but it was cumbersome and difficult to re-sterilize after use. We decided to try to design a simple, disposable kit that would perform a reliable anastomosis, and could also be used to join the end of a graft or vessel to the side of another, during bypass surgery and organ transplants.

We sat in a bar after work and sketched out a design that radically modified the Russian system. From parts of disposable surgical instruments obtained as samples at a medical conference, we built a prototype in the basement workshop of the house where I lived. It was crude, but it worked, and with it we successfully joined some bits of arterial graft-tube together, end-to-end and end-to-side. We showed our results to a designer from a surgical instrument company we had met at a symposium. He arranged a presentation to his firm, where an independent expert – a vascular surgeon at another hospital – advised the company that the concept had therapeutic potential. An agreement was drawn up that would give the company sole rights to assess the idea for a three-month period, in exchange for five thousand dollars. If the device proved worthy of development, we would share in patent and royalty rights with the company. Proudly, my colleague and I mentioned our achievement to the chief of vascular surgery at our hospital. The next day a letter arrived from the hospital lawyers, requiring our presence at an urgent meeting. Steve came with us.

I think we expected to be congratulated on our inventiveness, but it turned out that we hadn't understood certain rules regarding the concept of intellectual property. Though we'd built the device in our own time, we had done so while employees of the laboratory. This meant that the idea, and any potential commercial advantages it produced, belonged to the hospital.

'The concept is ours,' said the head of the hospital's legal team. 'You have no rights to it except those that we may decide to assign to you once the hospital has calculated its profit margin.'

'He's right, you know,' said Steve. 'It may not be written into the employment contract but those rules apply to all of us in research.'

We nodded, reluctantly. The lawyer, resplendent in a fawn silk suit, plumped the knot of his yellow tie.

'I'm glad you see reason,' he said. 'It would be embarrassing to have to sue you. Now if you'll just hand over your design notes, your drawings, and the prototype you've built, we'll take it from there.' He leaned back in his chair, savouring the moment. 'And I believe you owe us five thousand dollars.'

Perhaps I had been influenced by my exposure to American medicine more than I'd realized, for I was seized by what could only be described as pure commercial aggression.

My colleague and I had each worked hard for a share of that five grand.

'As the concept is entirely yours, you'll have a much better idea about its design than we would,' I said. 'Make your own prototype.'

In the end the instrument company announced, regretfully, that development of the concept would cost several million dollars, and that the specialized market for the device made its production unprofitable. The hospital renounced its interest, and the chief even gave us some recognition for the work we had done. He let us keep the five thousand dollars we'd earned.

⊕

By now, my co-worker Tim and I were correlating our final results. After prolonged follow-up, none of the heat-treated arteries showed signs of either recurrent narrowing or aneurysmal dilatation. It seemed that the heat technique might make a significant difference to the results of balloon angioplasty treatment for arteriosclerotic vessel disease. An incidental bonus was the fact that the equipment we had used to generate the heat effect cost around eight hundred dollars, theoretically making it accessible to patients in less affluent countries. Tim set out the results in the format required for FDA submission, while I wrote up my thesis.

When FDA approval was confirmed, Tim's company held a champagne party to celebrate. The executives appeared delighted, as well they might; the share-price of the company had rocketed. Tim and I were warmly congratulated. Steve was there too, and other friends from the laboratory. I looked around the gathering with sadness. I realized that I would probably never again be so closely immersed in a sector of knowledge – however specialized – or feel that pure, personal thrill of contributing to its advancement. I would miss the excitement of discovery and collaboration, where a casual conversation at the laboratory coffee machine might spin off all sorts of lateral associations, sending everyone away with new insights.

There would be no more creative drinking parties in the dark bars near the hospital, or fêtes on the Commander's lawn, or barbecues at Steve's rambling rural spread; whose boundaries he patrolled with a rifle at cranberry season to stop fly-by-night fruit pickers stealing his crop. Now that it was over, I realized that my two years of research had been the first interlude of relatively normal life – without night duty and insidious, draining exhaustion – that I'd experienced since I had been a medical student. I contemplated my return to the hospital life of a surgical senior registrar with a degree of dread.

Three months later, back in my hospital post, I heard from my university medical school that my Master of Surgery thesis on the effects and applications of heated balloon angioplasty had been accepted without revision. I called Steve to tell him the news and asked him to pass it on to the bosses of the company.

'They aren't in that field any more,' he told me, 'as soon as the news of their FDA approval got around, the company received an offer from its main competitor, an arterial laser manufacturer, and sold up its interest in the idea. All the executives pocketed very handsome pay-outs.' As far as he knew, Steve went on, the heated-balloon arterial device had been pretty much shelved by its new owners.

5

Namibia and Zululand

Master of Surgery. The title had a ring of Zen about it, as though I was now a sage of some martial art, a mystic bladesman. I had trodden the path of professional dedication, served the necessary years at the required levels of experience and responsibility; paid all my dues to date. A consultant post – the reward for all this industry – lay ahead, with attendant success and security. But I found myself beset by an odd emptiness. I'd really believed in the value of the research work I'd done to acquire my new standing, and it was little consolation that plenty of promising projects never passed into clinical use, for all sorts of reasons. Also, I'd had the disconcerting experience of meeting Stefan again.

He'd arrived at my hospital in London to fill in for a psychiatry registrar away on leave. He had seemed, at first re-meeting, the practical positivist I used to know, though he didn't acknowledge our old closeness, or offer any explanation about where he'd been during the last ten years. There was something about the way he sat, slightly forward in his chair, that reminded me of his tension at our last encounter in Cape Town: alert, but with a subtle inattention, as though throughout our conversation he was tracking some distant sound. Everyone else thought Stefan was fine. His patients seemed to find him understanding and sympathetic; his colleagues were impressed by the clarity of his diagnoses. The head of the psychiatry department offered Stefan a permanent post. He seemed pleased, but the following week he failed to turn up for work. The consultant, knowing I was Stefan's friend, sought me out: did I know where he was? I didn't say that I was as concerned as he was; there was no answer on the phone number Stefan had given me.

A week later Stefan called and asked if I would meet him in a bar. I arrived early, but he had clearly been there for a while already. He was drunk. He trembled, and his pallor was offset by a black eye and a vivid bruise that covered one cheek and disappeared beneath his collar. I reached forward – Stefan flinched – and gently hooked away the shirt. Dark marks encircled his neck, the shape of a pair of hands. I could see the imprint of each finger pressed into the skin. He tugged his collar closed.

'It's nothing,' he said. 'I got into a fight.'

He had wanted me to apologize to the consultant for him; he wasn't coming back. He'd found another job somewhere else. I asked him if he was still using drugs, if I could help him. He said he was fine but I could see that his distraction was worse, as though he was listening to a tumult of gibbering.

Stefan had been my first guide in how to behave as a doctor; he'd been perhaps the single greatest influence in the way I thought about the moral and social responsibilities of clinical practice. Now I felt as though some fundamental confidence had abandoned me. I was most aware of the loss when I had to reassure patients on whom I was about to operate that they could entrust their lives to me. After the detachment of research I was struck again by the amount of death I had to deal with: each morning, coming onto the wards, I would wonder who had survived the night and who had succumbed. My emotional energy seemed no longer sufficient to deal with the absurd extremes of hospital work.

I admitted a woman with intestinal obstruction. She had a history of episodic pains in her right side; these had become severe a few days before and then suddenly stopped. The next day her belly had begun to distend, and she'd started vomiting. I examined her in casualty with the aid of an abdominal X-ray. It showed multiple fluid-levels in the intestine that indicated small bowel obstruction. More unusually, it also showed the clear outline of her gallbladder and biliary system, inflated by air as neatly as an anatomy diagram.

Intestinal gas will not normally pass up the bile duct, so there remained another explanation: a large gallstone had caused her pain through periodic attacks of cholecystitis. Eventually the pressure of the stone had eroded through the gallbladder wall and the top of the duodenum to which the inflamed organ had become stuck. Relief had come as the stone had slipped through into the gut (allowing air to pass the other way, up into the gallbladder) but it had been short-lived. The stone, probably around the size of a marble, would have passed through her small intestine until it jammed at the narrowest part – the end of the ileum, just before the junction with the colon – and caused obstruction. Gallstone obstruction is not very common – early operative treatment of cholecystitis means that few cases progress to this stage – but whatever the cause of the gut blockage she still needed surgery, so I would soon find out whether my diagnosis was correct. I took her to the operating theatre.

Burrowing between blown-up loops of bowel, I found the place where the distension ended and felt a hard lump. A cut through the gut wall revealed the green, granular surface of a gallstone. I removed it and repaired the hole, then took out her troublesome gallbladder. At the end of the operation I placed the stone in a specimen bottle, asking the ward-nurse to leave it on the patient's bedside table for her to see when she awoke. When I reached the ward at the end of my daily round I found the woman lying in bed, looking discontented. I asked if she was in pain.

'My stomach was hurting terribly, doctor,' she said petulantly, 'and the nurses wouldn't give me anything. So I took that big green tablet on the bedside table. It was an awful struggle getting it down, and it really doesn't seem to have helped at all.'

Late at night, after I had finished opening and closing her for the second time, I walked down the hospital corridor, hearing the sound of my heels on the linoleum. I felt exhausted. The sky outside reflected the sulphur glow of London's night and suddenly I saw clearly that if my professional career proceeded to plan, I would be making this lonely 4 a.m. walk for the rest of my working life. I felt a great need to step outside the process for a while, to make a reckoning of what I had achieved and where I might be going. A steady predawn wind blew through the open window. It reminded me of Africa.

⊕

I arrived in Johannesburg by air. I had heard through exile contacts that the computer at the airport was unserviceable, a casualty of international sanctions that withheld replacement parts. Without its database the barcode in my passport would remain silent, with no telling record of draft evasion to come up on the screen. The immigration officer flipped open the document and bounced his stamp with a bang on the page. 'Welcome home.'

I didn't stay long. There was something desperate in the way I found myself trying to match what I saw around me with the country I'd known a decade before, for I hadn't realized how my exile's dreams had been altered, by the constant revisions of memory, into a place that had never existed.

Even the things I'd thought unchangeable – the intransigent militarism of Pretoria, the endless border war in South West Africa – were changing. The army had pulled back from its battle-positions on the Angola border, relinquishing them to a United Nations transitional force. Soon South Africa would leave the territory altogether, and Namibia would become – in 1990 – the last country in Africa to acquire independence. I imagined that the place could be a sort of half-way house, an intimation of how South Africa might feel once real change began. I had been in desultory contact with a university friend all through my years of absence, who had frequently urged me to visit him in Windhoek. Now seemed like a good time to go.

Windhoek had been the capital of the old German colony of South West Africa. My friend Rod and I sat in a café on Kaiserstrasse, eating Bavarian pastries. He was already anticipating the joys of freedom. With the departure of the South African military, the border area was, after fifteen years, no longer an operational zone. He proposed that we take his four-wheel-drive truck up through the desert to the Namibia-Angola border, to visit those parts of his country to which he had been denied access for so long. Rod produced a set of military maps – marked Classified, they showed fire-zones and mine-fields, plus every waterhole and track – and traced the route. It passed through Oshakati and Oshikango, the places of Stefan's war and of the experience that had seared his life. I wanted to see those places. If I hadn't left South Africa when I did, it would have been my heritage too.

We headed north, along dirt tracks that wound between the ribbed mountains of Damaraland. Where these ended we took to dry riverbeds, grinding in low-range until we reached the bluffs above the Cunene River. The Angolan bank was deserted apart from basking crocodiles that slid into the water as we tried to bathe. The South African army had had a hundred thousand men under arms in Namibia, in garrisons and bases along this border. Of their long occupation only ghosts remained. We slept a night in a ruined fortification that had once been the western bastion of the line. Weeds sprouted through the sandbags and perimeter wire, covering the red warning triangles that indicated minefields. The officers' mess had been cut into the rock of the hilltop as protection from artillery. It was roofless, blown up by the departing soldiers, but set in the walls were the regimental plaques of units that had done tours of duty there. The bar-counter bore, inlaid in semi-precious stones, the insignia of Northern Border Command with its uncompromising maxim: Hou Koers – hold your course.

South Africa's border war was now over, but the north of Namibia still roiled with its fallout. UN troops patrolled in white armoured personnel carriers and manned roadside checkpoints. They were trying to keep order among the orphans of the conflict, men who had been with this or that armed force until a month before. We gave lifts to demobilized SWAPO fighters who were returning to their villages. Some had been exiled for years and now they were walking home in threadbare canvas boots, their only possession a small pack. In the Ovamboland towns, ex-troopers of Koevoet – the South African police counter-insurgency force whose crude interrogation methods Stefan had encountered – sat in the bars and watched the dusty streets, their pistols hidden.

There were displaced Angolans who had been members of Three-Two Battalion, a semi-irregular South African army unit that had operated deep inside enemy territory. They would be away for weeks at a time on these infiltrations, and their dead had gone unreported on the official casualty lists. Just across the Angolan border were the bases of UNITA, the National Union for the Total Independence of Angola; more of South Africa's bastard offspring, spawned by the war and with nowhere to go. Operated by South African Military Intelligence – with CIA backing – to destabilize Angola's

MPLA government, UNITA still received American supplies through Zaire to the north, but the withdrawal of their South African patrons from Namibia had removed their main means of support and they were tense and uncertain.

We stopped one night to camp at the side of a track near the border. Rod, obeying instincts that I did not question, had taken the truck about thirty feet off the road into the bush, afterwards brushing away our wheel-marks. We made a fire and ate, then rolled ourselves into our blankets. At around 2 a.m. Rod woke me.

'Be quiet,' he breathed in my ear, 'listen.'

I heard the sound of a truck approaching, its engine muted. From where we lay we could make out the pale line of the road between the thorn trees. A man stalked by silently, the barrel of his weapon just visible. A minute later came the lightless vehicle, idling past at walking pace, and a group of marchers; soundless but for the clink of equipment and the whisper of their boots in the dust. No one spoke.

In the morning we reported the event at the next UN checkpoint, a Finnish base twenty miles along the road. The officer recorded the information in the margin of his map.

'We'll check it out,' he said. 'There have been attacks by ex-Koevoet elements on returning SWAPO people. UNITA forces are using the roads inside Namibia to move men and equipment, as there are no tracks in this region on the Angolan side of the border. You shouldn't be on this road, you know. There are still old mines around, and UNITA may be planting new ones.' He pointed at the white armoured trucks that stood in the courtyard of the base. 'We patrol only in mine-proof vehicles. Sometimes at night we hear explosions and shooting. We can never be sure what we'll find in the morning.'

Back in Windhoek, I got a job on a government survey being planned for the Caprivi Strip; a two-hundred-mile corridor of Namibian territory that stuck eastwards from the top corner of the country like a slender spear. Germany had annexed this cartographic anomaly in 1895 to drive a wedge between Portuguese and British colonial possessions, and it lay across the great game migration routes linking the Angolan savannah, the forests of Zambia and the rich papyrus swamps of Botswana's Okavango Delta. The Strip had been declared a game reserve in the sixties, and been sealed off by the South African army since the start of the Angolan conflict in 1975. Now Namibia's new government was sending a team of conservationists to survey the area and assess the results of years of military occupation. Their work would be documented by a film crew, on which I was to be the sound-man. I was also, informally, the survey's medical officer. As it turned out, my involvement there was not so much medical as anthropological.

The Caprivi was home to a population of Basarwa; the small, Asiatic-looking people who were known, slightingly, as 'Bushmen'. Nomadic hunter-gatherers, the Basarwa had been inducted into the South African army for their unique skills as trackers, to hunt down infiltrating SWAPO guerrillas. We found the remains of 201 Bushman Battalion in the centre of the Strip at Omega Base, a military settlement constructed literally amidst the thorn trees: these protruded through the roofs of the buildings, their spreading crowns providing cover from aerial observation.

Despite this appearance of contrived naturalism, the Basarwa themselves had long since lost their traditional life-style. The men and their dependants had been encouraged to see Omega as a permanent home; the army had deducted pay from married men to allow them to 'buy' their camouflaged quarters. In exchange the Basarwa received the benefits of army life: uniforms, rations, the habits of acquisition and of alcohol. 'We are not trying to destroy the Bushman,' a

South African army colonel had once explained on a government newsreel, 'but to build a better Bushman.'

The South African officers had departed two months before, packing their furniture and pets into the holds of transport aircraft. The battalion commander had left behind a delicate garden of ferns and tree-orchids that depended on hidden sprinklers to stop them wilting in the parched air. His Basarwa soldiers, abandoned in this outpost of a vanquished empire, still kept to the letter of the old order. Lights burned in the empty officers' houses and the flower beds were weeded and raked, though squealing Basarwa children had invaded the white officers' club ('Right of Admission Reserved') and splashed in the swimming pool's turbid water. In its shed at the airfield the generator thumped away untended. Army mechanics had left a few hundred gallons of diesel in the storage tanks. The generator was the heart of the settlement; when it stopped beating the houses would be dark, the frozen food-rations would thaw and rot, and pumps would no longer lift water from the deep bore-holes.

The Basarwa – dressed in a mix of brown uniform and grubby pastel polyesters, the gift of a Lutheran charity – appeared beaten down by misfortune. After fifteen years of fighting for South Africa, everything had altered; SWAPO – the enemy – now formed the country's new government, while the withdrawal of the army had left the school without teachers, the hospital unstaffed. I wandered through its wards and operating theatre. The fittings had been removed and sand had drifted in through the open windows. The only thing the military had left behind was piles of buff folders, the medical records of those who had been treated there. They recorded wounds and deaths, from combat or training accidents. The Basarwa had certainly paid in blood for this barren place, but the office of the Volkskas – the People's Bank –

was locked and the life insurance policies that the army had encouraged them to buy were worthless.

Hearing that I was a doctor, the Basarwa brought me their ill and injured. Most were trifling complaints; a sore throat, a thorn-scratch, a man with a bruised lip. I wondered if they would ever rediscover their hardy instincts. Those who recalled the old ways – a few of the elders – had already bundled up their spears and their scant possessions and melted away into the bush with their families, to try to recover the life they once knew. Many ex-soldiers were spending their last pay-packets on drink, brought in by the truckload by unscrupulous traders. Others had joined the Soutkerk – the Salt Church, an eccentric blend of Christianity and shamanism – and gathered in clearings in the bush outside the base perimeter. There, in robes embroidered with moons and crosses, they danced deep circles into the sand, spinning through the night to the monotonous beat of drums and the women's shrill wailing.

The Caprivi could still be a place of menace. We were driving near the Cutline – the arrow-straight, bulldozed swathe through the bush that marked the northern border of the Strip – when men appeared from the long grass that flanked the track and stood before our vehicle, weapons raised. Others filtered out of the bush, fixing us in the blank gaze of their mirrored sunglasses. One of our party had a brief conversation with the men in Portuguese.

'They're UNITA,' he announced. 'They say we're inside Angola.'

UNITA had a tradition of taking Western hostages whom they would hold for months as 'guests' in their network of bases deep in the country, eventually to be released in exchange for money or supplies or some international recognition. Perhaps the men decided that our abduction would be too provocative. They asked where we were going, and we pointed out the line of the track on our map; well inside Namibian territory. 'We will accompany you. For protection,' we were informed, and half a dozen men boarded the trucks in a clutter of guns and Chinese stick grenades. We lurched along the overgrown track as far as the bank of the Kavango River, where the soldiers dismounted. I asked to inspect the enamelled badge that one wore pinned to his bush hat. It carried a wealth of patriotic symbols – spears, rifles, ploughshares, ears of corn – and words like 'fraternity' and 'negritude'. I requested a translation of the slogan around the edge of the badge. 'We will fight everyone,' he said.

In fact, the main victims of UNITA's firepower had been Angola's elephants. Isolated by international sanctions, South African government officials had been desperate to find a way of funding the long conflicts on their borders. A solution was to pillage Angola's natural resources. The Military Intelligence Directorate had set up an elaborate sanctions-busting operation. Army trucks that carried supplies to the UNITA bases returned loaded with tons of ivory, which was falsely certified as having come from elephants culled in South Africa's Kruger Park game reserve. It was then sold in the Far East, or exchanged for electronic and communications equipment that South Africa needed for its military and aircraft navigation. The operation was eventually exposed by a South African army Special Forces colonel, horrified at the wanton slaughter, but not before the bones of a hundred thousand elephants littered the Angolan bush.

Now, with the end of the ivory war, the elephants were returning cautiously to the Caprivi, wandering in the thick forest that flanked the Kavango River. Falling asleep at night, the stars softened by my mosquito net, I could hear the thrash of leaves as they browsed. Hippo churned and snorted in the shallows. I felt strongly how much I had forsaken when I'd left this vast, intimate continent, and I revelled in my rediscovery of its prolific nature. There was something elemental about this life, a sense of reality that had eluded me all the time I'd been away. There was something, too, about the quality of human suffering here; more explicit perhaps, or somehow more comprehensible, than I'd been exposed to in the West. Returning to South Africa, I took a job at a hospital in Zululand, because I needed to understand my interaction with suffering: a sick symbiosis.

⊕

Medicine in Africa can be very basic, very visceral. It may involve things at which the spirit will quail; vomit will rise in the throat. This reflex must be suppressed, and the instruments and drugs laid out, for there is work to be done. On my first day at the hospital I admitted a child with a fever, of as yet unknown cause – tuberculosis or encephalitis, pneumonia or meningitis were among the possible diagnoses – and while I was examining the small, hot body I noticed something moving inside a nostril. Slowly the head of a worm appeared, blind and questing, and delivered itself inch by inch into a steel dish held beneath the child's face.

Ascaris Lumbricoides is Africa's commonest intestinal parasite: a muscular worm, up to a foot long, that twists in the guts of the continent's poor. Ascaris is so precisely adapted to live inside humans that it has a low tolerance for any change in its environment, such as a fever caused by other illness. It can present itself in other unpleasant ways. I took a child with gut obstruction to the operating theatre. His stick-like limbs indicated malnutrition, a common finding in this rural area. Once he was asleep the anaesthetist slipped a tube down into his stomach to drain the secretions that might otherwise be regurgitated into his lungs during unconsciousness. The gastric tube blocked at once, and the doctor withdrew it, muttering. Encased within the transparent tube was a worm.

'I know what you'll find in there,' he said. 'Look. And listen.'

He indicated the child's belly, now relaxed from the effect of the anaesthetic. Under the thin muscle something writhed like animated spaghetti, and from within came a strange, dry rustling.

'It's Ascaris,' said the veteran anaesthetist, 'a whole mass of them. They're covered by a sort of segmented shell, and they make that noise as they twist together.'

Inside, the intestine was packed with worms, dense knots that could not be untangled. I hooked them out through an incision in the gut, gagging behind my mask.

'You'd better pour in some piperazine,' suggested the anaesthetist, 'to kill any that are left. Otherwise they'll come wriggling through your suture line, and he'll end up with peritonitis.'

The hospital stood high on a hill, with a view of the Indian Ocean glinting in the distance. Once it had been run by medical missionaries, offering hell and healing to the people who lived in the nearby kraals. Gradually the bush had been replaced by rolling fields of sugar that stretched to the southern horizon and to the sea in the east. The villagers had ended up in the black township that grew beside the white settlement on the coast. Eventually the hospital had been taken over by the Zulu homeland government. Along the valley below it a scabrous crust of shacks and plastic-sheeting shanties extended in a creeping sprawl from the edge of the township, as more people left the hardships of rural life in the interior and came to look for work. Some found employment as domestics in the white town. The men generally ended up trading subsistence on the land for a stringent servitude, as labourers on the vast sugar plantations.

The sharp-edged leaves of the sugar plant caused wounds which festered rapidly. Untreated, the infection spread through the muscles of the hand, which – unless the pus was surgically drained – ended up contracted and useless; a condition we called 'canecutter's claw'. The township and its squalid environs, though, provided most of the hospital's patients: there, all the diseases of deprivation flourished. Tuberculosis was rife, transmitted from person to person in the crowded living-quarters. Meningitis, typhoid, hepatitis and dysentery – as well as Ascaris worms – came from the sewage-stinking streams where people washed and from which they took their water.

I was on duty in the outpatient clinic one afternoon when I heard shouting from the hospital entrance, and then the noise of an approaching crowd. From the door of my examination room I could see that its focus was an elderly woman being brought in by her extended family; carried in, actually, for they had lashed her to a door with many turns of rope, and her little grey head screamed and spat as she writhed against her bonds. The shiny skin of her legs was split by a network of cracks. I remembered suddenly that this was called 'crazy-paving' dermatitis and realized that I was seeing a case of Pellagra, the first I had encountered since medical school. Its other symptoms included diarrhoea and, as in this patient, crazy-raving dementia.

Pellagra is caused by a deficiency of a common B-group vitamin. In the misery of the township many residents drank themselves into oblivion. The cheapest source of alcohol was the government beerhall, a squalid hangar where quarts of sorghum beer were sold at a few cents apiece. It took a lot of the stuff to get properly drunk so turnover was quick, with new batches being brewed by the day. A by-product of the chemicals added to accelerate fermentation was that they blocked the uptake by the body of necessary vitamins. This patient would respond well to a period of alcoholic abstinence and treatment with vitamin injections and tablets, but first she had to be sedated, to prevent her injuring herself or anyone else.

The power in her skinny limbs was formidable. Despite the ropes, it took the strength of two hefty nurses to hold her flailing arm while I found a vein and injected an ampoule of Valium. The dose was enough to fell a big man, and gradually she slumped in her bonds and her eyes closed.

'Let's loosen the ropes,' I suggested. Her family, on the whole, was unimpressed.

'She is mad,' they chorused, 'she chased us with an axe.'

'She's sleeping now,' I said, looking at her wrinkled face creased in repose, 'I think it's safe,' and leaned over her to lift an eyelid. At my touch her eyes snapped open; her head lunged forward with the speed of a striking mongoose, and her jaws closed around the barrel of the syringe that I still held in my hand. Before I could pull it away the robust plastic had split under the pressure of her toothless gums. It took another entire ampoule to relax her enough that we could untie her and transfer her to a bed.

After the ordered progression of my surgical training and research, African medicine had an intoxicating weirdness. Any sort of improbable pathology could turn up at the hospital; with quiet suddenness, or heralded by a clamour at the entrance, where the families of those waiting to be seen were encamped under the flame-lily trees. One morning, quite early, a battered rural taxi drew up outside Casualty and a man emerged – with some difficulty – from the back seat. The four-foot handle of a throwing spear stood out from the centre of his forehead, and he moved his head carefully, like a wide-horned animal. He answered our concerned queries – he felt quite all right, thank you, apart from a slight headache –

and allowed us to lead him into the building, smiling shyly at the shocked exclamations that followed him.

The man came from an area to the north, where a feud was underway between two clans that dwelt on opposite sides of a valley. The origins of these vendettas were lost in the turbulent times that had followed the deposing of the last great Zulu king by the British in 1879. 'Faction fights', as the papers called them – sometimes with a scorecard of numbers killed and wounded – tended to follow a predictable path. Young men from one group would steal across the stream that marked their territorial border and pinch a few head of cattle from their traditional enemies; the other side would retaliate, until blood was spilled. The fighting season usually required the deaths of a couple of each clan's eldest sons before honour was satisfied.

The patient explained that he had woken during the night to a rustling in the thatch of his hut that sounded like rats. Then he'd smelt smoke and, realizing that the place was on fire, he kicked open the door and dashed outside into the darkness. Something had struck him solidly between the eyes, knocking him senseless. In the morning he had been found by some villagers and brought to hospital. He sat on the examination couch, eyes crossing as he tried to focus on the shadow of the spear-handle that projected just above his line of vision. By now the surgeons, and a number of other doctors, had gathered around. We could see that the spear-blade had struck him exactly in the midline of his forehead, cleaving the skin vertically into two ridges that puckered against the iron when he frowned. Its tip could be felt at the back of his head, a point that heaped the scalp at the centre of his occiput.

Astonishingly, the blade appeared to have travelled exactly between his cerebral hemispheres, missing all neurological structures. It had passed right through the great central vein –

the sagittal sinus – that ran from front to back of the cranium, effectively plugging the holes that it had made in the vessel. Clearly, removal would be too dangerous with our limited neurosurgical facilities. The spear seemed solidly enough implanted to risk transferring him to a specialist unit. Before the man left in the ambulance we braced his head against a table and carefully sawed off the handle, to make him more manoeuvrable. He thanked us, and added a comment in Zulu that made the nurses howl with laughter; he had asked to keep the wooden shaft so that he could rejoin it to the blade once it was removed, to one day fling it back at his attackers.

The Zulus are renowned for their stoicism; it is allied to a firm belief in the inexorability of vengeance, in human or spiritual form. One night, as I was waiting in the theatre to operate on my next case, a porter burst through the swinging doors.

'They need a surgeon in Intensive Care,' he yelled, 'come now!'

I ran, to find a scene of carnage. In one of the beds, connected to a ventilator that still sighed uselessly, was a dead man. His throat had been cloven by a great gash, and blood was sprayed high on the walls. A young woman sat head bowed in a chair, wrapped in a blanket, watched by a group of shocked nurses. On the floor was the heavy-bladed cane-knife that had done the chopping. The police came and took her away, while the nursing staff explained to me the inevitability of this death.

The woman had been raped by the man a week before. She had consulted a *sangoma* or witch-doctor, who – in a trance – had been assured by the woman's ancestral spirits that the man would die. These spirits had taken the form of a snake that had laid in wait for him, and bitten him that morning when he was cutting cane. Snakes were a regular hazard in the sugar-fields, and after it had been killed by a foreman, the farmer had placed man and serpent in the back of his pickup truck and rushed them both to hospital. Inspection of the snake confirmed the evidence of the man's symptoms; its poison was a nerve toxin, attacking the brain's centre of respiration, and as the man's breathing worsened he had been brought to the Intensive Care unit and placed on a ventilator. His victim had heard what had happened, and that the action of the doctors might save the man's life. Borrowing a machete from her brother, she had come to the hospital to do her duty to her ancestors by ensuring that their wrath was not thwarted.

Sangomas were consulted by the local people on matters of health as well as misfortune, and showed a skill in demarcating clinical signs. Children suffering from Bilharzia infections would arrive in outpatients with their enlarged spleens neatly outlined by a tracery of fine cuts. Their reason for attending hospital was usually not the original infection, but the sometimes fatal liver damage caused by the *sangoma*'s traditional treatment: a herbal enema made from the *Senecia* plant which was administered for most juvenile complaints. Some *sangomas*, though, were keen to modernize their therapeutic skills. They would attend outpatients in full regalia: inflated animal bladders, monkey tails and hide head-dresses. Reciting a litany of complaints – pains in the head, in the knees, in the chest, in the veins – they would direct an apprentice to be examined in their stead. The tablets we prescribed would be examined and their functions carefully noted, before being stored away in a jackal-skin bag; later to be mixed with ingredients of a more mystical nature for the treatment of the *sangoma*'s patients.

This dualism was shared by many of the hospital staff. One morning the outpatients corridor filled suddenly with a phalanx of frightened nurses, pushing at a run a metal gurney whose wheels shrieked and juddered over the uneven concrete. Then I saw the cause of their panic. A woman knelt on the swaying trolley, her hands clasping its edges to avoid being flung off, as she stared, transfixed, at the object that emerged from her open mouth. It lay on the blanket like a yard of off-white ribbon: a tape worm, half-vomited. To patient and staff the parasite represented an archetypal manifestation of spiritual malevolence, its head burrowed into the wall of the woman's intestine while its vile length undulated on the pillow. I put on a glove, reached down her throat and wrenched it out, while the nurses screamed as one and the patient, bug-eyed with terror, threw herself howling on the floor. It took half an hour of persuasion to calm her enough to take the tablets that would kill the head of the worm still inside her.

Medicine could not cure all the ills that afflicted these people's lives, even if it had been comprehensively available. The Kwazulu homeland, where the hospital was located, was one of those overcrowded rural slums where the Pretoria government corralled its unwanted black citizens. The populace were thus doubly victims: first of apartheid, and then of the inefficient homeland administration that spent its budget on grandiose offices, a vast civil service, and a murderously corrupt police force that gobbled up the lion's share of its resources. Like each of the homelands, Kwazulu had its own Ministry of Health whose bureaucrats and limousines consumed most of the money designated for healthcare. Much of what remained was systematically embezzled or re-routed into corrupt pockets, with a frank indifference to the sufferings of the people.

The hospital was a microcosm of the administration that controlled it. Some nurses were dedicated, but others were venal or lazy. Patients on the wards complained that they had to pay for their food; to be given bedpans; even to receive the drugs they were prescribed. During a midnight operation I needed a suture to close the abdomen. The theatre nurse searched desultorily through her stocks, and shrugged. The scrub-sister who was assisting me explained that the suture would have to be obtained from the store-room, and despatched the nurse to get it. A while later the other nurse slipped out, saying she would find the item. Then the sister herself left – to find the other two – and did not return. Eventually the anaesthetist and I could stand to wait no longer. Putting a sterile drape over the open belly, I left him alone to care for the unconscious patient and went in search of the theatre staff. I found the three of them sitting comfortably in the rest-room, drinking tea.

It was strange, then, that in this struggling hospital certain conventions of correct procedure were so scrupulously observed. On a quiet day, when a tropical storm was lashing the ground outside into muddy soup and keeping outpatients empty, a call came through to the doctor's duty room.

'You must come to the ward,' said the nurse. 'A patient is gasping.'

I knew that patients who were 'gasping' were usually breathing their last, and that such terminal situations could seldom be rectified on the under-equipped wards, but I dashed across the flooded yard to where the call had come from. It seemed clear, once there, that little could be done. Screens had been drawn around a bed where a woman lay, eyes open, her jaw sagging crookedly. Her face had the vacated look that the dead all share. I felt for a pulse on the still-warm wrist. My fingers left a slight dent in flesh that had lost the resilience of living skin.

'I'm afraid it's too late,' I told the ward sister. 'There's nothing we can do for her now.'

'I am sorry, doctor,' said the sister, appearing embarrassed. 'She was very sick. She came in three days ago with pneumonia, maybe plus TB. The doctor gave her intravenous antibiotics. A little while ago we noticed that her breathing was difficult. I don't know how long she'd been like that, we're so busy here. We gave her oxygen and called you quickly, but I think she was already gone.'

The woman's wide-dilated pupils, unresponsive to light, confirmed the sister's diagnosis. All that remained was for me to certify her demise, and note the date and time of death in her hospital records. As a final check, I clipped my stethoscope around my neck and lifted back the covers to ascertain that there was no heartbeat.

The appearance of her chest made me pause. The skin was raised in great, fluid-filled blisters that quivered slightly in a simulacrum of life. I turned to speak to the sister but she had gone. In her place stood the senior physician.

'What's this?' I asked him, pointing at the lesions. 'Bullous impetigo? I seem to remember that can be a cause of huge blisters.'

'Nothing that rare,' he said. 'The nurses are dashing around mid-morning changing bedding, and they notice that a patient can't be roused. When they look closer they realize that she's passed on hours before, during the night. They were supposed to have checked everyone's pulse and temperature at 8 a.m. but now it's eleven, and the doctor they call to certify her death will notice that she's already cold. So they run a hot bath and dump the body in, to warm it up and reverse the signs of rigor mortis. Then they put it back in bed and call us.' The physician drew the sheet up over the woman's face. 'This time, perhaps, the water wasn't hot enough, so they heated up the kettle. The poor stiff's been parboiled.'

There was no point in fussing about such minor things, he explained as we left the ward; a complaint would only antagonize the nursing staff at a time when everyone's workload was increasing. In the last ten years the township population had increased fifty-fold; part of a trend towards urbanization that would soon see half of Africa's people living in towns. AIDS was spreading exponentially, associated with an increase in virulent TB, while new, drug-resistant strains of malaria were tracking southwards from Mozambique through the lowlands of the Zululand coast.

There were other problems at the hospital, though, that had less to do with pathology than politics. Some of the white doctors on the wards were in army uniform, posted to this homeland hospital to do their military service now that the Angolan border war was over. The strange thing was that the war had followed them. The release of Nelson Mandela from prison had brought the prospect of change, and the tenuous grip of the homeland governments was cracking. Their leaders had truly believed Pretoria's promises that they were sovereigns of their piecemeal kingdoms of eroded earth and bursting shantytowns, and dreamed that they could somehow hang on to their ramshackle power. The KwaZulu government based its strength on Inkatha, a Zulu 'cultural organization' funded by Pretoria as a means of securing the backing of the homeland's traditional tribal subjects. The civil service, the police, the senior nurses at the hospital, were all Inkatha members.

But in Zululand there was burgeoning support for Mandela and the ANC, which the securocrats of Military Intelligence wished to undermine. Following the covert-action manuals they'd used in Angola and Namibia, they had brought destabilization tactics to the homelands. Under their direction, the KwaZulu police – equipped with automatic weapons from Israel, which ignored the international arms embargo – provided firepower for Inkatha warlords. Criminal gangs were armed and set loose to spread carnage in areas sympathetic to the ANC, whose 'self-defence units' retaliated with home-made shotguns against the subjects of pro-Inkatha chiefs. Indiscriminate attacks by hooded gunmen slaughtered families and ambushed buses on rural roads, with the casualties reported dismissively as victims of 'black-on-black violence'.

The police brought bodies to us for formal confirmation of death. They stacked up on trolleys near the entrance to the casualty department, each covered by a grey blanket. The cop would flick back the shroud, intone from his clipboard: 'Male Bantu. Name unknown. Found roadside Nongoma. Woman, same. Child, female, same,' and I would note the twisted faces, the sprays of bullet-holes, the smell of blood and of woodsmoke from the clothes of hut-dwellers who cooked over open fires. It was as though these random killings bared deep wells of primitivism, that fed the pool of suffering lapping each day around the hospital doors.

The township was being terrorized by violent robberies, whose knife-victims filled the waiting area of Casualty. In order to help the hard-pressed casualty doctors we would detour through the place between surgical operations. The critical cases we would sometimes bundle onto patient-trolleys, and rush them straight to theatre. Those who simply needed patching would be placed in a queue to have their wounds stitched by the nurses, a hasty note from the doctor pinned to their chests. SPS, TT + Pen IMI, read the shorthand: Suture please, sister, Tetanus Toxoid and Penicillin intra-muscular injection.

A little doctoring can go a long way among people so battered by deprivation and violence, but it has its limitations. On one such foray into Casualty I noticed a man among the overflowing crowd, sitting quietly on a bench. He might have been a sugar-factory worker, dressed in his Saturday best for an evening out in the township. He wore a jacket and tie and held his hat with dignity against his chest. His relative prosperity had evidently made him a target for the gangsters, for blood splashed steadily onto the floor, forming a widening puddle under his seat. I greeted him in Zulu.

'What happened to you?' I asked him. 'Where are you hurt?'

'It is a small thing, doctor. I have been cut.'

I asked him to let me see the injury.

'It is nothing,' he said, clasping his hat against him. I lifted it away and saw that his shirt was soaked with blood that welled from a wound below his left breast, just beneath his ribs. I called the sister.

'Could we get this man ready for surgery?' I asked her. 'Let's start a drip and get some blood cross-matched. He's been stabbed in the spleen. We'll do him as soon as the table's free.'

The woman spoke to him at length in Zulu but he answered briefly, shaking his head.

'He does not want an operation,' she translated, 'he only wants a bandage.'

I saw that the man rocked slightly on the bench where he sat.

'He's about to pass out,' I said. 'He's lost a lot of blood. Convince him that he needs the operation right away. I'll go and warn the theatre staff.'

The man never arrived. When I went looking for him the sister told me that he'd stood up, put his hat politely on his head, and walked out. I was soon preoccupied with another emergency, and only reminded of him the following day when the sister spoke to me.

'You know that man last night, who didn't want his operation?' she asked me. 'Well, he didn't get far. They found him this morning, sitting against a tree outside the hospital gate. He still had his hat on, and he was completely dead.'

I had come back to Africa in search of restoration, a sense of completeness. I had found that I was useful here in a way that did not happen in the hospitals of ordered societies. But I was aware of an obscure guilt about practising this kind of medicine, for the sense of worth that it gave me came at a cost. These patients were largely the victims of preventable suffering, inflicted by the policies and actions of their fellow humans. Working to heal them, I was finding personal and professional fulfilment – even an intensified sense of my own humanity – in the constant presence of brutality and pain. The reward was tempered with revulsion. I wondered what price I might end up having to pay if I stayed on in this paradoxical place.

I was staying with a colleague whom I'd known at Cape Town university. In our medical school days, I remembered, he had been a kind man, a humane man. He lived in a pretty hilltop cottage with a view over the sugar fields towards a valley where a patch of riverine forest survived. During the years he'd spent at this hospital he had developed an interest in ornithology, and when the pressures of work permitted he would go down to the small nature reserve that he had helped establish and spend the twilight hour netting and ringing the birds that flashed along the river's edge. Back at the cottage that evening I told him about the man who'd died alone with his dignity. We sat together on the veranda in the warm evening, sipping sundowners. My friend was caring for a tiny turquoise kingfisher with a fractured wing, and it marched cheeping across the drinks table like a broken clockwork toy.

'You win some, you lose some,' he said, shrugging. 'It's remarkable that we manage to save any at all, considering the daily anarchy.'

6

Kurdistan

It was sometime in the afternoon that they brought the boy down the far hillside, slumped inside a blanket fouled with blood. I waited on the river-bank that marked the Turkish border while the men paused on the other side to divest themselves of their weapons and cartridge-belts. Then, with their bundle hoisted shoulder-high, they waded into the icy torrent, clinging one-handed to the rope that was strung from shore to shore. The current foamed against their thighs as they staggered on the rocky bottom. At the near bank they lifted their burden up to me, their hands curled into the edges of the cloth. I looked between its folds and saw the boy's face, his brow creased with an inner concern as though anticipating each next lurch of his tortured journey. His jaw was fine and pale, blue-shadowed with the stubble of an adolescent's beard; the nose sharp, flesh pared away by pain. His eyes, bright with fever, were already sunken in their sockets.

He was conscious, and he moaned as they laid him on a stretcher in the tent. The Kurdish fighters who had brought him told his story. The boy had been shot through the groin during a fierce rearguard action against Iraqi forces two days before. His comrades carried him out of the line of fire. The bullet had passed out through his buttock, tearing a great hole which they stuffed with rags. Then, while others held off the attack, they had carried him over the mountains to the border, following the tracks of fleeing refugees. They had no drugs to give him apart from aspirin, which they had crushed into a paste and fingered into his mouth with dribbles of water. He was a brave boy, they said, a *pesh merga* – 'one who walks with death' – like his father; killed in action during Saddam Hussein's last big campaign against the Kurds in 1988.

I knelt beside the stretcher. The boy's eyes tracked restlessly, and the tip of his tongue fluttered between his cracked lips. Despite his fever his hands were cold and pulseless, and he was so dehydrated that the skin of his forearm, when pinched, stayed raised in a fold. His wound I dared not inspect yet, for any disturbance might start it bleeding anew. The rags that bound it were soaked with faeces. In the gloom of the tent his pale face glowed, like a pure spirit amidst the smell of shit.

The French doctors and I started to resuscitate him, placing a drip-line in each arm and pouring fluids into his veins. The wound gave out a smell of rotting meat that rose in waves, choking us. We added antibiotics to the drip bottles. Slowly his blood pressure climbed, and I wondered how we could save his life. If he didn't die from blood-loss, the hole in his buttock – contaminated with bowel bacteria – presented the dire complication of septic shock. He needed a blood transfusion and urgent surgery, first to find and clamp the vessels that oozed amidst the lacerated flesh, and then for all devitalized tissue to be cut away and the wound cavity packed with gauze. Intensive nursing would be needed, with oxygen and further transfusions and monitoring of his kidney function. If he survived, the wound should close by slow secondary healing, the dressings being changed each day under sterile conditions.

The boy needed transfer to a hospital inside Turkey, but I knew that the border troops would never let him pass. Although the Turks were part of the Allied Gulf War coalition that had just beaten Saddam Hussein, they drew the line at embracing the Iraqi Kurds – enemies of their enemy – as friends. For fifteen years the Turkish government had been trying to suppress its own Kurdish uprising – by guerrillas of the PKK (Kurdish Workers' Party) – in the villages and ragged peaks of Turkish Kurdistan; a secret conflict of ambushes, reprisals, imprisonment and forced relocation. The red star-and-crescent flag cracked above forts and bunkers all along the frontier. Turkish soldiers were keeping the Kurdish refugees on the Iraqi side of the river, camped under blankets and bits of plastic sheet amidst leafless poplar trees that were rapidly being felled for firewood.

When we'd arrived that morning I had waded across to visit the Kurdish encampment. Some of the displaced had been there for several days, and had tried to improve their rough shelters with stone walls and drainage furrows. Their only source of water was the river. It was almost freezing, run-off from the mountain snows, but its purity was deceptive; sewage from thousands of people flowed into it. Some had developed amoebic dysentery – the splatters of their bloody stools were bright against the mud – and soon the rest would have it too. The Turks refused to let us work inside the refugee camp but grudgingly allowed us to set up our treatment station on Turkish territory: a pair of grey, box-like tents, erected on a meadow by the river. Once our tents were up I had stood on the bank with my doctor colleagues Bertrand and Antoine, our translator calling across the churning water that the sick and injured should be brought to us. Refugees were allowed to cross the river for temporary treatment. Each patient had to pass the scrutiny of a Turkish officer. He didn't trust Kurds, so he made the process as slow as possible.

One tent now housed a half-dozen surgical patients on stretchers, the other containing children with gastro-enteritis who lay listlessly under intravenous drips. We had no lamps, so I had improvised an operating table outside between the tents to take advantage of the pale daylight; a canvas stretcher raised on a platform of ammunition boxes. There we worked, sometimes sheltered under a sheet of plastic as sleet-squalls scudded up the snow-rimmed valley. Bertrand performed the anaesthesia and I did the operating, with a basic set of surgical instruments that I scrubbed in disinfectant after each patient.

Until the arrival of the *pesh merga* boy my surgical cases had been minor ones; stitching lacerations, draining infected blisters, and cleaning and dressing bullet wounds to an arm and foot. There had also been a lot of little amputations: the removal of small, black, frostbitten toes from the feet of children who had come over the mountains of Iraq in pathetic patent-leather loafers, bought in quieter times by proud town-dwelling Kurdish parents. The toes particularly troubled me. How could Kurds – a people with a long history of conflict and dispossession – not have known to own good boots? They should at least, I thought, have been accustomed to betrayal; ready to run. They had a long history of getting involved in other people's wars – serving the Ottoman Empire, the Shahs of Persia, Russia, Britain, and later Iraq, Iran and the USA; each pursuing its own imperial objectives in the region. In each case the Kurds had been abandoned once those objectives were attained.

At the start of the Gulf conflict, US President Bush had called upon the Iraqi people 'to take matters into their own hands to force Saddam Hussein to step aside'. When the war ended at the beginning of March 1991 – with an Allied ceasefire that left the Iraqi dictator still in power – the Kurds rose up, hurling out Iraqi garrisons in the north of Iraq and declaring autonomy in the area they had liberated. They may have thought that their rebellion would have Western support, but Iraqi Republican Guard tanks had moved against the Kurds, unmolested by Allied aircraft. The recently liberated Kurdish towns fell quickly. Civilians fled northwards in buses, taxis, tractors and on foot, even while broadcasts from a CIA-funded radio station – the 'Voice of Free Iraq' – continued to call on the Kurds to depose 'the evil Saddam'. Refugees were now being attacked from the air by Iraqi helicopter gunships as they made for the dubious sanctuary of the mountains along the Turkish border, while lightly armed *pesh merga* fighters still tried to hold back the advancing armour. The wounded boy was a victim of this most recent betrayal.

⊕

The air was compressed by the thud of rotors. From under the tent-flap I saw three German airforce helicopters clatter overhead, their down-wash battering the canvas. The aircraft landed, bouncing, on the road above the meadow. A group of officers strode down to the tents, stepping carefully over the dirt in their smart grey flying-suits, heads erect. Their presence on Turkish soil marked the first time German forces had served outside their own borders since World War Two, even if they were here only in a 'support' capacity, and they posed before the backdrop of the refugee encampment while the event was recorded by a German airforce cameraman. I introduced myself to the Flugkapitän and took him to see our critically ill patient.

'He needs urgent evacuation,' I told him. 'One of your helicopters could airlift him to a military hospital.'

The Luftwaffe officer jerked away from the stretcher, his face twisting at the smell.

'He is war-wounded,' he said. 'We cannot take him. It is forbidden to give assistance to combatants.'

'He's just a boy,' I said, but the captain, now nervous and

unhappy, was already shepherding his crew back up to the helicopters. As they took off overhead, I saw – below the black crosses on each fuselage – the word HELP written in big white letters.

I'd arrived on the Turkish border a week before. Since then I'd seen lots of Turkish soldiers – combat troops and Jandarma, the blue-bereted frontier guards – trying to hold back the tide of desperate Kurds. I'd met the odd foreign representative of international aid organizations and some journalists, but of Western forces there had been no sign, nor of the vast logistical machine that had just transported, supplied and provisioned half a million ground-troops for the invasion of Iraq. But a recent change of policy must have occurred, for suddenly foreign troops were turning up; the Germans weren't the first. Early that morning, while we'd been en route to set up our treatment station, we'd encountered some Americans.

There were two of them, a major and a lieutenant in US army green, standing uncertainly at a Turkish checkpoint on the road. While our driver was trying to persuade the churlish Jandarma to let us through, the major had approached our jeep and introduced himself.

'Could you help us out?' he'd asked. 'We've been ordered to make an assessment of the refugee concentrations along the frontier, and these guys' – he indicated the Turkish troops watching from sandbagged bunkers in the hillside, and an armoured personnel carrier parked nearby – 'were supposed to provide liaison and transport. I showed them the orders from their high command, but there seems to be some problem.'

Our driver spoke to the Turkish captain.

'He says he is sorry, the machine is broken. You can go as you like, but they cannot transport you.'

I conferred with Francine, the French nurse. We weren't

supposed to be on this road ourselves; our medical credentials – flimsy papers adorned with photographs and stamps – had managed to get us through a first roadblock, but even if we made it beyond this one we didn't know how much longer our luck would hold. We were trying to reach a valley twenty miles further east where there were reported to be a collection of refugees. The presence of the Americans and their official orders might open the security barriers.

'Climb in,' we said, and the two army men folded themselves between the crated medical supplies on the back seat, tucking their weapons awkwardly beneath their legs.

'What are you doing here?' I asked the major as our driver pulled away.

'We've been based west of here, at Incirlik,' he explained, 'watching the refugee situation on CNN. It seemed kinda tough that we weren't doing anything to help; I mean we've been pouring aid into Kuwait ever since the fighting stopped a month ago, and these folks are a lot worse off than the Kuwaitis. Orders were the Turkish military had it all wrapped up – they were policing their border and it wasn't our concern.'

Eventually, however, the television images of the vast refugee migration must have unsettled the US State Department, for President Bush had indicated that a programme of assistance was being considered. The sudden appearance of Major Mike and his lieutenant on the border was the result.

'We've got to do a reconnaissance, see how badly off these folks actually are,' said the major, 'also try to get some numbers.'

'You're welcome to what I've been able to find out,' I told him. I pulled my journal out of my side-pack and passed it back, open at a page of place-names and columns of figures. 'Only the top one is reasonably definite. That's the concentration at Isikveren in the mountains, near where we picked you up. I'd reckon there are about three hundred thousand there now. The rest is pretty much based on rumours.'

The major began to copy the information into his notebook, braced against the bouncing of the jeep.

'Do you know where there'll be a smallish group?' he asked. 'Something representative of the overall conditions? We need to find a place for a, like . . . pilot study.'

'Maybe at Yekmol, the place we're trying to reach today to set up a treatment station. There are supposed to be around twenty thousand people there, in a bad way.'

'That sounds like what we're looking for, doc.' The major handed back the journal. 'Glad we met with you.'

The major's credentials did the trick. At each checkpoint he'd unwound his considerable bulk from the back of the jeep and marched up to the blockhouse, our driver skipping beside him. There was much saluting and handshaking by the Jandarma and each time we were allowed to go on our way. The truck carrying the rest of the team and our equipment was not even searched. When we reached Yekmol, the major and his subordinate set off to find the Turkish commander, their packs bulging with cartons of American cigarettes. While we set up the tents and saw the first patients, I noticed the pair of them moving along the road above with a Turkish officer. At one point they waded to the other side of the river and made a brief inspection of the camp. Then I forgot about them under the pressure of work.

The German helicopters had come and gone, and I was reassessing the wounded *pesh merga* boy when the Americans returned, barging into the treatment tent out of the rain. It was already crowded and the men filled it further, dripping water from their wet ponchos. The Turkish officer with them shook off his raincoat, spraying water on Kurd women crouched beside the stretchers on which their children lay.

'This is the commanding officer,' said Major Mike. 'He's been real helpful. Even speaks some English.'

The commander had spotted a group of Turkish conscripts in soaked uniforms, sheltering beneath the tent flap. The four soldiers – their bodies hunched with cold – tried to come to attention. The officer struck one, a stunted, bow-legged man, sending his cap flying. They fled out into the downpour, the last of them receiving a kick that sent him sprawling in the slime outside.

The Turkish officer turned to me and saluted crisply.

'I am sorry, doctor,' he said. 'Peasant boys. Very stupid. Not come in hospital,' and he marched out after them, screaming orders.

'Ask the helpful officer,' I suggested, 'whether there's a surgical bed in Turkey we can get this casualty into.'

'No can do, doc.' Major Mike shook his head. 'He told us that Iraqi citizens aren't supposed to be on Turkish soil. They shouldn't even be on this side of the river.'

'How about your base hospital, then?'

'Same thing applies: the Turks are our hosts, they make the rules. In fact we have to leave now. The C.O. says no Westerners are allowed in the border zone after dark; for security.'

I knew about this restriction already, from my time in the area. Among the refugees I'd found a Kurdish nurse who had worked at the hospital in the Iraqi Kurdish town of Zakho. I gave her intravenous fluid bags for the wounded boy, already primed with antibiotics, and an ampoule of morphine and a syringe.

'*Nif, varih e saharih,*' – half, evening and morning – I said, embarrassed by my scanty words of Kurdish.

'*Azanem,*' she answered: I understand.

'*Subeh,*' I said: tomorrow, and as we hiked up the slope towards where the jeep was parked I looked back and saw her wave from the door of the tent. Across the river the shelters of the refugees were already lost in a dusk of smoke and twilight.

On the way back our chauffeur pushed the bucking jeep as fast as it would go, the French doctors' truck rocking behind us through the potholes. Both drivers wanted to get back to town, for only Turkish military vehicles used the road after dark, and our small convoy would be an easy target for PKK guerrillas. Major Mike sat in the back with his pad and flashlight, making notes.

'You reckon that boy will be OK?' he asked me.

'I hope he survives the night,' I said. 'We'll find out in the morning.'

'You're going back tomorrow? Great,' said the major, 'we'll be going there too. Is there anything we can bring for you?'

'Medical supplies?' I asked.

'Sure, doc, we can get you anything you need.'

'Six units of Group O-negative blood, on ice,' I told him. 'Your medical unit will have it in stock. And a cold-bag to carry it. Also a bottle of oxygen with a line and mask. We'll need it if we have to operate on him.'

'No problem, doc. That'll be easy.'

From my bag I took a sheet of letter-headed paper from the medical organization I was working for, and wrote out my request in bumpy capitals. I signed it with my name and qualifications. Major Mike folded the paper into his notebook.

'You'll have it all, doc, first thing,' he promised. 'We'll be out there early, with our own transport.'

The next day we set off at sunrise on our return journey. The Turkish checkpoints were slower than ever, and I dozed in the jeep. Eventually we parked on the road and we walked down to the tents. There was no sign of the Americans. The Kurdish nurse met me at the tent door and led me inside.

During the night the boy had become even paler and more angelic. His blood formed a great, dark lake on the canvas of the stretcher, and the blueness of his fingers – where his scanty red corpuscles could no longer deliver a sufficient cargo of oxygen – showed that he was slipping into circulatory shock. Bertrand, Antoine and I conferred.

'We're going to have to open him,' I said. 'We can't wait for the Americans. They may not even come.'

The Kurdish fighters had attended him all night. Now they carried him out to the operating stretcher and laid him down in the weak sunshine. His body was light, the muscles already wasted by fever, and the shadows of his ribs stood out in unnatural prominence. Only his left leg was heavy – pale and swollen like the limb of a drowned giant – indicating damage to the major vein in the groin; it appeared, though, that some arterial blood supply must have survived or the leg would be dark and marbled with necrosis. Bertrand injected the anaesthetic slowly through a drip-line, and under the influence of the Ketamine the boy's face lost its clenched look and relaxed into an expression of questioning repose. His eyelids flickered as the vivid dream-consciousness of the drug took hold. With forceps, I hooked my instruments out of the detergent solution and laid them on a piece of sterile towel. The nurse poured water over my hands while I scrubbed them with iodine soap. Pulling on gloves, I looked over at the French anaesthetist.

'He sleeps,' he said. 'You may commence.'

The Kurdish nurse cut away the putrid dressings and laid open the boy's wounds, half-rolling him as she pulled the packing from his buttock. The exit wound was beside his anus, a huge soiled cavity that frothed shit and a pink ooze of blood. The hole extended down into shredded muscles on the back of his thigh, full of pus and clot. I hosed the area down with disinfectant, squirted from a plastic bottle, and transferred my attention to his front, where the bullet had gone into his groin. The puncture of the entry wound was puckered with dried blood through which a fresh trickle was starting. As I cleaned the wound it began to bleed faster. Antoine checked the boy's blood pressure. He seized a litre of Haemaccel and attached the synthetic plasma solution to the intravenous line. I heard the urgent puff of the blood-pressure cuff being inflated again. I was aware of Bertrand shaking his head.

I had to find the source of bleeding and control it. Quickly, I cut along the skin just below the bullet hole. My incision revealed a pulsing lump of clot; beneath it lay the lacerated femoral vessels that I had to clamp. Before my eyes the clot bulged and burst, and a brisk arc of arterial blood sprayed from the wound. Venous bleeding, dark and spreading, surged behind it. I pressed down hard, trying to compress the vessels against the edge of the pelvic bone, but my fingers sank without resistance into the void of the bullet-track. Warmth flooded my thigh; blood soaking through the canvas of the stretcher. I half-lifted him and saw that the wound at the back was pouring too, a rush of blood and dead meat and pus. I rolled a swab and forced it into the cavity, pressing front and back while Bertrand and Antoine squeezed the plastic Haemaccel containers with both their hands, trying to force the fluid into the boy's failing circulation. A helicopter passed low over the tents, showering us with blown debris.

Surgeons should never be too emotionally close to their patients. It's a defence mechanism that allows us to cut into flesh, to make rational decisions without being overwhelmed. Our feelings are blanked off, we function like logical machines. The feelings come later. That boy was a stranger. I had known him only briefly; I had spoken a few words to him while I had been tending to him, that he would not have understood. As I held his body pressed between my hands, trying to hold in the blood on which his life depended, that barrier of detachment broke. I began to cry. His body tensed and jerked, as his brain, starved of oxygen, began to switch itself off. Through my palms and fingers I felt him die.

'*C'est fini*,' said the anaesthetist.

I closed the wound I had made with a few small stitches, a meaningless restoration that would be the last service I would ever do him. The Kurdish fighters watched me. Then, their faces wet with tears, they bathed the body, cleaning it of blood and filth. They wrapped it in a cloth and placed it on a bier of poles. One man turned to me and touched his breast.

'*Tusach, daktur*,' he said: thank you.

I watched them lift the boy onto their shoulders and carry him down the hill. At the river they did not break their stride, but marched through the freezing water and back into the mountains of Iraq. As I gathered my useless instruments I seemed to hear the sound of cheering. I wiped my eyes on my sleeve and looked up. A mass of Kurds was gathered on the road, where I could see a big Sikorski helicopter. Turkish troops – who had apparently let them cross the river – stood on the hillside above the crowd and did not interfere. The Kurds began to clap, wildly. Above their heads appeared an American flag. The crowd parted and I saw that the flag was carried by a column of American soldiers. At their head marched Major Mike, his battle-greens neatly ironed. Beside him stepped a large man in a suit, trying to keep his shoes out of the mud.

As they neared the tents the major saw me.

'Hey, doc, how's it going?' he called, throwing me a half-salute. 'This is the US Secretary of State. He's here on a fact-finding mission. Secretary, this is the civilian, er . . . the surgeon I told you about.'

The politician switched on a smile of Angstrom-deep sincerity.

'The major tells me you're doing a great job, doctor,' he said heartily, sticking out his hand, though I saw him blanche a little at my bloody clothes. A TV cameraman orbited low, trying to frame us in his viewfinder. I ignored them both.

'Where's the fucking blood you promised me?' I roared at Major Mike, my voice cracking. 'Where's the fucking oxygen?'

Then I walked down to the river bank and gazed across at the mountain peaks of northern Iraq, where the Kurdish front line lay. That was where the wounded boy had come from: where I was supposed to be operating now, according to the assignment I'd received in Paris ten days before.

⊕

March in England had been miserable, and when I'd been approached to work as a volunteer surgeon for an international medical intervention group – active in trouble-spots such as Liberia and Sri Lanka – I had seen it as a chance of re-exploring the ambiguous fulfilment I'd found in Africa. Marc, the organization's founder, had met me in his Paris flat. The pictures on the walls showed him standing on a stony hillside with a group of Afghan fighters. In the photos he wore the same baggy trousers and wool tunic and rolled hat as the Mujahedin, and leaned with them against the side of a downed Soviet helicopter. Marc had started off working for Médecins sans Frontières, the original intervention group on which all others were modelled: efficient, organized, and able to put an army of medical staff, logisticians and equipment into the field. In the late seventies, identifying a need for a different sort of organization, Marc had developed his own: small and mobile, and ready to operate where other groups – for reasons of politics or security, or ethical complexity – would refuse to go.

With the Kurdish uprising underway, Marc planned to set

up a casualty treatment unit in northern Iraq just behind the Kurdish battle-front. The initial mission would be small; myself and Francine, a French nurse. We would be expected to organize our own communication links, security, food and transport through local co-operation. Once we had discovered a route into Iraq and a place to work, we were to report back with a list of our operational requirements. Paris would assemble the necessary material and personnel, and send them out to join us. Francine and I were to leave the next morning on a flight to Damascus along with Antoine and Bertrand, French doctors from an allied organization. They would be based in Turkey, and act as a referral centre and communications-relay for our forward unit.

Francine was a veteran; she had seen service in Iran, in Burma, Ethiopia and Armenia. I had met her that morning in the organization's offices, putting together the manifests for the medical equipment that would accompany us. She was blonde and slender, with a wicked smile, and I was sure that she would cope with whatever circumstances arose on this unpredictable venture. I hoped she'd be able to look after me as well. We ate dinner with Marc at his flat. He opened a second bottle of wine and poured us all a toast. I reflected on the impulsive assurance that had brought me here; it was now far too late to back out. 'I envy you, *mes braves*,' Marc said, embracing us through the smoke of his cigar. 'Perhaps I'll see you out there, in the field.'

We landed in Damascus in the small hours and drove through streets deserted apart from patrolling soldiers. Date-palms were outlined against the sky as we turned into a courtyard, to be met by a rifle-toting watchman. We clattered up the stone stairs of a transit house that belonged to a faction of a Kurdish exile group, for an hour of sleep. Then we set off on the five-hundred mile journey to Qamishli in Syria's north-eastern corner, the nearest town to the crossing point over the Tigris into Iraq. After half a day's desert driving the ruins of Palmyra were a sudden explosion of colour: ochre walls surrounded an oasis of palms, and arcades of yellow columns marched into the distance, the detail of their capitals still crisp in the dry air. On a sharp-edged hill stood a red citadel. The French doctors clambered among the nearest ruins, posing for pictures. I remembered photographs taken by my father here in 1943, on leave with colleagues from his army hospital in Egypt. In my pack I had a copy of Xenophon's *The Persian Wars*, bought at his suggestion as I'd left London; he had carried the same book with him then.

The streets of Qamishli were frenetic with bicycles and contraband cigarette sellers and groups of men in woollen jerkins, their weapons slung: Kurdish fighters from inside Iraq, given sanctuary by the Syrian government. An unmistakable tension seeped through the town from the Iraqi border a dozen miles to the east, where the Tigris river crossing was reportedly under shell-fire. The news was confirmed the next morning by a *pesh merga* representative who arrived at our hotel. Flamboyantly moustached, in black pantaloons, knee-boots and a chequered cummerbund, he had come from Zakho – the nearest town inside Iraq – expressly to find us. Our medical supplies, and the presence of Francine and myself, were eagerly awaited at the battle lines, but the prospects for our mission now appeared uncertain.

The Kurdish forces inside Iraq were in retreat. That morning a boatload of refugees, one of the last attempting to cross the Tigris, had taken a direct hit. Even if we could get ourselves and our equipment to the other bank, the road beyond to Zakho was under fire from Iraqi guns, and communication with the *pesh merga* guerrillas there was cut. Perhaps, the man suggested, we might be able to slip in from the north with a Kurdish guide, via a smuggler's route from Turkey. He would try to get a message to the interior to let them know that we were still coming. We sipped coffee in a shuttered reception room, beneath bucolic frescoes of shepherds and their flocks. The man spoke of ravines in Iraq's northern mountains where we might be able to set up a hospital. He mentioned place-names, guttural and exotic – I made notes in the margin of my journal – and gunships, bombs, mules and mountain paths. None of it seemed real. Above our heads a fan looped slowly, stirring the warm air in the shadows near the ceiling.

Additional information came from Suzanne, a tough, chain-smoking French journalist who had turned up at the hotel that evening. She'd heard reports that large numbers of Kurdish civilians in northern Iraq were fleeing for the nearest frontier, ahead of the advancing Republican Guards, and she was leaving the next day for south-eastern Turkey to try to reach the region along the Iraqi border. While Francine and the doctors awaited the arrival of our medical supplies from Damascus, it was decided that I should accompany Suzanne, in order to find out about conditions on the Turkish border and to discover what I could about access across the mountains into Iraq.

The Syrian border police stamped our passports, waving us on our way. We shouldered our bags and walked along the road to the Turkish customs post. There the officials denied me entry: I would have to get a visa from the embassy in distant Damascus. My claim to be a member of a humanitarian mission only hardened their refusal. I said goodbye to Suzanne – who could enter Turkey freely on her French passport – and I trudged back towards the pillboxes of the Syrian frontier. I had visions of being stuck in no-man's-land between opposing banks of rusting barbed wire, but the Syrian guards re-instated my visa and offered me a glass of tea before I returned, dejected, to the hotel.

We turned for help to the Armenian prelate, the local Man

Of Influence in Qamishli. Crisp in a black cassock, the priest made time for Francine and me amongst a constant stream of supplicants, letter-bearers and telephone calls. Boy-acolytes served us coffee and sweetmeats while he ranted in voluble French against the US, the Russians, and Les Juifs, 'whose presence disfigures the whole face of the Middle East'. But he could help, he assured us; a phone-call here, a telex there, even if our aim was to help the Kurds . . . For a moment he raged against them, too – they had massacred his whole family back in 1915, only his grandfather escaped – and then he was, as suddenly, forgiving: 'they are, like us, all God's children'.

He offered a suggestion: north of Aleppo there was a border crossing where the Turkish guards might be 'accommodating'. If I was to take a taxi there the following morning – the three-hundred-mile journey should take no more than six or eight hours – I could be in Nusaybin, the Turkish border town opposite Qamishli, the following day. There I could meet up with the rest of the team, who would have crossed with the medical equipment. If that rendezvous failed we would all meet a day later in the Turkish town of Cizre, close to the Iraq border.

I set off at dawn, through a khaki land covered with a faint scattering of yellow flowers. Villages formed grey nodes in the distance, and an occasional low hill stood out briefly before sinking back into the dreamy monotony of the plain. Gradually the land became folded. Scattered trees appeared, then a grove by the roadside, into which the driver vanished for a sustained crap. '*Tamaam*' – good – he said on his return; about the only word in any language we had in common. In Aleppo he stopped at a bus depot where, with a bow, and the touch of his hand to his chest, he handed me into the care of a charmingly villainous taxi-driver colleague with a gold tooth in his smile. From this man's speck of English, his *soupçon* of

French, his *schmatter* of German, I gathered that these border deliveries were a regular part of his work. Reversing blind into the demented traffic, he tore out of town on a back-road, keeping his foot flat for the forty miles to the frontier.

The Syrian border post was a lonely concrete hangar where my arrival seemed to cheer the men inside, who shook my hand. I walked through the gate to where the Turkish flag hung limply in the afternoon glare. Two crop-headed gendarmes inspected my passport without comprehension. Then they marched me half a mile down a road of crushed quartz from which the sun bounced painfully into my eyes. The police post contained ten men in variegated uniforms. There was not a working pen among them. My ballpoint was annexed, and one by one they each filled in a line on a complex form. A big policeman took me into an office. Hunting through the desk drawers, he produced an official stamp and flourished it above the document. I gathered that some sort of payment was necessary. I pulled out Syrian pounds. He harangued me in Turkish. I produced twenty US dollars, which he pocketed. I picked up the words 'Marlboro', 'whisky'. I had none of these. He folded his arms.

'*Visa ma'afi*,' he said: visa gone.

I contemplated the return trip to Damascus and the time I'd waste before I would be able to start my medical work. I began counting out more dollars on his desk. After a while he nodded. My visa was kissed by the stamp.

'*Turkïye tamaam*,' he said, waving me farewell.

I joined a small party of other travellers in the desolate little village that lay beyond the border post. The men spoke to me questioningly. I pulled out my map and pointed, tracing a line towards the Turkey–Iraq frontier. I added the word 'doctor' a few times, and received a flurry of exclamations and smiles; I hadn't yet realized that the population along this part of the Turkish border was Kurdish, or that '*daktur*' has the same meaning in Kurmanji, the main Kurdish language. They loaded me with them onto a bus. We reached a town where I was transferred to a taxi, carried to a different bus station, and delivered aboard another bus to Diyarbakir, the next place on my map that lay more or less in the direction I wanted to go.

I stared out of the window at pink twilight reflected in an undercut river bank, at a cluster of minarets, at a crossroad with black crows rising from the dusk-softened fields. Time appeared to be unreeling with increasing speed, delivering me eastwards into darkness, into war. I wondered how it must have felt for my father, with everyone in uniform: some sense of great, common purpose. Here I was alone, making my way to something incomprehensible. I didn't even know whether to be frightened. It was as though I travelled in the unknown territory of a dream, where intent and language were indecipherable yet obscurely familiar, towards some incalculable enlightenment.

Night fell, and we continued our headlong journey. The bus lunged and roared. A haze of light announced the approach of Diyarbakir, its high basalt walls silhouetted against the glow. Nine hundred years before the city had been the capital of a Kurdish kingdom, ranked in fineness with the royal courts of Cairo and Damascus. Now it was a garrison town from where the Turkish army governed their rebellious Kurdish provinces. At a hotel I secured one of the few unoccupied rooms in town, reserved by an American TV news crew who were in transit from Ankara. I tried the word *daktur* on the manager and brought out my map. He handed me a key; the room was mine. The next morning his son led me to the bus station. Turkish forces were on high alert, fearful that the PKK would take advantage of the uncertainty on the border to increase its attacks. Troops patrolled the streets, lining men against the shop-fronts and checking documents.

In the bus depot they were emptying suitcases out onto the oily ground. Amidst wailing children and shouted interrogations, the boy put me on a bus to Cizre.

We stopped at the Turkish frontier post of Nusaybin to pick up passengers, and I gazed across the border fence to Qamishli across the valley. There was no sign of Francine or the French doctors, nor of their truck loaded with medical supplies. The bus continued eastwards through low, spitting rain. After nightfall we rolled into Cizre, where dim streetlights reflected in the puddles. I made my way towards the glow of a hotel-front down the street. All the rooms were full, but I'd found a seat in the bar and bought a beer when a ringing slap on my back nearly flattened me. Suzanne, the French journalist, straddled the chair beside me, her face creased into a smile. She tossed her Camels onto the table and lit a fresh one, coughing like a graveyard of consumptives.

'Where is Francine, and the rest of your *équipage*?' she wanted to know. I explained that I had hoped to find them here in Cizre.

'We came this morning and I have not seen them,' she said. 'This is the only hotel.'

She called back to the bar and made a circling motion with her finger over the table-top. Two men joined us, carrying beer. Suzanne introduced me; Paul and Misha were from her press agency, and we began discussing what was known about conditions on the border. Some correspondents, who had escaped across the mountain frontier and arrived that day in Cizre, were claiming that the entire Kurdish population inside northern Iraq was on the move. A million people, the inhabitants of the towns of Kirkuk and Suleimaniyeh, were reportedly trying to reach Iran in the east; perhaps a million more from Mosul, Dahuk and Zakho might be heading north towards the Turkish border.

'There is a journalist who has just come from there,' said

Paul, pointing at a haggard-looking man scribbling at a table. 'He said he came across the mountains at a place called Isikveren, where there are already many refugees. He says the Republican Guards are still coming. Maybe the Kurdish fighters cannot stop them.'

I knew that these developments might signal the end of our medical mission: if *pesh merga* resistance had collapsed, there would be no stable front line behind which Francine and I could set up our casualty treatment station. I sipped my beer, trying to analyse whether my predominant feeling was disappointment or relief. The hotel doors flew open, admitting the sound of rain and swearing, and the lobby filled with a drenched TV crew and its equipment boxes. The leader, the hem of his overcoat splashed with mud, was berating the manager.

'What's wrong with this shitty country?' he yelled, his modulated anchor-man's tones cracking with rage. 'First some scumbag hotel in Diyarbakir gives away our room, then we reach this shithole and you say you're full! I know you've got a booking for us, we faxed from New York to confirm!'

One would have had to have a heart of stone not to laugh at this display of petulant temper. Even the exhausted-looking journalist in the corner snatched a moment from his writing for a pale smile.

'It was me who stole their room in Diyarbakir last night,' I confessed to my French companions, who were delighted. 'That reminds me; I'd better find a place to sleep.'

'Absurd, *mon cher,*' said Paul, 'we have a room. Of course you will share with us, if you do not mind the floor.'

He brushed away my thanks, while Misha ordered food and we began to eat. Between bites we decided that we should leave early the next morning to find Isikveren and the refugees. In friendly company, with a secure place to sleep, I felt a wonderful languor sweep over me. That was the last repose I was to experience for a long time.

⊕

The camp was more terrible than I could have imagined: a quarter of a million people crowded into an area of ridged mountainside by a cordon of Turkish soldiers that prevented them coming down into the valley. More refugees poured over the border hourly, an unbroken column of figures along the distant skyline – some leading mules so heaped with possessions that they looked like tiny tortoises – and down across high snow-fields towards this uncertain sanctuary. The camp was a welter of churned-up mud, rotting entrails of slaughtered animals and rivulets of liquid shit. Exhausted families lay packed like sardines under shelters made of plastic sheet supported by bits of string and tree-branch. There was no room for the men, who squatted outside in the mud with their heads on their knees, fast asleep amidst the constant din.

From along the crests that marked the frontier came bursts of shooting, as Turkish troops fired into the air in an attempt to turn back this human tide. Babies wailed, wood cracked as branches were torn from the scrub-oaks and fed into fires, and hoes thudded into the half-frozen ground as new graves were dug. It was mainly the children who were dying, of exposure and dysenteric illness. Mothers stood by the gravesides as the small bodies were wrapped in blankets and consigned to shallow holes, each resting place marked by a stone thrust into the earth at head and foot. But in the icy rain the grave-markers slid down the steep slope, and the margins of the burial grounds were lost continually under the tramping feet and spreading shelters of new arrivals.

We walked, dazed, through this inferno of misery. Mothers sobbed, holding out to us their dying babies; without any medical equipment I was utterly unable to help, and had to turn away. I saw a child, the skin of his face a weeping crust through which his eyes peered; we were told he had been burned when the truck in which he was travelling was hit by rockets from an Iraqi helicopter. There was an elderly man in a wheelchair canted in the mud, who had been carried by his family over the mountains to this desperate place. He seemed demented, asking those around him, over and over, to move him into the sun. A couple of Iraqi army deserters who had fled with the Kurds sat silently on a log, their hands thrust inside the pale flames of a fire they tended with sodden twigs.

We threaded our way up ridge after ridge, between shelters of canvas and blankets. The slopes were draped in a pall of steam and woodsmoke from fires in the clefts where snow was being melted down for drinking water. It was a dirty grey, and tasted of petroleum: fallout from the oil-field fires in Kuwait, eight hundred miles to the south. Every shoulder of the mountainside that offered any purchase had been occupied, and men with hoes were cutting platforms for new tent-sites into the slopes. The encampment spread below us over the bare ridges. Beyond loomed the ranges of the Taurus mountains like petrified waves, their tops crowned with white. At the crest that marked the border we found some shivering Turkish soldiers. They'd made shelters of stones that they had draped with their groundsheets to try to keep out the biting wind, and we stopped near their position, panting in the thin air, to rest. Suzanne sucked down a restorative cigarette. We expected the soldiers to prevent us going on, but they looked at us without interest, their pinched faces as disconsolate as those of the people they were trying to turn away.

Descending the Iraqi side of the mountain, we passed columns of refugees plodding uphill. The embroidered skirts of the women, inlaid with tiny discs of mirror, hung heavily under their coating of mud. Further down, the ground was littered with the debris of military retreat: ammunition pouches and belts and the curved magazines of AK47s, cast away by fleeing *pesh merga* as they took their families to safety over the final ridge. In places the metal bullet-clips lay in drifts covering the path, and we slipped on carpets of cartridges that rolled under our feet. The snow-dusted slope was studded with the remains of small fires where the wooden butts and stocks of rifles had been burned for warmth; only the steel barrels of the weapons remained, hammered into the ground, where they had served as tent-poles for temporary shelters. Perhaps nothing else indicated so completely the extremity of *pesh merga* despair, for I had been told that the men never gave up their arms except in death.

Beneath us lay the end of the road taken by the refugees in their escape from the Iraqi plains. A vast park of abandoned vehicles – trucks, buses, taxis, tractors and hijacked Iraqi army lorries – stood at odd angles where they had bogged down or run out of gas or stalled on the steep slope. The track that snaked up from the valley below was lined by the wrecks of more transport that had expired en route. People were living amidst this mechanized wasteland, inhabiting mud-bound saloon cars with blankets draped over their smashed windscreens, or camping in the shells of canted buses. An old woman occupied the scoop of a front-end loader, her door a flap of canvas that hung down over the metal teeth. Most of these people were here because they were too weak to make the final climb over the crest. But among them also could be seen the signs of preparation, of men returning to the fight.

A production line had been set up on mattresses spread upon the ground. Men were stripping springs and firing mechanisms from damaged weapons. Others were assembling and checking assault rifles, then stacking them in the bed of a mired truck. Children foraged for loose bullets on the hillsides and gathered them in plastic bags. A boy of ten or so, his nose dripping, brought an armload of AK47 magazines that he had found. Others wiped cartridges clean of mud and handed them to their fathers, who oiled the rounds and thumbed them into ammunition clips. Nearby, a group were testing weapons, firing single shots and short bursts at a mark on the hillside and adjusting the calibration of their gunsights.

It was clear that these men were not helpless refugees. Instead of thin sports-coats and sodden parkas, they wore the Kurdish dress that was the uniform of the *pesh merga*: short jackets and pleat-fronted trousers with buttoned cuffs, of woven goats-wool dyed in grey or beige. Around their waists they had fine-patterned cummerbunds, wound in many layers to spread the weight of pistol belts and hanging hand-grenades. Harnesses of ammunition pouches crossed their chests. Most wore checked kefiyehs, turban-style, on their heads; some had fur flap-caps, taken as trophies from Republican Guards. All the men shared an air of confidence, and carried their weapons with the ease of long handling. Bundles of AK47 rifles, rolled into blankets, were strapped onto pack-mules tethered to a ruined tractor. The slender shafts of rocket-propelled grenade projectiles stood up like quills along the animals' backs. A child played with the telescopic sight from an anti-aircraft gun. He held the device to his eye and aimed up at an imaginary Iraqi plane, making explosion sounds with his mouth.

'Saddam *khallas*!' he shouted: Saddam is finished.

One of the *pesh merga* spoke a little German, and I gathered from him that the group was about to move to the front. It lay approximately fifteen miles to the south, he told me – sketching a map in the mud with a twig – at a place called Qasrok. There the Kurdish rearguard held a *Festung* – a fortification – blocking the Iraqi advance up the road towards the border. The man told me that their group was off to reinforce the defences against the Republican Guards. I explained that

I was a doctor and asked if I could travel with the unit to the forward position. A brief discussion was held. I was told that the decision depended on the Kurd commander; he was at the front, so I would have to accompany them there to ask him. I explained my intentions to the French journalists: here was a chance to see the Kurdish position and find out whether it would be possible to set up our treatment station there. They shook my hand and wished me luck, then started back up the hillside. I stood with my small shoulder bag, watching my friends climb away. On a shoulder of the mountain they turned and waved, and were gone.

Some of the *pesh merga* had set off already, leading the loaded pack-animals south towards the foothills. The rest of the party, their weapons slung, waited for a tractor-and-trailer that ground its way up the slope towards us. One man went to the truck on which the guns were stacked and extracted an assault rifle – an AK47 with a neat, folding butt – which he presented to me. I held up my palms, declining the weapon: I knew that in the war, my father's war, medical personnel had not borne arms. I had some idea that this was an inviolable principle of all conflicts.

'Doctor,' I said to the German-speaker, patting my chest, '*keine gewehr*: no gun.'

He frowned. '*Wenn kommen* Saddam helicopter,' he explained stiltedly, miming with his hand the attack-dive of a gunship, '*mussen alle schiessen*.'

This was the price of joining the group; helping to defend it, for our common survival. The only small protection against helicopters was for all to fire together, spraying bullets into the air from as many guns as possible to try to throw off the pilot's aim. I took the weapon and removed the magazine. It was full. Working the action to see that it ran smoothly, I re-inserted the clip, leaving the bolt uncocked. By now the tractor had reached us and we piled into the trailer, squatting on the metal floor. The driver made a turn between the abandoned vehicles and we were off down the road to the front.

Around us lay a vista of extraordinary desolation. Tractors stood on end like monuments, their big drive-wheels swallowed by the lapping mud. Cars that got stuck on the steep track had simply been abandoned by their occupants. Long convoys of stalled transport had built up, until a bulldozer had been used to clear the route for the pressure of vehicles behind. Mercedes, Land Rovers, plush saloon cars had been rammed off the road into a rocky gully, where they lay twisted together. Taxis and buses had been shunted into concertinas of metal and glass. The road entered a gorge that cut through the foothills. Here too, vehicles had been left where they'd stopped; doors open, tyres flat, some burned out as though they had been strafed from the air. Drifts of clothes and bedding lay across the roadway, where occasional figures picked through the debris for anything usable. A fighter lifted his rifle and fired at a pair of dogs trotting over the shoulder of a far hillside; they eat the dead, my translator explained. Our tractor wound slowly between the obstacles.

The valley opened out ahead, revealing the ruins of what had been an Iraqi base. Roofless barracks enclosed a square in which were parked some wrecked army lorries. They had been pillaged, their batteries cracked open to extract the acid, their fuel-tank caps prised off. Beyond lay the fort, on a low rise amidst a field of barbed wire.

'Qasrok,' said my guide and translator.

Surrounded by a curtain-wall, the entrance guarded by pill-boxes, the structure looked like a child's rough rendering of a Foreign Legion outpost. Stumpy circular turrets stood at opposite corners. On one had once been painted an Iraqi flag, now almost obliterated by bullet-strikes that pitted the concrete. A pick-up truck and a shiny red Toyota saloon were parked in a hollow, and smoke rose from cooking fires in the courtyard. On the other side of the fort the road disappeared between a couple of low hills capped with defensive diggings. A single shot popped somewhere round the corner.

A group of *pesh merga* emerged to watch our arrival. The tractor halted amidst a flurry of greetings. We jumped down, stretching our cramped legs, and I returned the weapon I'd carried to the man who had given it to me. We walked through the courtyard, past the mouths of some deep bunkers that ran underground. A heavy Russian machine gun on a tripod guarded the entrance to the courtyard. My escort explained my presence to the resident fighters, who seemed pleased at my arrival; I was ushered into the fort to meet the *pesh merga* commander. He was young, dressed in captured Iraqi officer's battledress, with a lively smile beneath his beard. My German-speaking acquaintance introduced me and the man embraced me, chest to chest; I was clearly welcome. I explained my mission: to return with the rest of my team, to set up a surgical unit for the treatment of wounded near the front line. This is the front line, the commander informed me proudly, the Iraqis are dug in just along the valley; I ought to see the situation for myself.

Four men climbed into the Toyota, the commander taking the wheel. Sandwiched in the back seat, I watched more fighters push-start the pick-up and pile aboard. It fell in behind us with a clashing of gears. The cavalcade travelled for only a couple of hundred yards before the commander slowed to a cautious crawl, keeping his vehicle in the shelter of the steep roadside verge. I noticed that the men in the pick-up following us were crouching low. We stopped below where some *pesh merga* lay against the bank, looking over its top. The commander waved me up beside him, handing me his binoculars and pointing. A quarter of a mile ahead the road emerged from a fold in the ground and crossed the front of a bumpy hill. A belt of barbed wire encircled its slopes, enclosing some bunkers roofed with sandbags that were the same wheaten colour as the hill itself. On the ridges beyond, similar structures were silhouetted along the skyline, and through the binoculars I could see the heads of some Iraqi soldiers moving above the top of the fortifications. The commander slid down the bank and looked at me with his engaging smile. This was his sector, and his enemy.

We returned to the fort to eat. I offered some rations that I had in my bag but they were waved aside, and I joined the men reclining on blankets while we ate a meal of beans and flat bread from a large communal pot in the centre of the floor. More fighters left their boots at the door and crowded into the central room of the fort until the place was full of weapons and men. I had noticed that the *pesh merga* never engaged the safety-catches on their guns – they considered such a practice effete, even when I remonstrated with them later as I operated on men wounded by an accidental discharge – and I winced when a stack of rifles clattered to the concrete floor. Fading light filtered through a shell-hole in the roof of the chamber. The walls were covered with smeary slogans in red paint, overlaid on the names of previous tenants – Iraqi soldiers – scratched in the plaster. Through a doorway to an adjoining room a group of men knelt at prayer.

The commander began an explanation. Other fighters joined in now and then, clarifying points that my translator questioned. I gathered that further reinforcements would be gathering at this fort over the next few days for a planned attack against the Iraqi defences down the road. My hospital would be very welcome, for they knew of no doctor in all of northern Iraq to treat their wounded. *Insh' Allah*, said the commander, of course there would not be any wounded and they would be victorious; but a doctor would be good. Tea was served from a tray of tiny cups. I looked around the group of men, prayer-beads clicking between their fingers.

An oil-lamp in the middle of the floor, lit against the dusk, glinted off belts of bullets and hand-grenades and bronzed, moustached faces.

From somewhere down the valley came a faint rattle of automatic fire, and a detachment of fighters got up, adjusted their equipment, and left to take up their posts in the forward positions for the night. The commander indicated a tall, broad-shouldered man who sat beside him. This, he explained, was Nouri Abdullah, and he and my translator, who I'd discovered was named Saed, would be responsible for my safety, now and when I returned with my medical team. The tall man nodded, his face friendly. He showed me to a sleeping mat in one of the turrets, stuffing a blanket in the firing-slit to keep out the cold. I fell asleep listening to the wind keening in the barbed wire and the popping of gunfire among the surrounding hills. I was aware, above my fear, of a disturbing sense of exhilaration.

7

Kurdistan

'It is better to fight than to be idle', runs a Kurdish saying, and while I couldn't share their ready acceptance of war, I was becoming aware of its perverse seduction. Part of the experience of being in the line of fire – despite the terror of death, mutilation, brain-damage or blindness – is the incomparable rush of clarity that accompanies it, a liberation from life's ordinary, insidious dread. Returning to Turkey felt like taking a frustrating step backwards to responsibility, though one still complicated by unpredictable dangers. Having promised the fort's commander and my new *pesh merga* friends that I'd be back as soon as possible with my medical team, I had retraced my route over the mountain frontier and down through the refugee camp at Isikveren, and I was in a café in the small Turkish town of Sirnak when a truck drew up outside. Out of it climbed Francine, her blonde bob luminous in the waning light. Bertrand and Antoine were with her. They were excited that I had been inside Iraq; I was relieved to hear that the truck contained our medical supplies, for which temporary storage had been organized in Sirnak until we could get across the border. Francine had arranged accommodation for us in the town with a Kurdish family. She had even charmed the head of Sirnak's hospital, who had agreed to allow us to take one of his ambulances up to the Isikveren camp the next day.

That night – after I'd eaten and washed away the filth of the camp and the smell of gasoline that clung to my skin – I walked down the hill to the Sirnak post office, to fax a piece to a Dutch newspaper for which I sometimes wrote. Lamplight glowing through the windows of the low houses did little to dispel the darkness. The town's population was Kurdish, so there was a big Turkish army presence: the flashlights of a patrol picked out the thin rain in their beams.

I sat at the post-office counter, writing my copy and sipping tea offered by the kindly postmaster. Some Turkish soldiers dried their boots around a paraffin heater while they waited to telephone. From across the road, behind the wall that enclosed the electricity station, came an orange flash: an explosion buffeted the windows and the lights went out. Two more blasts thudded from the direction of the military base at the edge of town. The Turkish troops had dropped at once to the floor, weapons cocked and their radio crackling with urgent commands. The Kurdish PKK attack lasted only a minute or so while I lay beneath the counter watching red lines of tracer bullets flick past the windows. I hurried back through the blacked-out streets to the house, passing revving armoured personnel carriers preparing to set off in search of the insurgents.

The next morning the army was conducting house-to-house searches in the town as we left. Into the ambulance we had loaded a crate of drugs, a World Health Organization pack containing medication for ten thousand people. The road to the border wound down into valleys and over bridges that crossed racing streams of snow-melt. The poplar trees were beginning to show the first dusting of green. Traffic was heavy; convoys of army trucks on their way to the border. At the entrance to the Isikveren valley we were stopped while earth-moving equipment worked to improve the road up to the camp. Eventually the gendarmes waved us through. Gunning his engine, the driver charged his four-wheel-drive ambulance past the Turkish army post – the soldiers at the barrier stood aside uncertainly – and onward up the rutted track that led to the heights above.

We stopped in the middle of the camp and were instantly overwhelmed. A great crowd – mostly women with children – formed around the ambulance, pleading for help. Three Kurds appeared who had some medical training. They introduced themselves, and helped by unarmed *pesh merga*, began forming the people into groups. Antoine, Bertrand and I each took up station at a door of the vehicle, and, assisted by a refugee medic, began dispensing drugs for amoebic dysentery, for gastro-enteritis, for pneumonia and eye infections. One man needed cardiac medication – he showed me a pack from a US pharmaceutical group – and as I hunted through our stocks for an equivalent, I was reminded for a surreal moment of the struggle between the American medical companies for a lead in the multi-billion-dollar coronary disease market, in which I had once played a transient role. Then I was handing out packs of oral rehydration powder, explaining via the translator how mothers should prepare the solution for their diarrhoea-stricken children using clean water. I wondered where they'd find it in the camp.

There was no time for proper examinations: just a question about symptoms, medication with dosage instructions scribbled by the Kurdish doctor, then the next desperate mother with her baby so dehydrated that it was unlikely to last the night. Within a couple of hours our drugs were gone and we left in defeat, bumping down the track past a crowd mobbing a bread delivery truck. Turkish troops stood on the piled loaves, firing into the air and kicking out at the faces clamouring below them. I could see that Francine and the French doctors were horrified by what they'd witnessed, and I recalled suddenly my own reactions at first seeing the camp only a couple of days before. Those emotions now felt strangely remote: buried, somewhere, for later analysis. I had already learned – as they would – not to feel too much, to concentrate my energies on the immediate present.

I had a task to occupy myself. I was trying to work out how we could move our material over the mountains to the fort at Qasrok in time for the pending Kurdish attack. The track into the Isikveren camp ended in a morass of mud and shelters, and beyond it there remained a steep climb over the mountains and down to the vehicle graveyard on the other side where we might meet some *pesh merga* and their transport. A mule-train would be difficult to organize among the leaderless refugees in the camp, and would certainly be stopped by the Turkish troops that manned the pass which we would have to cross. And before Francine and I could start working across the border, we would have to help Bertrand and Antoine establish their tent-hospital: as well as treating refugees, it would be our referral unit for sending patients back to the border from our planned forward dressing station.

The next morning we set up the treatment centre beside the river at Yekmol, where I was to have my encounter with the groin-shot boy who died. His fate stressed the urgency of our mission. If casualties could be stabilized at the front before they were evacuated, they might arrive in better shape – with reduced shock and sepsis – at a place where proper care could be given. Even with such an arrangement in place I knew that the boy might not have survived, but there were likely to be many more wounded in the days to come who could benefit. I hoped I wouldn't have to preside over too many more avoidable deaths.

✪

As though the arrival of the US Secretary of State had switched on the spotlight of international attention, the Turkish border was suddenly flooded with TV crews, dignitaries and international aid groups. I'd just finished the last of my surgical cases at Yekmol when the networks arrived: I was relieved that they hadn't been around earlier to make a media event of my patient's death. Afterwards Francine and I went with our driver to Isikveren, to check that the medical equipment we would need across the border had been moved to a tent near the Turkish army base as we'd arranged.

We found the valley below the Isikveren camp overrun by visitors: the Turkish Prime Minister with massive security entourage; an Italian government delegation; and, at the next stop on their lightning smiling helicopter tour, the Secretary of State and Major Mike. The Non-Governmental Organizations were beginning to arrive in strength. Representatives from Médecins sans Frontières (Belgium, France, Holland and Spain), Médecins du Monde, UNICEF, UNHCR, Save the Children, the Red Cross and various Scandinavian church organizations huddled in secretive groups to discuss how they could steal a march on the competition and establish themselves in the camp on the mountain above. The experts of MSF Holland were winning: a convoy of white trucks with their distinctive red paint-splash was already inching up the track, while in the valley their logisticians set up a satellite phone-link direct to their Amsterdam headquarters. Francine and I hitched a ride up to their clinic site in the centre of the camp. Neat white MSF tents were going up amidst the sprawl of shelters, efficient Dutch logisticians cutting drainage trenches around their perimeters. We had heard from Paris the night before that two more personnel were on their way to join us, but our presence here was redundant: the only place a minnow organization like ourselves could be of use was inside Iraq – our true assignment – where no one else was going to operate.

Now that intervention was fashionable, the Americans

were leading the show. We were high on a spur of the mountain assessing possible crossing routes when a pair of A-10 jets came howling up the valley and flashed past us at eye-level. A drone of turbo-props from the north brought a line of C-130 transport planes, banking one by one into a drop-run. They flew over the ridge on which we stood, their flaps down: on the open cargo-ramps we could see the kickers in their harnesses pushing the pallets out. The loads hovered and then separated, popping parachutes of lucent plastic or olive-green, and began their descent into a deep valley below us. Among the shelters the people were galvanized, seizing knives, ropes and sacks and bounding down the slopes towards the drop-zones.

One 'chute failed to open and the huge pallet, the size of a minibus, smashed into a group of tents. Others struck the steep hillside and rolled, their canopies collapsing like wilting flowers. They were still moving when the refugees swarmed over them, hacking through the tarpaulin covers. Fights developed in the crowds swirling around each load, and blood flowed as desperate people lashed out at their neighbours in the fierce competition for food. Others climbed the trees to cut down canopies and line. Everything was borne away on the backs of men and women, loaded like mules under improvised packs of parachute-cloth and strapping. On the hillside there was a burst of gunfire and people fled from a pannier that some Turkish troops had hijacked, keen to fill their stomachs on NATO rations. A man was carried past me with a bullet in his leg; another, shrouded in parachute material, was dead.

The sun was setting as we returned down the mountain, past a late-arriving TV crew and a photographer who were posing some half-starved Kurds to re-enact the airdrop drama: they had them pull a piece of parachute from a tree and pass from hand to hand some of the empty ration boxes that littered the ground. In the valley the dignitaries were leaving, and we took the opportunity to approach the air-crews of some US helicopters sitting on a landing-ground near the Turkish army camp. With them was a communications officer, who spoke on his radio to a distant presence. Suddenly all was arranged: a Navy cargo 'copter would be doing a food drop the next morning, targeting isolated groups of refugees in the mountains, and it would lift us and our equipment and put us down across the frontier. Francine and I were elated, and we didn't even weep when we found the medical boxes being looted by Turkish soldiers. At first I thought they were looking for food, until I watched one hack open a sterile surgical pack with his bayonet to steal the scissors from the instrument sets. Some of the men had taken advantage of the tent's privacy to leave large turds in the corners. The sooner we were out of there the better.

⊕

In the gloom of the fuselage it was difficult to see the faces of my colleagues: Francine, strapped into the seat beside me, beefy Jean-Pierre and young Ernest buckled into their harnesses on the other side of the pile of boxes that filled the space between us. They had just arrived that morning from Paris via Ankara, and looked bewildered; apart from a snatched breakfast on the landing pad amidst a bout of strenuous box-hauling, they had had no time to acclimatize. These were not the doctors we had been expecting – Jean-Pierre was a dentist, Ernest a physiotherapist – but at this stage their addition to the team, as organizers and assistants, was invaluable. Eight US marines, weapons held across their chests, occupied the rest of the seats that ran along each side of the helicopter's hold: officially, no Allied aircraft were supposed to cross the frontier into Iraqi airspace – never mind touch down on enemy soil – so they were along as an escort.

I'd marked the drop-zone on the pilots' maps. The Navy aircrew were excited. They'd not seen combat in the Gulf War, but dropping a medical team inside Iraq was a mission, and they were gung-ho.

The helicopter lifted tail-first and shot upwards, engines bellowing: conversation was impossible, despite the yellow rubber ear-plugs handed out by the flight-sergeant. I watched the earth recede through the small porthole. Range after range of snow-etched peaks filled the view. As we gained height, the rear loading-ramp dropped into its locked-down position and a blast of freezing air lashed our faces. The flight-sergeant, silhouetted against the wedge of light, leaned far out in his harness to survey the ground below. He exchanged arm-signals with the cargo man, who started rearward, clipping his safety line to the running rail as he went. The helicopter banked violently, revealing a brown hillside and scattered shelters rushing by a few hundred feet beneath us.

The food drop began; the cargo kicker thrust at the rearmost pallet and it ran out into the void and vanished. The flight-sergeant gave him a hand with the next – a load of flour-sacks wrapped in netting – and together they rushed it off the ramp, their charge stopped with a jerk by the harnesses that prevented them plunging after it. They hung out over the edge, watching the load fall. Evidently its performance satisfied them, for they exchanged grins and returned for the next. Now they were in the swing, and box after box tumbled from the rear of the helicopter. Suddenly I noticed the grey sack containing our tent – cadged with much difficulty from the Red Cross – shoot rearward and out of sight. I shouted as loud as I could, but without an intercom headset no one could hear me. I tried to rise but the shoulder-straps pinned me in my seat: fortunately, as there would be nothing to stop me flying out of the tail after the packs of surgical instruments and dressings that tumbled out next. The chopper hopped over a ridge and between the legs of the kickers I could see the boxes explode as they hit the ground and scraps of white fly across the hillside.

Jean-Pierre and I managed to save the last part of our equipment from the crew's enthusiasm by locking our legs around the cases nearest to us. The flight-sergeant, embarrassed, unwound the cord of a headset and plugged it into the bulkhead beside me, and his contrite voice crackled in my ear. Ahead I could see, through the cockpit Perspex, the random cars and sky-reflecting puddles of the vehicle junkyard. I told the pilot that our landing-zone was below. The helicopter touched down with a jump and the marines dived out of the side doors to form a cordon just beyond the radius of the turning rotor. We unloaded our remaining boxes, watched by a handful of Kurds. I was relieved that none of them were armed, for the American troops were clearly not informed about conditions on this side of the border. Their officer listened to the sound of gunfire from the edge of the plateau.

'Who's doing the shooting?' he asked me.

'*Pesh merga*, Kurdish fighters,' I told him, 'testing weapons before they go to the front.'

'Oh,' he said, peering through his field glasses, 'bandits.'

The helicopter took off steeply. A pick-up approached, rocking over the mud. The *pesh merga* driver seemed happy to take us down the road to Qasrok, and we piled our equipment in the back, Jean-Pierre and myself perching on the top of the load. Our arrival at the fort was greeted with much excitement. Saed the German-speaker told me that the first part of the commander's offensive had already begun: the small hill that lay forward of the Republican Guard's ridge-top bunkers had been overrun in an assault the day before. The *pesh merga* had however fallen back to their previous positions straddling the road, as the newly captured dugouts were under enemy fire. I asked about the big man, Nouri Abdullah; Saed assured me that he was unhurt, though on duty in the trenches.

A few minutes later the commander returned, still smiling, and our equipment was carried inside the fort to a room that had been put aside for our use. It was getting dark as we unpacked the remnants of our equipment by the light of an oil-lamp. The anaesthetic box was gone, its drugs and airways scattered somewhere on the mountains along with the bulk of our surgical instruments. An emergency resuscitation pack had been saved, and a small surgery kit; apart from that there were some boxes of medicines, intravenous fluid, and sterile gloves and dressings. We had a bundle of tent poles but no tent. We sorted out the stuff and arranged it ready for use. I advised Francine and Ernest to get some sleep while they could. Then Jean-Pierre and I started work.

There were a number of men with wounds from the day before, on whom I operated – on the floor – in the beams of flashlights held by my *pesh merga* assistants. The first case was a fighter whose right hand had been mangled by an exploding grenade. It had blown off much of his middle and ring fingers and part of his palm, shattering his thumb. A fragment had struck him below the eye, taking away a neat, diamond-shaped piece of flesh, and the eyelid fluttered like a trapped moth. He had lacerations and punctures to the front of his chest. I listened with my stethoscope: there were breath-sounds on both sides, so I was reasonably confident that his lungs had not been penetrated. All of the wounds, however, had to be explored, and his mashed hand cleaned of dead flesh and the dirt that had been blown into it by the explosion. I was keenly aware of the loss of the anaesthetic box, and cursed the heavy-footedness of the cargo-kicker as I searched among the remaining ampoules for a substitute.

Eventually I was forced to use Nubain, a morphine-type painkiller that we had in relative abundance. Giving it intravenously until the patient was groggy, I tried to numb the arm with local anaesthetic injected around the nerves in his armpit – a technique I had read about, but never tried before – and set to work over a bowl of disinfectant, scrubbing the grit out of the lacerated tissue with a nail-brush. The patient didn't murmur, and anxiously I asked Jean-Pierre to check that he was breathing: Nubain in large doses can depress respiration. By torchlight I snipped away torn meat and shards of bone.

In the distance there was a series of thuds and then a tearing sound overhead: the Iraqi artillery had fired a salvo of shells, which exploded on the hillside behind the fort. Saed and Nouri Abdullah fled outside to man defensive positions at the ramparts. In their rush they took the flashlights with them and I was left in darkness, holding a dressing pad over the wound. Jean-Pierre and I wondered whether this was a prelude to a counterattack; by the small glow of his penlight torch he drew up some more Nubain and injected it into the now restless patient, while we listened for a sudden burst of firing from the front line. It did not come.

My assistants returned, laughing at the inaccuracy of the Iraqi gunners, and I continued my ragged work. The man ended up with two fingers amputated, though I managed to preserve his thumb by pinning the bone fragments together with syringe needles. I smeared the surgical sites with iodine ointment and dressed them, then gave the man a shot of penicillin and a tetanus jab. He was carried to a corner where he lay sleeping. Before I started my next case I carried the pieces of amputated flesh outside, and, lacking any other means of disposing of them, hurled the package of bloody gauze over the barbed wire. There was a rustling sound and a snarl as they were carried off by the feral dogs.

I was thankful that none of my patients were critically

injured – until I could replace the missing equipment, my resources were even more slender than they had been at the tent hospital on the border – but the commander explained, sadly, that the seriously wounded had not survived. Over the next few days I began to understand why. The Iraqi forces did not risk trying to regain their lost outpost and contented themselves with firing on the Kurdish positions: mainly at night, when they hoped to catch the fighters above-ground. Explosions and the sound of screaming – my wake-up call – would herald the arrival of casualties, and I'd stagger from my blankets and lay out my equipment ready for the first patient. Lightly wounded men generally made their own way back. Those badly hurt were hoisted onto a comrade's back and carried at a run along the sunken road that led back several hundred yards from the frontline trenches. This evacuation system acted as a crude form of triage: the seriously injured died before they reached the mattress on the floor that constituted my operating theatre.

The Iraqis also continued their sporadic shelling of the fort, with effects that were disruptive rather than dangerous. I would have preferred to work in the deep bunkers that lay beneath the building, impervious to shellfire, but the refugees streaming up this valley ten days before had used them as latrines, industriously filling every inch of floorspace with shit. Later arrivals had used the stairs, so that the dark shafts that led to these underground chambers vented an almost tangible stench. I prayed that we would not have to seek cover there.

Each morning a crowd awaited us: refugees from up the valley that led towards the Turkish border. Francine and Ernest took shoulder bags of drugs and made tent calls there with a *pesh merga* guide, treating infections and sending the more serious cases down to the fort. These arrived in a steady flow: neglected wounds, comatose babies, sick adults.

Amoebic dysentery was rife, for which we handed out tablets. We too were at risk of infection as our only water source – the stream that flowed past the fort – passed first through the festering sink of the refugee area near the border. The gully in which it ran was choked by the bodies of a flock of sheep caught in an airstrike, and among their carcasses was a bundle of rags that could have been the remains of their shepherd.

Life became pared down to its essentials; sleep – snatched whenever I had a spare moment – and food; though despite my hunger, I sometimes nodded off over the plate of flat bread and beans that was our staple diet. I had come to rely absolutely on my *pesh merga* assistants. Nouri Abdullah seemed able at any time to conjure up a tiny cup of hot, sweet tea; Saed rolled me cigarettes of fierce Kurdish tobacco. For moments on end I could immerse myself in these simple pleasures before returning to my exhausting work. Perhaps because of my fatigue, the question of our safety didn't trouble me. I knew that if an Iraqi attack came, these two men would do everything they could to ensure that we got away unharmed over the mountains. But the stalemate continued. The Kurds had not the force to capture the higher Iraqi bunkers, and the enemy facing them appeared reluctant to attack. Instead there was sniping along the trench line; tracer bullets fanned up against the night sky.

Then, abruptly, the mood changed. I was operating when a clamour arose outside the fort, and Saed rushed in to give me the news: *pesh merga* scouts had just discovered that the enemy had slipped away under cover of darkness, and the road to Zakho was open. At dawn the fighters loaded their heavy weapons – a small Russian quick-firing cannon and a mortar – into the back of a truck, and set off in their vehicles to reconnoitre the town. Later, glad of the rest, I was dozing in the sun against the fort's outer wall when Jean-

Pierre called out; soldiers were coming down the road from the border. I opened my eyes. A dozen men approached, weapons ready, scanning the land around them. They were Americans, in diverse headgear – jungle hats, camouflage bandannas, berets – and bearing a collection of armaments that included fighting knives, machine-guns, shotguns and a stubby grenade-launcher. I greeted them from my sun-spot.

The soldiers were a US army Special Forces team. They had not expected to find a surgeon in this place, and were surprised that we had been working in the shooting zone for the past week. They offered us MREs – Meals Ready to Eat; US army rations whose hyper-processed blandness had earned them the epithet 'Meals Rejected by Ethiopians' – while their communications man spoke on his radio. A short while later a pair of French airforce helicopters circled the building and landed on the road, followed by a British one. Then some American choppers touched down, disgorging a group of officers. Suddenly the area around the fort was crowded. Events had unfolded while we had been involved in this tiny theatre of war, cut off from news. The White House had announced the creation of 'Safe Havens' for Kurdish civilians in northern Iraq. Allied High Command had declared the first one around the town of Zakho, and were negotiating the withdrawal of the local Iraqi forces.

The *pesh merga* came roaring back in their motley cavalcade, Nouri Abdullah waving to me from the weapons truck. They had managed to get in a last blow, shooting up the Iraqi police post in the town and liberating crates of cigarettes and a large radio. Already it was pouring out nasal music in the courtyard, where the men swaggered about, fraternizing with the Special Forces soldiers and demonstrating the workings of their Russian quick-firer. A belt of shells was discharged at the far hillside in celebration, bursting in a chain of orange flashes. The Allied officers looked disapproving, as though itching to get the Kurdish guerrillas under military discipline.

Later a convoy of French army trucks came rocking up the valley from the direction of Zakho. The Legionnaire colonel in charge told us that transit camps were to be set up around the town to receive the mass of refugees squatting in the mountains along the Turkish border. They would begin returning soon, retracing the route of their flight along this road. With the colonel were a couple of army doctors; it would be their job to bring in a medical unit and establish a large tent hospital in the field beside the fort. In a short time, perhaps a couple of days, our presence here would be superfluous.

The colonel suggested that we might find new employment to the east, closer to the Iranian border. The Safe Haven plan didn't extend to that area, and he thought that fighting between the *pesh merga* and the Iraqis might continue there for weeks. Jean-Pierre and I wondered if we could repeat our Qasrok operation at another Kurdish forward position in the mountains. I remembered mention of a place called Suriya – it seemed an extraordinarily long time ago – by the moustached *pesh merga* when we'd first arrived in Qamishli, who'd suggested it as a possible area for a hospital. I paged back through my journal and read the notes I'd made. The man had described Suriya as lying towards the Iranian border, near the mouth of a deep gorge in which we could set up our operation free from attacks by Iraqi helicopters. We needed to discuss the proposition with our whole team. In the meantime, there remained the enduring problem of our shortage of equipment.

I left Jean-Pierre at the fort to await the return of the rest of our group and caught a lift with the colonel back through Zakho. We wound along the twisted road that had been no-man's-land, and up past the abandoned Iraqi positions at the head of the valley. The ridge where I'd seen the enemy soldiers through binoculars was bathed in sunlight that glinted off a litter of ration cans. The valley behind contained piles of empty shell-cases, where the artillery pieces had stood that had dropped their projectiles around the fort. Beyond, the road opened into the wide plains of northern Iraq, and we sped along through a deserted land. The approach to Zakho was blocked by some bombed tanks. We swerved past them through a field of red poppies, and back onto the road. The only people on the streets were groups of armed Iraqi soldiers in black berets, who stood in front of the looted shops watching us pass. Great technicolour murals of a beaming Saddam, paternal arm raised, flanked the main street. The eyes had been shot out by happy Kurds, in the carnival days when they still had an uprising to celebrate.

I travelled with the colonel under the tall watch-towers that marked the border, and on to Silopi, the big Allied base some thirty miles inside Turkey. I'd been told that the Kurdish relief effort – the rather tritely named 'Operation Provide Comfort' – was being directed out of here. I jumped off at the airport. Beside the runway was a town of tents and supply-containers, amidst which bustled quartermasters and transport officers and exhaust-spewing forklifts. In a goods-yard of medical equipment I asked a man with a clipboard if I could obtain some surgical packs and drugs. He directed me to a cargo container beside the runway where DART – the US Disaster Assistance Relief Team – was located. I strolled inside, introduced myself as a member of the only medical team operating 'in-country', and explained our equipment needs.

Gus and Ted and Ron were identical big men in jeans and cowboy boots and windbreakers, though Ron was distinguished by the lack of a baseball cap on his crew-cut hair. They inspected my rumpled khaki shirt and muddy boots, the

French army brassard that I'd worn to ride in the colonel's jeep through Zakho and forgotten to remove from my sleeve, and my week's growth of stubble. I described how the medical work we'd been doing at Qasrok had allowed little time for personal grooming.

'Well, you kin go home now,' said Ron. 'The US of A has it under control.'

I explained that we were after more equipment because we were thinking of moving our dressing station eastwards, to treat *pesh merga* casualties where the fighting continued. Where exactly, he wanted to know, looking more interested. I started towards a pin-studded wall-map to take a look at the area around the town of Suriya. Gus or Ted intercepted.

'Sorry, that's classified,' said his twin.

I noticed that he was wearing a pistol in a shoulder-holster under his jacket. The other, I now saw, had a combat knife in his boot. I suggested that they continue with their urgent humanitarian work while I attended to our small needs: surely no one would miss a couple of boxes from the huge stockpiles of medical goods outside.

'The United States,' said Ron sternly, 'cannot be seen to be supportin' a political faction inside Iraq.'

At least it was a promotion from 'bandits', I reflected.

'Stick around,' said Ted or Gus, pointing at a chair and a pot on a gas-stove. 'Have some coffee. I'll just get someone to debrief you.' He picked up a handset radio from the desk.

'Thanks, but I'm a bit pressed for time. I'll be running along.'

The horizon was a dusty rose over the lines of parked helicopters as I crossed the road to the army camp, hoping that I might find the Legionnaire colonel and some food and a place to sleep.

'Hey, doc!' yelled a voice, and I looked up to see Master-sergeant Harris of the Special Forces team that I had met earlier at Qasrok. He took me to his unit's tent – 'here's that crazy doctor dude that's been working in that frontline shithole we reconned this morning' – where I was invited to join their meal. They had made friends with the Foreign Legionnaires in the next compound – no MREs for them out of the field – and we sat down to a spread of delicacies from French army ration-packs, each worth ten US rations on the informal economy. The team members introduced themselves by name and speciality – communications, demolition, medical, intelligence – with the assurance of men comfortable in the certainty of their expertise.

Now they had the job of finding out what structures existed across the border in northern Iraq, in order to set up a Kurdish administration in the Safe Havens. I explained what I knew about the forces around Qasrok, and that we were considering moving to an area controlled by *pesh merga* in the mountains to the east. I also mentioned my failure to obtain medical equipment from the DART officials at the airport.

'You won't get anything from the fucking Christians In Action,' snorted the master-sergeant. 'Those guys have their heads so far up Washington assholes in search of funding appropriations that they can't function in the field. The CIA completely missed the fact that there was going to be a Kurdish uprising. They should have asked us, we had teams in there training the *pesh* before the ground war even started.'

After the meal the team applied themselves to the problem of where we should set up our next treatment centre. Maps were spread on the ground, and I found the location of Suriya. On the large-scale chart I could see that it lay around forty miles before the Iranian border, near a point where the gorge of the Shamdinan river wound down from the Turkish mountains to meet the wide transverse valley of the Great

Zab. I wondered who held the town: *pesh merga* or Iraqi troops?

'Recon is strength,' said Master-sergeant Harris enigmatically, and disappeared into the darkness. He returned some minutes later, accompanied by a man who wore the insignia of a colonel.

'Hi,' he said to the team, who stood at once: I couldn't tell whether out of respect for his rank or to fetch him some French coffee.

'Have you ever seen a case of cholera?' the colonel asked me. I acknowledged that I had.

'Good,' he said, 'a pair of Blackhawk helicopters are leaving tomorrow morning, carrying a civilian specialist from the Atlanta Centre for Disease Control to a place along the Turkish border.' He pointed on the map. 'There's been an outbreak of illness at the refugee camp here in Cukurça, reported by the MSF hospital at the site. We need to take samples for analysis. You can go in with them. Master-sergeant Harris will accompany you. On the way back here, the pilots will fly south along the ravine and you can take a look at Suriya. It will have to be quick; that's a restricted flying area.'

The colonel vanished, leaving me blinking. The Special Forces medic appeared, dragging a bulging duffel-bag which he propped against the tent pole. 'Don't forget your pack when you go back to join your group, doc,' he said. I rummaged inside. It was full of anaesthetic drugs, limb-splints, dressings, flamazine burn ointment, dried plasma packs and antibiotics, and on the top of the pile a canvas field-surgery kit that unrolled to reveal a set of gleaming instruments in sterile sleeves.

⊕

The MSF hospital stood just outside the barbed-wire perimeter of the Cukurça camp. Dust blew towards us from the packed shelters that flowed down the hillside, mixed with foul smoke from a nearby fire where contaminated clothes and dressings were being burned. The man from Atlanta and I entered the hospital tent and introduced ourselves to a doctor. He led us to the isolation area. Patients lay on the floor, on pallets of blankets. The smell of illness was overpowering. The doctor, his voice hoarse with fatigue, explained that the first cases had appeared a couple of days before: three members of one family with severe diarrhoea, who had suffered sudden collapse and developed violent and intractable vomiting. Yesterday there had been thirteen new cases. Four died during the night, and today there were twenty more and it was not yet 10 a.m.

I looked at the patients where they lay along the canvas wall, each connected to an intravenous line. Their faces had an ominous uniformity. The cheeks and temples, even the sides of their noses were hollowed, all spare flesh shrunken away by the dehydration of fever and the loss of fluids caused by the infection. Their sunken eyes gazed upward, unseeing; half-shuttered by drooping eyelids. Mouths sagged, baring teeth in a death's-head rictus. Some of the sick lay in pools of thin, cloudy liquid that spread and merged across the canvas floor. I had seen the condition once before, at a small coastal hospital in Sri Lanka. I remembered the doctor there pointing out the distinctive clinical feature that made the diagnosis; the 'rice-water stool', a continuous purging of intestinal fluid that could exceed ten litres in twenty-four hours.

The Atlanta man and I donned gloves and collected swabs and samples from each of the unresponsive bodies. As he completed the laboratory forms, I noticed that he wrote under 'diagnosis' the coy notation: 'Suspected Condition 001'.

'It looks to me like cholera,' I said.

'I agree,' he replied in an undertone, 'and the MSF doctors are treating it as that. But until we're sure what strain it is and can offer large-scale immunization, we have to avoid panic. At the moment the refugees – I'm told there are a hundred thousand in the camp – are too frightened to return home. If they hear that there is cholera here they'll run. The disease would be carried to other camps, to villages, and from there to the towns and cities. That would be an epidemiological disaster. There are no facilities in this region to treat a general epidemic.'

The specialist from Atlanta clutched his bag of sample bottles as the helicopter bucked in the turbulence. We passed over more refugee encampments tucked amidst the peaks, and dropped abruptly into the Shamdinan gorge. Over the door-gunner's shoulder I could see the other Blackhawk rising and falling in formation beside us as we swept along the ravine, our rotor tips skimming the rocky sides. We passed over a column of Kurdish fighters on the road below. The aircraft swerved low along the rushing green river, banking around shoulders of cliff and hopping suddenly over a steel bridge. We emerged onto the plain over Suriya and instantly the helicopters began to climb steeply.

'I think I understand why this area is restricted, doc,' came the pilot's voice in my headphones. As we rocketed upwards I glimpsed, among the town's roofless buildings, a line of tanks and armoured personnel carriers and Iraqi troops that conspicuously failed to wave. Master-sergeant Harris nodded at me from his position at the other door. His voice crackled in my headphones. 'Looks like they may be pulling out,' he said.

I returned to Qasrok with my bag of gift equipment and some other supplies that I had managed to scrounge, to meet three doctors who had arrived that morning from our organization in Paris. They stood with Ernest outside the new French army hospital that had been set up beside the fort: a capacious tent-ward staffed by sixteen military doctors and nurses. Francine and Jean-Pierre were there too. They had been running a small clinic among the refugee shelters up the valley, but their borrowed tent had been blown down again and again by Allied helicopters on the military tourist trail, flying low on their way to visit Qasrok. That day it had been conclusively demolished and the two of them were fed up. We sat on the ramparts and I told the group about my reconnaissance to Suriya.

I also explained that I had met in Silopi a group of newly arrived German doctors – equipped with tents, transport and a truck that contained a mobile operating theatre – who wanted to set up a hospital near the Iranian border. They had proposed that we travel eastwards together. Our group – especially the newest arrivals – were eager to continue the mission. Francine gave a tired smile.

'You don't need another nurse where you are going,' she said. 'I have received a signal recalling me to Paris. Now it is your job to look after the team. Be careful; don't lose any of them.'

We ate a last meal together in the room of the fort that had been our home and operating theatre. Now that it was no longer a fighting outpost, the camaraderie that had bound the place together was fading, and the *pesh merga* were starting to leave. Saed and Nouri Abdullah came to say farewell. They were heading for the mountains, to try to locate the families they had left behind in the refugee camps.

⊕

We sat outside a tent in the vast canvas city that had been set up on the outskirts of Zakho to receive half a million Kurds. Apart from some American army engineers and our party – six Germans, their translator (a Kurdish ex-*gastarbeiter*), five Frenchmen and myself – the place was deserted: the refugees were frightened to return without *pesh merga* protection while there were still Iraqi forces near the town, and the Allied high command still couldn't bring themselves to recognize that they needed the guerrillas' co-operation. To the east, American aircraft were lighting up the night with slow-falling white illumination flares. The red crosses on the German trucks and our borrowed seven-tonner looked black in the flickering light.

We studied my maps; a set of the US army's detailed charts of northern Iraq supplied to me by the Special Forces sergeant. The furthest point held by Allied soldiers was a British detachment at the village of Batufa: beyond them, on the road to Al-Amadiyah, was an enemy force of tanks and infantry who had so far not acknowledged the ceasefire. The region to the east of the town was terra incognita, with fighting reportedly continuing between the Iraqis and Kurdish guerrillas along the twisting route to Suriya, thirty miles beyond. The parachute flares continued their slow descent, leaving trails of smoke in the still night.

By sunrise we were on the road, a crumbling ribbon of tar pocked by Allied cluster-bombing that had transformed columns of vehicles into fused, fire-blackened metal. In places culverts and bridges had been hit, so that we were forced to do some energetic road-building and crater-filling before our three trucks could squeeze along the temporary tracks that bypassed these obstructions. In a narrow cutting we met the British jeeps. They were advancing cautiously, still about twenty-five miles from Amadiyah; the plan was eventually to establish another Safe Haven around the town.

'The Iraqis are somewhere ahead,' said the British officer, 'but it should be okay for you to drive on. They're unlikely to fire on civilians.'

We continued along the empty tarmac, following gouges left by the tracks of retreating tanks.

The Iraqi armour was encountered some miles further on, covering the road from an overlooking ridge. We stopped our trucks and I walked forward with Mart, the senior German doctor, to where a command post was concealed in the trees. With us was the Kurdish translator. An Iraqi officer stepped out and motioned us to halt. The translator was literally trembling with fear, his mouth too dry to speak. Mart murmured to him in German and the man managed a hoarse sentence or two, explaining our mission. The Iraqi commander appeared.

'To pass to Amadiyah is impossible,' he declared in English. 'You will need authorization from commander-in-chief, Zakho military district.'

We told him that Zakho was now in Allied hands: he began shouting into his radio, trying to raise some source of authority. For two hours we waited at the roadblock, eating canned peaches in the sunshine. The Iraqi troops watched us from their positions. Eventually, unable to raise an answer, the commander shrugged. 'You go,' he said. 'It is not my responsibility.'

The next roadblock was at Sirsenk, site of a military airfield and Saddam Hussein's summer palace. Darkness had fallen when we were halted under the barrel of a Republican Guard tank half-blocking the road. Through the Iraqi unit's medical officer, who spoke some English, their commander announced that we'd be taken to shelter for the night, and we followed an armoured car through the blacked-out streets. The town had been ravaged by Allied airstrikes and then by the Kurds, and further damaged when it was recaptured by the Republican Guards. Our trucks' headlights played across gutted shop fronts. Sirsenk's grand hotel, once used by diplomats visiting the Iraqi leader at his summer residence, had been partly flattened by a bomb. There was no electricity. The Iraqi commander announced that we would stay here as his guests. The manager made tea over a fire of smashed ammunition boxes on the floor of the kitchens and we drank it by candlelight, conscious of the soldiers in the lobby and the armoured vehicle parked in the driveway to block the departure of our trucks.

It seemed that I must have dozed for a moment, tea-glass in hand, for when I looked up I saw, standing before me, a delegation of my French team. The candle-flame flickered in the draught from the broken window; their faces loomed and faded, and I could see that they were worried. I placed the glass among the chunks of ceiling-plaster covering the table and asked them what was wrong. They believed that we were to be taken hostage and sent to Baghdad in order to be shown on state television shaking hands with Saddam Hussein. They would refuse utterly to be party to such Iraqi propaganda, they informed me sternly, and demanded to know my position on the matter. I suggested finding a room and going to sleep in a bed, the first I would have seen for a long time.

Water bubbled up through the bathroom floors from fractured pipes and flowed down the staircase. Squelching across soaked carpets, I found a room with a bed and fell onto it, losing consciousness half-way through the removal of my second boot. At dawn we awoke to find the place deserted, and resumed our journey. We had to pass the Republican Guard base again, but they waved us on; they were busy lining up their tanks and gun-carriers for transfer to the south. The summer palace – a many-tiered structure on a hill, surrounded by a high wall – was being left to the returning barbarians.

The countryside beyond Sirsenk was almost abandoned: in 1988 Kurdish villages throughout the region had been systematically levelled and their populations decimated by chemical weapons, leaving only overgrown foundations and untended orchards to mark their passing. In the occasional villages still standing the flat-roofed houses stood open, bedding and possessions spilled across the ground and dead animals lay bloated in the streets, tainting the spring air.

We stopped in the little town of Al-Amadiyah, its pale stone buildings and poplar trees crammed onto the flat top of a sheer-sided mountain. The main street was strewn with gutted Iraqi military transports destroyed by the *pesh merga* during their uprising. Amadiyah's normal population of ten thousand had shrunk to under a hundred souls, and most of them were watching the activity at the Iraqi headquarters, where the remaining garrison – some fifty soldiers – was preparing to depart. They darted in and out of the building, throwing bags and documents into a couple of trucks that stood with their engines running. On our way out of Amadiyah the mechanic of the German group improvised a repair to the water pump down in the valley. It started with a gush of exhaust smoke. A group had gathered above us on the edge of the town, and cheered as word was passed along the street that water was flowing from the taps. Again we took the lonely road east.

It ran beside the Great Zab River. A thin, clear light filled the valley, throwing the distant mountains into sharp relief. The sky was etched with the contrails of high-patrolling Allied jets. I was riding on top of the load in the back of our seven-tonner, bathed in a balmy wind intersected by bands of cold that made me shiver. The red fields of poppies on the hillsides seemed to pulse with a smouldering glow, and I realized that I had a fever: my muscles ached and I was wrapped in an enervating torpor.

We approached a village still under Iraqi control. Bunkers flanked the road, with posters of Saddam Hussein fixed to the sandbags. Perhaps these soldiers had not heard about the withdrawal, for they were cooking food and men were hanging clothes to dry on the wires of leaning telegraph poles.

They waved us through, even saluting our trucks. Ten miles on we swung north, crossing the river on a clattering bridge that was part-blocked by a burned Iraqi army ambulance. It leaked a heavy smell of charred meat. Beyond the bridge we drove through Suriya. The enemy armour had gone. A building smouldered, casting a haze across the rubble-strewn streets.

The road wound onwards through a deep valley, which I recognized from the helicopter flight a couple of days before. A few miles further on we were forced to stop: a tanker truck was angled across the road, its bonnet nosed into the hillside ditch while its rear hung out over the river. We switched off our engines and listened to the sound of rushing water. Figures stood up from cover on the hillside above us, others emerged from around the next bend: *pesh merga* who had been in ambush, anticipating that we were an approaching Iraqi convoy. The men put aside their weapons and greeted us warmly. They were an advance guard of the Kurdish force that controlled this area of mountains running to the Turkish border thirty miles to the north. They had chased the last of the enemy out of Suriya that morning, they told us – the burned-out ambulance was their work – and wanted to know about the Iraqi forces on the road from Al-Amadiyah, their next objective.

I thought of the scenes of army domesticity at the last Iraqi outpost, and the idea of it being attacked – of more dead and wounded at the tail-end of this dragged-out war – filled me with sick exhaustion. The Kurdish translator, though, was full of vengeance, and scratched on the ground an outline of the Iraqi positions. The tanker truck was moved so that we could follow it to where the road broadened out at a meadow on the river bank. There were a hundred Kurdish fighters here, many with their families, and a fleet of vehicles and browsing mules and piled possessions, like a gypsy encampment. Our arrival was greeted with jubilation; peals of celebratory gunfire were discharged skywards and an RPG rocket was fired across the water to explode against the far bank. The explosion clanged disagreeably inside my aching skull.

The Germans sat down to confer with our group. Mart had established that the road through to the Iranian border was open: there were reported to be a million refugees there, and he was going to take his medical group further east to help them. I proposed setting up our own treatment centre higher up in the deep valley that we had entered; reasonably placed to treat *pesh merga* wounded – though I hoped fervently that the Iraqis would have pulled back from their position by the time these fighters reached it – and to provide care for groups of refugees in the mountains. Mart and I shook hands; our brief, adventurous partnership was over.

'See you for a drink some day, some place,' he called, climbing into his vehicle.

⊕

We followed a *pesh merga* pick-up along a track cut into the side of the ravine. Iraqi army trucks had been tumbled off the edge and lay upturned in the torrent churning below. Ten miles further the road climbed to a tiny Kurdish village, set in a cup of hillside. The flat roof of each stone house acted as the front yard of the one above it, and sheep grazed amidst a grove of poplars. The place looked incongruously peaceful, though the civilian population had fled and only a contingent of *pesh merga* were stationed there. Their leader welcomed us – the only Western presence they had seen so far were high-flying aircraft – and after the firing of more joyous volleys into the air, he explained that our truck could go no further; within a mile the road became impassable.

Indeed, over the next ridge was a familiar sight: a

graveyard of tractors, taxis, cars and buses, empty of petrol and mired in mud. Beyond it, the commander told us, lay an enclave of some ten thousand refugees who had been surviving on airdrops of food. Dysentery and chest infections were endemic, he said, and many infants were dying. The village had clean water and a grassy area suitable for our hospital. The *pesh merga* stacked their weapons and the truck was rapidly unpacked, while an inquisitive American helicopter circled high overhead. Within an hour our tents were standing, the operating table – a canvas cot covered with plastic sheeting – ready for use. Gerard, the French surgeon, prepared his instruments. The first patients were starting to gather in the nearby meadow. Many more could be expected as the refugees returned from the mountains along the Turkish border.

⊕

My fever was worse, giving each moment the insubstantial intensity of delirium. I said goodbye to my comrades. My extraction was abrupt: a chopper to Silopi, a taxi to Sirnak to collect my bag – I found the ethos among the Turkish Kurds substantially changed, with taxi fares now a hundred dollars a ride (paid readily by free-spending TV crews) and my pockets picked by the Kurdish family in whose house I had left my things while I'd been helping their brethren across the border – then another helicopter ride to Diyarbakir. At the military airfield there I negotiated a seat on an air force transport leaving at dawn for England. The fleabag hotel in which I collapsed was beside Diyarbakir's market, through which the Turkish military were carrying out a *ratissage*: all night, megaphone voices and flashing lights came through the shutters from the street below, merging with my febrile dreams. I woke repeatedly, shivering, the sheets soaked with sweat as though all the microbes of Kurdistan teeming in my bloodstream were dancing in concert, pulling me back to the mountains.

The guards at the airport were blocking the departure of journalists – someone had antagonized Ankara by writing about Turkish soldiers selling food-aid to the refugees for whom it had been donated – and I held up the tattered identity papers from my medical organization, repeating numbly that I was a doctor until they let me pass. In the airforce tent I was fed tea and custard creams, then put aboard the plane. Some hours later we touched down at an English airfield and I took a train to London. I noticed the other passengers staring at my boots, that still carried a map of mud and blood-stains. My transition had been so rapid that I was still in front-line clothes. In one thigh-pocket of my combat trousers was a ration-meal, in the other, an intravenous giving-set. My shirt pockets contained ampoules of morphine, a selection of drip-needles, a spoon and a tin-opener. I stood at Victoria station in the midst of an incomprehensible bustle of people, staring about me. On the street the grid-locked vehicles were just a traffic jam – none were burned or wrecked – and among the rushing crowd the shapes of AK47s with their distinctive curved magazines were nowhere to be seen.

All I wanted to do was sleep, waking six-hourly to swallow the antibiotics that had been prescribed to rid me of my persistent fever. But after a couple of days the nightmares began. They revolved around fears that I had never had time to face when I was out there – preoccupied as I'd been with the intensity of each moment – and they always began the same way. I would wake up on the floor of the fort, in darkness, to the sound of gunfire and screaming. I'd know that casualties were coming and I'd hurry to ready my equipment by torchlight, running intravenous fluid through drip-lines and laying out my surgical instruments. But in a rush the noise would draw nearer, deafening: the door would burst open, and instead of one or two wounded being carried in at a run and dumped on the mattress, there'd be fifty or a hundred – too many to count – and there I'd be, alone, with my pathetic tray of instruments.

In my more lucid moments I wondered what I had achieved. After all, there were more effective ways to stop people dying than by being a surgeon. On my final helicopter flight I had sat next to a Swedish water engineer who told me about his work, while my body shook with chills. He built filtration plants, and the clean water that he had brought to the refugee camps had preserved probably thousands from death. By comparison I'd saved perhaps a handful of lives by operating to stop blood-loss or gangrene; improved the outcome of injuries in a few more cases where I was able to conserve a damaged limb or clean a wound, and possibly – just possibly – prevented some fatalities through the haphazard distribution of drugs among the refugees. In fact, I reflected, the most significant thing I did out there wasn't even medical.

I'd stolen a tent from the Turkish army and loaded it into the ambulance that we took up to the camp, because a man whom I had met the day before on my way back over the mountains – a mathematics teacher from Zakho – had asked me to help find shelter for his family. When the ambulance had reached the end of the road I'd seen him waiting amid the beseeching crowd. I'd beckoned him over, and together we pulled the staggering weight of canvas and poles out of the truck and loaded it onto his skinny back. Some days later, when I was passing through the camp again he'd come running after me and asked me to accompany him: there was something he wanted to show me. After a walk of a mile or so we'd reached the tent – it was a big one, solidly erected and quite weatherproof – and he pointed inside.

'These are my children,' he said. 'This is the family of my brother, who is lost, and this is the family of my other brother.' The man indicated the score or so of figures huddled out of the sleet and mud. A small fire burned at the entrance, on which a pot was cooking, and I could see that they were all dry and warm. 'These people are alive because of you,' he said.

Of course it was not because of me. It was due to the will of this man in his over-large parka, his teacher's hands blistered from the struggle to survive, that those people had been saved. But out of those weeks of desperate improvisation, that fierce exhaustion, I could claim something for myself. I had discovered that I could manage in the midst of turmoil, that I could work under adverse, even impossible circumstances. Henceforth, I imagined, I would be able to deal with almost anything that came my way in life; I, not the Kurds, had been the real beneficiary of the experience. But I'd lost as much as I had gained. In London, with the rich black soil in the park being drilled by invigorated earthworms and the trees bursting out in young summer leaves, I was depressed. I missed the exhilaration, that free-fall rush into unpredictability.

I tried returning to regular hospital work, but found it difficult to concentrate: the discipline and stability were oppressive. It seemed as though the values that had once ordered my life were now lost in a mist of irrelevance. My familiar neighbourhood felt strange: I would be talking to the friendly man who ran the corner shop and in a flicker his face would transform into that of a wounded *pesh merga* on whom I had operated for a bullet in the leg. I realized that my senses were elsewhere, still attuned to the subliminal sound of shell-fire, the distant screams of the wounded. I had not come home. I lacked the insight to understand what had happened to me. I believed that I'd found freedom, and a way of anchoring the meaning that otherwise slid from day to day as one forgot. I thought that all I needed to do was keep on travelling.

8

The South China Sea

Manila airport smelled like all the drains in the city had backed up, their contents cooked for a week under the equatorial sun. I stepped out into the 2 a.m. heat of the customs hall, beset on all sides by touts and importuners. Most were officials in pastel shades of crumpled, sweat-stained uniform, who looked as though they slept behind their battered counters in order not to miss the smallest unit of loose currency that could be wrung from travelling pockets. I spotted my name on a bit of paper being waved by a plain-clothes wheedler with the face of a tired pimp. Ostensibly an 'immigration agent', he wanted first forty-five dollars, then twenty-five, for the visa that – as a ship's medical officer joining a vessel – I didn't need. I demurred.

'Never mind, doctor,' he chirruped, 'you pay later.' In a corner, he produced a stamp and inkpad from his drooping jacket and smeared something in my passport. 'Now we pind transport.'

This was an elderly Dodge taxi with a missing headlight, and as soon as we'd entered the city's frothing traffic the driver started pressing me for medication for 'sexual tiredness'.

'Pucking, doctor, pucking,' explained the agent, while the man behind the wheel turned around to demonstrate with an index finger which he pistoned graphically through his fist. I muttered something about Vitamin E, but my expertise was immediately questioned: hadn't I heard that apricot leaves boiled till purple then drunk with sugar worked better than any vitamins? I settled back against the seat-springs as we zipped between hurtling Jeepneys – their names, 'God' and 'Jesus' in gaudy script on their windscreens saving me the need for exclamation – and swerved on two wheels through the port gates. Cranes swung loads overhead and arc-lamps gleamed on the flour-blanched bodies of stevedores piling sacks. We pulled up on the dock beside a long white ship, her mast-heads outlined in strings of lights.

I swung my seabag onto my shoulder and marched up the gangway. The agent skipped behind, his fingers nimble as spiders round my trouser pockets as he implored me for 'ten dollars, even five: a one, then, my prend, to keep as a souvenir of our blessed meeting'.

My feet landed on the deck-timbers with a thud.

'Who're you, then?' asked the duty officer.

'Ship's surgeon.'

He flipped through the crew list. 'Kap Lan? Thought you'd be a Chinaman.' He pointed through the lighted doorway behind him. 'In there, two decks down, you'll find the chop-room. Cook'll get you something to eat. Purser's mate will show you your quarters. Sailing at six.' He turned to the man who had brought me from the airport.

'Get off my ship,' he roared and the man scurried down the gangway, stopping on the dock to sneer up at me and wave a wad of banknotes to show that he didn't need my dollar after all.

The ship was a thirty-year-old Baltic-built steamer with a hundred and fifty crew and cabin-space for four hundred passengers; at the smaller end of the cruise-line trade. Its slim hull and high profile made it better-suited for the relatively sheltered waters of its birth, and it rolled like a bastard when the South China Sea got up. This discovery lay in the future;

for now I walked down rock-steady flights of carpeted staircase from which identical, empty corridors stretched aft and forward at each landing. The medical officer's cabin was in the bow, just above the water-line. A porthole was set in the white-painted plating. I swung it open. A smell of seawater and sewage seeped in from the darkness, and a blast of humidity that stuck my shirt to my chest. I peeled it off, ready for sleep. The wide berth, crisp sheets turned down, drew me strongly. There was a knock on the steel door.

'Settling in? Good,' said the departing doctor, just back from his last shore-night in Manila before flying home. He was an Australian, in a splendidly tropical shirt and pointy shoes, and a little drunk. 'You'll like it here. Good ship, captain's a demon, English-speaking officers mess together. Oh, and you better make sure that porthole is securely dogged shut when you get under way. Otherwise you'll find your stuff floating around the cabin once you hit open sea.' He opened a cupboard and pointed within. 'I've left my wank-mags; you might need them. Or again, you might not. Never can tell aboard ship.'

The drumming of the engines catapulted me from sleep and I went in search of instructions. Someone directed me away from the brightly lit passenger areas to a gloomy passageway that ran from bow to stern deep in the bowels of the vessel. This was where the business of running the ship was conducted. Forward, it connected offices, store-rooms and laundries; further back it grew wider and darker, a hazard of work-benches and hoists where machinists toiled amid the blue flash of an arc-welder. In the crew office, the purser – an arctic blonde, six foot two in her flat-heeled shoes – took away my passport, gave me a crew ID card, signed me on to the ship's manifest and told me the terms: a hundred dollars a day all found, plus twenty per cent of patient fees. I didn't argue. I drew my uniforms from stores; white tropical ducks for day-wear, a high-collared white tunic with brass anchor-buttons for evenings, and the formal rig, of black trousers with a satin side-stripe, a cummerbund, wing-collared shirt and black bow-tie, and a white mess-jacket fastened in the front with a brass chain that looped across the navel. A box contained three sets of epaulettes – a pair for each uniform – my introduction to the arcane ciphers of nautical rank. Small boards of black velvet, slightly salt-greened, they carried a gold loop and three stripes, separated by the red bands of a medical officer. I had taken my place in the chain of command.

The captain, a big-bellied, volatile Yorkshireman, wore four stripes. He directed his frequent, red-faced ire upon the three-and-a-half-striped shoulders of the lugubrious Anglo-Bolivian staff captain – his second-in-command – who dumped it in turn on the three-stripe first officer. Only the gruff Glaswegian chief engineer was supposed to be the captain's equal. He also wore four stripes and stood his ground, but muttered frequently into his whisky while drinking in the fantail bar with the other three-point-five stripers: the London-born passenger manager and the Irish 'reefer' engineer who tended to the electrical and refrigeration workings of the vessel. These constituted the English-speaking officers with whom, it appeared, I was supposed to share a table in the midday mess. They held themselves aloof from the three- and two-stripe French officers: the cruise director, navigation and radio officers and the first, second and third mates.

The rest of the officers were Filipino, as were the stewards, ratings, the ship's nurse, the band and the sublime crooner of the rear-deck lounge. The Chinese ran the laundry; an invisible lower-deck cabal who, if vexed, could starch the legs of trousers so severely that it was impossible to force a foot though them. The other staff were also divided along national lines; croupiers, dancers, entertainers and hairdressers were English, while the French looked after the housekeeping and tour services and operated the boutique. Subtle fault-lines ran vertically and horizontally through the social matrix of the ship, based on ethnicity, station and individual personalities – the icy Norwegian crew purser, for example, appeared to have no friends apart from a Swedish tour-manager of equal beauty and remoteness – a tapestry of human interactions that generally relegated the paying passengers to an almost two-dimensional backdrop.

The passengers came aboard for set cruises lasting seven days or ten, tucked up in this travelling hotel and unloaded en masse at exotic locations for gentle coach-view tours. Many had not travelled before; for these neophytes the experience was somehow both trivial and overwhelming: a stage-managed immersion in a world of new tastes, smells and sights in which they managed to get lost, over-excited, and fleeced by shore-side con-artists. Most were retired – Canadians, Americans and French – plus the odd Italian and Swedish couple, somewhat younger and a little bemused to find themselves taking a holiday at tea-dance tempo. For some the journey was more serious; a number were old war veterans, bringing spouses and middle-aged children to show them where they had undergone the defining experience of their lives. Among the elderly Dutch tourists were ex-colonists from Java, who'd not returned since they were released from Japanese internment camps in 1945 or been driven out by the independence uprising that followed; seismic experiences from which they had still not recovered three-quarters of a lifetime later. And for some it was truly a sunset cruise; odd souls with terminal illnesses who had followed Doctor's Orders and come to spend some of their remaining days aboard this floating sanatorium. I hoped that the refrigerated steel trays of the ship's mortuary would remain unused.

At this early stage of my maritime service, though, the most arduous of my duties were the formal dinners. Each senior officer was allocated a table that he would be required to host in the main dining room; the same set of twelve or fourteen passengers for the duration of their cruise. I would always select a later sitting, hoping that it might be the more grown-up travellers who would choose to eat after nine. The meals could sometimes be excruciating affairs; trying to make conversation with people who had no grasp of geography, history or cultural diversity. Some mistrusted the Filipino stewards – 'These Japs are all the same,' an elderly American woman told me darkly; 'remember Pearl Harbour' – or believed that they were cruising in the Caribbean. I would try to limit my attendance at these dinners, arranging with a bridge officer to call me away on my radio to deal with spurious medical problems. When I could not escape, the only respite lay in drink. Each officer had a monthly liquor allowance of several hundred dollars; I would use mine to order bottle after bottle of wine, until a certain gaiety was established around the table and the conversation flowed.

I had to be strict about refusing to conduct medical consultations during these meals, and even more so at the sunset hour, when it was the captain's wish that his officers should socialize with the passengers at the bars – the fantail bar at the stern, the lounge bar, and the one in the casino – to demonstrate their friendliness and accessibility. Drink was a way of life aboard the ship; as well as our bottomless liquor allowance, the crew could buy from the 'slop-chest', a below-decks cubby-hole stacked with cases of beer and bottles of spirits at three dollars each. At first I found the combination of tropical heat and alcohol enervating, but under a regime of regular enzymatic workouts my liver soon recovered its fitness, and I was able to coast through these duties with the help of the head barman who would ensure that a bottle of quality vodka was always in the back of the freezer for my personal use.

I reserved my professional attentions for my morning and afternoon surgeries, when I was usually besieged by a mass of coughs and colds and heat-rash. The Americans were demanding, the Canadians relaxed, and the French wanted treatment *par derrière*. I had not before encountered this preference for the rectal route to health, but Sandra – the salty ship's nurse – never wavered, producing medication in suppository form from our well-stocked pharmacy and slipping the dose deftly into the receptive patient behind a screen. At the end of each consultation I would scribble a receipt, receive twelve US dollars, clip them to the counterfoil and file them in the surgery cash-box for transfer to the purser at the end of the day. Shipboard general practice seemed a sinecure.

⊕

A rain squall swept up the Pearl River, over fleets of high-sterned wooden boats clustered around the cargo ships. Derricks unloaded slings of sacks into their open holds. Long barges piled with sand chugged across the smoke-coloured water, their wakes rocking the fish-nets which hung from bamboo cross-poles in the shallows. Small, sharp-prowed lighters with hulls of pink and turquoise cut the surface. The red stern-flags glowed in the diffused, milky light. On the dock a line of Canton customs men stood against a wall out of the rain, their uniforms a green stripe under red-banded caps. I loved it all, in an ecstasy of rootlessness: sailing up the harbour reaches towards a forest of cranes; watching from the rail as the hawsers were tightened and we were brought snug against the dock; disembarking into an intense world of bars and streets and new sensations; and then the ease – the delight – a day or two later of slipping our moorings and watching the port recede in our wake until all that surrounded us again was the open sea.

I became a connoisseur of our brief landfalls. The daytime passenger tours could be dull, conducted by coach to visit pagodas or sulky pandas in the zoo; Buddhas and museums and trinket shops where the consumers would buy carved ivory with conscienceless abandon. It was usually in the evenings, after my duties were over, that I had a chance to go ashore with other members of the ship's crew in search of diversion. Our party changed all the time. Its members were misfits, an odd collection of people looking to escape the claustrophobic intensity of shipboard society through adventure or alcohol or getting laid. It might include a literary Frenchman from the radio-room, referencing Graham Greene and Conrad in his search for the perfect place to drink; his sidekick the epicure pursuing regional delicacies; a couple of the dancers with a taste for bizarre sex-shows; an English entertainer, irrepressibly gay, who had originally welcomed me aboard with the offer that I should pop down to his cabin for 'a suck' if I was ever at a loose end; and sometimes the Scots chief engineer, tortured by his love for the fickle blonde masseuse of the ship's sauna.

We were stuck in Manila for thirty-six hours while a loading door, damaged in a collision with a harbour tender, had to be repaired. On the quay we piled into a taxi with a bottle of whisky, some plastic cups, and an eclectic itinerary that began with a visit to Imelda Marcos' shoe collection at the Malacanang Palace. Next stop was a horror show: the vast garbage dump on the city's southern fringes called Smokey Mountain where people survived by scavenging for recyclable trash. They dwelt on the slopes of the rubbish peak – amidst the acrid smoke of internal fires that vented through vales of plastic bags and old car bodies – in shelters made from the waste itself, or in stilt-shacks over foetid lagoons of filth. The chemical reek made us retch and turned the dancers' jewellery instantly black. As we were leaving a corpse was borne past on a stretcher out of the warren of hutches. The blanket slipped back, revealing a bloated face the colour of lead. We fled for an antidote of sanitized death; the Chinese cemetery, whose residents occupied grand miniature houses two or three stories high. The doors were fitted with letter-boxes, the interiors spotless, each reputedly containing a fully plumbed bathroom for the use of the dead.

Our whisky finished, we bar-hopped into the evening, stopping for a meal of ethnic authenticity eaten with the hands in an outdoor restaurant; rich, challenging and finally nauseating, as even the salad was spiced with fermented crab fat. We moved on to a drinking place staffed entirely by dwarves, who yelled their orders at groin height in the deepest of voices. The dancing girls were bored, and suggested a visit to a fuck-club; a place where human intercourse took place literally in one's lap. A naked woman curled herself gracefully over the edge of our table; a man, his body slick with oil, entered her from behind while the music thundered and spot-lights focused on the coupled pair. We clutched our drinks, repelled and mesmerized; an aroma of sweat and musk rose in the halo of light. Back at the harbour we saw out the night amid the dark panelling of the Manila Hotel taproom. 'Somerset Maugham drank here,' said the satisfied French-man. The ship's entertainer commandeered the piano and sang the blues, we knocked back great beakers of ice and whisky, and the dancers recounted ever more unlikely tales of penetrations they had seen.

⊕

The first day of each new cruise began with a lifeboat drill. These were signalled by the captain's voice echoing over bulkhead loudspeakers, and then the emergency bells would start shrilling through the vessel's decks. Boots thundered down passage-ways as the fire-teams and boat crews raced for their posts. In the sick-bay the nurse and I donned life-belts and broke out treatment packs, counting the seconds until our stretcher-bearers were assembled and I could report our readiness to the bridge on my radio. It also transmitted the muttered curses of the service staff, trying to chivvy grumbling passengers to their rally-points. Eventually everyone would be at their stations, the laggards excoriated by the captain as he watched the boat decks from his post on the wing-bridge. 'Jesus Christ!' his voice would crackle over the radio. 'Lifeboat six, your bosun's fucking useless! I could carve a better man out of a banana!'

I was pleased that there didn't seem to be any true emergencies. On this, the first eventful cruise so far, an elderly passenger had been laid up in her cabin following a mild stroke. Her condition was stable and the nurse and I visited regularly to see that she was being cared for by the capable steward, while the captain made speed for our next stop. A crewman fell down an engine-room ladder. I set his fractured arm and we prepared him for unloading into the care of the shipping agent when we berthed, who would arrange his flight home. We were still a day away from port when the first real problem surfaced. The ship was sailing through a strong gale and the sounds of breaking glass echoed from the bars as the passengers staggered to their cabins. I was doing the rounds with my black bag, giving injections for sea-sickness, when nurse Sandra asked me to visit two American women who had been ill in their cabin for the past three days.

I found them in their bunks, unwell and querulous. They hadn't felt right, they complained, since coming aboard in Hong Kong. Before the cruise they'd spent ten days there at 'the best hotel'. The city had been their first taste of the Orient and they had been charmed by its exoticism and eaten immoderately of its peculiar meats. Now one complained of diarrhoea and a cough; the other was constipated, with a moderate fever. Neither had any appetite, but pestered the steward for chicken soup which they then refused to touch. I visited them several times over the next twenty-four hours, puzzling over my clinical findings. The coughing woman had enlargement of the liver, the feverish one's temperature jumped in the evening but her pulse-rate remained slow and regular. I returned to the medical centre to consult a volume on tropical diseases. Sandra was there already, following the lines with her finger as she read.

'I think I see something like this before, on another ship,' she said, frowning. 'What do you think?'

The book was open at the chapter on typhoid fever.

I reported our fears to the first officer, who took me to the captain. He was on the wing-bridge, looking unrelaxed.

'This is a bad business, doc,' he said. 'How do we confirm the diagnosis?'

I explained about the Widal blood test which could be performed in a hospital laboratory. Cultures from the blood would also have to be made, to grow the infecting organism and find out what antibiotics it was sensitive to; an increasing number of typhoid strains were, according to the textbook, now resistant to the usual medication. Fortunately we would be docking in three hours, and I suggested that the ship's agent should arrange an ambulance to be waiting on the quayside.

'Out of sight, of course,' said the captain, mopping his temples. 'We don't want to worry the other passengers.'

As we docked I went for a final look at my patients. The Widal test was now superfluous. Their torsos were dotted with a delicate pink rash that blanched on gentle pressure with my finger; the characteristic 'rose spots' of typhoid. The ship's agent found me in my cabin, where I was writing a referral letter to the doctor at the infectious diseases hospital.

'I've got the ambulance tucked behind the warehouses,' he said. 'We'll wait for the other passengers to go off on their tour before we disembark the sick ones.'

I paced the deck, waiting for the laboratory's call. It confirmed the diagnosis: the Widal test was positive on both women, and they would be kept ashore for treatment. Their baggage was sprayed with disinfectant, unloaded for transfer to the hospital, and the cabin thoroughly cleaned. I reported to the captain in his office on the bridge.

'Any chance those passengers caught it on board?' he asked.

I explained that the incubation period of the illness made it certain that they were infected beforehand. He let his breath out in a sigh of relief, and tossed a sheet of paper onto the desk before me.

'Excellent, doc, whole thing's been handled very well. Countersign this.'

I inspected the document. It was headed: 'Maritime Declaration of Health' and had already been completed. I skimmed over the details about vessel name, registration, nationality and tonnage, noticing in passing that there was something called a 'De-Ratting Certificate' for which we apparently had exemption. The specific health questions required closer attention. Had there been on board any cases of yellow fever, smallpox or cholera? 'NO', the captain had written. Had there been any indication of plague during the voyage; for instance an undue mortality among the ship's mice or rats? 'NO' again. Had there, the form persisted, been any suspected cases of contagious disease on board? The captain had again recorded a firm negative.

'I'm not sure about this one,' I said. 'What about the typhoid?'

'It says "suspected", doc, "suspected",' growled the captain. 'Those cases aren't suspected, they're confirmed. And anyway, they're not on board any longer. Just sign.'

His finger stabbed below the Master's signature, at the line where the ship's surgeon had to make his mark. The ticking of the bulkhead clock was very loud. I signed. On my way below I found the staff captain and told him of my reservations. He looked harassed and in no mood for conversation.

'Captain orders you to sign, you sign,' he said shortly, and disappeared up the companionway. I returned to the sick-bay and recorded my unease in the medical log. I didn't feel that I had asserted my professional integrity very effectively.

We headed south, through days of dazzling sunlight. Flying fish exploded from our bow-wave and skimmed the tops of the slight swell. After lunch I was free to steal an hour of sunbathing on the top observation deck among the languorous girls of the entertainment staff. Their tanned bodies were clad in the threadiest of G-strings, and I'd have to force myself to think calming thoughts, or roll onto my stomach until the distraction passed. My afternoon and morning surgeries were as busy as ever. There was an increase in the number of passengers with diarrhoea and nausea – the result of a spreading wave of gastro-enteritis – that saw me called out through the night. I was relieved when we reached northern Borneo and tied into the placid harbour of Kota Kinabalu. Leaving the service manager to conduct a rigorous decontamination of the kitchens, I stood on deck with the young French couple who worked as onboard photographers, waiting for the vessel to be cleared by the harbour-master.

They had arranged ahead with the ship's agent for a boat and diving guide to be waiting for them, and had asked me to join them on their day-trip. A high-prowed wooden fishing boat bobbed at a nearby quayside. We climbed aboard and sailed out in the rising sunlight, leaving the white hull of the ship – our home – to be lost against the white buildings of the town. Small, perfect islets jutted out of the calm sea, encircled by rims of pale beachsand. While the others dived, I floated in the crystal water above vivid fish that darted among the buttes of coral. We picnicked on a small island, climbing through the jungle to its miniature peak while monkeys chattered in the high tree-canopy. During the photographers' next dive I lay on deck, smoking clove cigarettes and drinking coffee brewed by the crewman on a small charcoal stove. The blue pinnacles of Mount Kinabalu – 'The Revered Place of the Dead' – rose at the head of the bay, sticking up through a plate of cloud. The boat rocked gently, its rigging creaking.

By evening, that interlude of peace seemed a distant memory. We were already underway, slipping westwards along the coastline through the warm twilight, when I began my evening rounds. A number of passengers complained of upset stomachs – the gastro-intestinal bug was still making its presence felt – but I noted that two of them occupied the same cabin from which the typhoid patients had recently been sent ashore. Their condition gave me grounds for concern; feverish, with vague abdominal pain and a bit of diarrhoea. I was surprised to find that the cabin was in use again so soon – I had given instructions that it should remain empty for a week – but a decision had been made by the passenger office that an unused mid-deck cabin was a wasted asset, and when the couple had requested an upgrade from their lower-deck quarters to a more expensive slot, this was where they had been put. I went to discuss the matter with the staff captain.

'We'll be in Brunei port at first light,' he said, 'for a morning stopover to visit Bandar Seri Begawan. Do you want to get those two ashore for a blood test?'

I thought that was a sound idea, and the next morning found myself sweating in the heat of the country's pocket capital. While my patients had their tests at a pathology laboratory in the town I strolled towards the great gold-domed mosque that stood on the foreshore. In front of it sprawled Kampong Ayer – the water-village – a complex of tin-roofed houses, joined by bamboo walkways, that extended far out over the brown river. Water taxis jostled at the jetties and cut white trails across the surface. I watched them for a while, listening to the snarl of the engines and the clop of their wakes against the landing steps. I evidently stood there long enough to become a fixture. A busload of Japanese tourists disembarked, and their guide-translator, noticing my uniform, asked me if I'd mind having my picture taken. Amused, I agreed, and was posed against the railing while the tourists formed up: a solid phalanx of Bermuda shorts and floppy sunhats. The one at the end handed her camera to the man next to her, then came to stand beside me. A ragged volley of photo flashes travelled down the line, followed by the synchronized voom of motor drives. A belated flash came from the man with two cameras, taking a shot for the woman posing. She returned to the group, recovered her camera, and her place was taken by a companion. Again the whirr of shutters – and the delayed click of the extra exposure – and again the gavotte, as each of the party in turn relinquished his or her camera to the group and came to be photographed beside this maritime landmark. At the end the guide called her party to order. They faced me and bowed as one, before the bus whisked them off to Bandar Seri Begawan's next highlight.

I got talking to an elegant Englishwoman working for the Brunei Tourist Office, who told me that the placidity of the place was an illusion: the expatriate community, for example, was going barking mad – she gave a couple of fairly outré instances – from the heat and the boredom and a complete ban on alcohol instituted by the Sultan at the beginning of the year. There were scandals of nepotism and corruption; rumours of a revolution 'in six years or ten'. The Royal offspring were reaching their majorities, building new palaces, while the Kampongs remembered the communist uprising of 1963 put down by the British. If at any time the Sultan lost the protection of his battalion of Gurkhas, said my English friend, bloody revolution would tear through the place and no woman would be safe. She wondered if it might be possible to accompany me back to the ship for a drink and a bottle of gin. Despite her dark imaginings she seemed a festive soul and I would have been pleased to accommodate her, but we were sailing with the tide and I had to find out the results of my patients' Widal tests.

These were not forthcoming. Back at the vessel I was handed a note by the nurse who had accompanied them: the pathologist regretted that the results would not be available for a couple of days. The sick passengers had been re-embarked. We slipped our moorings and rounded the low headland into the South China Sea. I began my afternoon surgery, and my concern deepened. Now there were five people with similar symptoms of fever, lassitude and vague abdominal pain. A couple of them had enlarged, tender spleens. One woman had a rash, red and splotchy over her whole body, which, though it didn't resemble the rose-pink description of the textbook, did nothing to lessen my anxiety. The sickest patient of all was a crew-member; the steward who had served the cabin of the first two confirmed typhoid cases. I visited him in his quarters – in the warren of passageways deep below the waterline, near the engine-room – which he shared nose to armpit with three others. The dim orange of the bulkhead lights, the heat radiating from the steel walls, and the close, stagnant air, gave these lower decks the atmosphere of a purgatorial underworld.

The man lay on his bunk, listless and sweating. His bunkmates waited outside the tiny cubicle while I examined him, noting his fever and slightly enlarged liver. I looked for a rash, but I knew that it was difficult to see except in those of fair skin. On the threshold of panic, I asked him for a list of the cabins he serviced; if it matched the locations of the problem patients, I might have found the carrier of what could be the beginnings of an epidemic. It didn't. I ordered the man removed to the sickbay and started him on antibiotics, hoping that if he did have typhoid, I might prevent its sometimes fatal complications: intestinal perforation or haemorrhage, pneumonia and meningitis. I prescribed the same course of medication for his cabin-mates and the other afflicted passengers and, with the nurse and first officer, organized a system of isolation to limit the number of people exposed to the sick. Even if there had been time to go to bed that night I'd have had little sleep; I knew that if typhoid was indeed rampant on board, my precautions would all be too late.

Word had spread among the senior officers, and there was tension on the bridge when, at noon the next day, I finally saw the captain. His eyes looked baggy, as though he hadn't slept much either. He suggested that we talk in his cabin and stumped up the companionway ahead of me, his legs pumping like angry pile-drivers. He parked himself behind his desk, leaving me standing in front of him.

'You realize that if these cases are confirmed, we're fucked? We'll be quarantined, unable to leave port.' The captain hitched up his belly and leaned forward, his face reddening as the repercussions dawned. 'Christ, man, we'll all be out of a job, permanently. There'll be a maritime board of enquiry about why we didn't declare the last two cases. The ship will be finished when the word gets out; who'll ever want to take a cruise in her again?'

I couldn't think of an answer to that. He glared at me, while behind his head a computer screen dealt and re-dealt hands of cards, silently playing poker with itself. 'Tomorrow morning, doctor, when we reach Kuching, you go ashore with those passengers and take them to the laboratory. Make fucking sure that we have the results before we sail. Dismissed.'

During the afternoon and night there were no new cases, and my existing patients didn't get any worse. But they also didn't get noticeably better, despite the treatment, and I had little rest. At dawn I watched from the rail our slow progess up the Sarawak River. The water churned under our stern, the anchor-chains rumbled, and we swung to a stop a couple of cable-lengths from Kuching's small harbour-quay – our draught prevented us approaching any closer – while the ship's tenders were lowered to take the passengers ashore for their tour. A call came for me to report to the bridge. The captain was on the wing-deck, looking towards the inland horizon.

'Take a look out there, doctor,' he said. I followed his gaze to where a loop of river glinted between sullen flats of mangrove. 'You better hope those fucking tests are negative, or we'll spend the next six weeks moored miles upstream. No one will come aboard except the port health officers. No one will be allowed ashore.'

A stifling breeze brought the smell of rot from the mud-banks on the opposite shore, where teak-logs were beached around a lonely sawmill. 'If we get quarantined,' the captain continued, 'a lot of people are going to be very angry. And rightly or wrongly' – his thunderous expression made it clear which option he favoured – 'the person they are going to be most angry with is you.' He paused. 'If I were you I'd be very careful.'

I considered the prospect of spending six weeks inside this closed-down hull while it gathered weed in the distant reaches of the river. The vessel festered with grudges and conspiracies at the best of times; these sometimes boiled into violence in the crowded crew-quarters. Before I'd come aboard, an officer had been knifed in a dispute with a storeman over the favours of a Filipino stewardess. There had also been the case of a boatswain, involved in a vendetta, unaccountably gone missing at sea. My cabin – buried in the bow beneath the chain-lockers – was about the most isolated berth in the ship, and I wasn't sure that I could count on the protection of anyone on board. I couldn't even dead-lock my cabin door; it could be opened by anyone with a master key. For a moment I entertained a fantasy of escape; climbing over the forepeak at midnight with a bag of stores to shin down the anchor chain and swim to one of the canoes pulled up among the teak-logs, paddling it upriver into the hinterland. Sweaty paranoia gripped me; I didn't even have a weapon.

I disembarked our patients into one of the tenders. The shipping agent met us on the dock and accompanied us to the laboratory. After I'd helped the Malaysian pathologist take the blood samples, I discussed with him the antibiotic treatment I had given. 'If it's typhoid you've probably dealt with it, my good doctor,' he reassured me, 'if it's due to one of the other salmonella organisms, you've probably knocked that out as well. They don't look too ill;' and indeed it seemed that the patients had perked up somewhat. 'We'll have an answer in three hours or so from the Widal. Why don't you go and relax in the meantime?'

I was consumed with foreboding – if typhoid was confirmed in even one of the patients the ship still faced mandatory isolation – but the Eurasian shipping agent took a pragmatic view.

'If you're quarantined you won't be ashore for a long time,' he said, 'you might as well enjoy it while you can. How about a little private tour?'

And so it was that I saw Kuching pass before me in a

dream, in the company of my group of potential typhoid-cases. The agent whirled us through teeming streets of shopfronts, their upper floors enclosed by wooden shutters, past signboards of Cantonese characters over hand-painted images of bicycles and sewing machines. The carrion smell of durian floated up from piles of spiky fruit on the sidewalks, like an intimation of necrosis. At one point the roadway split around a Chinese temple where incense sticks as thick as tree-trunks smouldered on either side of an arched gateway, filling the courtyard with clean blue smoke. On the river front we stopped opposite the green bluff crowned by the Istana, the palace built in 1870 for Charlie Brooks – the greatest of the White Rajahs of Sarawak – who'd tried to suppress the antisocial practice of headhunting among the tribes of the interior and had built Kuching into a trading port. The agent whistled up a low-hulled sampan with a rattan cover and we were sculled into the current by the boatman in the bow, working his two long oars with cross-handed dexterity. A mist-shrouded mountain rose above the jungle. Clumps of slender palm trees sprouted in the grounds of Fort Margherita, built to guard against raids by Dayak river-pirates. On the way back along Great Bazaar Road I bought a heavy-bladed parang – a head-hunter's sword in a wooden scabbard – just in case I too would have to repel attackers in the near future.

The Malaysian doctor met me at the laboratory door.

'All negative, esteemed colleague,' he announced, beaming. 'I suspect that your problems have been due to an outbreak of simple food-poisoning.'

Back on board, I hung my superfluous purchase behind the door of my cabin and then reported to the captain, suggesting that he transfer his wrath to the kitchen managers. I stayed on deck as we glided down the river. Outposts of stilt-houses clung to the edge of the stream, hemmed by dark jungle behind and marooned amidst great rafts of teak logs floated down from the interior. Then the land receded, and we hit the slow surge of the open sea.

⊕

The ship was tired. There were repeated breakdowns of the kitchen refrigeration units and the air-conditioning, and the temporary repairs to the cargo door in Manila had yet to be completed, along with inspection of plates below the waterline where we had been charged by a rusty Russian freighter while at anchor off Hong Kong. Two of the four main engines were out of commission and a third had been kept going only by cannibalizing parts from the defunct ones. We were nudged into our berth at Singapore by fussing tugs, and our passengers – drained by the unrepeatable intestinal experience of their luxury sea-voyage – disembarked through the glitzy portals of the 'World Trade Centre' terminal.

We were overdue for dry-dock, but the vessel's owners had her down for one further indignity; a 'Jet-set Cruise'. These junkets were the bane of deep-water sailors; a twenty-four hour circuit through the islands south of Singapore, loaded with as many oriental gamblers – and their families – as the ship could hold. The passageways and stairs, so recently the haunt of sedate septuagenarians, now resounded to the shrieks of hyperactive children with pudding-bowl haircuts who hyperventilated in the close air below-decks and soiled their smart white shirts with vomit at our slightest roll. In the casinos their gambling fathers were oblivious; toiling over the tables through the baking night, their no-longer slicked-back hair shedding sweat and pomade onto the green baize.

Then it was over. Cleaners pushed brooms along the decks, dust-covers swathed the one-armed bandits, and the cabin staff were debarked on leave. With them went all the supernumeraries – croupiers, dancing girls, musicians and passenger service personnel – for a well-earned break or to be shipped home, their contracts over. Stripped down to a skeleton crew, the ship inched out of harbour and we steamed slowly through the Johor Straits towards the shipyards at Sembawang on the north side of the island. I watched from the bridge while captain and pilot picked a route through half-stripped supertankers, welding torches blazing on their decks, to aim us like a comb into the long concrete pocket of the graving dock. A freighter inched in behind us, the great lock gates squeezed closed, and the mechanical surge of the pumps took over, beginning their twenty-hour task of emptying our new berth. Imperceptibly the ship began to settle, the concrete dock-sides inching up our hull. The first work-gangs were already being swung aboard in a crane hoist, their steel cage deposited on the deck lightly as a leaf, while the captain threatened dire vengeance for any scratches to his planking.

I jumped into the lift and was raised high above the draining water between ship and dock-side. The cage rotated slowly, showing a red glow of sunset above a fence of harbour cranes and the darkening, jungled shore of the Malaysian peninsula. The shift-siren wailed, and red- and yellow-overalled men streamed below towards the shipyard gates while others headed in to work. On the canteen terrace I found a couple of my fellow officers drinking beer. I joined them, looking through the floodlit dusk at the white bulk of the ship looming above us.

'Captain hates dry-dock,' said one of them.

'Hates it,' agreed the other, 'too many strangers on board,' and the two of them gazed gloomily into their drinks. I began to realize that our passenger-free sojourn at Sembawang might not be as restful as I'd hoped.

I awoke, bathed in sweat, listening to the last, fraudulent sigh from the airvents. Halfway through my shower the water trickled to a stop. I left my cabin and found the vessel's interior utterly transformed. Fittings and furnishings were being stripped out, floors covered by lengths of carpet, its pink pile sullied by black boot-prints. Hammers echoed through the passageways. There was a cacophony of scraping and drilling and the sound of metal objects falling with a clang into the bottom of the now-empty dock. Breakfast tasted strongly of burned paint. With the ship's power off the medical centre was an oven, and I held my crew-clinic on the after-deck, in overalls (initially white, but rapidly assuming the colour of their besmirched surroundings) zipped open to the waist. My feet squelched inside the steel-capped safety boots that we were required to wear. The staff captain, obviously under pressure from above, stopped by for a bit of gratuitous harassment; why was I not using my hard-hat? I pointed out that it lacked ear-holes for a stethoscope and he left, a hunted expression on his face.

Dry-dock life soon shook down into a routine. I would be called on my radio, sometimes having to go down under the ship's hull to tend to minor injuries. The keel was supported on a row of wooden blocks where, in the dripping cave formed by the vessel's bottom, work-gangs scoured the plates with stream-hose and scrapers. Welders on scaffold-towers worked on the hull while crews replaced the water-tight glands around the propeller shafts and burnished the wide bronze blades. Weld-burns and abrasions were my usual fare, and patch-and-go the treatment expected; the shipyard workers lived by an hourly rate and were reluctant to be signed unfit for anything less than a fracture.

Below-decks too was a frenzy of labour. Through lifted hatch-covers, shafts of light shone into corners of the ship that seldom saw the sun. A filtered glow even reached the engine-room via the removal of higher sections of deck that let in the day. From these gaps rose smoke and the sound of cursing as the chief engineer harried the teams who hoisted up the great steel components. Despite the appearances of industry he did not look a happy man.

On the fifth evening I learned why. Going ashore, I'd been directed to the Terror Club, set on a hill beyond neat streets of ex-Royal Navy housing. The name seemed at odds with the welcoming pink glow of the bar, whose light reflected in the placid chlorinated waters of the swimming pool. Above the long wooden counter was the shield of HMS *Terror*; this was once its crew's watering-hole when Singapore had been the home port of the Asia fleet. The energetic Malay lady behind the bar tut-tutted at the late hour, but allowed me to sip whisky under the ceiling fans. I was sitting there when in walked the ship's engineer. I bought him a belt of Scotch and he began to talk.

'This refit's a fookin' waste of time,' he confided darkly. 'Fookin' owners won't pay for new parts, so refit's truly what it is; we pull the engine-heads, skim the blocks and toss the whole lot together again with some piece-of-shit slag-alloy bearings. And now there's a leak in one of the oil-bunkers, that they can't find. Whole thing's a fookin' disaster waiting to happen.'

The shutters were coming down over the bar and the landlady suggested that we relocate to the 'Jaws Lounge' down the road. 'Many sailor there, many girl,' she prompted us, 'I think you like.'

We followed her directions through the still, hot night. The disco could be heard from afar. Inside, strobes pulsed and classic rock 'n' roll numbers were being rendered with amplified phonetic unfaithfulness by a group of Thai musicians. The girl singers on the stage wore ribbon-wide black miniskirts that appeared spray-painted on their slender hips, and lonely boys off some US warship swayed like avid sunflowers six inches from their aura, beseeching something more than plastic smiles. At the door stood military policemen in white helmets, sipping ginger-ale. Periodically they swooped, hauling away any sailors who tried to lay a hand on the pert bottoms gyrating just before their noses. The engineer saw no poetry in this stylized longing.

'Fookin' Singapore,' he spat, and led the way back to the ship, down street-lit avenues where insects trilled in the bushes and crushed frangipani flowers on the sidewalk gave off their suffocating scent.

I hoped that the island might still have a subculture; that somewhere between the Spitting police and the Toilet police and the Chewing-gum police, some echo of the hedonistic vitality of the 'Crossroads of the Orient' might have survived. I had a weekend's shore leave to find it. I met up with my friend David, with whom I'd shared diverse adventures ever since we'd been medical students together in Cape Town. We checked into the Majestic Hotel in Chinatown and sat on the balcony, drinking frigid beer and catching up. Like me, David had become a medical vagabond; working his way around Africa, Madagascar and Southeast Asia as a doctor for oil companies, mining operations and expatriate communities. He had also worked on ships – he had previously held my current post, and would be replacing me on board in a few weeks – and I knew that if Singapore had an underbelly he would know where it lay.

It wasn't in Bugis Street, once a world-renowned synonym for debauchery and now a concrete plaza and some twee curio shops. The nightclubs along Orchard Road were sanitized beyond endurance. Somewhere around 2 a.m. we ended up drinking in Singapore's vestigial red light district, tucked between Jalan Besar and the canal. A monsoon downpour was churning the street into a lake and we sat at a table under a bar-front awning, feet up on the chair-rungs, chatting to a slender Asian-Chinese girl named Honey. In decorum, taste and sheer allure, she knocked spots off the women I came into contact with on board the ship. When Honey discovered that we were doctors her friendliness knew no bounds, and she invited us back to her place to give our professional opinion on the efficacy of her sex-change operation.

I rejoined the ship at Singapore's main harbour, to find unhappiness. Float-out from the dry-dock had been foiled by a non-functioning rudder, so that the ship had to put back for repairs. Then she'd been rammed by a tug along the starboard bow, scraping the new paintwork. The captain's face was already puce with rage when I came aboard, and the late arrival of the fuel-tender had him threatening to hurl junior officers to their doom from the wing-bridge. It was only on the second day at sea, with the wake curling away from the stern, that things returned to an even keel. By then I was settling back in to dealing with the foibles of my new passengers. Evidently some mild virus had been doing the rounds of the Singapore hotels, for every globetrotter had a slightly red throat and ever-so-marginally enlarged neck glands that they wanted cured. I became so tired of explaining that antibiotics were ineffectual against virus infections that the prospect of twenty per cent of each twelve-dollar consultation fee quite lost its pull. Reflecting that we were in the middle of the typhoon season, I began to pray for some bad weather to give them something else to think about. This, as any sailor will tell you, was inviting trouble.

It didn't come in the expected form – the sun rose each day in a cloudless sky – but as we slipped northwest along the coast of Sumatra, an elderly woman passenger became seriously ill. She'd been on medication for widespread cancer, and was dehydrated and delirious by the time I was called to see her. Through my stethoscope I heard the coarse, bubbling sounds of pneumonia. I began an intravenous drip with antibiotics. During the night she had a couple of epileptic-type seizures, and by dawn a dense paralysis had enveloped the right side of her body and she was deeply unconscious. Her slow pulse and rising blood pressure indicated haemorrhage in her brain. Her husband seemed resigned to her demise. He asked if a priest could be found to deliver the final rites. A retired padre was located from the passenger list. The solemn ritual was held in her wood-panelled cabin, while the dappled reflection of the sea danced and wavered across the ceiling. The woman's breaths came far apart, the silence between each groaning rattle so profound that I was sure that she was gone, but all that day and the next she hung on, her raddled body still preserving a tiny quotient of life.

It was strange how the nearness of death spread its presence throughout the ship. Only the officers were supposed to know about the woman's condition, but the passengers forgot their trifling woes and came to see me in the surgery, just to ask how she was getting on. The formal meal that evening passed in subdued conversation; even the sight of moonrise over the Straits of Malacca failed to raise the spirits of the cocktail-drinkers in the fantail lounge. We berthed at Port Kelang and the stretcher was carried down the gangway to the waiting ambulance under umbrellas, in the midst of a monsoon cloudburst. As I splashed after it in my storm-coat to hand over my patient to the Malaysian doctor, I glanced back at the vessel. Three hundred passengers lined the promenade-deck rail, bareheaded in the pelting rain.

They were restored to form by the time we got to Pulau Sepa. This was one of a cluster of low-lying atolls in the Java Sea, in sight of the orange flares of burn-off towers in the coastal oilfields. We anchored off the island and the passengers, eager at the prospect of a Christmas barbecue amid the coco-palms, were taken by tender to be landed at the palm-log jetty. Pulau Sepa was about half a mile across, a rough scallop of beach framed by mangrove headlands.

The family that owned the coconut plantation had set up an entrepreneurial venture: a tank of baby turtles, for which the passengers could pay ten dollars each to rescue them from imprisonment and release them back into the sea. The appeal was obvious. Tourists from the wealthy West – from countries that sustained twenty per cent of the world's population, while consuming ninety per cent of her resources – could now make a gesture towards restoring the balance. It was truly a moving spectacle. The four-inch-long creatures, their flippers moving like little clockwork paddles, plunged bravely through the foot-high surf and dived, clearly visible as they skimmed over the sandy bottom. Out towards the reef the current caught them and they were carried, swimming strongly, round the bay's end; once out of sight, to be netted again by the children of the enterprising islanders and returned to the tank.

An advance-party from the ship's kitchen had landed before dawn and built a fire in a boulder-lined pit. Whole sucking pigs had roasted through the morning, wrapped in banana-leaves, while the barmen set up their mixtures and shakers on trestle-tables over tubs of ice. Cocktails were served in coconut shells, adorned with skewers of fruit and little parasols. Champagne foamed in paper cups. The passengers carried their drinks and loaded plates into the shade or lolled in the shallows like basking cetaceans, their bellies forming a new archipelago. The more adventurous among them swam out to the reef, climbed among the mangroves, and fell over in the sand.

My evening surgery turned up many casualties who had disregarded the written warnings about sunburn and sea-urchins and now displayed scarlet knees studded with the black stubs of broken-off spines. For one man the freedom had been too much. While exploring, he had scratched his leg on a palm-frond, and wished me to treat and record his injuries in preparation for legal action. Someone, he assured me, was responsible; someone was going to pay for the pain and suffering he had endured at the hands of uncaring nature. I dabbed on iodine and wished him luck.

The gifts of Christmas were, as always, mixed. Most recipients just ate too much, or harvested a hangover. One woman, though, was still locked in weird festivities two days later when she entered my afternoon surgery. There was nothing wrong with her, she insisted, but her husband had made her come because she couldn't sleep. And she knew that the problem was not medical but electrical, even though the bastard reefer engineer had told her to come and see the doctor. Baffled by this introductory non-sequitur, I studied her as she lit another cigarette with shaking hands, ignoring the one that burned already in the ashtray. Then she threw herself back into the chair, panting smoke. She appeared to be in her late thirties, slim and blonde, though a glance at the birth-date on her record card showed that she was a good decade older. She clawed her fingers through her hair in an oddly deranged fashion, revealing, just below her ears, the telltale fine scars of an expensive facelift. I noticed that her whole body was trembling, and that her movements had the agitated choppiness of someone losing the battle for composure.

'Tell me how I can help you,' I suggested.

'It's those goddam cowboys,' she screamed, hurling her handbag across the room so that its contents scattered on the steel deck. 'At night, soon as the lights are out, they come out of the electrical fittings and ride their little horses round and round the cabin. All night. I can't sleep. Round and round and round and round and round.' Her head rotated jerkily, as though following a miniature rodeo. 'Little cowboys, about so high.' She stooped to indicate a level about six inches off the floor and fell forward to her hands and knees, where she began crawling about frantically, gathering her spilt possessions. I noticed that one of the items was a pint of vodka.

'Er . . . how do you know they're cowboys?' I asked, when she had sat down again.

'Because they've got little hats on, and little yellow vests,' she shrieked, the veins standing out in her neck. 'I know what cowboys look like, you stupid man! You're as stupid as my husband!' and she burst into shuddering tears and tried to light another cigarette.

'Where is your husband?' I enquired.

'Probably in the bar, getting drunk,' she told me, igniting her hair. 'He's an alcoholic you know.'

The ship was a gin-palace. Beside the three main bars, there was one at the pool-side, and booze could be had with every restaurant meal including breakfast. Somehow the woman would have to be kept away from these temptations, and the on-tap attractions of room-service. My first priority was to control her alcoholic dementia. With Sandra's help I escorted her out of the medical room, past the rows of fascinated faces in the waiting area, and back to her cabin. A tray of martini glasses stood outside the door. Within, the porthole curtains were drawn against the sunlight and clothing lay in disarray about the floor. Sandra soothed the woman and put her to bed and I gave her an injection of chlorpromazine, a powerful anti-psychotic. I waited with her while the nurse went in search of the first officer and the woman's husband. He stalked into the cabin a few minutes later, tall and imperious, his face engraved with the beginnings of dissolution.

'I demand to know what's going on here,' he said, with the controlled truculence of a drunkard.

'Your wife has delirium tremens,' I said. 'It's important that she has no further alcohol on this voyage.'

The woman started from her pillow and tried to hit me,

but the drug had taken the edge off her co-ordination and she fell back, babbling. The man looked furious.

'Listen, you little upstart,' he began, and a flush spread over his face as his voice rose, 'we have paid for this cruise and we will get whatever service we require.' He took a step towards me and lifted his fist, and I could smell sour gin in his sweat.

'If you strike my officer I will instruct the master-at-arms to put you under arrest,' boomed a voice from the door. It was, I think, the first time I had been pleased to see the captain up close. Sandra winked at me from behind his elbow. 'Your wife will be banned from the bars and the stewards will be ordered not to deliver any alcohol to your quarters,' he continued. 'If her behaviour causes any further disruption aboard this vessel I will have you both put ashore at our next port of call. I would suggest that you get rid of any duty-free stocks you have in the cabin, for both your sakes.'

'Some chance,' said the man stonily. 'The bitch has drunk it all.'

⊕

That evening I went to check on my patient. Her husband opened the cabin door, dressed in a tuxedo.

'How's she getting on?' I asked him.

'You're the doctor,' he said, with undisguised hostility, and pushed past me down the passageway, swaying slightly as he walked.

The woman was propped up in bed. She had managed to wash and brush her hair, and she seemed less agitated. Without her makeup her face looked curiously young and vulnerable, an impression heightened by the flouncy baby-doll nightdress that she was wearing.

'I'm sorry about this afternoon, doctor,' she said. 'I think maybe you'd better give me another of those injections. My husband has gone to the casino and he won't be back all night. I'm frightened of trying to sleep alone.'

She pulled a cushion from behind her head, and, placing it under her, turned over so it lay beneath her hips. Then she flipped back the bedclothes, revealing her bare, raised bottom. I drew up the medication and injected it into the muscle. As I placed a Band-Aid over the puncture she took my hand and held it against the smooth skin. She looked at me dreamily over her shoulder.

'Stay with me, doctor,' she murmured, moving my hand in small circles.

'Of course,' I said, and drew up the blanket. Then I sat beside her while she fell into muttering, sedated sleep.

For the rest of the voyage she sat alone in the lounge, or walked with invalid slowness along the promenade deck, her face pale beneath her sunglasses. Though her husband maintained his state of just-controlled inebriation, the woman made no observable attempt to get a drink, but I could see the ghastly intensity with which she concentrated on each tremulous step through the day. I suspected that it couldn't last much beyond the constraints of our floating world; her California dream-home must already be calling her back to the oblivion of its cornucopian cocktail cabinets. In the meantime she showed a brittle dignity. She kept herself together enough to avoid being off-loaded in Jakarta – where the harbour baked under a sky hot enough to fell a water-buffalo, and litter combusted spontaneously in the midday sun – and was still apparently sober by the time we reached Padang Bai, off the east coast of Bali, where she and her noxious partner were due to end their cruise.

At dawn the chains rattled in the forepeak and our anchors plunged into the placid waters. Through my cabin porthole I could see mist above the palm trees, and sunlight beginning to brush the tops of craggy mountains. A rust-bucket coaster and a small tanker rode the swell nearby, a regatta of out-rigger canoes gathered at their ladders where sailors haggled with the boatmen for fresh fish. I managed to escape ashore for a brief few hours, jumping onto one of the tenders taking passengers ashore. Some were off to the tourist shops of Denpasar and Kuta Beach, others to the airport to fly home, and I said goodbye to my dipsomaniac patient with a fondness born of our small, shared victory. Then I took a taxi through the switchback roads of the island's mountainous interior, stopping for refreshment at a teahouse overlooking jade-green terraced rice-fields. My brief rest over, I hurried back to the ship, for now it was the crew who were giving me problems.

⊕

Ted and Alicia were a married couple – both members of the entertainment staff – whom I had always found good company. Ted and I discussed books, Alicia teased me gently about the attractiveness of the dancers when we lay together sunbathing; of such little intimacies are the bonds of shipboard society constructed. Friendly with everyone, they appeared to be above the petty mistrusts that affected the rest of the service staff and we met regularly for a late-night drink at the fantail bar, under the stars astern. Then one afternoon Ted had come to see me at my crew surgery, slipping into the medical centre and sitting uneasily in the chair. What were the symptoms of AIDS, he wanted to know. I explained that the early signs of HIV infection were non-specific; tiredness, fever and enlarged lymph glands. Later, if it developed into AIDS, the disease would show itself through the appearance of other infections – pneumonia, gastro-enteritis, eye or skin conditions – that were the result of suppression of the body's immune defences. Wasting and weight loss were late manifestations. He nodded, staring at the floor. What exactly was troubling him, I asked.

'Well,' he said hesitantly, 'I've got a symptom, but it's none of the ones you've mentioned. It's like a funny scratching feeling in my penis.'

'You mean when you pass urine?' I asked. 'Is there any discharge?'

'No discharge, and it's there all the time,' he answered, 'like something burrowing inside me. It's been there for months. That's why I'm sure it's AIDS.'

He described how he had woken up with the sensation the morning after a night in Bangkok, when he had gone ashore with some crewmates and received a blow-job from a prostitute. Now he was convinced that the virus was at work, multiplying inside the organ of his sin. I examined him from top to toe, not excluding his genitals. I tested his urine for abnormalities. Then I elaborated to him carefully the many reasons why he was unlikely to have become infected from his drunken infidelity.

'Firstly, the virus seems not to be active in saliva,' I explained, 'tongue-kissing, for instance, has never been shown to spread HIV. Second, an HIV infection wouldn't cause the feeling in your penis that you describe. Third, even gonorrhoea and other infections of the urethra, which could conceivably be caught from oral contact, take several days to show themselves; you wouldn't have symptoms the next morning. And if you've never noticed any discharge, its unlikely that there has been such an infection.'

It was clear that Ted wasn't listening to me.

'It's AIDS,' he said, 'I know it is. And if, as you say, I couldn't have caught it from that prostitute, then there's only one other place it could have come from.'

With a certain incredulous dread, I began to realize the fixity of his obsession.

'Ted, it's most unlikely that you've caught HIV,' I said firmly. 'If you're that worried we can do a blood test the next time we're in a proper port.'

'It's too late, isn't it?' he said quietly. 'You know where I got it, doc. It's from that fucking whore, my wife.'

Alicia didn't sunbathe any more. I saw her on the lifeboat deck, where she stood hunched at the rail, watching the water curl along the hull eighty feet below. I noticed a bruise on her upper arm.

'Come and see me in the surgery,' I said, acutely aware of the limits of my job; patient confidentiality made it difficult for me to mention anything to her about Ted's problem.

'I'm fine,' she said, but I could see that she had been crying.

'You've been at sea for how long; fourteen months?' I asked her. 'Take some leave, go home. Get Ted to see a proper doctor.'

She said nothing. At the next port they were gone.

Other medical problems were more insidious. One of the radio operators came to see me, the head of his penis discoloured by a cluster of tiny, crusted blisters. I told him it looked very much like genital herpes, and asked at which dockside 'disco' he might have picked it up. The man was stunned.

'I do not sleep with *putains*,' he protested angrily, 'and the person I am with, it could not be her: she is very clean.' But through his bluster I could see the signs of doubt.

Was she a member of the ship's staff? I asked him. Reluctantly he mumbled the name of the blonde sauna-room masseuse. I prescribed treatment for him and advised that he ask her to come and see me without delay. He left, looking devastated. Among the crew's medical files I found the woman's records and discovered that her herpes had been diagnosed half a year before by one of my predecessors, who had warned her of the condition's infectivity. She had failed to attend for follow-up.

She was not at the next crew clinic, or the one after that. I saw her late at night in the fantail bar, where the officers usually gathered for their after-duty drinks. She was sitting with the Scots chief engineer who was in love with her, and she glared at me poisonously when I greeted them. When he had gone to get another round I asked her if she'd received my message.

'Leave me alone,' she hissed. 'It's none of your fucking business who I sleep with.'

'It is if you're going to spread yourself about,' I said. 'I don't need the extra work. Now come and get some anti-viral medication. I'll expect you tomorrow.'

She didn't come. Instead, the chief engineer himself stormed into the consulting room.

'What have you been saying to Amanda?' he demanded. 'She's right pissed off with you.'

'Didn't she tell you?'

'No she fookin' didn't,' he answered. 'You know I like that girl. I don't want you upsetting her.'

'Believe me, I really don't want to. But it's important that she comes to see me.' I hesitated, trying desperately to think of a way to advance the situation. 'If you like her, it's in your interests to get her to come along.'

'What do you mean, in my interests?' The man's eyes narrowed. 'Is this something that I should know about?'

'Look, I really can't say anything,' I objected. 'You know that doctors can't talk about their patients.'

He stood abruptly, the legs of the chair squealing on the deck. 'I thought you were a friend,' he said. 'You cunt.'

⊕

New Year plus three hours. It had been a rough night so far. We were beating southwards through a force eight storm, the tail-end of a typhoon lashing Bangkok. Beyond the deck-lights, water struck the glass with the force of stones, while from the bar came the sound, regular as a metronome, of smashing crockery where spilled dishes travelled from bulkhead to bulkhead across the slippery floor. The vessel had a peculiar yaw that I had never felt before, a sideways bow-down corkscrew motion that seemed always about to right itself, only to flick with a stomach-challenging lurch into the next wave-trough.

I had been busy this evening, ever since the formal dinner when my neighbour had suddenly assumed a look of rapt attention and ducked his head between his knees, vomiting lobster thermidore over his shoe-tops. The dining room cleared shortly after and I'd gone to work, travelling the length and beam of the passenger quarters with my medical bag. My radio crackled, calling me from cabin to cabin, where I gave seasickness injections to patients that prayed to their deities not to let the ship begin its next swooping fall. The passageways were deserted apart from a lone champagne bottle that trundled back and forth with each roll, and a steward glimpsed on Neptune Deck, smoothing down his uniform as he left the cabin of a buxom woman traveller. The singing of 'Auld Lang Syne' had been a sparsely attended affair, with only the die-hard revellers still on their feet; whooping as they stumbled like a display of synchronized drunkenness across the waltzing lounge-bar floor. By now almost all of them had succumbed to nausea or the bad champagne, and made their weaving way to bed.

I leaned at the bar and looked around at my fellow seafarers – officers, entertainers, passenger service staff – as they sat each in their exclusive groups, tossing back drinks while the off-duty nightclub singer hung onto a pillar and crooned into the microphone above the expert accompaniment of the piano-man. Beside me the assistant purser, his back propped against the bar-counter, updated me on the latest from the ship's ever-prurient rumour-mill, indicating with his glass-hand the subject of each new revelation: that one has body odour, this one comes too soon, the little dancer likes to take it up the rear. I felt already the repository of too many confidences, medical and personal. I knew the guts and the privates of this pathological society, its vengeances, inadequacies and betrayals. This was not a place for friendship to prosper.

Leaving behind the dregs of the party, I made my way to my cabin. The sea boomed against the hull; my reading lamp, directed at the porthole, showed swirls of bubbles as waves submerged the glass. Not even drunk, I climbed into my bed, wondering whether I had the energy to masturbate; the gift of the departing doctor had already proved its worth on this long voyage. There was a knock at the door. Standing in the glow of the corridor emergency light was a rather beautiful French girl. She was fresh aboard, as yet knew no one in the tour office where she worked. I dug a bottle out of the stowage locker and we drank to the quintessential sadness of a New Year's Eve spent alone. She asked if she could stay with me. I slept nose to nose with one of her cool breasts. By the time a couple of days had passed she had found her bearings and was again a stranger, subsumed into the incestuous mesh of shipboard relationships.

Such disappointments didn't last. I stood at night on the forepeak deck as we slipped south of the equator across the Flores Sea. Around us bobbed a fleet of squid-boats. Each carried a frame of lights that hung in a square around its hull from out-slung gantries. The sky was so rich with stars that there was no part of it that was truly black, and the lights of the boats were directed downwards into the green sea beneath them so that each vessel appeared to float atop a great pyramid of milky light in which flitted the ghost-shapes of teeming cuttlefish. The only noise was the rolling surge of the bow wave and the sigh of warm wind in my ears.

⊕

The lead limousine was long and black, with tinted windows and arctic airconditioning that chilled me through the cotton of my summer uniform. In front of us was a police black-and-white, roof-lights flashing; behind, a minibus carrying the captain's guests and family and a line of tour buses that contained the passengers, shepherded at the rear by another police car. We were on our way to Borobudur, an eighth-century Buddhist monument that lay a couple of hour's drive south of the Javanese port of Semarang. The convoy charged along the mountain roads, ox-carts and cyclists panicking before the howl of the police siren; the Indonesian government, anxious that a new massacre in East Timor was again generating unfortunate international 'misunderstanding', had pulled out all the hospitality stops. Even the platoons of soldiers, doubling along the road in full kit and rifle for an early morning training run, gave way to us. Eventually we pulled into the tourist village at the site. The plaintive strings of a welcoming Gamelan orchestra followed us up between the trees to where a grand confection of black basalt, a man-made hillock, towered above against a backdrop of blue mountains.

It took fifty thousand men and seventy years to build this geometric shrine, its terraces and galleries depicting the ascending spheres of the Buddhist cosmos. Borobudur's levels rose like a light-absorbing wedding-cake, the stone carved in friezes showing the ways of Enlightenment. The top terraces were dotted with trellis-work stupas, each stone bell housing the statue of a particularly enigmatic Buddha. Others, headless, directed their serenity over the surrounding paddy fields. Hordes of puffing tourists battled their way up the narrow stair-tunnels joining each level and were swallowed in the maze. After them dashed the postage-stamp sellers with their hundred different shadings of a glowering Suharto, and the photographers, flourishing portfolios of sun-bleached group-shots. After an hour one of the French officers on escort duty suggested that we slip away from this *bordel* and go in search of a drink.

A few miles from the temple complex was a nest of bars. It was difficult to tell whether they were flourishing; there were no tourists here, but a number of Indonesian men – some in military uniform – lounged at tables on the terraces, sipping whisky. Inside, scantily clad women wound themselves like cats around each occupied barstool. A pair attached themselves to us at once, the attentive maiden at my side slipping a breathily enticing murmur, and the tip of her tongue, into my ear. My fellow officer winked at me above the rim of his glass.

'I think I go wis zis pretty girl upstair, for twenty minutes,' he said, slipping an arm around his companion. 'This is better zan Bangkok.' He drained his drink. 'Good 'ealth, my friend, good 'ealth.'

Oh, the fecklessness of sailors. Bangkok may have had the reputation, but there was nowhere on earth like the flesh-pots of the Indonesian archipelago for the commingling of the afflictions of Venus: boils, chancres, buboes and encrustations, rashes and nodules and the multiple ulcers of lymphogranuloma venereum which produce the evocatively named 'watering-can' appearance of the genitals. A single indiscreet encounter could open the door to an onslaught of organisms: gonorrhoea, trichomonas, chlamydia, plus a selection of viruses. Pinned to the bulkhead above my desk in the crew clinic was a nautical cartoon. It showed a ship's surgeon being consulted by a sailor, a stereotypical old salt in the days of sail. The man bore an anchor tattoo and an eyepatch, and both his hands had been replaced by sharp-pointed steel hooks. 'Doctor,' the sailor was saying, 'it hurts when I pee.'

Clearly little had changed in the world of marine medicine, for these very words opened just about every male crew consultation I held, from the lowest low-deck Zamboangan garbage-handler to the most refined French radar officer.

Using the computer in the ship's tour office, I had put together an information sheet listing common types of venereal disease. Copies were put under the door of every officer, and distributed among the crew. Routes of infection, symptoms, consequences and treatment were all described, in simple yet graphic language. I tried to warn about the risks of self-treatment by taking a handful of the mixed antibiotic tablets sold at every Indonesian street-market; these cocktails, if not expired or dud, would only encourage the development of bacterial strains resistant to all future treatment. Even more useless were the slimy potions – Chinese herbal medicines – gulped indiscriminately by the Filipino crew for every affliction, from imagined impotence to secondary syphilis. My treatise had a salutary effect. Suddenly the crew-clinics were like the Trooping of the Colour; in rank and file they formed up to show me their private parts and reveal the green drip of gonorrhoeal discharge and the painless ulcers of primary chancres. Sandra laid out syringes and ampoules of antibiotics and we began our healing mission, plunging needles into buttock after wincing buttock.

⊕

The ship itself was failing. I heard that there were problems with the pumps that kept her bilges clear. There was now only one engine working, and the auxiliary generators ran all the time at full capacity to keep the aircon functioning. The refrigeration plant that chilled the gash-pit – the hold where the ship's accumulated garbage was stored until we reached port – was also faltering. As the sharp smell of rot began to climb the companionways, seeping inexorably upward towards the critical noses of the passengers, orders came for the trash to be dumped overboard and the garbage crews worked all night at this sea-burial. In the middle of it the last engine burned a bearing and was shut down. Morning found the ship motionless on a flat sea, a light haze trickling from her funnel. The passengers, gathering under the afterdeck awnings for breakfast, commented on the smell. Soon they found its source. Dotted on the water behind the ship, like the tail of a decaying comet, floated plastic garbage sacks inflated by the gases of their inner corruption. Beneath the stern they clustered thickly, seeping an oily sheen. Occasionally a small shark, attracted from the depths, ripped a bag in a flurry of splashing, releasing further satellites of floating debris.

By evening we were under way again, and my ex-friend the chief engineer appeared beside me where I held sundowner-station at the fantail bar. Despite his crisp white overalls and glinting stripes he looked so worn out that I bought him a triple. He hesitated for a moment and then knocked it back.

'I'm busier than a one-armed cab driver with crabs,' he said. 'I shouldn't even be here, but I had to get a look at the air.' He stared hungrily at the horizon. 'The old man's chewing fookin' horseshoes, says it's all my fault. Everyone else seems to think so too. I know you went through something similar with that typhoid thing, and that sort of makes you a mate; maybe the only one I've got on this shit-bucket.' He stuck out his hand. 'Sorry I gave you a hard time about Amanda.'

'Oh, yes, how are things going with her?'

'She's fookin' bad luck, that's what. Got some pox she's spreading around the ship. I made some enquiries after we spoke. You did me a favour, doc.'

'Another drink?' I suggested.

'Got to go,' he said, 'but I'd like to offer you one in my surgery. Drop down to the engine room tomorrow.'

Few people ever entered that infernal place unless they had to, and the black-gangs that worked there maintained their insularity. Some appeared occasionally in my clinic – suffering from respiratory problems – but they were seldom seen on deck. I found the chief in his office; a windowless, vibrating cubicle at the end of the main service passage. Technical blue-prints and wiring charts covered the desks. He brought a bottle of iced vodka from a freezer under the table and poured as he unhooked some overalls from behind the door.

'Have a shot of this,' he shouted over the engine-thump, 'and put those on. I want you to see my domain.'

We started down the steel steps of the companionway. The heat increased so that the air became difficult to breathe. I began to cough. We stepped out on a catwalk, above a dark pit of clamouring machinery. Spot-lights gleamed below off the oily flanks of the four great engines.

Two were running, their tappet-arms rising and falling in a dizzy dance. The others stood eviscerated amidst strewn parts, and from one the artificers eased a giant crankshaft with the aid of a chain-hoist. Deep beneath the gratings that formed the floor, a black pool of diesel rocked sullenly with the slow roll of the ship. I wiped my forehead with my sleeve. It, too, came away black.

'Still got that bunker leak,' the chief shouted in my ear. He turned to a console beside him, and, taking a rag from his pocket, scrubbed at the bulkhead above it. A panel of glass was revealed, covering a glowing neon strip-light. Immediately the glass began to darken, spotted by a fine oil-mist. The droplets coalesced until the light was again unnoticeable in the engine-room's gloom. The engineer said something that may have been about Amanda, but it was inaudible over the deafening noise of the engines. Sweat channelled through the filth on his face like tears. I coughed up curdled diesel on my tongue. I knew we stood in hell.

⊕

My redemption was at hand; my friend David was about to take over as ship's doctor. In Kuala Lumpur we lunched together at the Planter's Club, and I recounted the bizarre parade of shipboard life that I'd experienced.

'That Amanda,' he chuckled, shaking his head, 'I remember her well. Just when you think you're winning the war against venereal disease, she opens a whole second front.'

We took a taxi to Port Kelang and dragged aboard David's kit-bag and a box of books, diversions for his next six months at sea. David reported to the purser and was signed on. Then we repaired to the fantail bar for an afternoon tipple, while the ship made her imperious way out of harbour. We watched the pilot boat cutting back towards the port and I relaxed, knowing that I was no longer on duty; my last week on board would be as a non-paying passenger until we tied back in at Singapore and I left the ship. We had a drink to the durability of our long friendship, and then another. A sunset of pristine loveliness tinged the distant peaks of Sumatra.

'Why aren't you in uniform?' growled the captain at my elbow.

'Supernumerary, captain,' I said, indicating David. 'New doctor's come on board.'

'You'll become supernumerary when I say you are,' he bellowed. 'Until then you're still an officer on my ship.'

'Old bastard's still the same,' said David when we were again alone. 'Can't even be pleasant while he's doing you a favour.'

'A favour?'

'Well, you're back on full pay, with nothing to do. I'd call that a favour,' he observed. We drank to the captain as well. I told David about the state of the ship's machinery. He laughed.

'Things on this barge never change,' he said. 'The last chief engineer used to joke that there was a plot by the owners to let an engine-room explosion sink her in deep water, so that they could collect on the insurance. Though I actually doubt there is any.'

For the first time since I had come aboard I had enough time to myself. David ran the mildly remunerative passenger clinics – he was a kinder person than I, as well as being a better doctor, and actively enjoyed the formal dinners that I had found such purgatory – while I continued with the crew surgeries. These remained fascinating. A young man was brought to see me, a rather slow-witted dishwasher from the main galley. He'd been spending too much time polishing the knives, I was told, and had recently been found wandering through the lower decks, a meat cleaver in his hand. Also, he was hearing voices. The patient spoke no English, and the consultation was conducted through a Tagalog interpreter. The young man believed he was bewitched. One of the Chinese laundry-men, he claimed, had put a curse on him that was causing his penis to retract into his body, and only the death of the spell-binder would stop this inexorable process.

I thought the man was clearly schizophrenic, but David had his doubts; he had heard of this particular fixation before, he said, but only among animist jungle-dwellers in Peninsular Malaysia. How it came to manifest itself in a Catholic lad from Quezon City was an interesting diagnostic mystery. 'Delusional states are culturally determined,' said David. 'This guy should be chatting with the Virgin, like all the other Christian nutters. Maybe he really is bewitched. I don't suppose you could add a line to the referral letter that'll go with him to the Manila psychiatric hospital, asking them to measure his cock every day and keep us posted?'

A few days later, at the fantail bar, we had our farewell drinks. A small wooden angel, a piece of brightly painted flimflam produced for the Bali tourist trade, hung from the overhead. We toasted each other under this tacky symbol of destiny.

'To travel,' I said. 'To a varied life.'

'The thing I missed about this job while I was ashore was the routine,' said David. 'To peace and quiet.'

Below, the mooring gangs were moving on the dock, preparing to cast off. A rain squall threatened as my bags were landed ashore. I followed them at the last minute, jumping down from the end of the already lifting gangway. The storm arrived, veiling the cranes and gantries, and I watched the ship depart, her riding lights bright in the gathering gloom. David watched me as long as he could from the stern and then the rain drove him under cover.

His next communiqué was in the form of a newspaper cutting, and several postal re-directions had been scribbled on the envelope before it finally reached me in Mozambique some months later. Clipped from the *Straits Times*, it was dated exactly four weeks after I had left him and the ship in Singapore. 'Engine Fire Ends Bangkok Cruise' ran the header. David filled in the details in his accompanying letter. The alarms had been sounded during lunch and at first the crew response had gone like clockwork. Then the flames, fed by leaking bunker-oil, started burning back towards the fuel tanks and the fire-teams had fled, appearing rather obviously up on deck among the passengers waiting at their muster-stations. The chief engineer and some senior officers stayed at the hoses while the captain flayed the cowards over the ship's intercom. His blistering language had caused one of the passengers to faint, providing David with his only actual casualty. Eventually they had taken to the lifeboats, and been picked up at sea by a passing liner. With the ship in dry-dock for repairs for an indefinite period, David was out of a job. Was I doing anything interesting?

9
Mozambique

The man I was examining had a chain of scars that looped across his breast like a fine necklace. His left leg hung down over the side of the bed. It was long and slender, its dark skin unmarked. The right leg ended below the knee, in a bandaged stump that seeped a pink discharge. It was difficult to tell if he knew the limb was missing. He stared ahead, hands clenched on the edge of the bed-frame. An orderly explained that the young man did not speak; had not done so since the bullet-wound that had shattered his shin several days before. By the time he'd reached hospital infection had set in, necessitating an amputation. A patient with an artificial leg swayed through the ward, his metal knee clunking with each step. The orderly spoke to the young man, showing him that he would be able to walk again, but he showed no sign of comprehension. His faith was dead. The orderly pointed at the symmetrical scars across the man's chest.

'Marks made by the *curandeiro*, the witchdoctor,' he said, 'meant to protect him from bullets. But it seems that the enemy's medicine was stronger.'

Everyone who passed through Mozambique during the war years learned at least one word of Portuguese: *confusão*. Transport was *confusão*; communication was *confusão*; the war was, most of all, *confusão*. By any standards this was a strange conflict. It was called a civil war, though the rebel force – the Mozambican National Resistance, or Renamo –

had been created by neighbouring white-ruled Rhodesia to destabilize newly independent Mozambique's leftist government. It was an economic war, with South Africa using the rebels to sabotage the Mozambican transport network so that regional trade would have to pass through South Africa. It was a 'moral' war, with a weird collection of right-wing Christian and evangelical movements in the West backing Renamo as a crusade against godless communism. It was also a war of the witchdoctors, being fought by counter-armies of mystically inspired soldiers across the famine-stricken country.

Mozambique was a blank screen on which you could project anything you liked. Appropriately, perhaps, I was not there as a doctor but to make a film. Working in Kurdistan had left me aware of the limitations of medical intervention, and I wondered whether journalism might be effective in making a difference on a larger scale. In South Africa, when I was growing up, good journalism had been a weapon; the press was controlled by rigid censorship and revealing the truth was an heroic mission. I may have become a little cynical about doctoring, but I preserved a pristine naivety about the value of bearing witness. It didn't last long, in Mozambique. Wars encourage pillage, even if all you're stealing is images of suffering. And there was plenty of suffering.

After the Portuguese left in 1975, Rhodesia had set up Renamo to ravage the Mozambican countryside with random attacks. Civilians were abducted to serve as porters or soldiers. A new viciousness defined the war after 1980, when South Africa took over control of the rebel force. Its size was increased from two to ten thousand men and South African military intelligence specialists developed novel methods of extending Renamo's effectiveness. *Curandeiros* – traditional mediums who interpreted the utterances of ancestral spirits – were co-opted to spread the message that the tribal ancestors were sympathetic to Renamo. Areas where Mozambique's Frelimo government had popular support were chosen by Renamo's South African handlers as places of maximum destruction. Teachers and nurses were murdered, schools and clinics burned and transport repeatedly ambushed. And spiritual forces were used for terror, to expunge from these places not only government support, but the very population. Civilians captured by Renamo were symbolically mutilated – their lips and noses, even sometimes their eyelids, cut off to turn them into the unblinking ghouls of tribal folklore – then turned loose to haunt the ravaged countryside. The superstitious peasantry fled their lands, refusing to return. Hundreds of thousands became wanderers, hiding in the bush and emerging at night to forage for food, until eventually they reached some government enclave, starved and destitute and babbling of incomprehensible atrocities. Renamo's handlers appeared to have created an invincible force.

Then, in the devastated central province of Zambesia, a mystic leader appeared. Manuel Antonio claimed to be immortal, having died and been revived by God to free the land of Renamo and end the war. At ritual gatherings in jungle clearings, he treated his followers with a magical ash – rubbed into cuts on their chests – to render them impervious to bullets. Within a few months Manuel Antonio had transformed a loose group of village militia and refugees into an army of '*Naprama*', a word meaning 'irresistible force'. They advanced through the bush, shouting and rattling tin cans filled with pebbles. The Renamo soldiers fled, and soon large areas of central Mozambique were back under Frelimo government control.

Eventually Manuel Antonio was killed in a Renamo ambush, his body shot full of holes. Renamo had found a spiritual counter-force, a powerful witchdoctor from northern Zambesia province who led a rival magical army called the *'Mukuepas'*. His medicine was claimed to be even more effective than that of the *Naprama*, and his followers painted their faces with a white paste to distinguish themselves from their foes. *Makuepa* attacks had driven back government soldiers, and more refugees were arriving daily in the overloaded *barrios* around the coastal cities. The UN's Food and Agriculture Organization estimated that three million people were starving in the region, with the distribution of food relief being blocked by the continued fighting. In the war of the witchdoctors, Renamo had regained the upper hand.

✪

In Maputo, the Mozambican capital, the bar of the Cardoza Hotel was busy. The drinkers spilled out onto the terrace. Most worked for the parastatal agencies – the World Bank, UNDP, UNHCR, UNICEF, the Red Cross – and some two hundred other aid groups, charities and NGOs whose operatives had descended on the country in a plague of altruism. Twilight was falling and the fruit-bats wheeled in the blue air above our heads. Below the bluff on which the hotel stood, freighters full of food-aid were lined up to unload at the city's crumbling port. By this stage of the war aid was providing nearly eighty per cent of the country's GDP. The aid industry trade press always had a lot about Mozambique, the sort of headline-grabbing projects that attracted prestige and funding. The IMF and World Bank wanted Mozambique to accept an economic structural readjustment programme; reducing state expenditure on health and education, and abandoning government-subsidized prices for staple foods to the determinants of 'market forces'. Development agencies were offering 'tied' or 'bilateral' aid: subsidized programmes that locked Mozambique into service or spare-part contracts with suppliers from the donor nations, thus recycling the aid-dollars back home.

Lost children – orphaned, or separated from their parents in a Renamo attack – slept on the city's pavements and in a warren of ruined buildings near the market. They scavenged for food in garbage bins, forming a ragged, importuning throng that dogged the steps of walkers on the streets. Others played football in the courtyards of the over-filled government orphanages, or sat mute in the special rehabilitation centres set up for children who'd been forced to perform atrocities as child soldiers for Renamo. Around the capital the shantytown *barrios* now stretched mile on mile, a maze of flimsy shacks built by the displaced, of sticks and flattened oil drums. The bull-fight ring housed a clothing distribution centre for these *deslocados*. On the broken, potholed roads, fuming, battered buses fought their way between the army trucks and the handcarts of the charcoal-sellers.

There were also smart Mercedes and Toyotas owned by the sort of opportunists wars attract. These were the importers of luxury goods from South Africa and the owners of the incongruously plush restaurants and clubs where the United Nations staff could be found spending their hardship bonuses. The UN people probably felt they'd earned it, for the Mozambican capital was more or less besieged by Renamo forces that daily attacked outlying villages and ambushed traffic on the roads to the South African and Swaziland borders. Desperate for peace, Mozambique's government had been forced to the negotiating table for a year of as yet unproductive ceasefire talks, while the war ground the country further into ruin and bankruptcy. Hyperinflation meant most transactions involved bricks of banknotes bundled together with string. That didn't affect the UN staff, who got paid in dollars, or the businessmen, and Maputo's nightlife was surprisingly busy despite the frequent blackouts when Renamo blew up the power-pylons carrying the high-tension lines that supplied the city.

I was sitting on the Cardoza's terrace, drinking with a man. He worked for a subsidiary of Armscor – the South African weapons manufacturing conglomerate – that had a contract from the Mozambican government to lift the land-mines scattered by both government forces and Renamo along the route of the power line from the South African border to Maputo. Many of those now profiting from the war were South African. Renamo sabotage of Mozambique's hydroelectric production had prevented the country from meeting its own power needs, so throughout the war the South African grid had supplied Maputo with electricity at a premium price. Since 1984, South Africa had officially ceased support for Renamo – though mysterious military aircraft still flew at night over the border, dropping supplies by parachute – and Pretoria was now keen to stop attacks on the power line, which meant lost revenue to the South African national generating company, Escom.

I bought the de-mining expert a beer. 'Balzac' was an Afrikaner; tall, soft-spoken, and slightly menacing. He sported the full beard favoured by South African Special Forces and police counter-insurgency units. Following the South African withdrawal from Namibia, most of his old comrades had moved into private 'security work', but Balzac preferred life in Mozambique and the risks of his job. He had been ambushed a couple of times in the last two months; the week before, he'd run his armoured vehicle over a pressure-mine which had blown off a front tyre. Balzac mentioned that he was driving to the border town of Ressano Garcia the following day, and asked if I'd like to come along. I said that I would. The town contained a small hospital – dependent on medical supplies hauled along this dangerous sixty mile route from Maputo – that I wanted to visit.

I met Balzac at dawn in the compound of the mine-lifting operation on the outskirts of the city. We loaded our *'escorta'* – seven boyish government soldiers, with their AK47s, a pair of Russian machine guns of World War Two vintage, ammo belts, weapons-clips and packs – into the back of a sand-coloured Casspir. Even before Stefan told me of their use as torture devices, I had disliked the cruel outlines of these armoured vehicles. I'd seen them often in South Africa: the yellow police ones parked like mobile forts at the entrances to the townships, and the brown versions used by the army, hung with spare wheels and surmounted by an armoured shield around a big machine-gun. Now I was counting on the vehicle's durability, for the road between Maputo and the border town of Ressano Garcia was known as Ambush Alley. The steel doors were clinched shut, and with Balzac at the wheel we rolled out onto the quiet street. A roar came from the Casspir's high exhaust pipes. The soldiers checked their weapons, placed ammunition-clips close to hand, locked cartridge belts into the machine guns sticking through the gunports. One indicated a burned-out store by the roadside. 'The *bandidos* raided there six nights ago,' he said. 'They are attacking closer and closer to town now, so we must be ready.'

We sped along a sandy track, the service road for the power-line bringing electricity from South Africa. The twisted frames of destroyed pylons stuck up above the thorn-trees. Every few miles we passed a blockhouse, its garrison waving as we swirled by and covered them in a drift of dust. Beside the road lay the shell of an exploded tank, turret askew and bushes growing through its ruined tracks. I was standing in the back of the Casspir, peeking over the edge of the top opening. There was a sudden burst of fire and I tumbled down into the hull. The soldiers laughed, pointing at the brass cartridge-cases rolling on the vehicle's floor. Balzac congratulated me pointedly on the swiftness of my reflexes. 'Man, you came down like a sack of shit,' he said. 'I got hit here a week ago so I always order the gunners to give the bushes a few bursts when I pass this place.'

Moamba was the halfway point on the road to the border, and the last government-held post until Ressano. The roof of the station building was buckled from a mortar attack and armoured cars were parked along the avenues, escorts for a convoy of trucks that had paused in Moamba for refreshment. The road out of town passed between a pair of tanks whose crews waved at us as we drove by. Beyond, the fields were overgrown, the farmhouses ruined. Thorn-trees had encroached upon the edge of the road, turning it into a claustrophobic tunnel. Caravans of wrecked trucks lined the verges. We swerved among burst suitcases that had belonged to ambush victims. The body of a woman lay beside a burned-out pickup, her feet clad in bright lilac sneakers. She had been there for weeks, gradually mummifying in the baking sun, but it was too dangerous to stop and bury her. Our heavy vehicle slowed on the inclines and the soldiers cradled their weapons, scanning the trees in expectation of a sudden volley. On the outskirts of Ressano Garcia, Balzac exhaled with relief. 'I've been shot up there twice. But don't relax too much; we're more likely to get hit on the way back.'

The population of the border town was swollen by a vast settlement of *deslocados* that had sprung up on its edge. Renamo shelled the place periodically from positions on the surrounding hills. The wall of a trading store on the main street, washed red with mud splashed up by the rains, was scored with radiating scars from a mortar burst. A burned-out car stood at the curb. The hospital was a collection of bungalows on the side of a hill. Blood-stained stretchers were propped on a veranda and an orderly was trying to rinse the canvas clean with buckets of water. The doctor showed me around the treatment facilities and simple operating theatre.

Three women, one hugely pregnant, lay on sheets of cardboard on bare bed springs, their legs criss-crossed with dressings.

'These were hit when the *deslocado* camp was bombed last night,' explained the doctor. 'The other two died.'

⊕

The film I was working on was not about people's suffering. My faith in the value of reporting had taken its first knock in the process of trying to get the proposal accepted, for it turned out that the only way to get any interest from the television channels was to pitch Mozambique as a wildlife documentary. The organized elephant slaughter that I'd heard about on the Namibia–Angola border two years before was a feature of the Mozambique war too: South African supply flights landing at Renamo bases brought back piles of tusks, more came across the border on the backs of press-ganged porters, and the ivory was sold through Military Intelligence front companies to buyers in the Far East. Of Mozambique's pre-war herds of some fifty thousand elephants, it was estimated that only a couple of thousand still survived. It hadn't been easy to convince the Channel's 'commissioning editor, factual programmes' that there was a story here at all: 'Where are the visuals?' demanded the little media mogul. 'I don't want some soft human-interest shit, I want dead elephants. No one's interested in just another "War in Africa" piece.'

He was right. There was virtually no interest in the human victims of Renamo's war of spite. In fact Renamo was the pet cause of a small core of the British establishment. A Renamo office in London – the Mozambique Institute – was supported by the odd Lord and Marquess and some avowedly hard-right English financiers, one of whom periodically expressed admiration for Adolf Hitler's more extreme policies. Backing in England and the USA also came from right-wing Christian organizations. Renamo's Washington office (in the headquarters building of the Heritage Foundation) was run by an American evangelist who presented the rebels as a force for Christian revival in a country blighted by communist atheism. Fundamentalist churches in the USA such as 'Christ for the Nations Inc.' and the wackily named End-Time Handmaidens contributed funds for evangelical work in Renamo 'liberated zones', while the Jimmy Swaggart Ministries, part of the Moral Majority movement that had helped put Reagan in office, supplied religious tracts to Renamo bases.

My film assignment took me north from Maputo to a government-held town up the coast. It was not safe to use the roads; a food convoy had been attacked some days before, destroying a number of trucks and killing civilians on board a bus. The aircraft flew over the sea; inland stretched the war-ravaged, desolated countryside to which Renamo had brought Christian salvation. We circled above a bay of iridescent green shallows and dived suddenly to a landing on the dusty airstrip. The town, a grid of tin-roofed buildings, sat on a palm-fringed bluff looking out over the Indian Ocean. Wooden sailing dhows were pulled up on the beach. The film crew would be arriving a few days later; while I waited for them, I introduced myself to the young Médecins sans Frontières doctor who was in temporary charge of the small hospital. He had work for me; in one of the beds was a man with a bayonet wound in his back. The hospital's *técnico cirúrgico* was away and the doctor wanted to evacuate the casualty to the capital, but he was worried that it might not be safe for him to fly.

From the end of the bed I could see how the man fought for each breath, the tendons of his neck straining with the effort. The stab was just above his eighth rib at the back; an inch-long wound that sucked in air with every desperate inhalation. I felt the front of the man's neck. His trachea was deviated to one side.

'He has a tension pneumothorax,' I said. 'On the injured side of his chest the lung's collapsed, and with every breath air is being sucked into the space around it. The rising pressure in that side is pushing the airway and heart across so that breathing and cardiac output become increasingly difficult.'

'I have never actually seen a case,' said the young doctor. 'I don't know how to treat it.'

'We need to decompress the over-expanded side with a chest drain.'

He frowned. 'We don't have any.'

'Perhaps you could find the biggest cannula in the place,' I suggested.

He dashed off to the operating theatre, returning with a selection of intravenous needles for running fluid into veins. I chose the largest, peeled back its sterile cover and quickly swabbed the man's breast with alcohol. He flinched when I plunged the needle in below the collar bone. There was a pop as it passed through the pleura – the tough membrane lining the chest cavity – and then the whistling sound of escaping air. I withdrew the steel needle, leaving the cannula tube that had encased it still sticking in his chest. Quickly, I sutured the plastic hub of the cannula to the skin so that it would not become dislodged, then stitched the bayonet stab closed and sealed the wound with a vaseline dressing. The man's breathing was already easier, and the doctor eyed him hopefully.

'Now we have to make a Heimlich valve,' I said.

He frowned again. 'What's that?'

'That cannula will only equalize the pressure inside and outside the chest. It won't re-expand the collapsed lung. A Heimlich valve makes the lung re-inflate by letting air out of the chest cavity but not back in. I've never made one, but someone [it had been an American Special Forces medic in Kurdistan] once told me how it's done.'

From a rubber surgical glove I cut off the middle finger, and tied the open end of the digit tightly around the end of the cannula. The patient, happier now that his breathing had begun to ease, smiled and watched me work; he spoke only Shangaan, and throughout the procedure I had been unable to explain to him what I was doing. He was puzzled by the finger of pale latex that now dangled from his chest, and held his breath warily as I picked up a pair of scissors. Cutting carefully, I snipped a small hole in its tip. The man exhaled and the finger filled with a pop, quivering as the air escaped through the hole. As soon as he breathed in it sucked flat, collapsing like a joke penis. He laughed, and the balloon inflated in time with each chuckle.

A nurse would be flying with the patient back to the capital, where he would have an X-ray and a proper chest drain. I discussed with her how to look after the improvised valve. Then I excused myself from the hospital and went to find my contact in the town, a local trader who would be able to help me with the transport that I needed for the film crew. Suleiman was doing his accounts in his warehouse, seated among tractor parts and oil-drums and piled sacks of maize, cashew nuts, dried fish and coconuts that reached high into the rafters and mixed their sun-warmed smells in the dusty air. He was a smiling, bearded Moslem who owned the garage and repair shop, whose trucks brought in most of the town's food and carried away its scanty exports. Agreement on the cost of transport hire – a Land Rover and a motor-boat – was quickly reached, and Suleiman invited me home to lunch.

Later I accompanied him to the military post outside the town to meet the daily convoy. It rolled in late, a weary cavalcade of much-bashed vehicles with weld-burns in their paintwork. Some limped on tired suspension, or drove like crabs on chassis bent from old collisions, and all were piled to the utmost. Sacks were stacked on drums, bundles on the sacks, and on top of everything swayed a crowd of passengers, clinging to the cargo and each other. Suleiman surveyed the line. One of his transports was missing with its load of three thousand litres of diesel. He spoke to the crew of the escorting armoured car: the convoy hadn't been attacked; the truck might still turn up. *Insh' Allah*, agreed Suleiman. It might.

The local hospital ran a child-feeding programme in a refugee camp north of the town. They gathered from early in the morning: lines of children dressed in rags, sitting patiently on the bare sand. Each held a pot or bowl and did not move, even when the sun climbed overhead and the earth bounced back shimmering waves of heat. Now and then a baby moaned and was hushed by its mother, or some boys would run a few steps in play before subsiding again into their waiting immobility. Almost all the children had the swollen bellies and reddish hair of kwashiorkor – malnutrition, from a diet deficient in protein – and its attendant apathy. As the lines inched forward towards the weighing scales and the drums of beans and maize that cooked on fires beyond, the odd small figure would be left behind, too weak to raise itself from where it lay beside the pot that was its sole possession. I found the sight of these battered bowls – the utterly vestigial remnants of uprooted lives – unbearably sad. I helped to carry the feather-light bodies to the Land Rover that acted as the hospital ambulance. Where is this one's mother, that one's family, I asked the nurse. *Perdido*, lost, came the answer; the bandits took them, we do not know.

The MSF personnel showed real commitment. They had signed up for six months of this gruelling work, trying to drain a lake of despair that was endlessly replenished by the war. I envied them their youth and optimism as they sat around their compound, drinking sunset beers. Apart from their radio – which that evening brought news that a town a hundred miles to the north had been overrun by Renamo, so that they worried about their colleagues working in the hospital there – the MSF staff's main source of company was a half-dozen German and Norwegian aid-workers and the scattering of other expatriates who lived in the town or on islands in the bay. Most of the latter were dreaming of the return of peace and the reappearance of the holiday-makers who had once been the core of the town's economy; already an advance-guard of Afrikaners, big-game fishermen, occupied some bungalows on the closest offshore island.

An enterprising Australian was building himself a house above the sea, well-placed to catch the evening breeze. He had offered me a place to stay, and we were just sitting down to eat when a knock came at the door. Outside stood the driver from the hospital; I was needed at once. Outside the building I found the MSF doctor pacing under the trees. A woman had been brought in from a village clinic. She had apparently been in labour for twenty-four hours and then her contractions had stopped. She'd begun to bleed vaginally, so they had put her in a truck and rushed her here over fifty miles of axle-breaking road. I greeted the patient through a nurse-translator and asked her how she felt. The woman shook her head, looking frightened. Her gums were very pale, and a small pool of blood had clotted beneath her thighs. Her blood pressure was low, her pulse rapid; she was slipping into shock, and her collapsed state meant that we had some difficulty finding a good-sized vein to start a drip.

'Do we have cross-match facilities?' I asked the doctor.

'Yes,' he answered, 'but no blood. Usually we take it from the families, if we can convince them that it's necessary. She came alone. There's no way to find a donor at this time.'

The woman's womb felt a little smaller than I would have

expected if her pregnancy was at full term. She groaned when I examined her belly. I couldn't feel the baby moving or hear a foetal heart, but then the last time I'd done obstetrics had been as a medical student. I had some memory that her symptoms could be due to abruption – premature separation of the placenta – an event that could be catastrophic for the unborn child and even, sometimes, fatal for the mother.

'Do you know how to perform a Caesarean section?' I asked the doctor.

'No.' He looked distraught. 'Usually the técnico cirúrgico . . .'

'It's OK, I can do it,' I said, trying to sound confident. 'Let's get her to theatre.'

While the anaesthetic nurse put the woman to sleep I quickly scanned the only obstetric text – in Portuguese – and, as soon as she was unconscious, performed an internal examination. Her cervix felt only part-dilated, and my glove was smeared with meconium, the greenish-black intestinal excretion produced by a distressed baby. There was also a lot of blood. I scrubbed up hurriedly and draped the woman's belly, then opened it with a vertical midline cut that sliced through all the layers of the abdominal wall at once; there was no time for the neat, low, transverse incision used in Western hospitals. The lower part of the uterus bulged forward into the wound. I nicked it with a scalpel and, with my fingers shielding its delicate contents, slid my operating scissors across the front. The muscle-fibres split between the blades.

A tiny ear was revealed. Scooping my hand under the head, I lifted it gently, and at once the baby emerged in a slippery rush of blood and meconium. I clamped and cut the umbilical cord and handed the motionless body to the obstetric nurse. Immediately she started sucking out the baby's nose and mouth and pumping oxygen in to inflate its lungs. I knew I had to deliver the placenta before the uterus would stop bleeding. It came away easily – I guessed there must have been a complete abruption – but under it I glimpsed something that my surgeon's eye could not mistake. It was a loop of bowel. I brought the uterus forward so that I could see behind it. A huge, ragged tear passed obliquely down the back, and dark blood filled the abdomen. I felt a sudden chill of surgical dread.

'Of all obstetric complications, rupture of the uterus is perhaps the one most feared.' So I understood the opening sentence of the relevant section in the Portuguese text-book which the theatre orderly held up before my face.

'The baby is dead,' I heard the nurse say as she placed a towel over the lifeless little body. 'It did not breathe.'

I didn't have time to think about that; I was trying to save the mother. I sucked and swabbed the blood from her belly, restoring the bowel to its proper place. Then I repaired the uterine tear, cobbling it together with quick stitches, and closed the abdomen. The whole procedure had taken less than thirty minutes, but the woman's tongue was blue and her blood pressure was very low. With an oxygen mask we hurried her back to the ward – there were no intensive care facilities in the hospital, not even a cardiac monitor – and began a desperate resuscitation.

Without a blood transfusion our treatment options were limited. We raised the foot of her bed so that the blood in her legs would contribute to her circulating volume, and squeezed Haemaccel into her veins. The woman's tongue became a little pinker, but her gums remained almost white. Through a second intravenous line we added antibiotics to combat the sepsis that was compounding her shock. Then we sat and watched at the bedside, checking her blood pressure every few minutes. Ominously, the catheter in her bladder drained no urine; her kidneys had shut down, and slowly the pulses in her limbs dwindled and became impalpable as her heart output dropped. We tried a last-ditch infusion of adrenalin, the only cardiac stimulant we had. At 7 a.m. she ceased to live.

That was the time the aircraft was due, bringing the film crew from the capital. I sprinted down the hill to Suleiman's garage and hammered on the compound gate. His driver emerged, sleepy-eyed and smiling, his cheeks bulging with porridge. He was ready, he said, but the Land Rover was not – it had a puncture – and instead a fine truck was at my disposal. He pointed at an old blue Hanomag with a missing windshield. I watched him bolt down the last of his breakfast, my stomach growling. We swung out into the street as the plane passed overhead, wheels down, on its approach. Goats scattered before our blaring horn. We reached the landing strip in twenty minutes. There, outside the airport shed, stood the director and her crew of three with their equipment. The morning was already hot, and she was steaming.

'What is this pile of junk?' she demanded, glaring at the truck, 'and why are you late? You've had days to plan for our arrival and you still can't make it on time. We've been up since four, and I don't appreciate being kept waiting in the sun.'

I kept silent as I handed the director up into the cab. The film-crew, winking, helped me lift tripod, lens-case, sound recorder and provisions into the open bed of the truck and we set off for the port, the driver easing his vehicle delicately along the road. I was relieved to see the motorboat bobbing at the dockside. We piled ourselves and the equipment aboard. The director took her place beside the boatman in the stern, the mooring rope was cast off and we headed north, skirting the coastline of the placid bay. Beyond the shelter of the reef the boat began to rise and fall on the open sea. I felt annoyed by the rebuke I'd received, and a press of anger at the death of my patient and her baby. I decided to explain to the director the reasons for my late arrival. Moving to the stern, I gave her a graphic account of my last night's work. She appeared discomforted by the vessel's motion, and vomited moistly over the side. I sat back and tried to relax into the voyage. I didn't feel much better.

We were bound for an island about thirty miles to the north, a marine sanctuary whose isolation had allowed it mostly to escape the effects of the war. There were a few refugees from the mainland, but its natural resources – coral reefs, turtles, and a fresh-water lake full of crocodiles – made it a small beacon of conservation in a country otherwise so ransacked and degraded. The head ranger was a South African who had moved to Mozambique at independence. He had been imprisoned once by the government on trumped-up charges, and released through the direct intervention of the president. His research grant from a California university – augmented by revenue from hides and meat, from a crocodile farm which had been established at one end of the lake – kept the reserve alive, a project for which the hard-pressed government could spare no funds at all.

The dunes of the island rose gradually above the waves. By the time we'd reached the shallows and pulled the boat up on the sand below the lodge the director had recovered, but indicated by her demeanour that she had forgiven nothing. Even a cold beer under the thatch of the veranda did not cheer her, and I realized from her comments that she thought I'd made up the operation story. It took another small drama to redeem me. An open Land Rover came grinding up the beach, its engine bellowing. Nearly alongside us, it lurched and stalled. Its occupant, a young man in khaki shorts, did not get out.

'That's Grant, from the crocodile farm,' said the lodge manager. 'I wonder why he doesn't come in for a drink.'

'Come and help!' shouted his wife, who had gone out to the vehicle. 'He's been hurt!'

Grant looked very pale as he hung over the Land Rover's steering wheel. His left calf was shredded, and jellied blood coated the pedals and pooled in the floor-well. We lifted him out of his seat and carried him into the shade. He had been chasing a crocodile that escaped, he said faintly, and had grabbed its tail. Then, straddling the six-foot reptile, he'd yanked it backwards, intending to catch the snout as it passed between his legs. Instead it had caught him, taking a bite from his calf. After returning the croc to its pen, his workers – none of whom could drive – had placed him in the vehicle and he'd roared over here in first gear, unable to use the clutch.

I inspected the wound. There were deep gashes and a lump of missing meat. In the depths of the ragged hole an artery squirted. There appeared to be no nerve damage: Grant's toes and ankle wriggled to order. While my surgical kit soaked in disinfectant I injected the area around the wound with local anaesthetic, then trimmed away the ragged shreds of muscle. The bleeding point stopped with a catgut stitch, passed through the surrounding tissue and tied to compress the vessel. I brought together the muscle's sheath with a couple more of the dissolving sutures and used a silk one to align the skin edges roughly in the middle, leaving two big gaps for the underlying wound to discharge; I had never treated crocodile bites before, but if they were as contaminated as those caused by human teeth, infection was bound to follow. After dressing the wound, I gave him instructions for its care and a shot of penicillin. It was time for lunch. My beer had become warm. The director had mellowed too, and later during filming became extremely nice when I had to treat her for the excruciating pain of renal colic caused by the passage of a kidney stone.

For two days we enjoyed the island's peace while we interviewed the head ranger – he had direct knowledge of the extent of the elephant slaughter – and filmed conservation officers being trained for the task of rehabilitating the country's game reserves once the fighting was over. Then we returned to the mainland and the war. Beira had once been the choice destination of vacationing Rhodesians, who'd lounged on the beach, eaten seafood and visited the famed wildlife of the Gorongosa game reserve to the north. Now Gorongosa was a major rebel base and ivory hunting ground, and Beira's holiday charm had vanished. Freighters, beached by winter storms, rusted on the beaches. The town's taps were dry – Renamo had blown up the pumping station – and the only available water was a brackish, gritty soup that left a residue as unpleasant as the sweat that you were trying to bathe away. The collapse of the sanitation system left an effluvium of shit that filled the streets, unstirred by the sticky sea-breeze. The English film-crew were undaunted.

'Turned out nice again,' they'd quip each morning as we stepped out into the heat for another day's filming.

We interviewed officials and ivory dealers who could give us information about the trade in tusks. Our filming took us to Dondo, about fifteen miles to the west. Dust-storms wandered through the streets, whirlwind pillars of furnace-heat that plucked garbage off the ground and rattled the roofs before abruptly extinguishing themselves. The railway sidings were a scrapyard of damaged rolling stock that had been hit in Renamo attacks. Nearby lay camps of *deslocados*. The hills for miles were bare, every twig stripped to feed the cooking fires. Cholera was endemic in the camps. In a tent clinic mothers sat on the floor with their hollow-cheeked children while nurses placed intravenous drips in tiny scalp-veins. Dondo was a sort of front line, inasmuch as one could be said to exist in this hit-and-run war. After dark, government mortar positions to the north of the town sent desultory shells into the bush to discourage the approach of rebel bands. Dry lightning flared on the horizon, mocking their efforts. It should have been the height of the rainy season.

✪

But in Maputo, when we got back, the weather was changing. A bruised sky hung over the city, cleaved by crackling branches of light that arced to the horizon. With the thunder came the rain; pitting the dust, reviving lost colours in the bleached plaster of the buildings and rebounding off the gleaming gun-metal streets. Through lightning-static the radio reported progress at the ceasefire talks in Rome. A group of Renamo officials had moved into the Italian club along Maputo beach, accompanied by international advisers. The facilitators of the ceasefire negotiations – the South African president, the American Secretary of State, the Vatican – could hardly be seen as disinterested parties, for South Africa and the US had helped Renamo militarily, while right-wing Catholic groups had given it support.

But Renamo's backers were now having difficulty convincing Dhlakama, the rebel leader, that peace was necessary. He skulked in his Rome hotel, objecting to clause after clause in the agreement. The latest issue was the area of territory recognized as being controlled by each side. Renamo claimed eighty per cent of the country-side – this being the area crossed by their marauding bands – but held no towns; formed as a force of vandals and destroyers without a political agenda, they lacked the administrative skills to run a sweet-shop. While their negotiators stalled, Renamo launched offensives to try to capture district and provincial capitals. Frelimo found money to pay the government troops and airlifted them to the pressure-points to hold back the attacks.

Eventually the ceasefire was signed, but attacks and

counterattacks continued: the dying war still had a few synaptic twitches in its limbs. One area that remained dangerous was a region on the coast to the south of the capital that had once been the famed Maputo Elephant Park. In its prime it had supported about ten thousand elephant, but like Gorongosa Park in central Mozambique, the game reserve's wilderness had become the site of a major rebel base. The elephants had been hunted almost to extinction. Recently, though, twenty-six surviving animals had been reported in the coastal forests of the Maputo park. We went to see if we could find them.

For this we needed Balzac and a pair of his Casspirs, for the trip would take us right into the badlands. I met him at his usual haunt – the bar at the Cardoza – along with a couple of his sidekicks. Spider, Balzac's ex-sergeant, was a neckless crop-head whom, Balzac assured me, was steady under fire. Spider glowered. Also present was Micky, a Portuguese settler of angry temperament who'd been in trouble with the Frelimo government for pro-Renamo sympathies. He owned a struggling farm south of the city and knew the area towards the elephant park. Micky did not attribute the failure of Mozambican agriculture to economic destabilization by South Africa, but rather 'to the way the blacks have fucked up this beautiful country'. He would, he said, bring along an extra weapon for me to 'have a shot at the gooks'. I declined, and he looked at me oddly, as though unsure whether I was truly white.

We set off the next morning while it was still dark, the Casspirs' exhausts echoing off the shuttered shop-fronts. The director and Micky rode ahead with Balzac, while the film-crew and I followed in the second vehicle driven by the surly Spider. The *escorta* seemed relaxed, sitting up on the armoured coping in silhouette against the dawn's glow on the horizon. Our first stop was Micky's farm, and he bellowed at the labourers because a tractor tyre was flat. He raised his fist to administer a beating, the cameraman sighted through his Arriflex, and Micky stumped off into the farmhouse to scream up some coffee. Then we continued along the road, which deteriorated with every mile. By now the *escorta*'s weapons were cocked and loaded, their assault rifles and machine-guns sticking through the gunports.

The last government-held outpost at Changalane was a ridge astride the road, zigzagged with trenches and backed up by a pair of battered tanks. The commander at the roadblock wanted to know where we were headed, and one of Balzac's *escorta* soldiers kept up a cheerful chatter from the front turret as the armoured vehicles idled forward in low gear, until the men on the ground pulled aside the barrier of petrol drums to prevent them being crushed. They had been trying to extract a tribute – in cash – to let us pass, for they had not been paid for months, and sustained themselves through tolls extracted from the infrequent travellers.

Beyond that point the road was overgrown; abandoned farms and ruined agricultural projects lay by the roadside. The soldiers, tense at their weapons, let out a shout – '*bandido*!' – a rifle-carrying man had appeared on the edge of the track behind us, and now watched us out of sight. Hours of rough driving followed. We slowed often to circumvent deep trenches dug across the road by the rebels. Recent rain had thickened the bush and the green shadows seemed dark with menace. Eventually, the ruins of a gate-lodge and a gunshot-riddled sign indicated the park's boundary. With us was a warden who had worked in the park before its loss. He guided us along the wheel-tracks, barely discernible, between small hills that led to the Futi river. There were fresh prints in the mud of the bank but not an elephant in sight; the warden told us that he thought the gun-shy animals would stay well clear of any human presence. A freshwater lake shimmered in the distance; beyond it a bluff of dunes marked the sea. Apart from birds, we saw no living things at all.

We reached the Wildlife Service's offices and field school, where rangers had once been trained. Charred rafters stood above smoke-stained walls. Our escort kept watch from the top of the Casspirs while we poked around in the rubble. The long grass near the collapsed garages yielded a human skull and an AK47 magazine; the rounds inside it had exploded, so that the steel casing was ruptured into jagged petals. Balzac turned the items in his hands and began to speak.

'I was in a contact once,' he said, 'in the bush in Ovamboland. Bullets were flying around, you couldn't tell where from. Suddenly I saw this guy running across my front and snapped a shot at him. I hit the clips that he was carrying in his ammo pouches and they went off like a chain-reaction. Maybe he was carrying spirits in his pack, because next thing he's turned into this big yellow flame, still running. Then he fell over and carried on burning.'

'What did you do?' I asked him. 'Did you shoot him dead to stop him suffering?'

Balzac frowned. 'You know, doc, I can't remember.'

Much of what the man had done was horrifying – some years later he would apply for amnesty to the South African Truth and Reconciliation Commission, for his alleged role in the murder of some young black activists in the eastern Cape – but that day he saved our lives. I was riding in the front vehicle as we returned from the Elephant Park. The sun was low behind the trees and shadows barred the dirt track. We were at risk of violating that most basic rule of conflict zones – never be on the roads after dark – and the Casspirs bucked over the ditches without stopping. We roared along the track past a long-ruined agricultural college, near where we had seen the rebel gunman that morning. On a bend, a peasant couple in rags scrambled from our path onto the overgrown verge. Balzac waved at them through the armoured glass. The man raised a hesitant arm. The woman, with a look of fear, dropped her bundle of firewood and clapped her hands to her ears. Immediately Balzac wrestled the heavy wheel to one side. The Casspir jumped the roadside bank with a clang and crashed through a grove of saplings that bordered the track, the steel bumper bulldozing them flat. Thirty yards further we swerved abruptly and were back on the roadway, accelerating northwards through a pall of dust. Behind us I saw the second Casspir leap like a buffalo as it completed the same manoeuvre.

I rubbed my head where I had struck it against the bulkhead.

'What the fuck was that about?' I asked Balzac.

'Landmine in the road,' he said. 'When the old lady blocked her ears I knew she expected a bang. I looked ahead and because the sun was low I could see that the tracks we'd made this morning had been dug up and then smoothed over. They knew we were coming back this way. They would have put in something big – maybe a double anti-tank mine – that would have turned us all to fishpaste.'

⊕

Micky proved true to his political affiliations by helping us get access to the Renamo delegation at the Italian club. It was a charming place, set among a grove of palms beside the beach with a pleasant bar, thatch-roofed and half-enclosed, whose tables looked over an outdoor dance floor. This was the gathering-place of the city's gay community, all pomaded hair and gold earrings and tight, tight pants. The club also hid among its discrete bungalows the office of the Renamo delegation. Their bodyguards sat all day in an anteroom, watching television. They were simple bus-ambushers, apparently forbidden to go into the city in case they behaved in a way that might bring discredit upon their organization. An inner office contained the Renamo representative – a bland-featured lump of a man in an Italian suit – who had the power to issue the vital *credençial* that would allow one to be received by Dhlakama, now returned to his Gorongosa headquarters.

We wanted to ask the rebel leader his opinion of the evidence we'd gathered for our film: captured Renamo documents detailing ivory prices per kilogram and its exchange-rate for weapons; news footage shot after the government assault on a rebel base showing guns and piles of tusks; and most damning of all, the testimony of a senior South African Special Forces officer who had trained Renamo guerrillas and described how arms were supplied to them in exchange for ivory in a large-scale operation run by Military Intelligence. And we wanted to see the man himself – head of a force blamed for half a million deaths and four and a half million displaced, for mutilation and destruction – who now claimed to represent democracy for the Mozambican people.

There was only one way in to Renamo headquarters: on the food-aid flights that were due to start supplying civilians in the area following the end of fighting. We managed to find transport on the first plane in, an Antonov loaded with American corn and EU cooking oil supplied by the Red Cross. In the din of the engines, we perched on the food sacks that filled the hold. Sunlight, shafting in through portholes, lit floating motes of corn dust in the air. The empty khaki land passed below, a skein of dry river beds and abandoned villages. With a thump and a rumble we touched down on the dirt landing strip at Renamo's Gorongosa base, originally built to allow the landing of South African military supply flights. The Russian pilot taxied to the end of the runway and turned his aircraft, while the engineer engaged the mechanism of the rear loading-ramp.

It lowered to reveal a sea of faces. Thousands stood behind the plane, dressed in rags or bits of hide. Dark skin showed through the rents in their garments. The women all wore brassieres – stitched from bits of parachute cloth, or occasionally, second-hand pink lingerie with stiff breast-cones – a moral improvement enforced by Renamo's evangelist backers. The people were silent, their eyes unblinking in the propellers' dust-storm as they peered up into the gloom of the aircraft's hold from which the food would come. Behind them smoke rose amidst the thorn-trees from a hundred cooking-fires, started in the expectation of a meal.

We watched the unloading begin. A line of men jogged to the ramp. Each received a maize-sack on his shoulders and ran to lay it down, directed by young Renamo gunmen with pistols in their waistbands. Children dodged the guards and dived for single kernels in the dust, which they stuffed into their mouths while the soldiers whipped them back with sticks. A speck of dust at the far end of the runway resolved into a uniformed motorcyclist, who rode up to inspect us. A protocol officer and a couple of aides in snappy 'Viva Dhlakama!' T-shirts arrived on similar machines, and soon we were each perched on a pillion, clutching our film equipment as we swerved down narrow bush trails to the pair of grass huts that formed the Renamo nerve-centre. One contained a radio operator. We were requested to rest in the other, furnished with reed beds; the 'Doctor President' was on his way down from the mountain to see us. After a couple of hours we were led through to a clearing among the trees, swept smooth around a thatched shelter. Sitting in an armchair was the Renamo leader himself.

Dhlakama was a small man, with an open, engaging face and a disarmingly pleasant manner. While the camera crew made ready he asked the director and I to sit, and enquired courteously after our health. He looked quite dapper in his freshly pressed, tailored camouflage uniform. There was no sign of the large crucifix he was described by his American evangelist supporters as always wearing. Instead, his shoulders were adorned by large red epaulettes. Each carried the four stars of a general, three crossed arrows – a Spanish fascist symbol that also acknowledged the *flechas*, the notorious Portuguese colonial police from which many of Renamo's core had been recruited – and a lovingly embroidered guinea-fowl. This latter detail was reportedly the work of the wife of the Professor of Foreign and Comparative Law at UNISA, the University of South Africa, where Dhlakama had obtained his PhD. The Professor himself was thought to be the author of 'The Renamo Constitution' – glossy copies were distributed to us by one of the President Doctor's aides – a document that, I noticed, prohibited 'torture and other cruel or inhumane punishments'.

The director asked Dhlakama about the widespread atrocities attributed to his soldiers, mentioning that she had seen some of the mutilated victims in hospital. He looked immensely sad. 'Frelimo prepared all these people,' he said, 'put all these people in beds so they could say to the journalists: look at the atrocities committed by Renamo.' By now the camera was running, and he warmed to his task. 'It was easy for Frelimo to say to someone in the hospital: look, today some journalists are coming and you have to say that Renamo violated you; attacked you; set you on fire; even ate your children.'

The director quoted from a US State Department report in which Renamo was described as waging 'a systematic and brutal war of terror against innocent civilians . . . beatings, rape, looting, burning of villages, abductions . . . one of the most brutal holocausts against ordinary human beings since World War Two'. Beret straight and hands square on his thighs, Dhlakama spoke at length, despatching each allegation as proof of the disinformation campaign waged against him. On the matter of Renamo's use of child soldiers, for instance: 'It is Frelimo that recruited these children. Whenever a journalist arrives in Maputo the first thing that Frelimo does is to present a crowd of these children and these children say that they were soldiers . . .' He made his voice quaver like a whining infant. 'My mother is dead, Renamo gave me a gun, Renamo made me fight.' Dhlakama laughed. 'It didn't happen and there are witnesses to prove that.'

But the questions about ivory poaching made him sad again. The death of elephants was a tragedy he felt keenly, for Renamo was, in fact, a movement dedicated to wildlife conservation. 'Our soldiers were instructed during the war not to kill animals, not only elephants but even trees,' he announced; the claims of ivory found in Renamo bases were a complete fabrication. All the elephants had been killed by Zimbabwean and government troops because 'Frelimo knows that in the world there are certain human rights organizations that defend the environment, and so they did this as another way of destroying Renamo's reputation worldwide.'

I had often wondered what it would be like to meet one of the real architects of pain: not just a perpetrator of individual acts, but someone responsible for large-scale policies of brutality, someone whose works had added substantially to the sum of suffering in the world. And now I saw such a man, and he was impervious. After seizing the leadership of Renamo ten years before – during a night-time bloodbath in Renamo's South African base-camp that ended with all the rival contenders dead – Dhlakama was unlikely to be short on self-confidence. 'Victory is certain,' he said, quoting Renamo's official slogan. 'This will be testified at the end of the war by the people's vote, because I know that my party is going to win.'

Climbing astride his command-machine, Dhlakama set off at a regal pace to the airfield to show us how he moved among his people. We overtook him on the rest of the motorcycles, set up the camera, and filmed as he arrived and dismounted. A crowd surged about the ramp of the aircraft, that had since returned with a second load. The people seemed not to notice him until the Renamo soldiery began a rhythmic clapping. Dhlakama approached the sacks piled beside the runway and the crowd followed, streaming like an avid tide. He climbed the precious mound of aid and began to speak.

'I have brought this food for you, my people,' he announced. 'I have brought the international press to see your suffering. *Viva* Renamo!'

'*VIVA!*' came the attentive reply. Dhlakama beamed. Clearly this man had presidential potential after all.

✪

Editing the film was difficult. We had a story of *confusão*, in a ruined country whose prime natural resource – ivory – was being plundered by many individuals. Only Renamo, though, had the orders and the export route via South Africa to loot it systematically, and there was clear evidence that that was what they'd done. They'd done a lot more – all well documented, some of it much nastier – but the commissioning editor stuck to his principles: no human interest crap. He was annoyed that we didn't have the footage he'd demanded of running elephants, the slow-motion strike of bullets, blood on the long grass. He fired the director and brought in a friend who knew good film library sources, if not the story. Using images of the animals in their death-throes, this man conjured up a powerful documentary. I watched the film on broadcast night in a London living room. The audience included a number of acquaintances – thoughtful, committed people –

who worked for a high-profile global environmental organization.

'Such suffering, such slaughter,' said a woman sitting beside me. 'It's sickening. More must be done to protect the elephant.'

10

Transit Lounges

'Flying Doctors Wanted' read the banner advert. 'Doctors with broad range of medical experience required for remunerative work as aeromedical physicians.'

I had been studying, with a sense of despondency, the list of posts for surgical senior registrars in a medical journal when I'd stumbled on this gem in the 'miscellaneous' section at the back. Serious doctors regarded the section as somehow sinful; the jobs it offered – medical officer in the Solomon Islands, doctor on an ethnographic expedition to Papua New Guinea – as siren voices luring them away from stability. Such advertisements would be scanned furtively, or read out in hospital common rooms in tones of salacious envy. The medical journal even published a disclaimer – 'Warning: these posts are not recognized or accredited for training purposes' – in order to distance itself from responsibility for any life-altering consequences that might arise. My resolve to return to full-time hospital surgery was less than entire; I recalled that at one time when I was a medical student, I'd thought being a flying doctor was the most fulfilling work to which I could aspire.

⊕

During our second year of clinical training, my friend David and I had used one of our rare breaks to visit the Kingdom of Lesotho. Surrounded by South Africa, this small country had never been colonized; its rugged highlands were guarded both by the sheer escarpment of the Drakensberg range to the south and by the combativeness of the Sotho, who sniped at invading Boer commandos from high caves. The British, who'd fared no better at trying to subdue the place, nominated it a 'protectorate' and readily granted independence in 1966. Anglican missionaries had given Lesotho the highest literacy rate in Africa, as well as the foundations of a medical service. Among its stone-pillared, tin-roofed buildings, the capital Maseru now boasted a casino – patronized by whites from South Africa, where gambling was banned – and a general hospital, named after the English monarch and called Queen Two for short.

The kingdom's rugged interior still preserved its isolation. No roads served the villages huddled on the shoulders of precipitous valleys. The men, wrapped in blankets against the cold, herded their cattle from the backs of shaggy Basuthu ponies. They also provided the country's chief export, labour: every year, tens of thousands left the high mountains for the mine compounds around Johannesburg, to dig for gold in the deepest underground galleries in the world. In acknowledgement of the revenue they sent back, the Lesotho government provided a flying doctor service, supplying medical care to the men's home villages. Runways had been cleared by hand on hillsides or edges of riverbeds, and pairs of rondavels – circular, thatch-roofed huts – constructed as a clinic. These were served a couple of times a week by single-engined aircraft that would land a doctor and nurse in the morning and return to the airstrip before dusk to pick them up. My father worked sometimes as a visiting orthopaedic surgeon at the Maseru hospital, and his contacts in the country's health service served as an introduction. David and I were invited to join the Lesotho Flying Doctor Service as temporary assistants.

I remembered our first take-off, the aircraft climbing out of the grey pre-dawn light still pooled in the valley that enclosed the capital, and the rich rays of sun flooding the cockpit as we cleared the ridge. We headed south, over jumbled peaks separated by chasms of shadow, while the Australian pilot – in shorts despite the cold – flicked the dials of unresponsive instruments with his finger. David and the pilot were talking, but I could hear nothing above the engine's rattle. Beside me, in the cockpit's fourth place – where the other rear seat had been replaced by a stretcher that extended back into the fuselage – dozed a young woman doctor from New Zealand. The small plane rocked, the note of the engine seeming to falter as we dropped into a pocket of cold air and skirted a craggy buttress. The aircraft began to vibrate as the throttle was opened.

The mountain range ahead was split by a narrow groove. I watched it approach through the shimmering disc of the propeller. The cleft came nearer, and I could see the spiky outlines of aloes growing along its edge. The sides appeared much too close to permit the plane to pass. The pilot was pointing something out to David; a dark scar high on the cliff-side. David glanced back at me, a shaky smile on his face, demonstrating with his hands an aircraft striking the rock. I gestured forward urgently to where the walls were closing in on our wingtips. With a lurch that glued me to the cockpit-side, the pilot flipped the plane through a quarter-roll. We skimmed vertically through the narrow slot, shooting out of the cliff-face and over a sudden gulf of space.

The nose dropped, pointing down a valley cut through slabs of stone. The aircraft swooped over switch-back river bends. From a cup halfway up the flank of the opposite mountainside plunged the fine line of a waterfall. Now the pilot pulled back the stick and we swooped upwards and over its lip, and continued climbing above steeply-rising steps of grassland. Our speed was falling, despite the full-throttle bellow of the engine. The stall alarm began to shriek. Above the nose I could see only sky. For an instant the shuddering aircraft seemed to stand still. Then it dropped, precisely, onto the end of an airstrip that ran up to the brow of the ridge, and taxied to a stop. The New Zealand doctor woke up. 'Looks like a busy day,' she said. A crowd of umbrellas clustered about the plane, their shadows black in the sharp sunlight. More figures were approaching along a skein of paths that converged at the whitewashed walls of the rondavels. A man in a white coat stood beside the door of the nearer hut.

The pilot took off down-hill, his aircraft diving out of sight off the runway's edge and reappearing half a minute later to climb like a distant fly against the far wall of the valley. Around the rondavels, blanket-swathed women sat with their children in orderly lines. They had come a long way for treatment: the nearest village served by the clinic was two hours away, the farthest, a day's walk. With around a hundred patients to be seen before the plane returned, each consultation had to be brief. The white-coated nurse, who lived in a local village, introduced each case with a short history. The doctor performed a brisk examination and prescribed treatment, to be doled out by the nurse from the tin-trunk dispensary. David and I received a crash-course in mountain pathology: elderly women in mild cardiac failure who had walked from miles away on swollen legs; babies with pneumonia; and the commonest condition of all: venereal diseases, brought to the village communities by men returning for their annual visits from the gold-fields.

Despite the ubiquitousness of this malady, the wives and girlfriends of miners wore with pride the bright Perspex wristbands that were issued to their men as ID bracelets. David and I were installed in the other hut with a tray of syringes and a supply of penicillin, and a steadily lengthening list of patients. Even after the plane had returned and left again without us – wings catching the setting sun as it climbed out of the valley, its places filled to capacity with the doctor, a woman in incipient diabetic coma and a youth with acute appendicitis – David and I carried on, injecting antibiotics into the backsides that were paraded before us in the yellow light of a paraffin lamp. A group of coquettes invited us back to their village for a 'party': faced with a three-hour walk and the inhibiting knowledge of their venereal afflictions, we declined, and watched them file, laughing, out of sight towards the peaks silhouetted against the sky's last light. After showing us the contents of a second tin trunk – blankets and tinned food – and pointing out a stack of firewood under the hut's eaves, the nurse mounted his horse and was gone into the darkness. Our fire flickered in the night wind. It was very quiet in the mountains.

The next day was much the same. Another hundred patients confronted us when we awoke, stiff from the cold. The nurse rode up, followed shortly by the hum of the approaching aircraft. It landed with a thump and trundled up the slope towards us. The doctor stepped, stretching, from the cockpit and soon we were busy again. Every now and then she would call us to witness some pathology – the case of a youth, for instance, brought by his parents because he was 'hearing noises in his head'; despite the doctor's preliminary diagnosis of schizophrenia, these turned out to arise from a large cattle-tick that was suckled onto the edge of the young man's ear-drum, against which its tiny legs flexed in blood-satiated bliss – or to hold the heads of squirming patients while the doctor applied dental forceps and pulled their rotten teeth without the balm of local anaesthetic.

Over the following weeks we worked at a number of other airstrip clinics. Sometimes all the places in the plane would be taken by patients, or a gusting evening wind would prevent the pilot landing to collect us, and he'd circle overhead, waggling his wings before setting course for home. David and I never saw him disappear over the dusk-blurred peaks without a sense of excitement at spending another night in the mountains; it was, I believe, the first time that we had realized the full potential of our medical studies to enrich our lives.

⊕

The aeromedical physician work now being advertised in my medical journal was quite different. Instead of being carried in light aircraft to remote landing strips, my new conveyance was usually the economy section of a passenger jet; my patients, tourists who had become unwell on holiday. Their travel insurance covered the cost of emergency treatment, hospital admission if indicated, and – the first imperative of the underwriters – the quickest possible transfer back to the United Kingdom and the free ministrations of the National Health Service. It is a requirement of the airlines that passengers who have suffered certain medical problems – heart attacks, severe infections, strokes, some fractures – have to be accompanied by a doctor if they travel by air within a certain period after the incident. This was my job. To all but the seriously ill patients I was no more than a glorified flight attendant: looking for stray luggage, pushing wheelchairs through the aisles of Duty Free, reassuring accompanying family and seeing that my charge was comfortable for the trip home.

Most of the aeromedical assistance companies operated out of offices in the bleak tower-blocks of Croydon, that undistinguished area of south London colonized by carpet warehouses and used-car dealers and the headquarter-hives of government bureaucracies. My work-pattern soon became established. In the evening my telephone would ring. The company medical officer would give me a synopsis of the patient's condition and whereabouts – Atlanta, Buenos Aires, Wellington or Zagreb – and an operations manager would fax over a flight-plan. At 4 a.m. there'd be a driver at my door to race me through the city's empty streets to the company offices. There I would greet the night-staff amid the multilingual babble of the telephones and the telex's clatter; bolt a cup of coffee while I checked my equipment boxes and saw that the cardiac defibrillator's battery was fully charged, and arm-over-arm through yards of fax paper to find the patient's latest medical data. At the airport I'd allow my orange emergency medical pack and the red cross on the resuscitation box to waft me to the front of the queue, board the plane and go at once to sleep.

At the other end I would grab a taxi to the hospital to meet the patient – usually installed in a private room – to be greeted like a saviour come to deliver them from incomprehensible medical machinations and disturbingly tasty hospital food. I'd receive a status report from the attending doctor and establish that my charge was fit to travel. Then I would find my way to my pre-booked hotel and notify the London office that all was in order, or inform them of any complicating factors. Thereafter my time was usually my own until the repatriation flight the next morning. There was a peculiar intensity to these brief visits. Some places would be resort towns and I'd head for the beach and swim, or stroll the promenade among the throngs of holiday-makers. Others were great cities full of famous attractions, but my explorations would usually be circumscribed by how far I felt like walking. I'd be content to find an idiosyncratic quarter where I'd sit in a bar or on a café terrace and read or sketch, then walk again until drawn by the light from the door of some restaurant.

In the morning I would be back at the hospital to accompany my patient on the ambulance ride to the airport.

This could be an event of great theatricality. Having loaded us into the rear of the vehicle, the crew would grind out cigarettes and take their seats like bomber pilots. Siren and flashing lights engaged, the ambulance would launch itself headlong into the traffic, missing pedestrians by inches, swerving into the oncoming lane at every opportunity, and throwing great crops of palpitations onto the heart monitor connected up to my hitherto stable patient. Keeping up their momentum, the crew would browbeat their way through airport security and onto the runway, where they'd weave among the tenders to pull up with a dying wail of sirens and a screech of brakes beside the parked aircraft. Even patients well able to walk would be enjoined to stay aboard the stretcher, which would be manhandled with much dramatic grunting up the gangway. Once aboard, face frozen with embarrassment under the gaze of a plane-load of passengers, the invalid would be seated by the kindly cabin crew while I stowed my – hopefully superfluous – boxes of resuscitation equipment and sat down alongside.

Only at this point could my charge relax, and confide to me the joy of going home to the staid certainties of a bed in a British hospital. I never told them so, but often the facilities in the centres where they'd been treated were better-equipped and more modern than those they were returning to; eviscerated by opportunist politicians, the National Health Service had continued to decline. The ratio of doctors per head of population in the UK, even the quality of care for common conditions, was worse than almost everywhere else in Europe; survival rates from heart attacks – my patients' usual affliction – were lower than those in Poland or Mexico. Once back in Britain (sometimes after an additional flight from London to a secondary airport, and then another ambulance-ride) I would deliver them to their local hospital, where they would wait on a trolley in an overcrowded casualty department until a bed was found for them on a public ward. I would hand the patient over to a harried doctor and say goodbye, wishing them a speedy recovery. A couple of times a grateful relative even tried to push a twenty-pound note into my hand 'for my troubles'.

I didn't need any extra money. In fact flying-doctoring paid better that any medical work I'd ever done before, especially during the holiday season when there was so much demand that I made flights back-to-back, returning to find the message indicator winking on my telephone with news of the next assignment. I had already managed to pay back most of the debts incurred during my itinerant past. And the work was becoming more interesting. Some medical repatriations could not be carried on regular passenger flights. These were the serious stretcher cases that required a specialized air-ambulance: a twin-engined aircraft with a fully pressurized cabin, monitoring and resuscitation equipment and enough space for myself and a nurse to work at the patient's bedside throughout the flight. The planes operated from country air-fields to the south of London: a control tower, from the days when the place had been a wartime fighter base, a couple of hangars, and a small Customs post.

These flights did not include leisurely hotel stays. With an hour's notice a car would rush me to the airfield. Usually we took off after dark, climbing over the Channel through strata of air traffic whose wingtip-lights flashed beyond the cabin portholes. Once at cruising height the engine note would soften and the co-pilot come back from the cockpit with a stack of faxes: the medical records for the case we were going to collect. After the nurse and I had checked the equipment I'd read the medical notes in the yellow pool of light from a bulkhead lamp while dining on coffee and sandwiches from the small galley. Now and then one of the pilots would send back a radioed update on the patient's condition or a weather report.

We were always cleared to land at once, ahead of other aircraft – mercy flights had priority – and taxied behind the ground control truck to a corner of the airfield where the ambulance waited, its red beacon flashing. The co-pilot would crack the door seal and I'd walk down the steps, slightly deafened from the long roar of the engines that had now clicked to silence, towards the pool of light spilling from the windows of the ambulance and through the open doors at the rear. The doctor would be inside, his hand-over brisk; here were the fluid balance charts, the drug records and X-rays. Quickly we'd co-ordinate the patient's transfer to the aircraft – stretcher up the steps, the reconnection of his oxygen supply – together we would note the cardiac monitor's steady scroll. Then the doctor would be gone, with a handshake and a last instruction: 'Watch his airway. Good luck.'

As the door closed and the engines began their rising howl to take-off I would already be engrossed: measuring blood pressure, regulating the drip, checking cerebral responsiveness through a pupil's flicker in the beam of my penlight torch. All through the return flight the nurse and I would work together, sharing our observations and recording them on the patient's chart, and checking the settings – if assisted respiration was required – of the steadily sighing ventilator. At cruising altitude one of the pilots would come back to the cabin and enquire about the condition of our passenger. Wrapped in our respective roles, there was little conversation; just a feeling of quiet cohesion among the team, isolated high above the earth on this homeward journey.

Often the patients were young, victims of an urge for risk that had culminated in the motorcycle accident or hang-gliding fall or bar-fight that had smashed them up. I would sit beside the stretcher, watching their faces in the dim glow of the cabin lights and wondering who would bring me home if I was ever hurt in the course of my work: travel insurance policies didn't cover injuries incurred in war zones. But then the next blood pressure check or injection of medication into the drip line would take up my attention, and banish the thought from my mind.

⊕

Air ambulances, because of their speed and fuel capacity, were only suitable for trips of short to medium length. Long-haul repatriations of serious cases depended on scheduled passenger flights, using a stretcher fixed along the rear-most seat-rows in the tail of a Jumbo jet. Although this corner could be curtained off, it was seldom peaceful: on long flights via Los Angeles to the Antipodes, for instance, which could take twenty-four hours or more, the tail area became a sort of informal gathering-place. The party-types, the drinkers and smokers, even resting cabin crew, jaded and jet-lagged, would congregate there through the extended darkness of the westward-flying night. This circus could be diverting – I'd have little chance to rest anyway if I was tending to a seriously ill patient – but it could also be distracting during a demanding medical repatriation.

I was escorting a man back to Tasmania. He had been working in London when he'd developed weight loss and abdominal pain, and was admitted to hospital. Investigations revealed that he was suffering from a virulent form of leukaemia. The cytotoxic drugs given to suppress the production of malignant white blood cells had also affected his body's immune response, laying him open to secondary infections – bacterial and fungal – while a deficiency of platelets from his malfunctioning, cancerous bone-marrow meant that he was prone to gastrointestinal bleeding. His condition had been stabilized with difficulty, and now a race was on to get him home to his family before he died.

I was travelling with a nurse, and the man's precarious state meant that neither of us would have much rest. His blood pressure, fluid intake and urine output had to be monitored closely. Pressure sores would develop unless he was helped to change position at regular intervals throughout the long flight. Medication had to be given frequently, both by mouth and intravenously: two anti-fungal drugs, four antibiotics, three cytotoxic agents, gastric acid suppressants to stop his stomach bleeding and diuretics to rid his body of excess fluid that threatened to flood his lungs. Pain-killers and anti-nausea medication were also required. Besides my usual drug-kit and resuscitation box, I also carried a cool-bag containing twenty-four packs of concentrated human platelets to maintain his blood's ability to clot; one to be infused each hour through his drip line.

Shortly after we had taken off our patient had a bout of diarrhoea, a side-effect of his medication. Then the cardiac monitor started showing bursts of rapid heart beats. Dealing with these developments, alongside the regular observations and injections, required our full attention, and our world had contracted to the small lighted space enclosed within the drawn curtains: the soft-spoken, quietly suffering man on the stretcher, the drip bottles hanging above him and the catheter bag below. The main cabin was in darkness following the in-flight movie, and most people were asleep. A murmur of voices came from the tail-section where the insomniacs were gathered. I had little idea how long we had been in the air when the first extraneous problem began. There came a thud and a cry, and an agitated stewardess stuck her head through the screen, asking urgently for my assistance.

A man had been standing down the aisle, sharing his bottle of duty-free brandy with some new acquaintances. The stewardess dragged me over to where he now lay on the deck, apparently in the midst of a full-blown seizure. Placing a life-jacket under his jerking head and recruiting his drinking partners to prevent him injuring himself as he threshed about, I searched rapidly through the man's pockets. There was no tell-tale bottle of anti-convulsant medication, nor did his wallet or a wrist-bracelet carry any indication that he was an epileptic. I called the nurse to bring over our drug kit, found an ampoule of Valium and injected it gradually into an arm vein. The man's fit slowed and stopped and he began to breathe deep and rhythmically, a fine line of blood at the corner of his mouth trickling from his bitten tongue. A crew member helped me place him safely on his side in a position that would keep his airway open, and offered to watch over him. I returned to the interrupted care of my patient.

A short while later the stewardess was back. A client in business class had complained about the noise, which had caused her to wake with a start. Since then she'd been having chest pain, and demanded a doctor: it would be greatly appreciated if I would come and take a look at her. I found the passenger – a large woman, travelling alone – leaning forward in her seat, her face contorted by fear and pain. Her hands were pressed to her sternum; it felt, she said, as though something was crushing her heart. I felt her rapid pulse, noting the sheen of sweat on her face. Suddenly she began to retch, and I had just enough time to open a sick-bag under her mouth before she filled it with regurgitated business class cuisine. While the cabin attendant went to get my drug kit I laid the woman on a row of seats, propping some cushions behind her for comfort and others under her knees to raise her legs a little and reduce the workload on her heart. Then, from the orange pack that contained my emergency drugs, I took a tube of glyceryl-trinitrate spray and squirted a dose of it under her tongue. Within a few seconds the pain was fading, and her rapid breathing had slowed to a more normal rate.

The stewardess shared the woman's relief, but I did not: her response to the spray – which dilates the coronary arteries supplying the cardiac muscle – suggested strongly that she was having a heart attack. I persuaded the woman to swallow half an aspirin – its clot-dissolving properties could prevent thrombosis further blocking the coronary arteries – and to don an oxygen mask. She objected strongly, insisting that she was fully recovered: I had to use that old lie – 'I know you probably don't need it, but it's for the doctor's peace of mind' – to get her to keep it on. Then I excused myself to confer with the senior cabin attendant, the aircraft's purser.

Out of the woman's hearing I explained that she needed to be hospitalized urgently; the plane should be re-routed if necessary to get her on the ground as soon as possible. The purser went to talk to the captain and returned with the news that we would be landing at Los Angeles in under thirty minutes; we had already begun our descent, and any diversion at this stage would not significantly reduce our time to landing. I requested that a message be radioed ahead for an ambulance to meet the flight, and proposed that the apparent epileptic be disembarked as well. In view of my own patient's fragile condition, I could not undertake the additional responsibility of attending to him if he had further fits on board.

The nurse was clearly relieved when I reappeared at the stretcher-side. Our man was due for his next intravenous medication, which I had to supervise. I examined him – his lung-bases crackled softly at each breath, warning of an accumulation of fluid, so I added a small dose of diuretic to the infusion – and then, apologizing to the nurse for abandoning her again, went to explain to the woman with the suspected heart attack what was happening. With me I took the defibrillator, parking it discreetly behind a nearby seat. I sat down next to her and asked how she was feeling.

'Fine,' she snapped, 'I don't need this thing any more,' pointing at the discarded oxygen mask.

'Well, I'm still worried about you,' I said. 'I think it would be better if we had your heart checked over in a hospital in Los Angeles. With chest pain–'

'There's nothing wrong with me,' she interrupted. 'I'll see my GP in Australia when we arrive. If you think I'm going to get off this plane in Los Angeles you're very much mistaken.'

'If the doctor says you're not fit to fly then I'm afraid we have to disembark you,' explained the purser.

The woman turned on me furiously. 'How can you say such rubbish?' she demanded. 'As a doctor, it's your duty to look after me on the flight. If you put me off this aircraft I'll have you sued.'

'It's airline policy,' interjected the purser gently. 'If there's any possibility that you've got a heart problem we can't carry you.'

'I'll sue you too,' shouted the woman. 'I paid for my ticket and I intend to use it!'

We landed and taxied to the terminal, where an airport medical team boarded. I introduced my chest-pain patient to the attendant doctor, explaining the basis of my diagnosis. The woman interjected that I was incompetent and probably not even medically qualified.

'You're probably right, ma'am,' said my American colleague, giving me a wink. 'We'd better get you somewhere where you can have proper care.'

Still arguing, she was loaded onto a stretcher and carried out. On the way back to the tail I passed a second stretcher bearing the man who'd had a fit, snoring gently.

⊕

We took off again, and when we were high over the Pacific a man fainted. I laid him flat, gave him oxygen, and was then called to see a passenger with violent vomiting. She responded to an injection of an anti-emetic. I was beginning to hope that the last distraction of this jinxed journey might finally be over when the curtains were twitched aside and the cabin stewardess stood there again.

'We need your help, doctor,' she said. 'A man has locked himself into one of the rear toilets with a fifteen-year-old girl. We can open the door and drag him out, but we were wondering whether you could try to talk to him and get him to come out quietly.'

This didn't seem to be a medical matter, but I felt that I couldn't refuse: I had met the girl in question a few hours earlier, when, unbidden, she'd materialized outside the curtains with cold mineral water for the nurse and myself. Christine had heard from the cabin staff that I was from South Africa and wanted to say hello; later, during a break from caring for my patient, we'd talked about Cape Town where she lived. Despite her youth I'd been struck by her air of containment, and also by the aura of innocent sensuality that she projected. I had noticed the effect this was having on a man nearby, a gently drunk Australian in his forties who was watching her with moonstruck attention, a foolish smile on his face. I'd asked her if the man was bothering her.

'Oh, that's Munroe,' she'd answered. 'I met him on the flight. He's pretty harmless. He says he's in love with me.'

Munroe, unabashed, had stepped forward and shaken my hand. 'Isn't she beautiful, doc?' he'd asked, and Christine had laughed with a surprisingly adult tolerance.

Leaving the nurse – our patient was asleep, and his condition temporarily stable – I joined the group of cabin staff gathered at the toilet door. The flight engineer held a master key, about to put it into the lock. I motioned him aside and pressed my ear against the panel. From within came a murmur of voices.

'Are you okay, Christine?' I asked.

'Yes,' she answered, 'Munroe is just telling me something.'

'Munroe, I think you should come out of there,' I suggested.

'In a moment, doc.'

'Listen, Munroe, help me out,' I said. 'Christine is an old friend of mine from Cape Town.' I hoped he was drunk enough to find this plausible. 'As long as she's in there with you I have to wait outside this door to check that she's okay. If you come out I can go back to looking after my patient.'

There was a pause. 'Right-o, doc,' he said sadly. The door opened and Christine appeared, followed by a contrite Munroe. While a steward escorted him back to his seat, I asked Christine if she'd been hurt or frightened.

'Nothing like that,' she answered, with her usual composure. 'He just knelt on the floor and asked me to marry him. I told him I'd think about it.'

Thankfully, the remaining hours to Sydney passed without further interruption. The nurse stretched out on a row of seats and rested while I sat beside the stretcher, modulating the man's intravenous infusion. I was so tired that the calculation of his fluid balance – including the volume of each platelet pack plus the content of the accumulated ampoules of drugs injected into the drip line, minus the amount excreted in various forms including insensible loss through sweat and exhaled water vapour – took an interminable time. Shortly before we landed I gave him another small dose of diuretic; the higher atmospheric pressure at ground-level would increase the load on his heart and the tendency for fluid to collect in his lungs. He was still alive when we touched down, and smiled when we landed for a second time – after a low-level air ambulance flight along the coast – in Tasmania. His family were waiting for him in the haematology ward at Hobart hospital. His daughter embraced him, tears streaming down her face, and then turned and hugged me too.

'Thank you,' she whispered. 'The doctors in London told us he might not make it.'

'Everything was straightforward,' I said, through a sudden tightening of my larynx. 'We had no problems at all.'

⊕

By now I was beginning to know the aeromedical business thoroughly. I'd found that British Airways was my least favourite airline – surly ground staff, aircraft that I was travelling on delayed at take-off with passengers kept sitting on board for hours, then returned to the departure hall for hours more without explanation – and learned to appreciate those carriers whose consideration and helpfulness made my work easier. I had discovered that a few of the company medical officers were such pompous prima donnas that any suggestion by the flying doctor of a change to the organized itinerary – a hotel in a city centre, perhaps, instead of one at a distant airport, or proposing that a local connecting flight might be less tiring for an ill patient than a two-hundred-mile road journey – would be taken as personal criticism and result in the troublesome doctor being struck from the company's list of aeromedical practitioners.

Of more positive value was the clinical experience I was gaining. I looked after patients with unstable spinal fractures whose each transfer – from hospital to ambulance, ambulance to aircraft, and back again on the receiving side – required meticulous choreography to prevent further damage. I escorted people with malaria, shouting in delirium, and restless psychiatric cases who had to be soothed into compliance with improvised psychotherapy and in-flight sedation. Once I was part of a mass repatriation of casualties from a holiday coach crash, in an aircraft whose cabin had been modified into a flying ward housing fifteen stretchers. The only one of my patients who died in the air – an elderly woman, unconscious from a massive stroke – slipped away quietly somewhere over the Atlantic, and all that had been necessary was to draw the curtains around her berth and inform the captain, according to protocol, before ordering the small whisky otherwise denied me while on duty.

My readiness to fly at short notice, and to escort – trepidation notwithstanding – even seriously ill cases, made me, after a year, a sort of veteran in the aeromedical field. Yet each flight seemed to me a wild improvisation, an exercise in medical decision-making without a manual. Occasionally one of the larger assistance companies organized a training course for their doctors, held at a country airfield. I attended one and found it an eccentric mixture of theory – about differential oxygen pressures at various flight altitudes and the management of electrical and fuel fires – and scanty information about clinical practice. After lunch we tried putting out sample blazes on the edge of the runway, then donned life jackets and jumped into a nearby swimming pool. A multiple-choice test was administered, followed by drinks. Attendance at the course was considered a significant step up the short ladder of aeromedical expertise.

For those who wished to rise further in the business, the top post to aim for was that of company medical officer. These were the doctors at headquarters who made the decisions about repatriations: assessing patients' fitness to fly through telephone consultation with those caring for them in distant countries, organizing the required medical personnel and equipment for the flight and arranging the eventual admission of the patients into their home hospitals. A big company would have three or four medical officers, a small operation only one, and duty rotas ran day and night. The job offered various benefits and generous rates of pay. My friend David, the habitual traveller, had begun working as a flying doctor a year before me but flew no more. Temporarily beguiled by the company car and the pension plan, he now commuted to work in Croydon, from where, during his times on duty, he would offer me first choice of the plummier flights.

The aeromedical assistance business was fiercely competitive, with companies manoeuvring to undercut each other's contracts with the travel insurance adjusters. Competent company medical officers were a major asset – they made the repatriation business run smoothly – and these individuals were regularly poached by rival assistance providers with offers of improved salary and perks. Then, in order to guard their profit margins, the companies would have to find an area of saving, usually by paring away the money they paid the flying personnel; suddenly, hotel sleep-time on an overseas assignment would attract only half the hourly rate, or be transformed into a luxury for which they'd decided you should not be paid at all. Unprotected by contracts, the doctors and nurses who did the actual patient repatriation work – by nature, footloose independents – had little say about their conditions of service.

David suggested that I free myself from the uncertainties of this episodic employment by trying the company medical officer route myself: a small assistance company, looking to enlarge its share of the market, had offered him a job and was looking for another staff doctor. The idea was superficially attractive, but then I visited David at his office and observed the strange mixture of deference and resentment that characterized the attitudes of the company executives for which he laboured. Hustlers by nature – hybrids spawned of the travel and insurance industries – they appeared to regard medical professionalism (and probably, any other kind) as some sort of subversive weed that undermined commercial competitiveness. Worse was the spectre of having to socialize with them at after-work get-togethers and summer barbecues; a prospect, I noted, that set even the normally gregarious David blanching.

I contemplated other options for making a living. Working as a doctor in war zones was voluntary and unpaid. My hospital surgical career looked increasingly uncertain – my curriculum vitae was a curious patchwork of jobs that shocked the sensibilities of staid consultants – and I was considering a full-time post in accident and emergency medicine, where I hoped a varied résumé might be less provocative to the interview committees. Between repatriation flights and spells of employment in Casualty I continued to work as a freelance journalist, pitching news and feature stories to magazines and news-agencies. I would be gratified when they were accepted, despite the derisory pay rate; an eight-hundred word piece, which might require several days to research and write, might net me a hundred and twenty dollars. A glycerine-tongued acquaintance – a successful freelance advertising copywriter who derided my lack of financial acumen – proposed that I go into business with him.

He'd applied his confident glibness to the marketing of most things from hygiene products to holidays, but had recently become aware of a lucrative and expanding field: the health industry. My ability, as he saw it, to explain medical ideas in an accessible way, was a commodity from which he felt we both could benefit. I was sceptical until I saw him at work, selling the concept to a neophyte biotechnology company involved in the identification of fungal compounds for the treatment of cancer. Thrilling the executives with pungent phrases – 'focus-enhancing', 'vision-expanding', even 'mould-breaking' (no one laughed) – he landed us the commission to write the annual company prospectus.

I laid clinical flesh on the bones of their research data while he imbued the outcome with the sort of breathtaking investment-of-a-lifetime hyperbole designed to have venture capitalists lunging for their chequebooks. Flushed with our success, he paid me handsomely and began to look further afield for a place to market our combined skills.

A few days later I was being lunched – sumptuously – by the senior partner of a leading international public-relations company. After boasting about their global standing – a major account was the Indonesian government, who employed them to counter the 'negative impressions' induced in the public mind by certain massacres in East Timor – the man made me a proposition: to head their newly created 'health sciences' division and lead a team of dedicated concept-pushers. My first brief would be to advise a certain client on the effective presentation of complicated medical issues.

'Who's the client?' I asked.

He concentrated on unwrapping a large cigar. Had I read, he enquired, the report on passive smoking by the International Agency for Research on Cancer? I told him I'd seen a synopsis of it in a medical journal, recalling that it revealed a predictable increased incidence of lung cancer in those exposed to other people's tobacco smoke.

'That's exactly the sort of misconception you'd be working to correct,' he said, smiling benignly. 'The number of cases examined was actually too small to be statistically significant, so no solid inference can be drawn from the findings. In fact the margin of mathematical error was such that passive smoking could be interpreted as having a protective affect against lung cancer. Your job would be to make the public aware of this controversy.'

'It's hardly a controversy,' I objected. 'The fact that there is a health risk from passive smoking has been well established by other studies.'

'Look at the figures,' he said, pulling from his briefcase a number of large show-cards of the sort used in client presentations. 'Statistically, the actuarial risk of dying from inhaling the smoke of someone next to you is less than that of choking to death on an oatmeal biscuit.' He pointed at a picture of the lethal cookie over a block of artfully fonted text, then flipped to the image on the next card. 'You're more likely to die from drinking a glass of tap water.'

Taking my mute response as evidence that he had made his point, the man continued in a voice of winning reasonableness. 'As head of the health sciences division, your role would be to report the true statistical validity of these and other studies that appear to denigrate our client's products. Your medical qualifications make you ideal for the job.' He leaned back, spreading his fingers on the tablecloth. 'You can, within reason, name your own price.'

I stood up. 'Thanks for lunch,' I said.

'Look at the figures,' he yelled after me as I walked out. My brief foray into medical copywriting was over.

⊕

A good lunch can taste even better when a real prick gets stuck with the bill, and I'd needed the reminder that if being an aeromedical physician didn't always involve serious medicine, it was, at least, relatively honest. It also seemed to suit my desocialized state; I'd become a habitué of transit lounges, of taxi rides and ambulance races through the streets of foreign cities whose geography would remain always unknown. I escorted further repatriations to Australia and New Zealand, all of them arduous. Sometimes the insurance adjusters would require that the nurse and I spend less than forty-eight hours on the ground to reduce hotel expenses, leaving little time for recovery before facing the long haul back.

Some of the assistance companies for which I worked would agree to me breaking my return journey in Singapore – unpaid, of course, and providing that they did not require me for another flight – for a few days of relaxation, while the nurse returned home with the equipment. I made a habit of staying at the same Chinese hotel that I had used when my ship used to dock there. The elderly couple that ran it always gave me the same first-floor room, and, gazing on the hectic street below, it began to feel as much home as anywhere else. I would walk through the neighbourhood to eat at the outdoor tables of the nearby hawkers' market, wondering whether any of the stall-holders had begun to recognize me. Then I'd return to my room and sit on the balcony through the warm evening, reading and sipping duty-free Scotch.

Before I slept I would lean on the rail, glass in hand. With the clarity of mild drunkenness I'd review my rootlessness, the state to which my wandering existence had brought me. I had accumulated nothing: no pension, no property, no life insurance, no lasting relationship. I was living from one assignment to the next, relishing the peculiar mixture of fulfilment and frustration that they provided. There were even opportunities for intense and transient meetings. I'd spent an evening talking to a girl in a London bar. Before we parted she had offered me her phone number in Düsseldorf and I'd scribbled it down, not expecting to see her again. But a repatriation a week later had, by chance, taken me to that city. Two months later I was back again, and three weeks after that. Each time we'd have an evening and a night together before I accompanied my patient back home; not much to go on, but for a time the nearest thing to a relationship I had.

Yet stranger conjunctions presented themselves. Once I flew into Zakinthos to pick up a woman from the Greek island's small hospital. On the second day of her holiday she'd suffered a miscarriage and had been admitted after losing a significant amount of blood. The pair of representatives from the travel company who met me at the airport looked drawn and exhausted, and said they had spent most of the past week in attendance at the patient's bedside. I was met at the hospital by the woman's partner. He too was pale under his tan, and looked as though he hadn't had much sleep. The patient greeted me through lips that had almost no colour. I asked to see the doctor, and the latest blood-test results.

The haemoglobin level – an indication of the oxygen-carrying capacity of the blood – was around a third of normal: just sufficient to cope with the respiratory demands of lying in bed at sea level, but not with low oxygen pressure in an aircraft cabin at thirty thousand feet. The hospital doctor arrived, flustered and apologetic: over the past few days the woman had received ten units of blood by transfusion. This should have raised her haemoglobin to a level where it was safe for her to fly, but she had bled again. The hospital was down to its last blood packs, and could not release them unless new donors could be found to replace them. Suddenly I began to understand the cause of the wan appearance of the travel reps and the woman's boyfriend: they confirmed that each had given a pint or more over the course of the week to top up the hospital blood bank's reserve, as had several other guests at their hotel. Now they were running out of people to tap. The doctor looked at me appraisingly: would I consider offering some of my red corpuscles to the cause?

I had given blood as a medical student when I'd been younger and fitter, and I remembered how drained I'd felt for a day or so afterwards. I promised to consider the idea while I conferred with my employers, though the prospect of tending to a seriously ill patient in the air when I didn't feel entirely well myself, was unappealing. I phoned from my hotel. The London assistance company office – unsurprisingly – was all in favour of my sacrifice, though less enthusiastic when I explained that once enough blood donors had been found, the new transfusion would need to be given slowly over a period of twenty-four hours or more. It then had to be in the recipient's circulation for a further day or two before the new red blood cells began working efficiently; this meant that I would have to stay on the island for several more days before I could safely bring my patient home. The adjuster might balk at the further hotel expense, argued the company medical officer, and asked for time to think about it. I decided to go to the beach.

Afternoon sun lay warm across the rocks of the small cove. I dived into the sea and swam down as deep as I could over the sandy bottom. When I emerged and walked back to the hollow amidst the boulders where I had left my towel, I found two women lying there, examining the book I had been reading. They were Dutch and very attractive; one blonde, the other dark-haired. We began talking about Amsterdam and the newspaper there for which I sometimes wrote. They took off their T-shirts and stretched out beside me, bare-breasted in the sunshine. I tried to sketch the fall of light across a rocky headland. We arranged to have dinner together. When I returned to my hotel there was still no word from London. I met the women at a restaurant on the harbour wall, and we ate with the small waves splashing at our feet and sending an occasional ripple across the flagstones under our table.

The evening had an air of charmed perfection. Phosphorescence curled around the hulls of the fishing boats that rocked at anchor a few feet away. The food was excellent, and even the local wine seemed to lose its harshness in the soft night air that carried an iodine tinge of seaweed from the rocks. We talked of writing and philosophy and travel, and laughed immoderately at each other's wit. The girls invited me back to their pension and the three of us walked up the cobbled alley arm in arm. With the shutters open to the sleeping harbour, we sat on the bed sipping ouzo, the soft mattress tumbling us together in an intimate tangle. They didn't seem to mind. We drank some more. I stroked the delicate skin of an arm that lay across my lap. The owner – the dark-haired girl – giggled. Her friend placed her arm alongside and I played with the ticklish area inside the elbow. Their firm bodies lay close against me. I looked at the delicate shadows of veins that coursed just beneath the translucent skin.

'Could the two of you,' I asked, 'each spare a pint of blood?'

✪

I had to fly to Dubrovnik to pick up a British resident. A retired nuclear physicist, he now lived in a small apartment near the port. According to his medical notes the man had chronic emphysema, probably from the forty cigarettes he smoked each day. An attack of pneumonia had put him in hospital. Now, gathering signs of war in the Balkans had persuaded his family back in England that he should be brought home. I flew in to the small airport in the mountains and a local agent of the insurance provider drove me along the winding road that skirted the Adriatic coast, past limestone islands capped with pines. At the hospital I found my patient on the balcony, wrapped monk-like in his dressing gown. He gesticulated with his cigarette.

'This place is paradise, doctor,' he said in his wheezy voice, 'even the nurses are beautiful.'

He added some comment in Serbo-Croat and the solid faces of the two white-smocked female orderlies cracked into grins. Their answer made him roar with laughter, which degenerated into a fit of coughing so prolonged that I thought he'd never regain his breath. He seemed much livelier than I'd expected considering the ninety years attributed to him in his medical records.

From my high room at the Grand Hotel Imperial I could look over the full circuit of the city's Venetian walls and massive bastions, to the sea beyond. Late sun lit the roofs and domes and church-towers above the shadowed valleys of the streets. I had an entire top floor suite: the fighting in Slovenia and in the Krajina enclave further up the coast had already chased away the tourists, and the hotel – a nineteenth-century watering-hole of European royalty, with a coach-drive and casino – was almost empty. In the old town I had a drink at a café table in one of the piazzas. Pigeons fussed on limestone paving that shone from the polish of centuries of feet. I envied the old Englishman his place of repose.

The next morning on the way to the airport we stopped by his apartment. It was at the top of a narrow alley, full of cats, that climbed up towards the city wall. The husky ambulance-men carried his wheelchair up the long flights of steps as though the man weighed nothing. His lodgings were small; a bedroom, a sitting room full of books, a kitchen that opened onto a tiny terrace where geraniums glowed in a pool of sunlight. An aged neighbour handed me a small suitcase that she had packed. He gave her his keys and they kissed on both cheeks. I turned away so I wouldn't see them crying.

As the aircraft climbed, the old man peered through the window, trying to catch a last glimpse of the town. The 'no smoking' sign went off and he asked if he could have a cigarette. Considering the dwindling store of his life's pleasures, I told him to light up.

'I doubt I'll ever get back there,' he said, through his racking cough. 'When Tito died I think we knew the dream was over. I was a communist, you know. In 1934, when I was studying at Cambridge, I went to Soviet Georgia to help bring in the harvest. There were volunteers from around the world. We worked all day, cutting wheat and piling it in wagons. At night I'd lie with a girl in the middle of the wheat fields. Such a beautiful girl. We didn't know then that there was a famine coming, that so many would die in the purges. Stalin destroyed that dream, and Tito managed to revive it. When I retired to live here in the seventies I felt as though I was young again. Now it's finished.'

I handed him over to the doctors at the London hospital where he was expected. The X-rays I carried with me showed a malignant mass in his lung that I knew would not be operable. Three weeks later I saw Dubrovnik again. This time it was on the evening news. Flames gouted from the balcony of the room I had occupied in the hotel, and thick smoke rose from the roofs of the medieval city where Serb shells were landing.

✪

I'd once thought that human evolution would halt the progress of disease, that science would provide new cures. It was true that some forms of medical care were now available globally via a phone line, so that with an hour's notice I could find myself, equipment in hand, flying off to another country to carry out a complex repatriation. But all the time, across the world, new wars were starting. Wounds and deaths multiplied, epidemics spread, social systems collapsed and the cries of refugees and orphans rose to the heavens, on and on without end. I might have hoped that it would be possible to take a holiday from war – even to have lost interest in it entirely – but war, as Lenin had warned, remained interested in me.

11

Burma

This was undoubtedly the most ostentatious birthday party that I'd ever had. Five hundred guests, the absolute cream of local society, filled the banqueting hall. One side of it was open to the warm night where the partygoers, had they been less constrained by formality, might have strolled the lawns under a tropical moon. There was even an honour guard, standing to attention along the garden terraces. Each soldier held a bamboo torch that flared and crackled in the still air, and reflected in the strip of red cloth bound around the barrel of his rifle. Within the hall, slender Chinese girls in side-slit dresses served trays of Regency Grape Brandy to the most important guests, Hsan Loi rice-whisky to the rest. Captive bears grunted in cages at the bottom of the compound. It wasn't my house, or even my guest list. I just happened to share a birth-date with the host, and he had been emphatic that I come along.

Khun Sa was not the sort of man that you argued with. At his Ho Mong headquarters in Burma's southern Shan State, he was 'The General', Shan leader and protector of his people. The guard at his party was formed by troops from his twenty thousand strong Mong Tai Army, and the encircling hills, above which the moon was rising, concealed anti-aircraft guns and missiles in case of a Burmese air attack. In December 1993 Khun Sa had declared independent the enclave that he controlled – a rough rectangle of territory bordered by the

Salween River in the north and the Thai frontier to the south – with Ho Mong its capital. Since then his Free Shan State had been besieged. Fifteen miles away, Burmese troops were entrenched on the heights of the Salween's north bank, blockading the ferry crossings that brought jade and gemstone traffic – reportedly worth a million dollars annually in tax revenue – through Ho Mong. More enemy divisions were advancing on the Free State's eastern edge, their progress marked by the smoke of burning villages. Captured peasants – terrorized by rapes and killings – worked in labour gangs, cutting jungle roads for the Burmese army that brought their artillery and tanks ever closer.

These atrocities evoked only muted protest from the international community, for Khun Sa was effectively without friends. He had been indicted by a US Grand Jury for running an international opium network that stretched from his jungle base to America's inner cities, and had been elevated to the status of Global Public Enemy. An official of the Drug Enforcement Administration in Washington had dubbed Khun Sa 'the Prince of Death', for the delectation of the media and his own organization's glory. The Central Intelligence Agency, anxious to justify their mandate after the end of the Cold War, had moved into counter-narcotics work and was also plotting Khun Sa's downfall. Even Burma's military junta – the State Law and Order Restoration Council, or SLORC – claimed that its attack on Free Shan State was an anti-drug offensive, though cynics noted that eighty per cent of the country's opium was now being harvested in regions under Burmese army supervision, where production had recently doubled and new refineries were springing up to convert the crop to heroin. Khun Sa remained the last independent trafficker still outside their control.

If he felt the precariousness of his position, there was little sign of it at Khun Sa's birthday celebration in Ho Mong. His guests included Chinese businessmen, Thai intelligence officers, Shan nationalists and MTA (Mong Tai Army) commanders, arranged in ranks of armchairs according to precedence. Khun Sa – hair pomaded back, elegantly sharp in a sharkskin suit – moved from group to group, toasting each with brandy, his glass instantly refilled by hovering orderlies. He had written to the American president proposing US investment in a poppy eradication plan, and to the United Nations Development Programme, pleading for agricultural advisers and aid for crop-substitution. He had received no response. His composure remained undented as he joined his family to blow out the candles on his cake and entertained the gathering by singing Karaoke vocals to Thai pop songs. 'The General is happy tonight,' murmured an official as children gathered in an alcove to kneel before Khun Sa and receive glossy red envelopes containing gifts of money. 'We are all happy.'

I wasn't so happy. I was in Free Shan State to carry out a medical evaluation, examining people suffering from malaria, amoebiasis, liver flukes, Filaria worms and leprosy. Some were refugees, hungry and destitute, their homes destroyed by the advancing Burmese. The hospitals of the MTA contained young men with bullet wounds and missing limbs. The inhabitants of Khun Sa's small enclave were being ground down by pressures from every quarter: they were pawns in a power-contest between rival government agencies in Washington and they were items of barter in shady deals between Burmese and Thai generals. The major humanitarian organizations didn't want to get involved in this tragic absurdity. Even the intentions of the medical NGO under whose direction I was conducting the evaluation seemed oddly ambiguous. The Shan and hill-tribe villagers looked like losing out in every way. It was a frustrating business.

⊕

I had first heard of Khun Sa a year before, during the editing of the film I'd worked on in Mozambique. The office of the television production company housed a documentary maker who had been visiting Shan State since the seventies, recording the complex career of this Shan nationalist leader, drug warlord and international criminal. The film-maker had heard about my work as a doctor with international medical groups, and asked me for advice. Khun Sa's subjects lacked basic health services and were in need of assistance to establish a civilian hospital: did I know who might help? I gave him the addresses of medical organizations that I'd worked for and explained that formal requests for aid would have to be directed to them by the Shan. It had taken a year for the proposals to be drafted, sent and declined: these bodies were unable to help, claiming, regretfully, that they were already involved in medical missions to other Burmese minority groups – the Karen, Karenni and Mon – displaced to refugee camps along the Thai border.

There was, however, one organization that was eager for the opportunity. I had first encountered MIAOW (Medical Intervention At Once Worldwide) shortly after I returned from Mozambique; indeed, had been directed to them by a supporter who'd heard that they were considering a mission to that country. MIAOW was a young organization that had already been active in Armenia, the Sudan and Sarajevo; but the aid and relief field is a competitive one, and in crowded intervention areas such as these it was difficult to get noticed among the many other groups at work there. Now MIAOW's leadership was looking for a high-profile mission that would attract publicity and funding. Free Shan State was virgin territory – so far without international intervention – where an enterprising NGO could make its mark. MIAOW wished to send a team to conduct a medical evaluation there, and they asked me to lead it.

The publicity aspects of the mission did not interest me; what swayed me was a plaintive letter brought back by the film-maker from his latest trip. It was written by a human rights foundation called the Volunteers for the Displaced Shans. 'The people of Shan State flee in all directions with haste, leaving their small possessions, having no time to collect them before the onslaught of the occupying SLORC Burmese forces,' it read. 'This has prompted us to look for help from the international NGOs . . . May God help the people who are trying their utmost to bring an end to the cruel and horrible events happening to the innocent and pitiful people of the old Union of Burma.' The foundation added that they were ready to start erecting a hospital building at once, a thirty-bed unit of teak-plank walls and tin roof with an operating room and staff accommodation. They would supply volunteers to be trained as nurses and medical auxiliaries. They had even chosen a site near the Thai border (a hand-drawn map was appended) and simply awaited the go-ahead and the guarantee of medical staff.

MIAOW's evaluation team would consist of a doctor (myself), a logistician named Stevie who had worked for other NGOs in Ethiopia and Afghanistan, and Virginia, an operations manager from MIAOW headquarters. Because of Khun Sa's notoriety, the mission demanded considerable circumspection in any dealings with his administration or his army. This delicate diplomacy was entrusted to Virginia. She would also run the negotiations with the Volunteers for the Displaced Shans regarding the planned hospital. I was disconcerted to discover that her field-experience had apparently been gleaned in Kenya, where she'd acquired a fund of knowledge about the difficulties of dealing with domestic servants; 'house-boys', she called them. My brief was straightforward: to assess pathology, collect statistics and make the medical evaluation. It was inevitable that I would get my hands covered with the usual secretions – sweat, snot, shit and maybe blood – but I carried no supplies of drugs and only a tiny surgical kit, so whatever suffering I saw I would probably be unable to intervene.

A couple of days before our departure for Bangkok I was asked to supply an equipment list for the mission. Remembering the near-impossibility of finding proper maps in places like Kurdistan or Mozambique, I had specified the importance of getting detailed charts of the border region and southern Shan State. On the eve of our flight I'd visited the MIAOW office for a final briefing. The person responsible for our necessities had conferred with Virginia, and they'd decided that such maps would be easier to obtain where we were going. However, they told me proudly, they had secured sponsorship from a maker of designer boots, in the form of a pair for each of us; all we were required to do was to organize some high-quality transparencies by the 'team photographer' (myself) of the boots being worn in Shan State in poses that could later be used for advertising purposes. It was now too late to look for maps, but the boot-supplier had promised over-night delivery. By the time we left for Bangkok they hadn't arrived.

⊕

At Chiang Mai in northern Thailand we met Kya Nu, the author of the Shan's plea for help. He was a small man, entirely bald, who resembled a Buddhist monk in every aspect of his serene demeanour. Only his white moustache, neatly clipped, suggested a tiny vanity. Swathed in a pale brown wrap, he sipped tea while he explained the intricacies of Thai support for the Free Shan State. Currently rice, medicines and fuel were allowed to reach Ho Mong in exchange for teak, felled and trucked out by Thai logging companies. The military governors in Thailand's border provinces had a stake in the trade: if not owners of the timber companies, they claimed a cut of tariffs levied on both the loggers and the Shan. But back in Bangkok the Thai generals of the National Security Council took a longer view, favouring partnerships between their own companies (construction, power, hotels) and those operated by the SLORC military inside Burma. A vast development involving highways, industry and hydro-electric power from the Salween river was being planned for the area with Chinese government backing, and all the generals wanted to be major investors.

To this end the governor of the Thai border area adjacent to Ho Mong – considered sympathetic to the Shan – had recently been transferred, reducing the chance of our medical group obtaining permits to cross the border legitimately. It might instead be necessary for us to be guided on foot into the mountains to the north, said Kya Nu; there to meet Mong Tai soldiers who would escort us, and whose mules would carry our equipment, over the frontier.

'If only we had those boots,' said Virginia, possibly imagining a picture of herself astride a noble pack-animal, gracing the pages of *Vogue*.

'Perhaps we should look for some maps,' I proposed, having searched for them fruitlessly in Bangkok. Four hours of trawling the shops of Chiang Mai confirmed that sale of sheet 47-2 of the international map grid – the Thai border and southern Shan State – was forbidden 'for security reasons'.

'How very odd,' said Virginia.

Chiang Mai contained the headquarters of a number of NGOs that split, merged, aided and obstructed one another in much the same way as did the various ethnic factions across the Burmese border that they aimed to assist. Some organizations were excellent, others (older groups with links to the US Agency for International Development, and some missionary groups) were tainted by reputed CIA connections, and some were just dire, the so-called 'bubble' NGOs. These had generally been set up by backpackers, whose calling had been suddenly revealed to them among the misty hills and plentiful intoxicants (emotional and pharmaceutical) available in northern Thailand, and who had never gone home. Some described themselves as environmental consultants, others as development workers, and those who didn't have a sideline exporting local hill-tribe handicrafts dealt in the esoteric currency of 'information exchange'.

We started with the most effective NGO, one that supplied medicine and rice to refugees along the western border. The organization operated out of a hillside bungalow that looked over Chiang Mai's rooftops, now blurred by the afternoon's accumulation of smog. The part-Shan woman who ran it had recently made an unpublicized trip to Ho Mong to examine the founding of a maternal and child health programme. Her group had also managed by quiet industry to truck some food to the points bordering Free Shan State where hill-tribe people, displaced by the Burmese offensive, had gathered. She suggested that hardening attitudes in Bangkok would prevent a medical group working 'officially' inside Shan State. This would not be a problem as long as MIAOW, like other international organizations working among Burma's ethnic minorities, operated without embarrassing the Thai government. It was only when this understanding was violated – a group of doctors working in Manerplaw, the Karen 'capital', had recently featured in a television documentary whose screening in Europe had brought official objections from the Burmese government – that the Thais were forced to act by withdrawing visas.

I looked through the maps in the organization's office to find the sheet we needed, and dashed into town to have it duplicated. Then, while the evening closed in and Stevie and Virginia retired to the guesthouse to discuss the implications of the operating restrictions – how MIAOW would derive publicity and funding from a project that could not be publicized – I went along to visit another of the NGOs that flourished in Chiang Mai. A blattering tuk-tuk took me to a house on the edge of a canal, where fireflies flitted in the reeds and mosquitos swarmed. I knocked on the door and was admitted; an earnest group sat on the floor being addressed by a stout woman in a sarong and many ethnic shawls. She ran the Asia Centre for Data Distribution, and she believed fervently in her work. I could only imagine that the Thai authorities tolerated her because of her ineffectiveness, since she was less than reticent about her doings.

She had just taken this group of concerned persons – some American Green activists, a Swiss pharmacist, an Australian optometrist, a New Zealand pig farmer and a 'qualified alternative therapist' – 'inside, to Rebel HQ', where they'd had 'a wonderful time; very dramatic and very heart-rending'. They were now being lectured on the best way that each might Distribute the Data to publicize the plight of these wonderful, suffering people. When she'd finished I asked her what she knew about the conflict in Shan State. She launched into a lecture of hyperbolic generalities which contained nothing about the Shan. Then, rendered slightly hysterical by the thrill of her authoritativeness, the woman proposed a toast. A nasty wine of Bangkok provenance was splashed into our glasses.

'Down with SLORC!' she shouted. Her acolytes responded with cheers and whoops, as though already drunk.

'To all my wonderful friends!' she sobbed, and threw back her drink, quite overcome. I excused myself. The woman accompanied me to the door where she embraced me, stiflingly.

'What you don't realize,' she breathed into my ear, 'is that they're practising *genocide*!'

The town of Mae Hong Son – our step-off point – was a

cool haven, tucked into the foothills of the mountain range that formed this corner of the Thai–Burmese border. Kya Nu took us to see the sacred carp that cruised indolently in a lake below the Buddhist temple. On the little jetty he produced a rice-cake from his sleeve and crumbled it into the water. The fish boiled about the wooden pilings like piranhas, while Kya Nu revealed the next stage in the delicate counterpoint of our mission; the town administrator could not actually accede to our entering Shan State, but he had let it be discretely known that he would be out of town the next day on official business. During that time we expected to make our crossing over the northern pass that connects with the Ho Mong valley. Mules would not be involved; a four-wheel-drive truck had been arranged.

We departed early, the driver leaving the main road a few miles north of the town to take a side-track that rose and dipped through scattered villages and then wound up the head of a steep valley. Forest covered the fluted slopes below us. The road was a trough of boulders and dust gouged out by logging trucks; one threw a wave of sand over our windscreen as it descended. A Thai control post at the top of the ridge appeared unoccupied, and we passed under the raised boom and through the bare, tree-stump-studded no-man's-land that led to Free Shan State. Three miles on we pulled up at the Shan border post. A soldier in jungle green manned a radio set inside a bamboo hut. On the wall was the Free Shan State flag; horizontal bands of yellow, green and red – Kya Nu explained that the colours represented Wealth, Love and Courage – overlaid by a white moon denoting Peace. We were given tea, and a meal of rice and boiled leaves that was to be our staple diet, with odd alarming variations, for the duration of our stay.

The road to Ho Mong clung at first to the edge of a snaking ridgeline, with a cursory handrail on the curves that seemed unlikely to stop us plunging over the edge. Patches of jungle had been clear-felled, leaving stumps and degraded scrub. Small settlements of bamboo and thatch hugged the hillside, the same colour as the orange dust. The road descended gradually. Files of soldiers trudged along the verge, each bearing on his back a basket of soil. A wall of earth curved across the valley floor where work gangs were completing a concrete sluice-way.

'This dam will bring water and hydro-electric power for Ho Mong,' said Kya Nu , 'as the General has ordered. Over there' – he pointed to where a bulldozer worked among dry paddy fields, raising a cloud of dust – 'will be the golf course.' He looked a little embarrassed. 'It is for the Japanese and Korean visitors. They come to buy the gem stones. I suppose it is part of our development.'

Ho Mong was no furtive jungle hideaway. Ten thousand civilians and a similar number of MTA troops lived beneath tin roofs that stretched along the valley and lapped between the surrounding hills. Gem-cutting workshops, schools, a hospital and a number of Karaoke bars testified to its affluence. Red earth roads formed a haphazard grid, and banana and papaya trees flourished among the dwellings. We were shown to the quarters arranged by our hosts, a group of huts on a hillside terrace. After splashing the dust away, we went to our first meeting: with Free Shan State's Foreign Liaison Officer. He joined us at sunset in a bamboo-roofed pavilion that looked out over the town, now veiled by smoke from cooking fires. Somewhere in the distance a generator came falteringly to life and white street lights flickered.

The official's fluent English was tinged with a noticeable America accent. I knew from the film-maker's comprehensive pre-mission briefing that this man – like Khun Sa himself – had once worked with the CIA-run Battalion Speciale 111, a unit made up of Kuomintang (KMT) Nationalist Chinese forces who had fled into Burma's Shan State after their defeat by the Communists in 1949. Directed by the Americans to reinvade their homeland, the KMT generals had proved more interested in the hill-top poppy harvests. The opium sap was exported through a network of Chinese syndicates across East Asia, with CIA complicity: the start of the modern narcotics industry. The KMT force degenerated eventually into banditry and was destroyed. Meantime Khun Sa, impressed by the drug's potential, had set up his own opium business, and used the profits to build a private insurgent group that had combined with other Shan forces to become the Mong Tai Army.

'The Shan do not grow opium,' explained the official rather disingenuously. 'We only tax its passage through our territory. It is the hill-tribes that grow it, and the more unstable the situation the more they will grow. Unlike rice it can be carried easily and turned into cash for food, a necessary thing if the Tatmadaw, the Burmese army, are likely to come and burn their villages and make the people into refugees.'

He quoted a recent speech by President Clinton, stating that the American government's efforts should concentrate more on reducing demand for narcotics than interdicting supply; interpreting the nuances of US drug policy was the main function of Free Shan State's Foreign Liaison Office. Then he clapped his hands, and dinner – rice, greens and unidentifiable pig parts – was served, with fragrant tea.

On a parade ground below us a festival was underway, from where the cacophonous strains of Shan traditional music had been floating up the slope as we ate. We strolled down after supper, passing silhouetted figures with slung rifles watching from the hillside. The track was bordered by candle-flames where hill-tribe families sold bundles of Shan cheroots and bottles of cough mixture, rice-wine and Mekong brandy from mats on the ground. On a stage a traditional play was in progress, with singing actors in brocaded robes. Significant moments of slapstick or pathos were punctuated by a front-row orchestra: an egg-shaped drum, a one-stringed zither and a man who spun like a top in the centre of a circle of small bronze cymbals, striking out on all sides. Yellow stage-light flowed over the crowd who sat, transfixed, on the dry earth. Most were Shan, tawny-skinned with high cheekbones; here and there some Chinese from Yunnan province, smooth-faced and paler, their children in red felt hoods against the night's chill. The light glowed on the faces of young MTA conscripts under peaked caps and glinted from the M16s of the sentries in the shadows.

We were braced for a further series of meetings, and they began after breakfast – rice and greens – the next morning. It soon became evident that it would be impossible for us to operate here entirely independently, for the Volunteers for the Displaced Shan were part of the Free Shan State administration and answerable therefore to the General; attempting to establish a moral distance from his organization was like insisting on perfect hygiene in a mud-bath. Strategic decisions regarding a new hospital involved the army, the Ministry of Health, the Economic Ministry and the Foreign and Interior Ministries. Each minister had his bungalow in a different section of Ho Mong, with a shaded terrace and a small contingent of soldiers. We raced from one to the next, our driver making high-speed turns through compounds where indignant black pigs cantered from under our wheels.

Each meeting involved a subliminal setting out of positions: what we hoped to do here, what they expected us to do. My request to the army's Chief of Staff, for example – that I be allowed to visit the front line to study their methods for treatment and evacuation of casualties – was, as he and I both knew, an attempt to assess the solidity of the defences, for the security of our future hospital. Kya Nu sipped his tea, translating with delicacy and tact, while the Chief of Staff studied me with the slow blink of a seal and a small smile, and deferred the matter for due consideration. I'd experienced this sort of stylized, discursive conversation from working elsewhere in South East Asia and I rather enjoyed the ritual. My MIAOW colleagues did not, and were annoyed by the way things never seemed to be explicitly confirmed or refused.

I was, however, anxious to begin our assignment. The prospective hospital was intended to serve the civilian population of Khun Sa's domain, both valley Shan and hill-tribe minorities. I needed to know what diseases prevailed among them. There were reported to be several thousand refugees displaced by the advancing Burmese and scattered inside Free Shan State. They would have to be found, to assess their numbers and state of health. We needed to evaluate roads and likely evacuation routes, so that any hospital could be placed for ease of access by the local populace, and so that its staff could escape quickly should a Burmese breakthrough occur.

I consulted Mister Johnny, the man employed by the film-maker during his visits as his facilitator and interpreter. Johnny had acquired his name and impeccable English at a mission school in Shan State, and his understanding of local power-politics was intimate. He'd once been an officer in the Chinese-backed Burmese Communist Party insurgency against the government in northern Shan State. In 1988, when the army's slaughter of pro-democracy demonstrators on the streets of Rangoon brought international isolation, China had dumped the BCP and become instead the Burmese military government's main supporter. Johnny had made his way to Khun Sa's domain. Tall, trim and fit despite the forty non-filter 'Moon 33' cigarettes he smoked daily through an ivory holder, Johnny undertook to organize our travels through the territory. In the meantime he took me to visit the Ho Mong hospital; the condition of its patients would give an indication of the pathology I would see during the rest of the medical evaluation.

The hospital had been started by American medical missionaries in the 1950s. The operating theatre and surgical unit dated from then; a low structure of concrete, recently painted white in the hope that the Burmese might not bomb it. Now, expanded to a hundred and fifty beds in teak-plank wards set on terraces up the dusty hillside, it was the military hospital for the Mong Tai Army. There were four doctors. One was a Chinese anaesthetist from Yunnan. The others were Shan, but neither Doctors Chai nor Seng had completed their training at Rangoon University before it was closed following the 1988 pro-democracy demonstrations. At medical school Dr Myint had been a student activist, imprisoned and tortured by the Tatmadaw. When eventually released he'd followed his classmates along the underground networks to the border area and into Free Shan territory.

I was shown the X-ray machine and the basic operating theatre. The Chinese doctor knew a little orthopaedics, but the management of battle trauma – Dr Seng's responsibility – was mainly self-taught. Leg wounds, from landmines and shattering bullet injuries, generally went straight to amputation; the staff lacked experience of methods of bone-fixation and wound care that might have allowed some limbs to be saved. Abdominal surgery cases did not do well, either. If the jolting stretcher evacuation from the front line did not kill them, the long delay in reaching hospital guaranteed infection, and the principles of bowel repair – what sort of perforations could be simply closed, and which needed to be exteriorized through a colostomy – were not fully understood. Even simple techniques like skin-grafting, for the extensive jungle ulcers and the infected soft-tissue lacerations that formed a large percentage of the surgical wounds, could be improved. But the main problem was disease.

The dispensary held an array of drugs that had been manufactured in America, England, Thailand, Burma and China. Dr Seng explained that the pathology was seasonal: respiratory and eye infections and diet-deficiency diseases in the dry season; dysenteric illness and malaria during the rains. There had been a recent outbreak of meningitis among the troops that had killed twenty, and infectious hepatitis, amoebic dysentery and cholera were endemic. The commonest diagnosis, however, was 'fever', and if a blood smear examined in the primitive laboratory failed to show malaria parasites, a haphazard cocktail of antibiotics, steroids and Chinese herbal medicines was administered, with unpredictable results.

The wards were filled with golden light, diffused through gaps in the rough plank walls. On bamboo bed-platforms the patients were martialled for inspection; shorn-headed boys and men cross-legged on their blankets, their backs straight, each with a sheet of paper – his medical records – square before him. However variable their care, these men were relatively lucky; they at least were getting treatment. The hospital doctors also ran a small clinic for civilian patients on Ho Mong's main street. Serious cases could sometimes be shipped across the Thai border to Mae Hong Son, but the majority of the patients stayed put, to survive or die. Doctor Chai explained that, away from Ho Mong, the Shan and hill-tribe villagers had little access to healthcare. Unless there was a village store-keeper with a rudimentary knowledge of illness and some tablets, or a Thai logging camp had a charitable manager prepared to dispense from the workers' medicine chest, the afflicted suffered on their own. It was these people that our prospective hospital was intended to help.

Johnny had organized a truck – a battered, shock-absorber-deprived four-wheel-drive pick-up – and, before it was light, we piled into the back and were driven through the wakening town. Oil-lamps glowed in the market stalls and a file of soldiers, returning to quarters after guard duty on the surrounding hills, appeared to be wading waist-deep through the low-lying mist. The road twisted up the valley side past the guarded gates of the rehabilitation centre of Free Shan State's Drug Control and Eradication Agency. Despite the twenty million dollars that he acknowledged receiving annually from his stake in Burma's opium harvest, Khun Sa forbade the use of drugs among his subjects. I'd heard that rehabilitation consisted of ten days in a pit, and that repeat offenders were sometimes taken into the forest and dispatched by a single blow with a club.

The village of Kun Lung lay in a valley that led north to the Salween: a collection of thatched houses and banana plants beside a small stream. Johnny took Stevie and Virginia on a household survey to ask questions about water supply, rice prices and crops. I went with Kya Nu to the school, interrupting their English lesson. Under a thatched shelter some twenty children read from Burmese textbooks – 'My name is Za Za. This is my kite' – and all put up their hands when I asked who'd had malaria. The young woman teacher told me that three adults and six children in the small community had died from the disease in the past few months, the most recent fatality occurring only two days before. The front of her neck was distorted by a bulging goitre, the result of iodine deficiency. A couple of her charges showed signs of malnutrition, and several had coughs that shook their small bodies into breathlessness.

The road ended at Num Lung, from where a steep mule path and a two-hour walk led down to the Salween bank. On the shaded benches of the tea house a solitary elder puffed on his pipe. Until a few months ago the village had bustled with commerce – gemstone and jade dealers, opium mule-trains and sellers of Chinese cigarettes, radios and sewing machines – but the ferry had been sunk and the Mong Tai Army post collected no more taxes. Instead it had been reinforced and fortified with a sprawl of trenches dug across the nearby hillsides; if the enemy managed to cross the river, this track would offer their most direct route to Ho Mong. High overhead a Burmese airforce reconnaissance plane glinted against the sky, but none of the troops bothered to look up; all knew that the aircraft carried no bombs. The Shan shop-keepers allowed me to examine themselves and their children. They complained of a proliferation of illness. Having lived on a busy trading route with regular consignments of medication passing through, the inhabitants now found themselves at the end of the road. The decline in trade had affected everyone's health.

There were different problems in Mae Ark, a Pa-O hill-tribe settlement on a high ridge. The huts were raised on stilts, each capped by a wide thatch roof that came almost to the ground. Women in bright sarongs and black turbans were returning from the fields, cargo-baskets on their backs. Men coming back from hunting carried long-barrelled muzzle-loaders; one showed me how the gun was fired by the application to a touch-hole of a smouldering cord. My system for medical examinations was now established: Johnny called up to the people sitting at a hut doorway and, invited to join the family group, we kicked off our boots and climbed the notched log that served as a ladder up to the raised bamboo platform. Taking our seats on a mat, half-shaded by the thatch that formed a low eave over our heads, we were offered tea from the kettle simmering on a flat stone hearth. Bare-bottomed infants and puppies tottered around, licking each other's faces. Small boys, in trilby hats like their father's, sat cross-legged in the shadow of the doorway.

Johnny explained the reason for my visit, and one by one the children gravely offered themselves up to be examined while their siblings peered over my shoulder at my clinical notes. The parents conferred about their off-spring's medical history and then their own – how many babies had died of dysentery, how often they'd had malaria – and allowed me to look at their tongues and eyes, and place my stethoscope on their chests. The grandmother went last, unselfconsciously peeling off her blouse to reveal her withered breasts. Finally a bowl of water was produced containing the seed-pods of an acacia, in which I was invited to rinse my hands. They all hoped that I would soon return with a hospital, for they suffered much sickness.

Once these people had lived on the other side of the Salween where they'd had rice fields, but after being press-ganged by the Burmese army and having their harvest repeatedly commandeered, the whole village had relocated. Now they grew poppy. Occasionally one of the men might find employment with the loggers and bring back enough pay to purchase a few month's worth of rice. But contact with the Thai workers had significant drawbacks. A number of the villagers had developed coughs that produced bright blood-streaks. Weight-loss and night-sweats, and the resonance of breath-sounds through my stethoscope, indicated that they had become infected with tuberculosis.

It was in that place – as I wrote the date in my journal above the record of my examinations – that I realized it was my birthday. I mentioned the fact to Johnny as we drove back to Ho Mong, the dust road glimmering in the twilight. Johnny announced that it was the General's birthday too, and on the outskirts of town instructed our driver to stop outside a guarded compound. He disappeared through a gate, returning after a few minutes with one of the General's aides: the significance of our shared birth-dates was deemed propitious, and our group was expected at once inside Khun Sa's mansion to attend his party. Water was brought for us in an ante-room to wash off our travel-dust, while Virginia protested that she had nothing to wear. Then we were ushered to a table in the banqueting hall. Johnny poured me a glass of Hsan Loi rice whisky – its label showed a mountain peak, tipped by the setting sun – and offered me a Shan cheroot, eight inches long and thick as a finger. He stood to attention as his Commander approached. Khun Sa and I shook hands, fellow Aquarians. He made a short speech. 'If we were free we would not need opium,' Johnny translated, 'but they make war on us. We thank you for coming to help our people, for we need assistance from the West.' Khun Sa held his glass with both hands, his fingers forming a neat triangle, and lifted it before his bowed head in a toast. The Shan nationalists and Chinese money-men clapped.

The next morning we set off on our survey through Khun Sa's domain. Three valleys traversed the seventy-mile-wide enclave of Free Shan State, running northwards from the mountain range that formed the Thai border through rugged hills to meet the Salween river. Mule tracks along these trade-routes had been converted by Thai loggers into roads, providing access into Thailand. A transverse track followed tributaries and coiled over sharp ridges to connect the valleys – a means of transport for troops, supplies and soon, we hoped, medical services – across the Free State. Ho Mong lay in the western valley, which we had already surveyed. Further populations lived in the central valley along the Nam Me Mark and Nam Me Pate Rivers, and the eastern one supported a large settlement and rice-producing area at Mong Hta on the Nam Pang Hang River with more villages upstream around Mai Soong near the Thai border. We needed to visit them all.

A reliable pick-up truck had been placed at our disposal,

and Johnny and I stood just behind the cab as we drove out of Ho Mong in the early coolness. The load-bed was packed with women and children taking advantage of this opportunity to visit and trade. Near the tailgate, stretched out comfortably among piles of sacks and baskets and live chickens, were Stevie and Virginia. A short distance north of Ho Mong we swung east and started climbing along a road of wondrous views. It skirted crests, ran along the tops of razor-back ridges and zigzagged down the sides of plunging cliffs. In valley bottoms our truck thumped across boulder-strewn river beds – in one an elephant worked, piling logs at a timber depot beside the track – then inched its back-and-forth way up the other side. Always we trailed a column of dust, fine as flour, that roiled about the rear of the truck and turned the passengers a blotchy ochre. With a bandanna across my face I watched ahead as we passed through shadowed groves of high bamboo and verdant jungle, the trees covered in white blossom, then broke into the clear on skylines to look over range after range of blue ridges that faded into the blue haze of the distance.

The smell of smoke, from fires set by loggers to clear the undergrowth, accompanied our progress. Grey palls shrouded the valleys, lit from within by the flash of exploding bamboo, and dense white columns rose from distant hillsides. Barefoot children crowded round the truck in hill-tribe villages where we stopped to do our survey. East-facing slopes, so steep as to be almost vertical, held the spiky remains of last season's poppy harvest, their seed-pods scored by the parallel claws of the sap-collectors' forks. We slept in the rear of a trading store in a valley settlement, on the edge of a desert of just-cleared jungle. The sound of chainsaws rose from the loggers' camp where they were trimming tree-trunks. Garbage – plastic bags and Coke tins – clogged the steam. We breakfasted on rice and greens and snake-meat fried in chilli-oil and started off again, weighed down by yet more passengers. The road climbed through another range of mountains. Now and then a billow of dust would herald the approach of another vehicle: a truck loaded with cut timber and thatch and a teetering cargo of men in MTA uniform with red rags fluttering from the barrels of their weapons. Logging rigs, their trailers piled high with teak, inched past us on hairpin bends on their way to the Thai border.

Around Mong Hta the valley broadened into a veritable oasis. Bubbling irrigation ditches flowed between rich green paddy fields and the white bell-shape of a Buddhist stupa glowed on a hill above a grove of fruit trees. We conducted our survey knowing that this community might soon be evacuated. The Burmese advance was only some fifteen miles away and they were bound to try to take this valley and its industry; a heroin refinery guarded by Khun Sa's men operated still in Mong Hta. As we drove south the valley closed in again and with it, the night. Red lines of fire snaked up the hillsides and marched across distant peaks. Our route crossed and re-crossed a stream; the truck's head-lights, softened in the mist that rose from the water's surface, becoming bright and hard as the road rose and the beams flashed across the bamboo walls of the settlements. Candles, lit by the villagers with the approach of darkness, glowed inside miniature spirit-houses at the roadside. Eventually we saw electric light on a distant hillside: the house of the Shan forestry officer at Mai Soong, with whom we would be staying. Our vehicle ground up a rough driveway. Dogs barked, light flooded across a courtyard from an opened door and, cold and dusty, we climbed down to meet our host and be offered tea.

✪

The normal population of this eastern valley had been swollen by refugees fleeing the Burmese advance. Mainly

Palaung hill-tribe people, they had gathered at Mai Soong as close to the Thailand border as they could reach. The Thais prevented them from crossing but allowed some sacks of rice to pass in the other direction for the displaced. These poor people owned scarcely a pot to cook it in; most had been working in the fields when gunfire and the sight of flames rising from their villages had alerted them to the arrival of the Burmese army. Those who could had fled into the jungle. It had taken a week or more to find their way here over the steep ridges, hiding in the daytime while small parties went out foraging for food. Some had not returned and were feared captured or killed. The survivors now occupied crude lean-to shelters of bamboo and grass, erected in wavy lines across the hillside. They stood outside in family groups, each a knot of colour. The green jackets and deep red sarongs of the women smouldered in the sunlight. It glinted off silver bracelets and the lacquered hoops of silver and bamboo that encircled their waists like life belts.

We climbed up to the shelters. No one spoke. There was a tinkling sound from the small silver bells that the women wore stitched in a band around each upper arm, but up close their brocaded jackets were stained and filthy. The shelters stank of sweat and smoke and diarrhoea. The women's bare feet were caked with dirt and the tiny babies at their breasts suckled weakly, seemingly without nourishment. I passed among them, cataloguing illnesses – malaria and dysentery, pneumonia and tuberculosis – an agency as inscrutable to them in its motivation as the weather or the Tatmadaw. With the resignation of the dispossessed they answered my questions in quiet, exhausted tones, and let me see their tongues and listen to their chests and ask about their babies, living and dead.

The Mong Tai Army ran a small hospital in the valley nearby, a bamboo room on a rise beside the road. Inside, in the light that filtered through the slatted walls, patients huddled under blankets on wooden beds. I asked the medical assistant if I could look around his establishment, and was welcomed with an effusive gratitude that only added to my sense of helplessness. Most of the soldiers looked like boys. Some were flushed and restless, sweating through malarial nightmares; others, hit in the current fighting, were still shocked by the brush with oblivion that had knocked them helpless to the ground. One had had his leg blown off and now had gangrene in the stump. Flies clustered on the foul dressings, as the medical assistant waited for permission to evacuate him over the border to a surgical facility in Thailand. Other men had enlarged lymph glands or distended bellies; the victims of tropical fevers whose cause and treatment – lacking any diagnostic facilities – I could only guess at.

Afterwards we sat in our host's summer house, an open-sided pavilion of bamboo on a bluff at the end of the garden. He'd brought out bottles and glasses and we sipped Sun Thip whisky and slapped at the mosquitoes that rose from the paddy fields, now gleaming with the last of the sky's fading light. I was exhausted by the sadness of examining people whose pain I'd been unable to ameliorate. Yet each tragedy carried with it a balancing note of hope: each pathological statistic added to the information we needed to achieve the establishment of a civilian hospital in Free Shan State, with committed staff and a training programme for village health assistants. I hoped that it might help the survival of the hill-tribes, their very existence now threatened by disease and war. I could feel the whisky burn its way down my gullet. I decided that I would volunteer to be among the new hospital's first doctors.

We had been joined by the local Mong Tai commander, a boorish individual with a revolver on his hip. Between gulps of whisky he announced that he wished to have the hospital placed here at Mai Soong to treat the local refugees. Through Johnny, I attempted to explain that if the Burmese captured Mong Hta the road would be cut, isolating this eastern valley from the rest of Free Shan State, and the hospital staff – and the refugees – would be forced to retreat into Thailand or be captured. The commander interrupted angrily. The Shan were invincible, he declared (Johnny translating in an undertone); did we perhaps not believe that the General would defeat the Tatmadaw? I demurred; of course we had full confidence in the MTA . . .

'The General is in control of the situation,' announced the commander. 'I too am in control,' and he pulled out his revolver and waved it drunkenly.

Everyone but Johnny flinched and made fluttering gestures with their hands. Clapping an arm around the commander's shoulders, he poured the man a huge jolt of whisky, adding a similar dollop to his own glass. Then he lifted his drink, proposing a salutation. The man reached for the brimming tumbler. Finding the pistol in his way, he fumbled for the holster and missed it, dropping the weapon in the dirt. Johnny covered the gun with his boot, simultaneously placing the glass in the officer's hand. Both men threw back their drinks. The empty glasses thumped on the table and Johnny at once refilled them. The commander had been searching for his gun, striking about his waist with wild slaps, but now – matching Johnny's toast – he drank again. Then he stumbled to his feet and retched over the pavilion's handrail. Johnny picked up the weapon and flipped out its cylinder, ejecting the cartridges. Automatically he blew the dust from the barrel and action before stepping round to help the commander back to his vehicle. As he handed the man's slack weight over to the driver, Johnny slipped the empty pistol back into its sheath.

✪

We retraced our path westwards to complete our survey in the central valley. A cluster of settlements, the largest called Nam Cut, lay in a fertile hollow that carried a track from Thailand northwards to meet the main transverse road. It took several days to complete an assessment of all the villages in the area, assisted by Johnny, while Kya Nu, Virginia and Stevie made enquiries about transport links – the road apparently remained passable in the rainy season – and the quality of the water. Nam Cut seemed an ideal location for the hospital. It lay astride a clean stream that was spanned by a series of slender bamboo bridges, and was sufficiently far from the front to be spared an MTA garrison. Water buffalo grazed beneath a pagoda that marked a small Buddhist monastery. We stayed in the house of a retired Thai logger who had become a monk, and now ran a small centre for the treatment of malaria. After our evening meal of rice and greens and smoked monkey – the small hands, pressed upon us as a delicacy, were cartilaginous and stringy – Johnny would play the guitar and sing old blues numbers; it turned out that he had been a nightclub singer in Rangoon at one stage in his complicated life.

Bang Kank was the last settlement to be surveyed in the Nam Me Kun valley. I sat in the tea-house, prey to the attentions of a species of biting fly that favoured delicate skin – the ankle or inner arm – raising a pin-head sized red blister. A dessicating wind gusted down the street, flaying the eyes and raising small dust-storms. I had just completed my medical assessment, finding some distinctive pathology in the last man I'd examined. His toes and fingers were blunted stumps and a deep ulcer had eroded his heel, revealing the underlying bone. There was thickening of the ulnar nerves, which could be felt like cords on the insides of his elbows: the man had leprosy. I recorded the clinical findings in my journal, and made a note that treatment for the condition would have to be included in the services of the prospective hospital. Kya Nu was engaged with the MIAOW staffers on an economic assessment of each household. He had been talking to the tea-shop owner about where we might find accommodation for the night, but Johnny and I, our work done, were ready to move on.

A pick-up truck, top-heavy with drums of diesel, rattled along the street. It was on its way to a logging camp near Nong Aw, a village on the road back to Ho Mong, and Johnny negotiated a ride for the two of us perched atop the cargo. The driver raced his engine, we threw our bags aboard, and fled from the sober weight of the rest of the company. The truck leaped over bumps and ploughed deeper the existing ruts, while we sat high on the shifting drums, swathed against the dust – Vitamin D, Johnny called it – and exulted in the joy of moving. Eventually, after a few hours of wild hill-driving, the vehicle pulled up in the compound of a logging depot beside the track. We shouldered our bags and began walking over the long ridge that led to Nong Aw. Up the road towards us came a marching column of MTA soldiers. They walked in two files, keeping to the thin cover of the overhanging teak branches. The incline was steep and the men, burdened with rifles, rocket launchers and packs, plodded like draught animals, their eyes on the ground before their feet.

At the top of the ridge the commander, riding a large-boned mule, ordered them to halt. The men threw themselves down by the roadside. Johnny spoke to the officer while I sat on the verge, watching more men toiling up the slope below me. Some wore bonnets of fresh green leaves as sun-hats, most the square-fronted MTA cap. Baggage mules were in the column too, their wicker panniers loaded with rocket-shells. As soon as the soldiers were no longer driving the mules they stopped in the middle of the track, straddle-legged.

'They are on their way to Mong Hta,' Johnny explained. 'In the next few days they will launch a counter-attack to try to push the Burmese back. The dry season will end soon.

When the rains come nothing can move, and we will have some months to prepare before the Tatmadaw's next offensive.'

The track dipped down towards the settlement that lay below on a saddle of hillside, its outline dissolving in the dusk. Our feet made no sound in the thick dust. The moon showed over a ragged fringe of trees that the loggers had left, the clean aroma of resin wafting from cut stumps beside the track. Roosters and dogs called among the huts and cooking fires flickered behind the wooden stockades. We passed the first dwelling, half-buried in the jungle's edge. A tiny flame showed low between the bamboo slats and a cloying, acrid smell, like burning peaches, seeped across the path.

'Opium,' said Johnny.

At the village centre, where the road turned, a paraffin lamp hung below the eaves of the tea-shop. We dropped our packs and sat on rough benches around a little table. We ate and drank as the stars came out and the evening cooled. Then, with a bottle of jungle whisky – harsh rice-spirit – and a pack of Xinxing cigarettes before us, Johnny began to talk.

'I have used opium,' he said. 'It was when I was with the BCP [Burmese Communist Party forces] in the east of Shan State near the Yunnan frontier. We had positions in the hills, and the Burmese were trying to come in to the zone we controlled. They were boys from the cities and the plains with no experience of the jungle, and they were frightened to leave the paths. I would take my men through their lines and lie in ambush. We shot many of them. At night, when we came back to our base I would report on the radio how many we had shot and then go and bathe. Then I would smoke opium, a couple of pipes, and ask forgiveness from the spirits of the men I had killed.'

⊕

Our quarters that night were in the back room of the tea-shop. I lay under my blanket and thought of the young soldiers I'd seen that afternoon, trudging uphill on their way to the front. Apart from a notion of Shan identity – perhaps no more substantial than the miniature Free State flag on their sleeves – they were preoccupied with simple things: their feet, bruised through the thin soles of their canvas boots, the weight of the rifles grinding on their shoulders. Yet they would, if ordered, die for Khun Sa, a man categorized by many as an amoral gangster. I considered my own situation. By sheer good fortune I had managed to avoid ever having to shoot at anyone, or to become canon-fodder for someone else's cause. I'd been able to make the choice of coming here of my own free will. Too cold to sleep, I lay on the bamboo platform and thought about how that choice entailed a responsibility to try to help these people. I could do little to alter the factors acting against them; even my medical assessment might make no difference. Under such circumstances, a doctor should at least try to treat the person in front of him. So far on this trip I had not managed to improve the lot of a single individual.

The next morning Johnny and I conducted our medical survey in the village. The Pa-O people were impoverished, their children snot-nosed and in rags. These hill-tribe families all grew opium and some brought out their harvests to show me; malleable balls of dark sap, each of one *wis* – a traditional measure of crude opium, around three and a half pounds in weight – wrapped in the dried red petals of the poppy flower. In a good year a family could harvest four *wis*, enough to pay for their food requirements. In a bad season they would have to borrow rice from the shop-keepers, mortgaging their next year's crop against the debt. Even if Khun Sa's hope for crop substitution was successful, it was hard to imagine that these hills would support much more than subsistence agriculture.

There was no medical service in Nong Aw. The shopkeeper had a small stock of tablets, but most people depended on the local herbal practitioner. I met him at the tea-shop where he spread his armamentarium for my inspection; bags, tins and boxes containing bits of horn, bone, galls and roots that would be filed into powder and mixed with red and black potions made of dried blood and opium. His most precious remedies were some fragments of ancient Chinese pottery, their colours still bright but the edges rubbed smooth where they had been ground away for medicine. A shard of sea-green celadon-ware he pronounced a cure for poisoning; I wondered if he knew that celadon platters were once used by Chinese emperors because the glaze was reputed to change colour in contact with poison. Generally the man's potions were for the treatment of fevers, which he differentiated into 'wet' and 'dry' types; each of these had further subdivisions which were not easy to distinguish.

Suspecting that most fevers were likely to be due to malaria, I asked him how he knew which type he was treating. That was simple, he told me; if one combination of ingredients did not work he tried another, until the patient responded. When he'd found the right prescription he knew the diagnosis. A firm empiricist, he was scornful of people he'd heard of who tried to drive away fevers by thrashing the afflicted with leaves. In fact I'd heard about this very treatment from Dr Myint, who had described how in northern Shan State a traditional treatment had been for sufferers to lash themselves with branches of a particular shrub. Chinese researchers studying this unlikely therapy had found that it was often very effective in bringing down temperature. They'd isolated a compound absorbed through the skin from the broken leaves; a natural anti-malarial agent called artesenate, which was now being marketed worldwide in tablet form for the treatment of the disease.

I noticed that the man's eyelids twitched continually; his greyish skin and constricted pupils indicated that he was an opium addict. He admitted that he smoked twenty pipes a day, and offered – noticing my curiosity as a fellow physician – that I accompany him home to watch him light up, and to partake if I wished. His hut was the one on the village edge that Johnny and I had passed the night before. Inside it was dark and low, furnished only with a sleeping platform and a kettle. From a beam he brought down a bag and laid its contents on the floor. He lit a small spirit-lamp that sent flickering shadows across the woven mat. Braced on one elbow, the man placed a chip of opium in a ladle and heated it over the flame until it was soft. He tore open a tiny plastic sachet and blended its contents with the black sap, twirling the mixture onto a long iron needle. I questioned the added ingredient and he handed me the wrapper: a dose of 'Red Cross Painkiller Powder'. The man brought out his pipe – a slender, brass-bound length of polished ebony with a soapstone bowl – and warmed it over the lamp. Into its recess he stroked the sticky substance from the needle; then, lying on his side, he sucked the flame into the bowl. His cheeks hollowed, the pipe wheezed and bubbled. His eyelids closed. His head lowered gently on the pillow, and I stole away.

✪

The next day the truck arrived with Virginia, Stevie and Kya Nu on board, and we returned to Ho Mong. They plunged straight back into their round of meetings while I made for the hospital in the hope of doing some proper work. I was met by Doctors Seng and Myint, who proposed that we make a comprehensive round to see all of the hospital's patients. We started in the isolation cubicles – like large plank packing-crates – that held the sickest cases. In one was a boy of fourteen with cerebral malaria, half-covered by a blanket that gave off a sour smell of sickness. He snored, face uptilted, sweat running like tears from his swollen cheeks. His limbs were lashed to the cot-sides to prevent them thrashing about in his delirium, while into one thin ankle ran an intravenous drip, the chloroquine infusion that might save his life.

The hospital's major surgical cases had been transferred across the border to Mae Hong Son – with the payment of a generous squeeze to the Thai officials – in the expectation of new casualties from the MTA counter-offensive. Those that remained were low-priority cases, mainly men with flesh wounds and jungle ulcers. Blow-flies had laid their eggs in the wounds so that maggots looped and swarmed under the dressings, cleaning away the slough of dead meat. I suggested that the wounds, once clean, should be skin-grafted. Dr Myint said that his attempts to use this treatment generally failed. He'd tried pinch grafts, taken from a distant site – usually the inner arm or thigh – by raising a nip of skin between thumb and fore-finger and slicing off the small peak with a scalpel blade. These patches of skin would be transplanted to the wound and laid on to the raw surface, then covered with a bandage. Few of them took, while the donor sites themselves sometimes became infected as well.

I explained that pinch grafts took the full thickness of the skin, including its deepest layers and even some underlying fat: often, before a new blood supply could grow into the implant from the wound's surface, the skin had died. A better technique was to take only the thinnest outer layer – a split skin graft – but that required a piece of special equipment, a Humby knife or dermatome. Dr Myint shook his head.

'Among our surgical instruments we don't have any special things, only scissors and clamps and retractors.'

'I've read of a way to make a skin-graft knife,' I said, 'from a safety razor. We need a metal one, the type that screws apart to take a Gillette blade. And a small file.'

An orderly was despatched to the market. He returned with a solid-looking Chinese-made razor, a package of blades and a Palaung metal-worker with his tools. We examined the razor. The flat base on which the blade rested had a smooth, curled-under edge to slide along the shaver's face. Parallel to the edge ran a slot that, during shaving, allowed the scum of foam and bristles to escape. A small bar bridged the slot at its midpoint. Following my directions the artisan filed away the metal bridge, so that the slot ran uninterrupted for its full length of around one and half inches. I also had him grind off the edge of one of the blades so that it was completely blunt. Then I placed the disassembled parts in disinfectant while Dr Myint looked for our first skin-graft candidate.

One of the boy soldiers on the nearby ward had a great, raw area on the back of his thigh. The wound looked clean but, because of its size, would take weeks to heal by skin growth inwards from the edges. Our patient had not yet had his breakfast rice and the anaesthetist was ready to dope him right away; the boy, who had already spent a week lying on his face, was keen to try any treatment that might shorten his stay in hospital. Once he was asleep on the operating table we turned him on his side to reach the wound and cleaned it vigorously with gauze and saline, rubbing the granulation tissue – the rough mat of new cells and small capillaries that had formed in its base – hard enough to make it bleed. Then we covered it and cleaned the donor site on the other thigh, scrubbing the skin with antiseptic soap. I put together the parts of the razor, placing the blunt-edged blade as a spacer beneath a sharp one, and screwed in the handle that locked the assembly together. While Dr Myint stretched the outside of the healthy thigh between two spatulas, I laid the edge of my improvized graft-knife against the smooth skin that he held under tension. Angling the razor as though shaving, I drew it downwards.

A translucent fringe of tissue emerged through the slot and rumpled there in fine folds. Behind the blade's progess a swathe appeared, as broad as the razor, where the brown surface of the skin seemed shocked into paleness. Then a blush of fine pinpricks of blood emerged, that grew and coalesced until it seemed I was painting the limb with red. Dr Myint slid the spatula downwards, flattening the curve of the thigh ahead of the advancing blade. At the end of a six-inch sweep I stopped and lifted the razor. From it hung a diaphanous band; a superficial membrane of skin. Dr Myint looked at me, his eyebrows rising above his surgical mask.

'A proper split-skin graft,' I said, impressed. 'That spacing blade set the thickness so we took off just the outermost layer. You could tell from the fineness of those first bleeding points: they showed that we cut through the very tips of the tiny capillaries supplying the sweat glands.'

Using scissors, I carefully snipped the strip of skin from its attachment to the thigh. It felt no more substantial than moist tissue paper, and I spread it gently with forceps over a square of saline-damp gauze. Then Dr Myint wielded the razor, skimming off a second and third strip of thigh skin alongside the first. We covered the raw surface with a pressure dressing to stop it oozing, and returned our attention to the original wound.

The granulation tissue in its base had stopped bleeding and was covered with a layer of sticky plasma. Dr Myint pointed out that the raw area to be covered was quite a lot larger than our available grafts. I showed him how the sheets of skin could be expanded, by draping them carefully over a wooden spatula and incising the surface with many small, parallel scalpel-cuts; gentle sideways tension made the skin strips expand into a mesh that reached the dimensions of the wound. Just in time I remembered that the spilt surface of the graft was shiny, so that it had to be applied with the dull side – the original outer surface of the skin – outwards, or it would not take. The fine membrane stuck readily to the clotting plasma, small beads of which began to emerge through the holes; these would drain fluid, preventing it accumulating under the graft and lifting it off. I tacked the new skin to the wound edges with a series of small stitches and padded it with moist cotton wool, before bandaging the wound and the donor area on the other thigh.

The patient was waking up, and I asked the anaesthetist to keep him sedated for twenty-four hours so that he would not disrupt the dressings. This was the crucial period when delicate capillaries would be growing into the new skin and proliferating epidermal cells would fill the gaps in the mesh, as well as re-covering the donor site.

'You can leave the bandages on for seven days,' I explained. 'Just inspect them daily to see that they haven't become wet or begun to smell. Then at the end of a week, soak the dressings off with saline so that the graft doesn't get detached. You can take the sutures out then, and after that keep the wound protected with gauze until it's completely healed.'

Dr Myint was delighted with the new technique, though perhaps not even so pleased as I; my improvised instrument had worked, and operating had banished the frustration I had been feeling about the clinical limitations of my evaluation mission.

Not even the disappointment of the rest of the team could undermine my satisfaction. Virginia and Stevie reported that a day-long, difficult meeting with the Shan officials had reached an impasse, with the Health Minister stating that the new hospital would be placed south of Ho Mong on the road near the Thai border. As this part of Free Shan State was relatively well supplied with medical services, and with Mae Hong Son hospital in Thailand only twenty miles to the south, such an establishment would offer little increased benefit to the local civilian population. Exasperated, the MIAOW staff decided they would return forthwith to Chiang Mai. I elected to stay for a couple more days, to speak again to the Minister. Also, to my surprise, my request to the Mong Tai Army chief to let me visit the front had suddenly been approved.

Dr Myint and I left early the next morning in the hospital's battered truck. It did not need to take us far; at Num Lung, ten miles north, the road ended and we would have to start walking. In the back sat two boy soldiers with our packs and provisions. We drove up the hill out of town, the truck rocking over the ruts like a surf-boat. The road stretched ahead, barred with shadow. Jungle ridges rose above it, soft in the rising light. On the switchbacks we passed a descending caravan of mules, their panniers empty after delivering rice to the front line. The muleteers rode seated sideways on their pack-saddles. The rear-guard was a boy on a tall roan horse. He wore a white shirt and a red bandanna, and had his carbine cross-slung on his chest; riding through a bar of sunlight, he seemed to glow against the dark fringe of the forest.

At Num Lung village we hid the truck in a banana grove near the army post and started walking. The path dived into a valley that fell steeply towards the Salween gorge. We followed mule-tracks and the imprints of the canvas boots of MTA troops. Under the trees the air was still and hot. Birds called, and from over a shoulder of mountain to the west came the sound of shots, muffled by the jungle. A couple of hours of walking brought us to a small defile. Bamboo shelters were set into its slopes, their raised floors carrying the sleeping forms of soldiers. An officer greeted us and received gratefully, on behalf of his men, the gifts of cigarettes that we had brought. Then he led us down a gully that emerged behind a deserted village, its bamboo walls splayed and great divots of thatch gone from the rafters. A hundred feet below, the sapphire-green waters of the Salween slid between rocky banks.

'Burmese guns hit this place often,' said the officer. 'They are up there.' He pointed at the heights of the opposite bank, clad in thin, dry forest. 'We must stay hidden.'

Keeping behind the cover of the houses, we filed downhill. The path ducked into a grove of trees, where the officer stopped at a small, roofed platform – a shrine, whose dark recess held some flowers on a red-checked cloth – to light a candle. He bowed and clapped once, softly. Then, beckoning us to follow, he leapt into a hole that appeared to open at his feet.

The jungle along the riverbank was laced with defences. Crouching, we followed the officer along a trench that skirted tree roots and embraced the curves of buried boulders to link the log-roofed bunkers. It was dark inside the dug-outs and the earthen walls gave off a damp, fermenting smell like sour dough. It mingled with the wood-smoke odour of the soldiers' uniforms. Some men kept watch, staring through firing slits across the dazzle of the river's surface. Others slept in trench bottoms or in rough niches cut into the walls. The officer indicated a couple of malaria cases, shivering in their blankets; he had no medic and no drugs, but the condition was so common that the sick stayed on duty, sweating out their fevers in the forward positions. However, he told us, evacuation of the wounded was a problem. A week ago the Burmese had tried to cross the Salween, losing three boats and the ferry which they had commandeered as a landing-craft. Its wreckage, said the officer, lay just around the bend. There had been MTA casualties, and the only way to get them out was through the village which had been under mortar fire the whole time; they'd had to wait in the bunkers for two days until the shelling stopped. Dr Myint promised to discuss the allocation of a medic with the Chief of Staff back in Ho Mong, though he didn't appear hopeful. The Tatmadaw's main offensive in the east was drawing off most of the MTA's resources.

Back in Ho Mong I arranged to see the Minister of Health. Johnny accompanied me and gave the man a summary of my history; that I had worked in other war zones treating wounded and that I'd been assisting the doctors at the Ho Mong Hospital. The minister appeared pleased that I had visited the Salween front, and after the usual circumlocutions and cups of tea, asked me what conclusions I'd reached regarding the provision of a hospital in Free Shan State. I explained the advantages of the Nam Cut Valley: its central location, its civilian and refugee populations and, delicately, the fact that there was no MTA base there that might lay our operation open to accusations of aiding Khun Sa's forces. The minister laughed.

'Those two that came with you were so nervous, always shouting. We thought it would be better to have their hospital near Ho Mong, so we could protect it. You can put it wherever you wish. Just give us the date of your return with your medical equipment and the people will start building.'

I met Johnny at the market-place the next morning, and we drank hot soy milk and raw egg while we waited for some transport. A pick-up truck arrived, heading across the border to Mae Hong Son. Johnny checked with the driver that he would be keeping to the back roads, and I put my pack aboard. I shook hands with the man whose comradeship had helped so much, and whose motorcycle driving had the night before provided the most dangerous moment of the mission: after a party with the hospital doctors that had taken in most of Ho Mong's bars, we'd been so drunk on rice wine that we'd ridden straight into a ditch. The truck was filling with hill-tribe women on their way to Thailand, and I climbed amongst them as the driver pulled away. I watched Johnny waving through the cloud of dust until he, and the houses of Ho Mong, were out of sight. Then I leant back on my bag and, surrounded by the swaying bodies of my fellow passengers, fell into a hangover-leavened doze.

I was awoken by a sudden hush; the chatter about me had stopped and the truck was slowing rapidly, the driver using gears and brakes to decelerate. The pall of dust that we'd been trailing caught us up, wrapping the back of the vehicle in a yellow haze. I peeped over the top of the cab. Some trucks were stopped ahead of us, blocked by a barrier across the track. It was manned by Thai Army Rangers in camouflage. The women motioned me to keep my head down; I huddled among them as the soldiers walked slowly along the verge, peering into the backs of the trucks. No one spoke or looked up. The cooling engine ticked in the stillness and from the front of the column came the metallic voice of a two-way radio. There was shouting as someone was pulled from a truck and led away. A murmur, like a soft groan, rose briefly from the women around me. They crouched lower, effacing themselves under the shadow of their black turbans. Beside our truck an order was barked and they flinched; a hand appeared above their bowed heads, pointing directly at me.

I climbed down. My pack and shoulder-bag were dropped onto the road. A soldier nudged them with his foot, indicating that I should pick them up. Another took up station behind me, and I was marched along the line of vehicles to the check-point. An officer looked me up and down, shouting questions in Thai. I shrugged, indicating my incomprehension. A rifle barrel struck the pack out of my hand. My shoulder-bag was tugged away and I was pushed towards the trees, where a small group of captives squatted on their haunches under guard. I crouched among them, my elbows on my knees. Near the road a table had been set, screened by bamboo mats, where the officers sat beside the radio-set directing operations. These men wore black uniforms, the mark of Thai special forces. I'd heard that the unit responsible for this sector of the frontier was notorious; reputedly recruited from jails and blamed for a massacre of civilians in Bien Luang some years before. Now one of them, with shoulder-length hair and sunglasses, was looking through my passport. He called out and a soldier hustled me over to the table where the contents of my shoulder-bag had been dumped.

'What you do in Shan State?' he demanded, his eyes invisible behind his shades. 'What you work?'

'I'm a doctor.'

'You friend Dzao Mong Khawn' – I recognized one of Khun Sa's pseudonyms – 'You sell guns.' He patted the pistol he wore in his armpit.

'No, I'm a doctor.' I pointed at the stethoscope that lay atop my possessions.

'You mercenary maybe.'

'I'm a doctor.' I picked up the battered copy of *A Simple Guide To Trauma* that always accompanied my travels and flipped it open, at a graphic on amputations. He didn't look at it. A second man, in a black T-shirt and baseball cap, slapped it from my hands.

'You narco dealer maybe.'

'No, I'm a doctor.'

The T-shirt man had found my maps and was examining them intently, trying to decipher the notations about road conditions and village populations. The other was leafing through my journal. He gave an order. I was told to pick up my pack. Flanked by two soldiers, I was pushed along a path behind the command-post. It ended at an earthen wall, where a sort of quarry had been cut into the valley's side. I was stood against the bank. The black-shirts emptied out my pack in front of me and began, meticulously, to arrange its contents; clothes and boots, photographic film, books and my small instrument kit, opened out to show its array of steel. My mosquito net and waterproof were military surplus and they examined them closely, then laid these out too. My camera bodies and lenses were marshalled in a row, the medical texts and documents opened to selected places. My hat was plucked from my head and added to the front of the display. The man with the shoulder holster produced a camera from the pocket of his combat trousers, and I and my possessions were photographed from every angle. Between shots a subordinate would dart forward to turn a page to a more incriminating anatomical diagram, or to open slightly my surgical scissors so that their sinister intent should not be missed.

When they'd used up a roll of film I was directed to repack. I carried my luggage back along the path. The group of prisoners still squatted under the trees. One man's face was puffed and blood dripped between his upraised knees; it appeared he had been beaten. On the road the trucks waited in the sunlight, their occupants with eyes downcast in that still air of menace. Back at the table another pair of sunglasses was reading a letter I'd written to my girlfriend that I'd not been able to post. The long-haired one, who seemed to be in charge, thrust forward the canvas wallet in which I kept my travel documents.

'Passport, ticket, moneys, all correct. You count.'

I looked inside the compartments. The items were there, even the foreign currency, but the wedge of Thai Baht that formed my ready cash had thinned to a single note. The man was staring at me with his impenetrable shades. 'All correct,' he said emphatically.

I nodded, throwing my things back into the shoulder-bag. I knew a bargain when I saw one.

✪

I wrote up my medical findings, which were incorporated into the Free Shan State Evaluation prepared by MIAOW. 'There is an immediate need for reinforcement of the existing limited medical resources,' it read. 'Endemic tropical diseases, and the continuing conflict . . . have left the civilian population exposed to readily treatable conditions. The lack of public health services, the inaccessibility of treatment centres and the absence of foreign aid organizations, has isolated a vulnerable population.'

MIAOW also published a newsletter requesting donations. It led with poignant pictures of hill-tribe folk and highlighted the organization's unique access to the area: 'The political implications of the opium and logging trade create a sensitive environment where only a neutral non-political organization such as MIAOW could carry out low-profile civilian assistance.'

Neither of these documents brought any benefit to the people of Free Shan State. The government officials responsible for dispensing overseas aid – MIAOW's main source of funds – refused to support an operation there: apparently, pressure from the US State Department had vetoed the setting-up of a humanitarian mission in the territory of an 'enemy' of American foreign policy. I met the film-maker for a drink and told him the result. He was disappointed at the news, but not surprised. He had been present in 1975 when Khun Sa had made the first of several well-publicized offers to sell his opium stocks to the Americans at a fraction of their market value. He had filmed the meeting with the team of US Congressional Narcotics Commission officials, flown by Thai military helicopter from Bangkok to Khun Sa's base.

'Khun Sa offered the entire crop to the Commission at the "border price" of twelve million dollars,' said the film-maker. 'Considering that at the time the US was spending seven hundred million a year to suppress the opium trade along that border, it didn't seem a bad deal.'

Instead, the Drug Enforcement Administration had received an additional allocation of funds, with which they'd supplied helicopters and crop-spraying aircraft to the Burmese army to attack Khun Sa's poppy production areas in Shan State. Agent Orange-type defoliants had been sprayed over rebellious ethnic minority villages as a counter-insurgency weapon, destroying food crops and creating a local famine. Now the anti-narcotics agencies in Washington were again invoking Khun Sa's name to obtain funding for drug suppression in the region; indeed, some were pressing the Clinton administration to resume material assistance to the Burmese army's 'drug eradication' programme, frozen by the US since 1988 in protest at the military government's abysmal human rights record. I remembered something Khun Sa had said to me at his birthday gathering, while below in the compound the bears howled in their cages. He was talking of the DEA, but his words applied just as well to all the other organizations who exploited him to justify their functions. 'They use me like a Christmas tree,' he said, smiling sadly. 'When they need more budget they shake me, Khun Sa, and the money comes falling out.'

12

South Africa and Brazil

Durban sweltered under a pall of moist heat. Outside the medical school's Industrial Health Unit wing, mynah birds screamed in a grove of avocado trees. Mark and I sat in a windowless room, in the flat light of a bank of viewing screens. On each screen was a chest X-ray: the struts of the collar bones, the parallel curve of the ribs. In every one the dark translucence of the lung-fields was marred by drifts and snow-storms of white.

'Compensation claims,' said Mark. 'Mesothelioma from the asbestos mills, chrome-workers' fibrosis from the plating chambers, lung cancer from the aluminium smelting plants.'

At his elbow were stacked more X-rays in yellow dust covers: the ghosts of workers, consumed like raw materials in the manufacturing processes. These damaged human by-products produced in Mark an un-industrial compassion.

'Here is a textbook case of mercury poisoning,' he said. 'Such a severe case should never occur in modern industry. I doubt if such a case has been seen in an industrialized country in fifty years.'

He pushed a tape into a video player.

'Peter was twenty-two years old, perfectly healthy,' said Mark. 'He went to work at the company and within a month or two he started having dizzy spells. After three months he was dismissed. His family took him to hospital. He was having difficulty walking and talking, numbness in his hands and feet. We drew a blood sample and found massively high levels of mercury.'

On the screen a figure appeared: a slim black man, swathed in too-large hospital pyjamas, shambling towards the camera down a neon-green corridor. He could barely lift his feet; his knees shimmied, his arms danced, and corkscrew, writhing motions twisted his spine and neck.

'This is Peter, when he was admitted,' said Mark. 'It took him a year and a half to die.'

⊕

It was through the network of South African exiles' tales that I'd first heard of the matter: a peculiar outbreak of madness, among black workers at a chemical factory halfway between the cities of Durban and Pietermaritzburg. Apparently fit young men, after a spell at the plant, were reportedly being possessed by paranoid delusions or frank psychosis. These reports of bizarre symptoms provoked considerable medical interest – Mark, an occupational health specialist at the Durban medical school's Industrial Health Unit, thought that they might be due to some form of heavy metal poisoning – but the company refused permission for him to examine its workforce. It was implied instead that the epidemic was due to bewitchment, or a localized ethnic predilection for schizophrenia.

The factory belonged to a British transnational chemical company called Thor – named after the Norse God of Thunder, whose symbol was the element mercury – and the judgement banning the Industrial Health Unit doctor had come down from UK headquarters. Thor's South African operation was already in the local news after mercury had been found in routine testing of a nearby river, the Umgeni, that provided the main water supply for Durban. Environmental investigators trying to assess the severity of the contamination sent samples to be tested in international laboratories. The mercury content of sediment from a stream in a valley below the factory was reported to be hundreds of times above the concentration that would classify it as hazardous waste in the USA. The company had responded by threatening its detractors with legal action, while the South African authorities seemed unprepared to pursue the matter, either as a risk to workers' health or as an environmental hazard.

I was becoming accustomed to seeing the blatant consequences of war and political strife in different parts of the world, and treating its casualties. Mercury's toxic effects, by comparison, might be more insidious, but they were happening in a place that I knew. The wide vista of the Umgeni valley – its river brown with topsoil eroded from the small maize-fields along its banks – had been part of my childhood. Later, as a doctor, I'd worked at a hospital in the sprawling township outside Pietermaritzburg, and knew something of the urban deprivation – and the inferior education available to black South Africans – which the workers would have had to overcome in order to obtain skilled employment in the chemical industry. It seemed bitterly ironic that poor subsistence farmers and diligent scholars should be those paying the greatest price for the country's industrial growth. I began to follow the story closely.

Thor Chemicals had originally manufactured mercury compounds in England at a factory in Kent, one of a chain of subsidiaries the company owned around the globe. Through the 1980s – at a time when South Africa's police cells were full of torture victims, blood flowed in the streets of the townships and international businesses were disinvesting from South Africa as fast as they could – Thor greatly enlarged their operation in that country. The manufacture of mercury compounds was relocated to their South African factory, and with the blessing of the government a mercury waste recycling plant – the largest in the world – was built, to process mercury-contaminated material from Europe, the United States, South America and the Far East.

With most industrialized countries facing legislative pressure to halt discharges of this hazardous substance, South Africa was a logical place for such an operation. Environmental laws, and those protecting workers – particularly black ones – were rudimentary. Pretoria was trying to find ways of circumventing international sanctions against the sale of military material to South Africa; some of Thor's mercury products had strategic applications, and its clients included defence companies that were part of Armscor, the South African government's weapons manufacturing conglomerate. It seemed unlikely that the operating standards of such a vital industry would be too closely scrutinized in that country.

It was only when men who'd worked for Thor started turning up in hospital that Mark finally got to examine them. His clinical assessment was backed by neurologists and psychiatrists; the men revealed signs – loss of balance, personality changes, tremor and forgetfulness – diagnostic of severe mercury poisoning. An official enquiry was convened. Medical evidence was presented that the men's symptoms indicated sustained, chronic exposure to the toxin. Hydrologists stated that sediment samples suggested ongoing contamination of ground water below the factory. Then the enquiry was addressed by the British chairman and owner of the international Thor Group, who had flown from his home in the south of France to testify. He offered a startling thesis: that 'environmental terrorists' were responsible for deliberately releasing mercury contaminants into the ground water; the same shadowy force had poured mercury into the compressor that pumped air into the workers' protective breathing-masks on the production floor. These actions had been carried out in order to disrupt production by discrediting the company, part of ' . . . a long series of events, events which we know are sabotage'.

In another country such ideas might have been ridiculed, but in South Africa – among the white officials conducting the enquiry, who had grown up on conspiracy theories about the Total Onslaught of Global Communism – they had a certain resonance. The company was acquitted of significant responsibility and allowed to continue the production and recycling of mercury compounds. Over the following year the first Thor worker to have been admitted to hospital progressed inexorably through a vegetative state into a coma and then died. An autopsy examination by a state pathologist recorded massive amounts of mercury in his brain tissue. A second man lay on a hospital ward, slowly deteriorating. Treatment was unavailing, as the neurological effects of cumulative exposure to the metal could not be reversed. Now the legal authorities acted.

Two senior executives and the plant engineer of Thor's South African subsidiary were charged with culpable homicide, plus forty-two counts under various occupational safety acts that included causing injury to twenty-nine of their employees. All of the accused entered pleas of not guilty, apparently confident that they would be acquitted. Whatever the outcome of the pending legal action, it would not benefit the afflicted workers: South African industrial law effectively prevented them from claiming damages against their employer. Their only recourse was to the Workmen's Compensation Board, which was not known for its generosity. The family of the dead man received a non-negotiable stipend of nine hundred Rand – around one hundred pounds – a month. The Thor Chemicals group had an annual turnover of over fifty million pounds, but it was unassailable; previous judgements in British courts had ruled that parent companies registered in the United Kingdom were not liable for the actions of their overseas subsidiaries.

I set out the events in the form of a documentary proposal and approached the commissioning editor of *World in Action*, a British television programme considered a byword for investigative journalism. My suggestion was for a film that would explore issues of industrial culpability and the lack of protection for workers employed by the overseas branches of transnational companies. There were indications that the mercury poisoning problem might actually have originated in England. For seven years, inspectors of the UK Health and Safety Executive had criticized the standards of Thor's mercury operation at Margate in Kent, citing significant air contamination and high mercury levels in the urine of their English workforce. Finally, in 1987, the company had been warned that it faced prosecution for repeated safety contraventions. Thor shut down its mercury operation in England and relocated the entire manufacture of mercury compounds to South Africa, moving the British plant engineer to that country to oversee the process. Shortly afterwards, the first bizarre symptoms had been reported among South African workers. The plant engineer was one of the local Thor management now facing charges. *World in Action*'s editor wanted names named, guilt apportioned, the suffering of the victims shown. I was flown to South Africa to research the story.

⊕

My first meeting was with Mark, the occupational health specialist. He took me to the hospital where the latest victim lay; a strong man rendered mute and shrunken under the sheets. A nasal tube led into his stomach, instilling a feeding compound. A catheter drained his bladder. The patient stared upward, unresponsive, his eyelids flickering in the state of withdrawal that indicates profound neurological damage. The nurses had encased his hands in boxing-gloves of clean white gauze, taped at the wrists, so that he could not grasp the tubes in his half-coma and pull them out. Each day they were supposed to spend some time stretching his limbs to prevent flexion deformities, but the nursing staff were greatly overworked. His wife did it instead, travelling for an hour on the township bus to sit beside him and stroke his cheek and straighten his stiffening legs and arms.

I met Chris, an environmentalist who'd been threatened with legal action by the company's lawyers, who accused him of inflating for political ends the discovery of an 'insignificant' taint of mercury waste in river silt. He was a big, quiet man, with the solidity of a farmer. He showed me the factory, which stood on the rim of the watershed that drained into the Umgeni valley. The plant was a gleaming maze of ducts and pipes that rose above steel pressure tanks. Chimneys vented a grey haze downwind.

'That's the "recycling" part of the operation,' said Chris. 'They burn the waste. Very little mercury is reclaimed. Most of it is vaporized and drifts off down the valley on the prevailing wind, along with other toxic compounds like dioxins.' He pointed at the factory compound. 'Those warehouses and storage ponds are full of thousands of tons of mercury effluent. That's what's polluting the water.'

Other smoke-belching factories stood along the edge of the plateau; below them the land undulated downward into the wide-pleated rift – called, in Zulu, 'the Valley of a Thousand Hills' – of the Umgeni river. Conical thatched roofs of rondavels stood in clusters on the slopes, each adjoined by a small rectangle of crops and linked by paths that met at the streams from which all drew their water.

'Many of the newer residents here are refugees from political violence,' said Chris. 'They moved into this valley to escape death-squads in the townships. But in a way the environmental hazard they have found here is also political.'

He explained that this densely populated rural area had been demarcated as part of the Kwazulu 'homeland'. The positioning of these factories along its edge was not coincidental. The old apartheid planners dreamed that once all the country's black population had been corralled into their independent tribal homelands – and were therefore no longer citizens of South Africa – they would be used as labour in these 'border industries'.

S'bu, an organizer for the chemical workers union that now represented Thor's work force, drove me through the dangerous streets of a township in the valley. On its outskirts, up red-earth roads cut by rain gullies, lived some ex-employees who had been permanently disabled. Albert had once been a piano-player and footballer; now he could no longer tie his shoe-laces. Eric, twenty-five, talked with laboured difficulty. 'I was shaking from my toes to my head,' he stammered, as though his twitching tongue would not obey him, 'my gums went blue. They said I was mentally disordered . . . that I must sign a letter of resignation.' His mouth trembled. 'It was my first job, and my last,' he said. 'They have destroyed my life. I am ruined now.'

I visited the mother of the man lying in hospital. She lived in a concrete cube – a standard township dwelling unit – along with seven members of her family. Once they had depended on the salary of her son, a rare boon in a community where work was hard to find. Now, while their case was being considered by the Compensation Board, they lived on charity. She was busy cooking when I got there; a big, sad woman in her fifties, just back from church. A parishioner had given her a treat for the children's midday meal, an economy tin of baked beans and a loaf of pre-sliced white. The kids were outside playing gangsters. One boy had a toy pistol tucked into the front of his trousers, covered by his threadbare jumper. He pulled it out and held it to the head of a younger brother. The house stood on a little rise above a crossroads. It was a strategic position in the township war. Their side of the settlement supported the ANC; across the road was Inkatha territory. These children, playing tough-guy in the bare yard, were on lookout. Up the hill stood the 'self defence unit', a group of youths outside an iron-barred store, with home-made shotguns under their coats made from lengths of piping.

This was a front line that had no place for me. I retreated to the apartment I was using on Durban's beachfront, that looked out along the serried rollers of the Indian Ocean. Each afternoon it rained, a plunging downpour that washed the blown beach-sand off the streets. Then the sun would reappear, bathing the city in a misty, ethereal light through which the curling crests of the breakers appeared to smoke as they advanced on the pale beach. The repeating rumble of their collapse reached me on the nineteenth floor where I pored over toxicology texts, learning about mercury poisoning.

Mercury appears on the World Health Organization's 'Red List' of the twenty-three most toxic substances known to man. It affects human beings in diverse ways. The madness of hatters had been described in the late eighteenth century, due to the emotional swings and behavioural disturbance caused by mercuric compounds used in the setting of felt. The first treatise ever written on occupational illness, by Paracelsus in 1520, had described psychological and physical symptoms among miners of cinnabar, the reddish oxide of mercury that is its most common form in nature. I learned how the metal is deposited in the motor centres of the brain, causing diffuse symptoms of imbalance, tremor and physical deterioration. In severe cases, personality changes include psychosis, delusions and paranoid fear: I remembered Eric telling me that he had to sleep with someone watching over him all night, for he would wake in terror and try to flee, barefoot, through the township streets.

I reported to the commissioning editor on the information I had gathered, and said that I thought there were sufficient issues of medical and moral culpability to make a worthwhile documentary. The director, producer and camera crew flew out to join me. We filmed the damaged men trying to survive in the hopeless environs of the townships, the bereft, impoverished families of the sick and dying. With the local chief, we visited people living in the valley below the factory. They told us how they used the water of the stream for washing, and blamed it for the way the skin of their arms had become white – mercury is a component of dangerous skin-lightening creams sold widely as a cosmetic in Southern Africa – and for the deaths of their livestock. We arranged for a biologist to set traps in the nearby valleys, and the small mammals he captured were tested for mercury in their systems. The levels present below the plant were seven times higher than those in adjacent valleys, indicating that the contamination was continuing.

At the factory, we presented our evidence to Thor's South African managing director. He was a tall man with a dense, close beard that fitted his face like greasepaint. He sat in his office, arms folded, apparently unperturbed by the camera.

'There's been an ongoing campaign against the company for a long, long time,' he said, 'which goes back to when we were accused of polluting rivers and drinking water. This in fact wasn't the case. We were also accused of poisoning a large number of workers. Again, medically, that wasn't the case.' He was prepared to admit only to a single 'incident' – the sabotage event claimed by Thor's British owner. 'That's the only mercury poisoning incident that's occurred at Thor despite lots of accusations that have been made.'

As he talked, the reflecting face of his wristwatch blinked like a heliograph, betraying a fine flutter of nervousness, or the physical tremor of mercurialism. Now the director was stressing the company's exemplary record in caring for its workers. Each was tested regularly for mercury intake; those whose urine samples occasionally showed an unacceptably high level of the metal (the standard he used was four times above that considered the danger level by the World Health Organization) would be taken off the production floor and given orange juice to drink. This was supposed to help mercury excretion. Then, to prevent further exposure, they were assigned for a week or two to work in the gardens around the plant.

I knew a little of this man's background. In his teens he'd played guitar in a blues band with a couple of friends: in the affluent white Johannesburg suburbs where they lived, they'd been kids with a conscience, performing at impromptu parties attended by the black domestic workers. Of these events and many others, one of the group, Rian Malan, had later written *My Traitor's Heart*, perhaps the most penetrating exploration of white South African guilt ever published. I wondered how the managing director had made the transition from youthful social awareness to becoming this defender of corporate values. We'd obtained copies of the company's own monitoring records of their workers' mercury levels. These appeared to indicate that in the period prior to the poisoning 'incident' there had been over five hundred instances of the men's urine samples exceeding the company's standards, and some had had over twenty times the World Health Organization's safety limit. Even men who were sent to do ground work sometimes maintained their excessive levels; one ex-worker had told us that the contents of the mercury waste ponds were used to water the landscaped gardens in front of the modern brick-and-glass frontage of the plant.

We continued our filming in England. Thor's plant lay in an industrial park beside the seaside town of Margate, and its wide drive and lawns, as well as the shining façade of the building itself, suggested that the same industrial architect had been involved in its design. Here the managing director was a bluff, no-nonsense type who rebutted all questions about mercury mishaps at the British plant. We asked him about the inspections by the Health and Safety Executive, and their reports of persistent safety infractions over seven years: airborne concentrations of mercury in the plant had exceeded allowable limits by twenty times, mercury levels in workers' urine were found to be 'inexcusably high'.

'I don't know of any report where mercury in urine was higher than the HSE would recommend,' he said confidently. 'There was never any problem with the workers.'

But an advertisement we'd placed in the Margate paper had uncovered some ex-Thor employees who claimed they'd suffered mercury poisoning at the factory. One had told us how he'd tried to sue the company after developing symptoms – emotional changes, tremor, and blue discoloration of his gums – which had been medically identified as due to mercury poisoning. Thor had settled out of court, without admitting liability. The managing director showed us round the plant, an arrangement of pipes and tanks similar to the factory we'd seen in South Africa. As we passed through the processing rooms I noticed we were being shadowed by an anonymous figure, tall and silver-haired and dressed, like the workers, in hardhat and protective jacket. He circled behind us, listening to our questions and the managing director's replies. I nudged the film director; here was the chairman, the British owner of Thor's global operation, the man who'd testified to sabotage being the cause of the mercury problems in South Africa. She confronted him but he refused to make a statement or to be filmed; all we were doing, he claimed, was propagating lies.

The documentary showed in *World in Action*'s usual weekly slot. It attracted viewing figures of around 2.7 million; a respectable enough figure, said the commissioning editor, in these ratings-competitive times. Just before transmission, a long letter full of subordinate clauses arrived from Thor's lawyers threatening the television company with High Court proceedings for broadcasting 'material which is defamatory to our client'. The network's solicitors replied by return of post. I was told that their answer was a model of legal succinctness. 'Dear Sirs,' they were reported to have written, 'With respect to your communication of the twenty-eighth inst., we would refer you to the well-known statement by defending solicitors in the case of Goldsmith vs. Pressdram, 1976.'

The text of that famous letter, also written in reply to a threat of legal action for alleged defamation, had been even more simple and to the point: 'Fuck off.' Nothing more was heard from the Thor group's lawyers.

They may have had their hands full elsewhere, for two legal actions were now pending that involved the question of Thor's responsibility. In South Africa the company's executives were finally facing the charges of culpable homicide. Their confidence in the outcome proved well-founded. Called to the stand, the state pathologist announced unexpectedly that he wished to retract the findings of his original autopsy report: the body tissues did not in retrospect show 'evidence of massive mercury accumulation' as he'd previously stated. The judge then decided not to hear testimony from the prosecution's expert witness, an international authority on mercury toxicity who believed that the workers showed signs diagnostic of chronic mercury poisoning. Instead he allowed the accused Thor management to plead guilty to charges of negligence. The South African company paid its fine promptly – the equivalent of around one and a half thousand pounds – and continued its operations.

It took three years for the other trial to come to court. A firm of London solicitors, armed with evidence and testimonies that we had collected in the research for our film, applied for South African ex-Thor workers and the families of the dead to be granted British legal aid funding to sue Thor in the English courts. They argued that the company had used certain mercury manufacturing procedures in the UK until forced to cease them when its operations had been judged unsafe; transfer of these processes, and the plant engineer, to South Africa did not diminish the responsibility of the UK parent company and its British chairman and owner. In a landmark precedent, legal aid was granted. Thor, faced with the prospect of huge damages, offered the plaintiffs an out-of-court settlement of £1.3 million. The sum represented only a fraction of the chemical group's declared annual turnover, but it was accepted by the twenty ex-workers and family members in the class action as a vast improvement on the negligible pay-outs available through the South African Workmen's Compensation Act.

For some the settlement came too late. Three of Thor's South African ex-workers were dead. But the hard-won precedent meant that overseas employees of United Kingdom-based multinationals now had the right to challenge the parent companies in British courts. Subsequently, several hundred South Africans were granted legal aid to mount a group action against the UK company Cape Asbestos, alleging that at least two thousand workers and local residents had been affected by asbestos-related illnesses from exposure – inside the mineral plants and from living near them – decades before, and a further twenty of Thor's ex-workers have received settlements from the company out of court.

⊕

A few months later I was flying over the Amazon. A sheet of silver marked the main channel of the river, its surface dappled with the shadows of small, spherical clouds that stretched away at the same height as the aircraft. The far bank of the river could not be seen. My friend and colleague Rob sat at a window seat, engrossed in the view. Rob was a specialist in infectious diseases, conducting an international research trial into a new means of treating kala-azar, a destructive tropical illness. One of the centres where the trial was being run was a small hospital in the river town of Santarém, approximately five hundred miles upstream from where the Amazon poured its great volume into the sea, and that's where we were headed. Infectious diseases, though, weren't my field. I was here because of mercury.

Of all the Amazon's great tributaries, the Tapajos has long been famous for the clarity of its waters. Travellers come to Santarém where the rivers meet to marvel at the merging of the clear stream of the Tapajos with the café-au-lait waters of the Amazon, and the great swirls of light and dark that extend for thirty miles downstream. But the waters of the Tapajos, despite their apparent purity, are polluted by huge quantities of mercury. Three hundred miles upriver, beyond the river-port of Itaituba, lie extensive gold-diggings. The unlicensed miners – the *garimpieros* – use crude methods of alluvial gold extraction: high pressure hoses are used to turn the river banks to mud, which is sluiced down wooden chutes containing troughs of liquid mercury. The dense flakes of gold sink into the mercury, where they form an amalgam. Rocks and debris float over the pools of metal and are washed away, but tons of liquid mercury go with them each month into the Tapajos and its tributaries.

Once free in the environment, the metal becomes a serious and persistent threat. Bacterial action changes it into highly toxic organic mercury compounds such as methylmercury, which accumulate in fish and other forms of river life. Consumed by humans, the mercury concentrates in the blood and nervous system. In the brain it affects the centres of balance, hearing and sight. Prolonged exposure leads to sensation loss, ataxia – staggering gait – and eventual blindness. The final stages of organic mercury poisoning are coma and death. Methylmercury is particularly toxic to unborn children. It damages embryonic cells in the womb, causing miscarriages and developmental abnormalities. In the 1950s methylmercury was responsible for one of the world's most graphic environmental disasters: a spate of monstrous birth deformities at Minamata Bay in Japan, from villagers eating fish contaminated by mercury discharged into the sea from a nearby factory.

The hospital in Santarém belonged to a medical NGO, a local organization that had started off running a river-boat clinic serving villages in the Amazonian tributaries. With donations, land had been bought on the edge of town for wards and an operating unit. Visiting doctors stayed in an adjacent compound, where hammocks hung between flowering trees and gaudy pet macaws screeched from the verandas. I sat in on Rob's out-patient sessions, snipping biopsy samples from the edges of crusted ulcers and the lurid skin lesions of tropical fungal infections. An American ophthalmic surgeon let me assist him for an afternoon while he did cataract operations. A dentist taught me something I had never been shown at medical school; the art of pulling teeth correctly. And an English sociologist, writing his doctorate in

Santarém, explained the study he was co-ordinating on the local prevalence of mercury toxicity.

He had already investigated the problem in miners and buyers on the gold-fields, amongst whom poisoning was commonplace. The standard method of separating the amalgam of gold and mercury was by playing the flame of a blow-torch over the mixture. As the volatile mercury metal vaporized, large amounts were inhaled into the lungs and rapidly absorbed. The men appeared to consider these symptoms of acute poisoning – trembling, salivation, bleeding gums, memory loss and mental derangement – as an unavoidable occupational hazard of the gold-mining business.

Now, with doctors from the Santarém NGO and physicians from the medical school in distant Manaus, the sociologist wished to assess whether mercury was affecting the vulnerable populations of fishing villages along the Tapajos. Rob and I joined the researchers who were travelling up-river the following day to conduct this next stage of the 'Projecto Mercurio' survey. We passed the boxes of diagnostic equipment down ladders from the top of Santarém's river wall and stacked them on the beach. Then we helped to carry them over bouncing plank gangways to a wooden river-boat, that floated in the shallows like a white-layered wedding cake. At dusk the vessel slipped its moorings, the eddy-current turning us slowly away from the bank. The engine drummed into life and we edged around the headland and into the ten-mile-wide mouth of the Tapajos. To the west could be seen the faint shadow of its opposite bank, outlined by a sliver of sunset.

The captain leaned from the window of his wheelhouse atop the upper deck. Smoke streamed from the chimney of the little galley in the stern where the cook was at work. We ate around a table on the deck, the wind of our passage whisking away the night-insects before they could begin orbiting the Primus lamp. Our empty hammocks, hanging between the roof-posts, billowed in the steady breeze. I had slung mine as far forward as I could, for coolness, and was late to fall asleep, stretched out in the diagonal position that makes hammock-sleeping as comfortable as any bed. The harsh bellow of the ship's siren woke me. From the wheelhouse stretched a bright finger of light, the beam of the searchlight which the helmsman used for detecting snags and floating logs. It was focussed on a vessel wallowing across the current a half-mile away, coming straight towards us. The beam played across the empty wheelhouse, glinting off the eyes of cattle packed into the hull, that swayed as the boat plunged and rocked. Our captain hung on the siren-cord, unavailingly, and his helmsman threw the wheel around as the boat sheared past us and charged onwards into the darkness.

Brasilia Legal, a fishing village of some eight hundred souls and a dozen regal mango trees, slumbered in the mid-morning heat. It owed its grandiose name to a period during the eighteenth century when Brazil, riven by uprisings and secessions, was under the rule of several contending governments: during one such convulsion this sleepy backwater had – for a few months – been proclaimed the official capital of the entire country. Few signs remained of this brief glory. A once-grand villa, its figured stucco flaking and discoloured, stood among the tin-roofed buildings that stretched along the high river bank. Women stood waist-deep at a line of wooden tables set in the shallows with their tops a foot or so above the surface of the water. At some the women laundered clothes, others washed pots or bathed. Here and there a canoe was tethered to a table leg, with a catch of fish and turtles being cleaned and gutted.

We formed a line up the beach, passing our equipment from hand to hand to where it was stacked outside the community's rustic clinic. At one point the chain was broken by a party of villagers on the way to the cemetery. They carried a small, blue-painted coffin; the body of a child, dead of fever the day before. These people were well aware of the precariousness of life; malaria, dysentery, meningitis and snake-bites took a regular toll, while insect stings, parasites and fungal infections were endemic nuisances. They knew nothing of the potential danger, invisible and tasteless, that came with each mouthful of sustenance taken from the river. A group gathered around our clutter of equipment. The toxicologist from Manaus explained to the villagers what we were researching. At once there were exclamations: this woman had suffered three miscarriages, that one had borne a deformed child.

Over the next three days almost every individual in the community presented themselves for examination, even the reclusive Amerindian families whose thatched huts lay in hidden clearings in the surrounding jungle. Hair, blood and urine specimens were taken from each person, and carefully stored – along with samples of the river water and the daily catch – for later assay of mercury levels at the medical university in Manaus. All histories of miscarriages and birth defects were recorded. Everyone received a full physical examination, with the children – particularly susceptible to the effects of mercury accumulation in their developing nervous systems – being comprehensively tested for signs of damage to balance, memory and concentration.

The sun, filtered through overhanging branches, suffused the wooden cubicles of the clinic with a green light. Children watched from the window as, one by one, their fellows carried out the programme of neurological tests. In simple tasks – placing coloured rings on pegs – they were slow and uncertain. Co-ordination was poor. Asked to stand on one foot with their eyes closed, the children would at once begin to waver, and unless caught by the arms of the examining doctor, would stagger and fall. The methodical recording of results helped to conceal our sense of helplessness: these were unequivocal signs of nervous system damage, yet little could be done to arrest the cumulative effects of mercury exposure except removal from all further contact with the poison. But beyond the clinic's doorway flowed the wide, steady flood of the Tapajos.

The world impinged on this place only in the most remote way. A few households had televisions sets that at night spilled blue light down the river-bank. Most of the time the screens gave out only a dancing snowstorm and a wash of static. Periodically a voice would emerge through the interference, a hazy picture would form, and at once all were engrossed: for perhaps ten minutes in forty a satellite, passing over-head, bounced down a weak, deflected signal from far-off Rio or São Paulo, a segment of an episode in some interminable soap-opera. Then the slipping image would fade, the transmitted voices scramble back to a hiss, and a buzz of conversation would spread from house to house as everyone tried to puzzle out the plot-developments they had missed.

The young men of the village gathered instead in the trading store called the Casa do Povo, where they shot pool at a battered table and drank warm Antarctica Beer and listened to the stories of those who had worked on the gold-fields far upstream. For them the mining town of Itaituba represented the outside world, with its saloons and gold-dealers and the possibility of striking it rich, and with young men's bravado, that's where they wanted to go; shit on this mercury thing.

Itaituba, that place of dreams, lay a half-day's journey away in a motorized canoe. The boatman kept to the edge of the river and in the jungle's shadow the turquoise wings of morpho butterflies flashed like signal-lamps. Gradually the banks began to open out, the trees hacked back to make way for new settlements. Gold-mining barges spouted flumes of mud from outflow pipes where they hoovered in the shallows. The town could be seen from afar. The landing stage was crowded with trucks, and supply boats from the diggings were nosed in all along the beach. Two- and three-storey concrete emporia stood above the river, bold painted signs indicating their trade – 'Casa Rurale', 'Casa de Garimpo' – and from big sound-trucks that cruised the waterfront came exhortations to buy, and the speeded-up guitar-beat of local ethnic rock. A great wall of smoke rose into the sky along the opposite bank where the jungle was being cleared.

We came ashore on a ferry ramp and climbed among the vendors to the town's main street. Faded plastic bunting fluttered in the wind. Every shop sold mining gear – prospecting pans, picks, mule panniers and water barrels – and all purchases could be paid for in gold: scales for weighing out nuggets stood beside the cash registers. There were racks of rifles, shotguns and sidearms for sale, and I noticed that many of the miners passing along the crowded pavements wore pistols at their hips. They made way for a man who shouted and staggered in the street. Saliva trailed from his chin as he raved, throwing a flailing punch at the ribs of a passing horse. The rider fended him off with his boot, leaving him spinning disjointedly until he fell into the dust.

'Mercurio,' said the gold-buyers, standing at the doors of their shops and tapping their heads.

OURO OURO OURO was painted everywhere; on building-fronts, windows, even lamp-posts. Inside each establishment a gas-jet flared, where the traders cooked off the last traces of mercury from the gold they were about to buy. I watched the bright gleam coalesce in a crucible and be decanted into a mould to form small ingots. The dealer was telling a story in rapid-fire Portuguese.

'Bandits held up the passenger flight this morning,'

translated the English sociologist. 'As it was taxiing to take off, some trucks came roaring down the runway and headed it off. They pointed guns at the cockpit and forced the crew to open the aircraft door. Then they stole the bags of gold it was carrying and drove away into the jungle. The police will never catch them.'

The writ of the Brazilian government was shaky in the mining towns, and ran out entirely in the gold-fields: officials here limited their activities to trying to register the *garimpieros'* land claims and collect taxes on mined gold from the largely unlicensed diggings. Though miners had some idea of the hazards from the mercury they used, the same pressures of poverty that had forced them to undertake this dangerous work gave them a fierce independence. When the government had tried to take control of the main gold diggings in Para State in 1984, the miners marched on Brasilia, the national capital, threatening an uprising. The government surrendered and left the *garimpieros* alone; it seemed unlikely that legislation to control the release of mercury into the environment would be enforceable.

✪

The results of the 'Projeto Mercurio' survey, when they were eventually published, made depressing reading. In the villages along the Tapajos, samples from more than eighty per cent of children showed mercury concentrations at levels known to affect brain development. The tests administered for attention-span and balance revealed clear evidence of neurological damage that correlated with the amount of mercury in the tissues. As distressing was the presence of deficiencies in younger children with lower levels of the metal, suggesting that exposure before birth might be responsible for lasting changes. Could Brazil – the richest country in Latin America, its economy the tenth largest in the world – continue to ignore the poisoning of its rivers from the gold-fields by ten tons of mercury every month? I wondered what cataclysmic weight of environmental and social damage would have to accumulate before people's health would be considered more important than the nation's desperate scramble for wealth.

Any change that did occur would come about through the work of people such as Mark in South Africa and the English sociologist and the Brazilian researchers. Their dedication was unquestionable. Resisted by political pressures and vested interests, they ploughed on resolutely, and sometimes they were rewarded with victory. Their fields of expertise – occupational medicine, epidemiology, public health – were those that as a medical student I had considered the dullest of academic backwaters, compared to the excitement and rewards of acute clinical practice. I'd ended up choosing the most intense sector of all: surgery. I tried to calculate some comparative value of what I'd achieved since then, but was brought up short by the memory of the water engineer I'd met aboard that helicopter in Kurdistan, whose bore-holes and pipes had probably saved more lives in one refugee camp than ever I would in the course of my clinical career.

I didn't even have the consolation of a definable professional standing. By contrast, most of the doctors with whom I'd undergone my training were now established in tenured hospital posts and esteemed in their fields.

'I look at Tim [a consultant surgeon colleague] for example, and myself,' said Rob the infectious diseases specialist one night, when rather drunk, 'and I realize that we've made it. And then I look at you, and I realize that you haven't made it and you never will.'

I sometimes assisted Tim with his surgical cases in the gleaming operating suite of a private hospital. We'd discuss the latest technological advances. Developments in laparoscopic instruments were allowing a new generation of high-achievers to carry out sophisticated 'key-hole' surgery: frontiers were moving on. My skills were more suited to the crude extremes of suffering I had first encountered all those years before, when I'd stepped from my career path to seek that intimacy with pain at the hospital in Zululand. There was little other market for them, or for the eclectic philosophy of disaster existentialism of which I found myself a sole, curmudgeonly exponent. I was just a doctor, with uncertain clinical detachment, the vice of restlessness and some tarnished shreds of idealism. It was only in the world's murkiest places that they had any chance to shine.

13

Eritrea

All through the night they brought the wounded along the road from Barentu. They filled up the military hospital in the old Italian fort on the hill above the town and then the civilian hospital, also built by the Italians, on the main street. The morgue was just inside the courtyard where the trucks turned. The area in front of it was where the new arrivals were sorted and categorized for treatment. I saw men lifting bodies from the backs of mud-smeared trucks – their heads lolled back in that dislocated way unique to the dead – and carrying them into the damp-cement smell of the morgue. There was a drum at the door, full of blood-soaked dressings and bits of uniforms cut along their seams by the medics. Nearby, against the wall, waited the less severely wounded; smoking in the early sunlight and picking the crusted blood off their skin and clothes with filthy fingernails.

The Eritreans had the best casualty treatment record in the world, I'd been told. During the Liberation War – thirty years of struggle against the occupation of their country by neighbouring Ethiopia – astounding feats of trauma-care and battle surgery had been commonplace, survival figures among wounded Eritrean guerrillas exemplary. This proud claim had been related to me by almost every Eritrean I had met – some of them ex-fighters – and repeated by journalists, with statistical or technical embellishment, as evidence of Eritrean resourcefulness.

'The average time elapsed between fighters being wounded and receiving medical treatment was less than thirty minutes,' a correspondent for Agence France-Presse told me, 'faster than American casualty evacuation in the Vietnam War.' Another eulogist described the difficulties encountered by Western intelligence analysts during the 1980s in assessing Eritrean losses by satellite photography, because of the Eritreans' ability to get their casualties off the battle-field 'more quickly than all but the most sophisticated armies'.

When I first visited Eritrea, the Liberation War had been over for seven years: in May 1991 the victorious fighters of the Eritrean People's Liberation Front, the EPLF, had reclaimed their capital Asmara. Colonel Mengistu, the head of Ethiopia's Derg military government, had fled into exile, and a few days later the main Ethiopian resistance group, the Tigrayan People's Liberation Front (TPLF) formed a new government in Addis Ababa. In 1993, in the continuing euphoria that followed their common victory against the Derg, Eritrea's independence was restored. The EPLF found itself ruling a devastated country – two hundred and fifty thousand Eritreans were said to have died in the conflict – but one endowed with an ardent nationalist spirit and a folklore of sacrifice. The signs of their long struggle were everywhere. The port of Massawa showed extensive bomb damage, and in the northern highlands – the heartland of Eritrean resistance – the tracks remained part-blocked by lines of wrecked Ethiopian tanks destroyed in ambush.

I was trying to reach Orota, site of the Eritreans' mountain headquarters during the 1980s. Every well-wisher, aid worker and journalist who'd visited the EPLF at that time had been taken to Orota, and all had described scenes of extraordinary industry and cohesion. Schools and storehouses were concealed in ravines, safe from aerial attack. Factories had produced medication – chloroquine and penicillin – as well as spaghetti, sanitary towels (for the thirty thousand women in the guerrilla movement) and the black plastic sandals known as 'Congos' that were the virtual badge of identity as a fighter. Orota was also the site of a hospital famous for sophisticated trauma-surgery performed with improvised equipment, and I hoped to visit the subterranean operating rooms where surgeons had worked on the wounded, protected from Ethiopian bombers. En route, however, the water tank in my four-wheel-drive truck had split under the battering of boulder-strewn mountain tracks, and I had stopped near a village to examine the damage when a man appeared from the hillside and offered his assistance.

Lieutenant Berhane's uniform was soft with wear, and the leather pouches around his waist – made from the uppers of Ethiopian army boots – marked him as a veteran fighter. He invited me up to the command post, a group of bunkers half-hidden in the rocky slope, while a replacement water container was found and filled. I was introduced to his comrades, men with whom he had served as a fighter in the EPLF for fifteen years. As shadows inched across the valley, and we drank cup after tiny cup of coffee from an earthenware flask boiling on the charcoal brazier, the men talked of the freedom for which they had fought and the war that they had won.

'When the Italians ruled us, from 1885 to 1941, they made Eritrea the most industrialized country in North Africa,' declared the captain. (This was nearly true; the territory had been Mussolini's show-piece colony, enriched with subsidized investment and development.) 'We have always been advanced, even as fighters. It is us who taught the Woyani [a disparaging term for the Tigrayans] how to defeat the Derg. Now that we have our independence, we will make our mark again on the world map.'

In fact Eritrea hadn't existed until Italy established the colony on the Red Sea coast as a base from which to invade the Ethiopian hinterland. Their first attempt in 1896 failed disastrously, but a few years before World War Two Mussolini was able to restore the honour of Italy with the help of tanks, poison gas and a substantial force of Eritrean levies. The Italian conquest was short-lived. By 1941 British troops had driven them out of Ethiopia, reinstated Emperor Haile Selassie on his throne, and taken Eritrea. After the war a UN commission placed the ex-colony under Ethiopian control, and in 1962 Haile Selassie incorporated Eritrea into his empire as its fourteenth province. Eritrean resistance grew, and the Americans provided Haile Selassie with billions in military aid, much of which was spent on garrisoning the restive province. In 1975 the Emperor was deposed in an army coup. Ethiopia's new military government, the Derg, approached the Soviet Union for assistance against the Eritrean rebels. When two years later the EPLF began what was expected to be a decisive assault on the port of Massawa, Russian naval vessels shelled the attacking guerillas, newly supplied MIGs strafed them from the air, and within six months the Eritreans had been forced back to their bases in the rugged highlands.

Berhane's unit was located below a range of red mountains that had been the EPLF's frontline for the next ten, bitter years of the Liberation War; trenches scratched into the rock where the fighters had kept watch through gun-slits on the enemy below. It was only in 1988 that the EPLF had been strong enough to launch their new offensive, capturing strategic towns and eventually advancing on Asmara to end the war. Combining remembrance and preparedness, Berhane and his soldiers still patrolled daily over these mountains, much stained by the blood of Eritrean martyrs. On a bank in front of the command post they'd constructed a patriotic map of their country outlined by heavy machine-gun shell cases hammered into the ground; an appropriately bellicose cartographic medium, for the five years since independence had not been tranquil.

Asserting its new borders, Eritrea had faced down Sudan to the west, Djibouti in the south and even Yemen across the Red Sea, over the possession of some islands in the Bab el Mandeb Straight: none of its neighbours wished to go to war with this small country and its battle-hardened army. As its confidence increased, the EPLF government began to question, and then to spurn, the projects of the aid organizations that had swarmed into their country with offers to rebuild its infrastructure, economy and health services. Eritrea objected to the attached conditions – tied aid, interest-incurring loans, the imposition of expatriate consultants to run grand schemes where small, indigenous projects would better serve – and at the beginning of 1998 began to boot out the foreign organizations. Their projects were closed down, their equipment forfeit and handed over to Eritrean agencies. The UN High Commission for Refugees' fine trucks and its depot of thirty thousand tents became the property of the Eritrean Relief and Refugee Commission.

But the biggest problem facing the young country remained its relationship with Ethiopia. Within two years of independence Eritrea had expelled 150,000 Ethiopians and their dependants, confiscating their belongings and property. The introduction of Eritrea's own currency, the *nakfa*, in place of the Ethiopian *birr*, separated the economies of the two countries. Free access to the sea through the southern port of Assab – granted to landlocked Ethiopia as part of Eritrea's 1993 independence agreement – became less free. Cross-border relations deteriorated. In 1997 Ethiopia published a map that claimed three frontier areas – Badme to the west, and the central villages of Tsorena and Alitiena – as lying within Ethiopian territory. Clashes were inevitable. Two days after I'd left Eritrea, on the sixth of May 1998, a new war – really, an extension of all the old wars – started.

And with the implacable bitterness of a falling out between brothers – the EPLF in Asmara and the TPLF in Addis spoke the same language, and had struggled shoulder-to-shoulder to destroy the Derg – this new war had ground on remorselessly. It was now two years old, a stalemate fought between trench lines six hundred miles long that snaked across desiccated plains and over mountains, where the two armies faced each other across a no-man's-land ploughed by artillery shells and pointlessly fertilized with thousands of corpses.

Throughout these two years Berhane and I had exchanged letters; his written from a bunker on the Badme front, mine sent to him at an address in the highland town of Keren, from where they had been brought to him on the supply trucks that conveyed food and ammunition to the forward positions. My letters contained heartfelt wishes for his safety. Berhane's replies harked back to the conversations we'd had during the couple of days I'd spent with him and his comrades, when I'd described my experiences as a surgeon in Kurdistan and Mozambique.

'I believe that you very well know the result of war,' he wrote. 'War is bad. But we have one choice, to protect our country from the enemy. We do not hesitate.' His last letter, however, had been written from his home in Keren: 'I arrive from the front one hour ago. I have twenty days' leave, and I want to use this time to marry. My girlfriend Ariam and I have known each other for five years, and now we will marry on 14th of May 2000, because perhaps I have not chance another time. I expect with every hope that we will meet in Asmara and that you will be there on my wedding day.'

I had long wanted to return to Eritrea, and Berhane's

invitation provided the final justification. But as well as attending my friend's wedding, I was professionally curious to discover how the medical services of the EPLF guerrilla force had been re-organized to deal with casualties in this most old-fashioned of wars. In the last year of the twentieth century, the conflict between Ethiopia and Eritrea was unique. Besides its echoes of World War One – not least in its massive casualty lists – it was the only war being fought between sovereign nations; all the others raging across the globe were civil wars or insurgencies. Also, with three hundred thousand men under arms in Eritrea, and more than twice that in Ethiopia, it was the biggest. Over the telephone I recruited my friend Guy – a photographer with whom I had travelled often in the past – to join me, and within a few hours we had arranged a rendezvous in Cairo to fly together to the Eritrean capital.

✪

Asmara was a little more run-down than I remembered it. The resumption of fighting had stopped development and curtailed a planned restoration of the city's historic buildings, though the Italian architecture – Deco, Futurist, Fascist Monumental – still looked bold and striking. There were no high-rise buildings: the skyline was dominated by minarets, the spires of the Catholic and Coptic cathedrals and the twin square towers of the Ethiopian Orthodox Church. In the cafés under the palms along Independence Avenue prices had risen, but the value of the *nakfa* had dropped and now there was an inflated black-market exchange rate for the dollar where there had been none before. Another new development was the hordes of children hustling on the streets, selling chewing gum, facial tissues, or simply begging.

I met Berhane in an Asmara café, and received the fighter's greeting: an arm-clasp and five firm embraces, collar-bone to collar-bone. He was tall and open-faced as I remembered him, beaming with delight at the re-affirmation of our friendship, and only the slight recession of his hair at the temples indicated the stresses of two years' service in the trenches. 'My friend, my good friend,' he said, 'you have come. I cannot believe it.' Together we walked through the streets to the house of his fiancée. Ariam was tall and graceful, a research chemist whom Berhane had met when she'd been posted to his unit during her period of military service, and his pride and love was obvious. She introduced me to the rest of her family: her dignified father, her serenely beautiful mother in traditional white robe and head-scarf, with an indigo cross tattooed on her forehead and a gold tooth glinting in her smile, and her lively sister Paula, half-way through a degree at the Agricultural faculty of Asmara University. All were excitedly planning the celebrations that would follow the wedding service on Sunday, in a week's time.

The next day I began making the rounds of government ministries. I had brought with me a letter explaining my professional interest in casualty treatment and asking for access and assistance. The Director General of Protocol was my first call. He had been a fighter – it was unheard of for someone to occupy office within the administration who could not make this claim – but had spent the latter years of the Liberation War as an EPLF representative in Europe. He read the letter through and pressed a bell. A secretary took it away for filing.

'Of course I understand why you should come here to learn about treating wounded,' he said, 'but you do not need my assistance. You can go anywhere in Eritrea, see anything you like.'

'I'd be very interested to observe how the army cares for their casualties.'

The Director General beamed. 'Of course, of course.' He

spoke into a phone, and scribbled a note on a piece of paper which he handed to me. 'Tomorrow you will visit the Minister of Health. Show him this. Now you must speak to the Media Organizer. Everyone will be pleased to help.'

The Media Organizer listened to my preamble. 'Do you have a letter?' he asked. I explained that it was in the possession of the Director General's secretary. Annoyed, he left the room and returned with a photocopy of the document, which he read through carefully. Then he keyed the intercom and his secretary removed it.

'Our medical service is superb,' said the man. 'On the Tsorena front there are underground hospitals run by trained women fighters, where the wounded get immediate treatment.'

'That's exactly the sort of thing I'd like to see.'

'Unfortunately the front is completely quiet,' he said with a shrug. 'There is nothing to see. But you must talk to the Ministry of Information.' He wrote a note for me. 'They will arrange credentials for you.'

The Information Ministry was housed within the old Italian fort, whose cactus-buttressed walls occupied a hill on the west side of the city. The man from Information asked if I'd brought a letter for him. I produced the Media Organizer's note, and a secretary took it away for filing.

'I understand that you can give me some sort of document to help me get around the country,' I said.

'Of course. You must have credentials, so people will know who you are.'

'Will they get me into the military hospitals?' I enquired.

He considered the matter. 'There is the main army hospital at Dekemhare, another at Barentu. But there is no point in visiting them. More important is an information programme about our medical services during the Liberation War. I will arrange for you to meet someone who can tell you about it.'

The Health Minster seemed my best hope. After relieving me of the note from Protocol, he offered me tea.

'Your professional interest is perfectly understandable,' he said affably. 'Our casualty treatment is excellent. But all our military services are excellent. The Eritrean Defence Force is winning the war. The front is quiet; the Woyani are losing, and they are frightened to attack us. If you visited the front there would be nothing to see.'

I asked if, lack of wounded notwithstanding, he could obtain approval from the army for me to visit their medical units.

'By all means.' The Minister waved an expansive hand. 'Just talk to my Director of Clinical Services. He will arrange everything.'

⊕

The Director was the first doctor I'd encountered in the hierarchy, but any expectation I might have had of a professional rapport was undone at once. Behind his glasses he had the lean face of a zealot. 'You will get all the information you need in Asmara,' he stated flatly. He began writing on a sheet of paper. 'This is a list of people who served as doctors in the Liberation War, at Orota and other places. You must make appointments to see them. They will tell you how it was. There is no need to leave the city.'

I described my work in other conflict zones, and explained my hope of meeting practising trauma doctors in order to learn how they were dealing with casualties in this current war. Perhaps, I proposed, the Clinical Director might make approaches to the army medical services on my behalf. In the meantime I was interested to visit the refugee camps established along the country's southern border for those displaced at the start of hostilities two years earlier, in order to learn about their healthcare too.

'If you have the time you can go to every camp there is,' he said dismissively, 'but most of them are very hard to reach.'

Transport was not a problem, I explained: my colleague Guy had been commissioned by MIASM, the Medical International Assistance Service Movement – one of the overseas aid groups recently allowed to return to the country – to take pictures of conditions in the camps where they were working, and they would give us access in their vehicles. The Director was suddenly stung out of his reserve.

'MIASM have only just arrived,' he snapped. 'They know nothing, they administer nothing. Anything they tell you is without authority, and their opinions are worthless. The only way to know what is happening in the camps is through the Ministry of Health.'

In a rage, he pressed a button on his desk, and, when his secretary appeared, rattled off a letter to her in double-quick dictation speed.

'Here is your credential,' he fumed, as he stamped and signed the document. 'It will get you access to all civilian medical services and all the camps. The military is another matter. There is nothing to see there.'

The MIASM crew occupied a bungalow in a pleasant quarter of the city that was rapidly being taken over by arriving aid organizations. The Eritrean government had held to its resolve not to let in foreign agencies until the recent drought and famine – affecting some twelve million people in Ethiopia, Somalia, Eritrea and the Sudan – had forced them to relax the embargo in order to qualify for international food-aid. In the previous months a host of assistance groups – including Oxfam, Save the Children, the US Agency for International Development, the World Health Organization, the Food and Agriculture Organization, Médecins sans Frontières, Swiss Disaster Relief, the World Lutheran Federation, Italian Co-operation and Africare – had arrived. The UN had come most recently, moving into a building down the road from their old compound. That address was now occupied by the Eritrean Relief and Refugee Commission, and outside it were parked in constant mockery the big white trucks they used for food deliveries, that still carried UNHCR markings on their sides.

MIASM's Country Representative was endowed with the sort of patient courtesy that I imagined would be vital in dealing with stiff-necked Eritreans. We met the rest of his group: a couple of friendly nurses, a logistician and a water engineer. And we encountered the probable explanation for MIASM's poor standing with the Ministry of Health: a square, intense woman who was neither a nurse nor a doctor nor a logistician but the Medical Organizational Overseeing Co-ordinator or something similar. She came from Kansas and spoke with a high-pitched lilt, as though trying to sound like a little girl. I was required by her to give an account of my presence in Eritrea. I mentioned my interest in trauma surgery. Sri Lanka was the only place to see real trauma, she countered; she had worked there with a surgeon who was the greatest trauma expert in the world, and until I had met him I couldn't claim to have the first idea about the subject. I assumed that her excruciating condescension might be reserved for people that she didn't like, but I found that it was one of her two standard means of address. The other was worse.

MIASM were going to visit refugee camps near the Ethiopian border, where they were planning a vaccination programme. On the basis of Guy's photographic commission from the organization's European HQ, the MIASM head offered us passage in the organization's vehicles and access to their operations. We left the next day, piled into the back of their Land Cruiser. The Co-ordinator wore purple lipstick and one of those many-zipped-and-pocketed explorer's waistcoats that shouted intrepidity. In the southern town of Mendefera we visited the offices of the Eritrean Relief Commission and the health administrator. At a district clinic further south we met the health assistant, and at our first destination, a refugee camp about eight miles from the border, we were introduced to the Eritrean personnel who ran it. In each instance the Medical Organizational Overseeing Coordinator pitched her ingénue voice a notch higher and spoke to the Eritreans in a sort of oh-so-forbearing baby-language, as though she considered them profoundly retarded. I could see how her tone would get right up the collective nose of an independent-minded government.

The refugees occupied faded ex-UNHCR tents scattered among thorn-trees and boulders. Some of the camps lay within range of Ethiopian fire, though they were placed on the lee-side of hills to prevent direct hits; the twisted body of a Katyusha rocket lay not far from the tents and a jagged sheet of shrapnel, suspended from a thorn-branch, served as the school bell. The classroom was a pool of shade under a tree, against the trunk of which the teacher leaned his blackboard. The kids were all on the scrawny side but looked healthy, and the communities had a general air of stability and sound administration. Some inhabitants still returned to their fields to plant and harvest, but for the rest there were deliveries of food and cooking oil. And of course there were the visits from the foreign NGOs: quite a lot of them.

It was easy to see why the aid organizations all wanted to work in Eritrea. The government was untainted by corruption, its people were highly motivated, and there was a functioning local infrastructure. But there just weren't quite enough refugees to go round. Each NGO needed to show that it was active in order to justify its budget and overheads and to give its publicity department something to publicize to attract further funding. There appeared to be a tussle underway between different organizations to help the displaced. In one camp where MIASM were planning a vaccination programme, many of the infants had recently been inoculated against the same illnesses by Save the Children, others by the Swiss, and quite a number by both. Mothers pulled out the coloured cards that indicated their children's vaccination records, but to no avail; MIASM's Medical Organizational Overseeing Co-ordinator was going to do them all again.

We had authorization from the Eritrean Relief Commission to spend some days in the camp: Guy, in order to take the pictures that MIASM's head office had requested, and I to see what sort of facilities existed to treat the malaria, chest infections, amoebic dysentery and measles that were endemic among the displaced. The MIASM Land Cruiser dropped us off among the tents and we watched with relief as the vehicle drove away towards its base. Agraa camp was spread among the thorn-trees at the foot of a steep escarpment. On the heights above could be seen a distant village and a tiny church, their roofs glinting in the afternoon light above an avenue of ancient cedars. Tsehai – her name meant 'sunshine' – was the camp's health assistant. She explained the local geography: the high village was called Adi Keshi; beyond it was Adi Quala, the nearest town, two hours' hard climb away; and ten miles to the south lay the central battle front. Then she invited us to her tent for coffee.

The smoke of roasting coffee beans rose from the brazier. Groups of children skipped past on their way to the river, sun glowing through the plastic of their water jars. Tsehai looked to be in her mid-twenties, but said she had been a fighter – this was not a claim to make lightly; everyone seemed to know who'd really been with the EPLF during the Liberation War – and been trained as a medic. She was now responsible for the health of the six thousand people in the settlement.

She insisted on us taking her tent – she had a perfectly comfortable examination cot in her dispensary, she said – and, although we had come supplied with food, she conjured out of nowhere a fine meal of the sour, spongy bread called *injera*, wrapped around a spicy lentil stew. The tent-canvas boomed in the dry night wind that gusted down the valley. From somewhere in the camp an affronted donkey brayed, and joyous ululations rose from the shelter of a family whose soldier son had arrived on leave from the almost-peace of the front line.

The next morning Guy was up before dawn to take pictures. Later he joined me at Tsehai's dispensary, and we were watching her administer to the small gathering of children with sore throats and coughs when a vehicle came rocking up the track between the tents. From the front window leaned the MIASM driver, with grim news: that morning the Ethiopians had launched a huge offensive on the Badme front twenty miles to the west, and we should return at once to Asmara. Tsehai said she thought the whole camp would soon be packing to flee, but the administrator was confident – as were the old men of the camp guard, the metal-work of their rifles shiny with handling – that the front would hold. On the road below Adi Quala, where the tarmac began its winding climb up the escarpment, the Eritrean army was establishing a defensive strongpoint. Three venerable T-56 tanks, camouflaged with straw, were being backed into gullies beside the road to cover the approach from the south.

As soon as we reached the capital I called Berhane. His leave was to be cut short: the wedding in two days' time was still on, but the honeymoon had been cancelled. That evening Guy and I joined the small group of resident journalists – a Reuters reporter, his cameraman, a freelance photographer, and Alex, the BBC World Service correspondent in Asmara – around an outdoor table at the American Bar, under the palm trees on Independence Avenue. They were discussing animatedly the latest developments, while passing Eritreans with contacts in the government took Alex aside to whisper updates.

The news was bad. The Ethiopian attack had fallen on a section of the western front that was thought to be impregnable: along the mountain-crests above the Mereb River, the confident Eritreans had only a single trench line with no rear positions, for everyone knew that each Eritrean soldier was worth ten Woyani. Somehow the despised enemy had managed to bring two hundred thousand men up to the front without being detected. At night these troops had crossed the Mereb and ascended fifteen hundred feet of rocky mountainside to overwhelm the Eritrean positions. Now, supplied by trains of mules, they were consolidating their bridgehead.

The next day was Saturday, and in Asmara the International Committee of the Red Cross was throwing a garden party at their villa. It had been planned long in advance, to commemorate the departure of a much-respected Head of Mission back to Geneva, but the circumstances gave it an added piquancy. I met workers of all the assistance groups, including some new ones I'd not heard of – German Agro-Action, Dutch Interchurch Aid, Cooperazione Italiana, the Organization for Co-ordination of Humanitarian Assistance – plus several other sub-agencies of the UN. We stood in the dappled sunlight of the grape-vine arbour, being served gin-and-tonics and canapés by uniformed waiting staff.

A couple of shots rang out from the army compound up the hill, but the assembled guests were too refined to notice them. Instead, the UN's Country Director was boasting of a boat he'd hired in Massawa to take a scuba party diving on the corals of the Dahlak islands the following weekend. Everyone wished to be invited; this would be an unmissable event on the expatriate social calendar, and the only other way to get there was on one of the usuriously priced 'tours' of a swinish Massawa entrepreneur named Mike, who had cornered the monopoly on leisure access to the Red Sea archipelago. There was much bonhomie, back-slapping and cosying-up to the UN rep, much sloshing down of booze. No one seemed to feel that the war would significantly incommode their pleasure.

⊕

Berhane's wedding service the following day had an almost unbearable poignancy. The voices of the choir rose plaintively into the high rafters of the church. The bridal couple exchanged their vows in low, solemn voices. I noticed Berhane's distraction as people in the pews whispered fragments of news, gleaned from passers-by on the street; there was fierce fighting on the central front fifty miles to the south of Asmara, and reports that the Ethiopian advance had broken through in the west at Badme. Berhane's unit was there, and I knew that he was thinking of his comrades, now struggling in the thick of the assault. I remembered his grizzled sub-lieutenant and the captain who'd talked so confidently of an Eritrean renaissance. I wondered if they had survived.

May was the lucky month for weddings, but as the cavalcade of cars wove their way through Asmara's streets they were greeted only with muted waves and nods rather than the usual ribald shouts of good luck. In the gardens of a hotel outside the city Berhane and Ariam posed for pictures. Ten other wedding parties were there, the dresses of the bridesmaids glowing in the pools of shade under the trees. Knowing that there would be a shortage of car-space on the return journey to Asmara, I walked down the hotel drive to hitch a lift back to the city. The road was almost empty of civilian traffic. Convoys of trucks were heading south for the front, piled high with crates of mortar shells and the long green crates that contained Katyusha rockets.

After some minutes a solitary vehicle, a small red Fiat, came speeding from the direction of the distant fighting. The driver saw my wave and stopped with a screech of brakes, his momentum carrying him well beyond where I stood. 'Come quickly,' he called, and I sprinted to the car and jumped into the back. Lying in the front passenger seat was a wounded man. Blood was dried brown on his sand-coloured T-shirt, and his face had the preoccupied look of pain endured silently. A blanket covered his body, from beneath which a catheter tube drained dark-red urine into a bag at his feet. The driver did not speak, concentrating on swerving through the traffic of horse-carts and cyclists on the outskirts of the city. He dropped me at a bus stop and roared away before I'd thanked him, his horn blaring to clear his route.

Throughout the rest of the day the wedding celebrations continued with a sort of fierce gaiety. Praise-singers from the two families outdid each other in eulogies to the food, the beer and the couple's charm, to be rewarded with banknotes stuck to their sweating foreheads. I stepped out of the heat of the tapestry tent to swallow a cold drink at a bar down the road. Inside the men were listening to Ethiopian radio claim the capture of a number of villages, cutting the transverse road along which the Eritrean army had in the past been able to rush reinforcements to any threatened point on the line. The party ended at midnight, and Guy and I said goodbye to the wedding couple in the small room, freshly whitewashed, that had been prepared for them in the house of Berhane's parents. They sat on the bed beneath palm fronds and sprigs of purple bougainvillaea flowers, surrounded by the presents – a boxed cooker, a fan, a radio, a set of plates and cups – with which they were going to set up their new life. Berhane would be returning the next morning to the front.

⊕

Two days later we were in Keren, the highland town that Berhane had considered his home. Amber evening light bathed the courtyard of the Hotel Sicilia and birds sang in the vines above our heads. During Italian rule Keren had been the colony's agricultural centre, famous for the camel market which still took place each morning in the riverbed below the town. The Sicilia retained the atmosphere of a caravanserai, with our vehicle – a four-wheel-drive Lada Niva that leaked petrol and bounced like a jackrabbit – parked, alongside those of other travellers, within its enclosing compound. People were discussing the latest news. Ethiopian radio had announced that its forces were now advancing in both directions along the road they had gained; to the east they threatened the town of Mendefera, while westward they were driving for the provincial capital of Barentu. Eritrea's Ministry of Information counter-claimed that the Ethiopian advance had been smashed, leaving twenty-five thousand enemy dead and nine tanks aflame on the field of battle; an Eritrean counterattack was now underway.

Earlier that day, while we'd still been in Asmara, the Foreign Affairs Ministry had suddenly forbidden all foreign journalists in the country to leave the capital until the situation 'stabilized'. Guy and I, tipped off by a friend, had escaped just in time. With the services of a translator – a middle-aged Eritrean who claimed to have served through the Liberation War as a battlefield cameraman for the EPLF – and my Health Ministry credentials, we'd passed through the checkpoints and taken the road to Keren. We had shared the route with lines of tank-transporters, each carrying on its bed the solid mass of a T-56. With the loss of the border road,

Keren lay on the only open supply route to the western front and men and material were flowing in a constant stream to Barentu to block the Ethiopian advance. Berhane was there already, reunited with his comrades of the 23rd Division.

On our arrival in Keren I had visited the civilian hospital, and on the neat wards I'd been shown a scattering of wounded – women with shrapnel injuries, old men with bandaged legs, a wide-eyed eight-year-old with a gashed face, crouched at the foot of a stretcher on which his mother, hit in the head, groaned and flung out a hand – casualties of an Ethiopian bombing raid, evacuated from Barentu. I asked the Eritrean surgeon in charge if I could be of any assistance. He'd declined the offer courteously; it had been clear that he felt the situation was under control. I might find it more interesting, he suggested, to drive on to Barentu hospital the next day, where I might see something of the treatment of military wounded.

It was almost midnight when Guy and I were woken from sleep at the Sicilia by a pounding at the door. Outside stood our translator. Throughout the drive from Asmara he had bored us with boasts of how Eritrea's counter-attack would grind the Woyani into the dirt, but the news he'd just heard had evidently shaken his nerve.

'Barentu has fallen,' he said, his voice trembling. 'The army is in retreat. We must leave at once, while the road to Asmara is still open.' In the courtyard people stood around a TV set, watching incredulously as the evening's programme was interrupted by a government spokesman. First in Tigrinya and then in English he made the same solemn announcement: 'Our forces have made a strategic withdrawal from the town of Barentu, in the face of heavy Ethiopian attacks. Approximately half a million people, occupants of the refugee camps plus the populations of the towns of Barentu and Akurdet, are being evacuated to Keren. Massive reinforcements are moving to counter the Ethiopian advance. The soil of our homeland will become the graveyard of the aggressor.'

'There you are, a strategic withdrawal,' I reassured the man. 'Your whole western army is between us and Barentu: we'll be perfectly safe. In the morning we can go as far as Akurdet and find out what's going on. Maybe the hospital there will be busy.'

At dawn we were driving down the mountain pass that led out of Keren towards Akurdet and beyond. The Eritrean positions beside the road were unmanned, and at the sight of the empty emplacements the man's nerve broke entirely. 'We must go back,' he gibbered. 'The Ethiopians are ahead! We'll die!' He began beating against the seat-backs with his fists, frantic with fear. Nothing would convince him that the enemy was at least forty miles further on, and I knew that we would have to turn back; his hysteria would prevent us getting through the checkpoints that lay ahead, for without the translator's help my credentials from the Ministry of Health would be useless. Back in Keren, desperate civilians pounded on the doors of the vehicle, pleading to be taken to safety in Asmara. 'Yes, yes,' our translator shouted. 'Let's go!' We found him a place in another car returning to the capital and sat on the terrace of a café in the central square, to drink coffee and absorb what was happening.

A mood of uncertainty appeared to have taken over the town. Shutters were lowered on shops and restaurants – their owners had fled – and from the gasoline station at the bottom of the hill came a cacophony of hooting as angry drivers fought each other to reach the pumps. Truckloads of soldiers roared through the main street, churning up dust and scattering people who were converging on the bus station in a fruitless search for escape; all transport had been commandeered by the army. It was no longer easy to make calls from

Keren; the public telephones had been disconnected by the exchange to prevent 'spies' sending information to the enemy. At the café I was writing in my journal when a suspicious citizen at the next table pulled the book from my hands. He stabbed his finger at a sketch I'd made the previous day, showing the square in which we sat and the rough mountains rising behind the town.

'Why are you making this picture?' he demanded. 'Why are you showing the Telecommunications Palace?'

I explained that I was a doctor and a friend of his country. I showed him other drawings I'd made; of the Deco interior of a coffee bar, of Asmara's rooftops. These only increased his officious truculence. I took the journal back and stuffed it in my shoulder-bag. 'I have to go now,' I said, before he could effect some sort of crazy citizen's arrest. 'I must return to the hospital.' The man and two of his friends followed me up the street and watched until I turned inside the hospital gate.

The ordered calm of the place had entirely disappeared. The once neat gardens were a mess of rent uniforms and discarded plastic Congos, and trails of blood showed where dripping stretchers had been rushed along the walkways to the treatment areas. Trucks were pulling up in the courtyard, unloading more casualties from the collapse at Barentu. The civilians had been moved from the wards, which were now full of military casualties. Other wounded men were lined up on the corridor floors, awaiting assessment by the triage doctors. Many had multiple injuries. They'd been hit by bullets and grenade fragments in the street-fighting inside the town, and had suffered further wounds when the casualty treatment posts to which they'd been taken were shelled. Some had been hit again when the trucks carrying them across the plains were attacked with cluster-bombs by Ethiopian aircraft, so that casualties wounded three days before also bore new injuries only a few hours old. Most lay still, their eyes staring; some with head-injuries moaned restlessly beneath their bandages. The hospital's senior surgeon seemed relieved to see me. 'Come with me to surgery,' he said. 'There are many to treat.'

✪

My first patient was unloaded onto the operating table. His uniform stank of blood and sweat, and the theatre nurse helped me strip off his rancid shirt. He had been hit twice in the left shoulder; an exit wound below his right nipple showed the path of one bullet. The man breathed with short, grunting coughs, like a wounded ox. I tapped his chest with my fingers. On the left side below his clavicle it resonated like a drum, but lower down the same test produced a dull sound as though striking stone. His X-ray confirmed the findings of a left haemo-pneumothorax: solid white indicated blood filling the lower part of the chest, with a black emptiness above where the lung had deflated. It also showed a bullet lying against the top of his heart, which would have to be left where it was, for we had no facilities for thoracic surgery. I painted iodine onto the left side of his chest below the armpit and felt with my finger-tip for the dip between the fifth and sixth ribs. Taking a syringe of local anaesthetic, I instilled some beneath the skin, then advanced the needle inwards between the ribs, injecting as I went.

The soldier groaned as the needle's tip passed through the pleura – the membrane lining the chest is extremely sensitive – and a swirl of dark blood sucked back into the syringe. With a scalpel I stabbed through skin and muscle, feeling the resistant pleura part under the tip of the blade. A pair of forceps, opened gently, widened the knife-track – the wound bubbled air – and I slid six inches of a plastic chest-drain tube through the hole and stitched it to the skin to prevent it being dislodged. At once the tube gushed blood – a litre, two litres –

as the man gasped and coughed and a cold sweat of agony pearled his face from the pain of pleural irritation. The haemorrhage continued, overflowing the bowl held by the nurse and splashing on my boots. For a moment I felt a wave of nausea – it was a while since I'd seen a lot of blood – and thought I might faint in the theatre's overheated air. But the feeling passed, and with every gasp the man was breathing more easily as the pressure left his chest.

A nurse connected the chest drain to a tube that led down into a bottle on the floor. It was half-filled with water, which acted as a simple one-way valve; with each exhalation, air and blood bubbled out of the submerged end of the tube and the lung started, by increments, to expand. I peeled off my gloves and placed them in a basin so that they could be washed. Writing up my operation notes, I prescribed painkillers and antibiotics for the patient and directed that another X-ray be performed in a couple of days; if this showed that the lung had reinflated, the drain would be removed. Someone mopped the mess from the floor and the anaesthetic nurse prepared her equipment for the next case. Orderlies swung the patient across to a patient trolley to take him back to the ward. He shook my hand. Another man was already being rolled in through the swinging doors, and I helped lift him onto the operating table. He seemed very light, his body hot and dry. On the red flash of the pulse-rate monitor his heart pattered like a bird's.

This fighter had been wounded in the flank, and his rigid belly muscles indicated the probability of peritonitis. A needle, stuck into the side of his chest, drew blood – he also had a haemothorax – and I inserted a chest tube to drain it so that the anaesthetist would be able to inflate the man's lungs properly during surgery. The Eritrean surgeon cleaned the skin and draped the abdomen. Gloved and gowned, I joined him as he opened the belly cavity, revealing dilated bowel and cloudy peritoneal fluid. As we parted the loops of gut there came the sudden barnyard smell of faeces and the crescendo hum of the flies as they swarmed above a punctured piece of colon. It had been traversed by a jagged steel fragment that had ended up embedded in the back wall of the abdomen, right beside the pulsing iliac artery. With forceps the surgeon drew it out and dropped it tinkling into a metal dish. Then we formed a temporary colostomy, bringing the injured loop of large bowel to the surface of the abdominal wall through a separate cut. Once the original surgical incision had been closed and dressed we opened the exposed colon, stitching its everted edges to the skin.

My next case was a young fighter, his cheeks carrying the three vertical scars that showed he was from the Tigré tribe. He had been hit at Barentu three days before, and a blossom of omental membrane stuck out through the wound on the right side of his belly like a yellow-pink rosebud growing from the smooth skin. The man lay on the operating table as though crucified, his outstretched right arm receiving an intravenous drip, the left extended for the blood-pressure cuff. The anaesthetist put the mask over his face and, once he was asleep, injected the drugs that would relax the abdominal muscles to make surgical access easier. These drugs also paralyse respiration, so she slid a tracheal tube down the man's throat and connected it to a rubber bag; without a mechanical ventilator, she would have to squeeze the bag over and over to pump air into the man's lungs for the duration of the operation.

I tied off and excised the piece of omentum that had plugged his wound, then opened the abdomen. Its contents were anointed golden-green by a tide of clear green bile that welled up and rained onto the floor. The source of the leak was marked by a fine coil of blood rising like smoke in the lambent lake, where a shard of shrapnel had nicked the liver and sliced through the gall-bladder, performing a rough cholecystectomy. I washed out his belly – sucking two litres of the fluid from the folds and hollows between the bowel-loops – and sutured the stump of the gall bladder. A couple of small bowel punctures were quickly oversewn, a tube placed below the liver to drain any further ooze of blood, bile or bowel contents, and I closed him up and went in search of the next.

A receiving ward had been set up on the veranda beside the operating rooms. Serious surgical cases were carried there directly from the triage areas and between operations we would pass along the line of stretchers, assessing the casualties and assigning each a place on the surgery list in order of urgency. Some needed immediate attention; some could wait their turn. Occasionally one of the receiving doctors in triage would have a case stretchered directly into the theatre vestibule and dumped at our feet, in the hope that immediate intervention might save a life. These were usually beyond help.

I lost count of the number of abdomens that we opened – perforated by bullets or bearing the ragged lacerations of shrapnel wounds – or of chest tubes inserted to drain blood and allow the re-expansion of collapsed lungs. My awareness narrowed to the infernal heat of the theatres, the stench of shit and pus and the familiar fatigue of endless surgery. The tin roof of the two operating rooms radiated heat; under the glare of the theatre lights my surgical gown was soaked with sweat and I worked light-headed from dehydration until I acclimatized. Flies rode in on the putrescent dressings of the injured and droned around the room, alighting on wounds and on our gloves, and being swatted by the nurses when they landed on our sweat-damp backs. Our facilities were basic. Disposable surgical gloves were washed and resterilized; we would have quickly run out if we'd discarded them after a single use. Instead of pre-packed sutures, needles were re-threaded from a roll of black silk before each stitch. Anaesthesia was not much more advanced than that used during World War One; patients were kept asleep by inhaling halothane or ether through a mask, and the nurse-anaesthetist would hand-ventilate with the red rubber gas-bag throughout each two or three-hour abdominal laparotomy.

Of the three of us doing the surgery, the most experienced was a sixty-year-old, granite-featured Russian with short-cropped, steel-grey hair. His hands had the square competence of a mechanic's, whether holding instruments or pouring a glass of tea as he wrote up his notes after operations. His surgical technique was briskly practical, as was his perspective on the current war; between sucks on the cigarettes he chain-smoked between cases, he recalled his experiences of working as a surgeon on the other side. In the 1980s he'd spent five years at the main hospital in Asmara when it was held by the Derg, operating on Ethiopian battle casualties helicoptered straight from the battlefront. By contrast, most of the patients we were now seeing had suffered several days of agony before reaching proper surgical care; there had been no lightning evacuation of Eritrean wounded.

Perhaps the system had collapsed under the sheer pressure of the tide of wounded, or perhaps its efficiency had rather been mythical. At the forward dressing stations some patients had received intravenous drips and antibiotics, but as a result of the time that had elapsed since being hit, almost all were dehydrated and feverish with peritonitis or sepsis. Even those with limb injuries were sometimes in a worse way than they should have been, because they'd had their wounds neatly stitched by diligent front-line medics. By the time we saw them the wound underneath would be tense and bulging with pus. At least one man I saw had developed gas gangrene, and despite intravenous antibiotics he was dead a few hours later.

Almost all battle wounds are contaminated with soil or

shreds of clothing, and with the dreaded Clostridium bacteria. These organisms proliferate in dead flesh and muscle, producing bubbles of gas in the tissue and powerful toxins that cause bacterial shock and death. Once established, only amputation can prevent its inexorable spread. Only in the second half of the nineteenth century, with the advent of antisepsis, had military surgeons stopped the practice of amputating wounded limbs automatically to prevent the gangrene that was otherwise assumed to be inevitable. But attempts instead to stitch battle injuries – so-called primary closure – also resulted in suppuration and gangrene. In the overflowing casualty centres of World War One there evolved a diametrically opposite policy, called wound excision or debridement. Instead of being closed, all wounds were opened – surgically explored, the extent of the damage defined, and all foreign debris cleaned out along with devitalized tissue – as the first line of treatment, performed as soon as casualties reached the forward surgical units. Later their injuries would be treated by regular re-dressing, allowing them to heal from within outwards – a process known as 'secondary intention' – or sutured once infection-free.

Wound excision worked – though the lesson had to be relearned by military surgeons in each subsequent war – and deaths through gas gangrene became negligible. The subsequent development of antibiotics had not altered its effectiveness; the drugs did not penetrate dead tissue, so all battle injuries still had to be debrided. If there was a lull in the arrival of emergency cases I would take patients to the operating room and open their wounds, cutting away damaged tissue until a raw, bleeding surface was exposed. As I assessed the men's injuries before surgery, I would ask each one if he knew my friend Berhane, lieutenant in the 4th battalion. None did, but they all had something to try to communicate: the incomprehensibility of what they had seen. 'The bombs fell like stones,' said a soldier, waving his bandaged arms like a man drumming. 'Bodies were everywhere, ours and theirs, all mixed together.'

⊕

As soon as the post-operative cases were well enough to be moved they would be transferred back to the care of an army hospital, where the priority facing the military doctors would be to get the wounded fit enough to be returned to combat. Though the soldiers seemed dedicated to their country's survival and eager to take part in its victory, I was pleased that I didn't have the responsibility of sending them back into the mincing machine of the front line; most of my surgical patients would be invalided out of active service for a long enough period of convalescence to keep them out of harm's way. But it also seemed possible that the war might continue for a long time.

New Ethiopian attacks were said to be building on the central front south of Asmara. Foreign embassies were advising their nationals to leave Eritrea, and already the Germans, Dutch and Scandinavians had gone. All scheduled flights into and out of the country were suspended. The BBC repeated US State Department warnings of 'security concerns in the capital' – a euphemism for bombing raids, or an Ethiopian breakthrough – and announced that special flights were underway to evacuate American citizens. Already the Eritrean state media were beginning to talk of another thirty years' Liberation War, with the Eritrean people retreating once again into the fastness of the northern mountains; in which case the men I was treating would find themselves back in the line – with their children and perhaps their grandchildren – before the next cycle of this protracted clash had played itself out.

14

Eritrea

With Ethiopian forces now occupying much of the south-western province, and the Eritrean army withdrawn to defensive positions, the flow of casualties began to ease. I met up with Guy for an evening drink at the rooftop bar of the Keren hotel. The moonlit mountains around the town stood sharp against the sky. Below, troop-trucks and artillery pieces were flowing through the square towards Asmara; the forces here in the west were being stripped of equipment and personnel to meet the threat to the capital on the central front. On the roof-terrace a television set, tuned to the Eritrean channel, was being watched raptly by a score of drinkers. Normal programming had been replaced by exhortative speeches, interspersed with patriotic sequences – the same shots of tribal dancers, gliding camels, Katyusha-rocket salvos and stern-faced fighters running, firing, and leaping out of trenches over and over again – and vox-pops of white-draped matriarchs ripping the microphone from the reporter's hand to denounce the depravity of the aggressor.

The newscaster spoke. The audience clapped. A man next to me translated the claim that a hundred and twenty thousand enemy troops were encircled at Molki, on the road to Mendefera. 'Of course we must kill them all,' said the man. 'Even if one Woyani surrenders he must not be allowed to live.' The broadcast began showcasing examples of self-sacrificial citizenship. The Association of Eritrean

Workers had donated its assets to the National Defence Fund; each member would also contribute thirty per cent of his earnings and already they had collected a hundred and sixty-four grams of gold. The United Shoe Workers had given five hundred grams of gold and six hundred quintals of macaroni. On the international news, fat-faced children of the affluent Eritrean diaspora– in France, Switzerland, Germany and the USA – were forgoing their weekly allowances for the cause; in home-video-quality inserts they strummed guitars and declaimed emetic homilies to 'Mother Eritrea' and 'The Dove of Truth'.

On our return to Asmara I found that the functionaries at the Ministry of Health were waging their own campaign for Truth. I went to ask whether, considering the fierce fighting, it might now be possible to visit the main army hospital at Dekemhare to see the treatment of wounded. I was misinformed, said an official; such a place did not exist. Could I go to a forward treatment station then, or a front-line aid post? No, for there would still be nothing to see; the Eritrean army had suffered no significant casualties. I countered that I had just spent most of the past week operating on those casualties, and that the hundreds of injured I'd seen had been only the overflow with which the Keren military hospital had been unable to cope. On the man's face appeared a look as though I had just uttered some gross indecency.

The old EPLF's ideology had been doctrinaire Marxist, and the current Eritrean government retained an absolutist streak – perhaps less totalitarian than the Addis regime, whose TPLF guerrillas had been adherents of Albanian communism – but few Eritrean citizens seemed to object to being told what to think. If their leaders called on them to walk fifteen miles into the city for a patriotic rally, then that's what they'd do. In Independence Avenue signs were being distributed from a Ministry of Information truck to a crowd, being formed up in ranks for another spontaneous demonstration to 'Condemn the TPLF's Naked Aggression'. Film crews from the Ministry's TV station were standing by to record the march, which would appear as a story on the national news. This was a small prelude to the evening's main event. Ladders stood against the palm trees all along the avenue where work-crews were stringing final decorations for the ninth anniversary of Liberation Day. Friezes of coloured lights – portraying the camel that is Eritrea's symbol, and the national flag – awaited nightfall, when the boulevard would be packed with revellers celebrating the eve of the birthday of Freedom.

The expatriates were seated under the palms at the American bar, discussing the war. It was a significantly smaller crowd than usual; the Irish, British, German, Canadian, Dutch and United States consulates had closed and UN emergency flights had evacuated all non-essential personnel and any other foreigners who chose to go. A short-wave radio stood among the beer bottles, tuned to the BBC: World Service correspondents, in the field with the advancing Ethiopians, were describing tens of thousands of troops moving forward with rocket launchers, helicopter gunships and ground attack aircraft in close support. Addis was claiming that their offensive had not been stopped at Molki but was far beyond it, threatening Mendefera; a town only forty minutes' drive south from Asmara on a good tarmac road. Ethiopia was also reporting victories along the central front at the towns of Tsorena and Zalambessa – key points on the Eritrean defence line – which their forces claimed to have smashed. Alex and the other journalists were fuming; they had again been refused permission to leave the capital.

At dusk we joined the crowds streaming towards the stadium at the end of Independence Avenue and, armed with invitations from Foreign Affairs, were directed through the barriers. A marching band played with bass-drum emphasis as people filled the seats; a tribal dancer swirled a giant flag against the fading sky. We waited at the foot of the stands among the wheelchairs and motorized tricycles of legless veterans, lined up for a front-row view. Officials stopped by to tell Alex that especially good news should be expected in the President's speech. A tinted-window Land Cruiser ghosted up and out stepped the man himself, to chanting, thumping cheers.

He mounted the podium and spoke lilting Tigrinya into the microphone. 'Today, on the Zalambessa front,' a voice translated beside me, 'our brave airforce shot down three MIGs of the Ethiopian aggressor. In the west–' The rest was lost in howls of jubilation. The police girls on the steps clapped frenziedly, mouths wide with delight; the entire crowd was on its feet. Their shouts were cut abruptly, rent by the perfect note of a solo saxophone that wailed out the national anthem. Soldiers grounded the butts of their weapons and came to stiff attention, the first-aiders clapped their white bus-conductor caps to chests that heaved with pride, and boy scouts gave their special salute. The amputees stared straight ahead, eyes glistening, until the last plangent notes had died away.

The whole event was choreographed patriotism. Dancers and fighter-singers paraded before the lights. They were menaced by three cardboard tanks and soundtrack gunfire, until fighter-actors rushed forward and from the turrets abject Woyani waved surrender. Grateful women in tribal dress flung popcorn to the troops and were replaced by a mass gymnastic display of schoolgirls in white stockings and little blue skirts with a yellow glove on one hand and a white one on the other. Then more dancers, more children, more swirling callisthenics. Guy, myself, Alex and the Reuters team slipped away, filled with a keen foreboding; the evening had the poignancy of a last-ever independence celebration, a lost war. The next morning the authorities took us to the central front.

⊕

We were driving across the wide bowl of a valley floor. From beyond the ridge came a clatter of rotors and a sand-coloured helicopter emerged, another in formation just behind it. The Eritrean airforce had two choppers, the Ethiopians many, so statistically these were likely to belong to the enemy. They skimmed overhead, ignoring our vehicle: they were Ours. It is said that there are three possible perspectives to have on a war. You're for it, you are against it, or you're in it. I suppose that third perspective accounted for the way the Eritrean cause had got under my skin, no matter how loopy their logic or arrogant their suppositions. After the independence festivities the previous evening we had been approached in a bar by an articulate, drunken soldier in camouflage fatigues. He'd announced that Eritrea would win this war 'because we have the Truth', and demanded to know of Alex which side he was on.

'I'm a journalist. I'm impartial,' said Alex, though I knew he loved the country passionately.

'You cannot be impartial if you know the Truth,' said the soldier. 'Therefore you are ignorant.' Disdainfully, the man helped himself to Alex's cigarettes. 'It is true, as our President said, that the foreigners they send us are not intellectuals. Instead they are lumpen, fools.'

Despite his contempt, it was difficult not to admire this soldier, his president and the whole stubborn Eritrean people. The country had a population of some three and a half million, confronting sixty million Ethiopians. Addis had invested hugely in new tanks and battle planes, and in the services of staff officers and pilots on cash-secondment from the Russian military. The Eritreans, by contrast, were on their own, and most of their equipment was a generation older, captured in the Liberation War: they had eight computer-aimed T-72 tanks, a tenth of the number possessed by the enemy, and just two high-performance MIG fighters against the enemy's squadrons. The vast Ethiopian forces were mainly conscripts from Ethiopia's tribal minorities – Oromo, Wollo and Ogadeni – while every Eritrean boy and around a third of the girls went straight from school into a year of compulsory military service. From teenager to fifty-year-old reservist, each Eritrean soldier was endowed with an unshakeable conviction in the rightness of their cause. The impartiality I might have started with was now long gone; every wounded man I'd treated had heightened my sense of involvement.

That was one of the reasons why I came to be in that truck watching the two helicopters climb away, their shadows slipping up to meet them as they disappeared over the mountain. I had elected to join the group after Alex and Guy had said that they would be pleased to feel there was a person along who would know what to do if someone got hit, but I wasn't there just to be a doctor. From the time of Berhane's wedding service, while I'd sat in the church as the street outside seethed with news of the Ethiopian offensive, I'd been aware of the front pulling like a vortex, drawing in the energy of the whole country: its people, its material, its thoughts. Men who had been there returned transformed – through wounds and through the horrors that my patients at the Keren Hospital had tried to tell me about – and I wanted to try to comprehend some part of what they had experienced; of what Berhane was probably enduring at that moment somewhere in the western sector.

The road switch-backed up a winding pass; road-gangs, their heads turbaned for the sun, pounded rocks into drop-aways where the lip had crumbled. Along the slopes below us stretched tented camps of refugees, established in the safety of these deep valleys two years before. Sen'afe town lay in the shadow of a great granite outcrop that towered a thousand feet above the flat rooftops. Our guide was a young man from the Foreign Ministry in jeans, dark T-shirt and a slung AK47. He suggested that we eat a meal while our vehicle was taken to the river bank for a camouflaging layer of mud. Troop trucks rumbled by the restaurant door, heading for the battle line; the other diners stepped out into the street to cheer them past. While we waited for our food I joined them outside. The view to the south – the direction that the troops were going – was blocked by a rocky ridge. From beyond it came a rhythmic thudding, like the slamming of a distant, giant door.

Our truck returned, an even ochre shade with only a small patch of windscreen left uncovered for the driver to see through. We climbed inside and began the climb up the steep southward road. Just below the crest of the ridge we pulled off the track behind a bulge of hillside honeycombed with dugouts and shelters. A radio truck draped with netting was backed into a sandbagged recess. A colonel approached us, flanked by some soldiers. The thuds had become louder and more frequent and the Foreign Ministry minder, evidently concerned that our neat Asmara Land Cruiser might get damaged, asked the officer to arrange some army transport. I thought an armoured vehicle would be ideal, but instead we were piled into the open back of a khaki four-wheel-drive pick-up. The Ministry man and the colonel seated themselves in another truck and we set off at speed across the high, treeless plateau. Smoke rose in columns near the road, where Ethiopian jets had made an air-strike against the Eritrean positions. I tried to deflect my face from the searing wind. I felt very exposed.

The trucks roared through Serha – once the Eritrean border town, now deserted – and crossed a trench line of stone and earth that ran away in both directions along the escarpment's edge. The road began a long descent, the driver racing at speed down the die-straight, pitted tarmac. Four miles further we swung into the Ethiopian town of Zalambessa. It had been captured by the Eritreans early in the war and since then all the buildings had been comprehensively destroyed, their pink and green-blue insides open to the sky. The trucks swerved around a tumbled wall, turned into a side-street and stopped.

'Out, out,' shouted the minder, waving his arms. We climbed down into the roadway and the vehicles left at once, rushing up a lane and out of sight.

'Spread out!' yelled the colonel. 'Scatter! Take cover!' And now that the engine-noise was gone we could hear from the facing hillside the 'blam blam . . . blam blam' of artillery fire and see the smoke from the Ethiopian guns. Projectiles screeched overhead, or cooed like owls. They burst among the ruins behind us with a stomach-wrenching slam, hurling fragments that clattered amidst the fallen bricks.

Our entry into Zalambessa had been noted, and the guns were searching for our vehicles where they were hidden amid the ruins. Grey smoke and brown dust sprouted over the nearer buildings. I dived into the wreckage of a roofless house. More shells arrived, dislodging new masonry-falls down the slopes of debris. I peered out through the doorway along the shattered, sunlit street. There was no one in sight, no voices audible, just the ringing echo of the guns and the clang of the explosions. Between each salvo I could hear birds singing in a fractured fruit-tree across the way. Enemy MIGs patrolled overhead, looking for targets; despite knowing that the pilots were too high to see me I cowered in the hollow of the roofless building, transfixed with fear. A shell burst up the street with a sound that rang through the earth. Stones tumbled off the top of the wall. A haze of brick-dust eclipsed the sunlight.

My medical training had taught me to believe in a systematic approach to information – assessment, say, of a patient's clinical history, examination findings, facilities available for treatment – and from these factors to calculate a course of action. I depended on a similar trust in logical inference to deal with each circumstance in which life placed me: to deduce, to understand, to negotiate my way through. But now this faith was revealed to be invalid. It didn't matter which side of the wall I lay, even whether I stood or crouched; the chances of being hit remained incomputable and terrifying, for the next shell could fall anywhere in the grid of rubble that made up the town. I had been frightened often before, but this fear was different; a negation of all my experience. Succumbing to the mortal loneliness which affects everyone under fire, I went scrambling to look for my friends.

I found the man from the Foreign Ministry on a rubble-strewn corner, in conference with the colonel. Some officers of the Eritrean unit holding Zalambessa had joined them in the shadow of the buildings. It seemed that it was time to leave the town – since whatever mysterious purpose that had brought us here had apparently been achieved – and the authorities were discussing where to take us next. The front line at Menekusetyo was proposed. This would require returning to Sen'afe and then a two-hour walk down from the plateau to the trenches; because of the risky access it could be undertaken only after dark. The journalists had emerged from their bolt-holes and were lighting cigarettes. The guns banged on the hillside and things fluted overhead and everyone ducked as though wired to the sound. A bracket of shells – I'd been told they were from 122mm howitzers – exploded in the next row of houses. An object struck the ground at Guy's feet and spun in the dust. It was a fragment of steel, jagged as a part-fused lump of razor-blades, too hot to touch. I picked it up with my bandanna and buried it in my shoulder bag, next to the satchel containing my medical kit.

Our truck came reversing at speed out of the alley where it had been hidden. We leapt aboard, hunching low in the precarious open back of the pick-up. It took off with a jump – the ruins flashed by on either side, receding behind us like film rushing in reverse – and then we were out in the open, running up the long, exposed road. As the slope steepened our speed began to drop. The driver shifted gears, hunting desperately between third and second. Shells exploded on the hillside behind us, unfolding in slow blooms of dust from the rocky fields. Their echoes reached us a moment later – blang blang – and I laughed aloud in relief that we were out of range until the tyres skittered over loose stone and we swerved past a shell-strike on the verge, still smoking; a white scar on the road and the sharp smell of shattered rock. Then we were over the crest and running fast across the level plain.

Back in Sen'afe – the sound of explosions from where we'd come now heavier and sustained, like drum-roll thunder that compressed the air – truckloads of fresh reinforcements were being sped forward to feed the fighting. Cheering towns-people lined the street, throwing cigarettes and fruit up into the men's outstretched hands. A group of schoolgirls, dancing round a drummer, serenaded the packed trucks. The fighters – in variegated camouflage, with lengths of cloth twisted around their brows and trailing down their backs that gave them the wild look of freebooters – appeared eager, elated even, to be going into action. The sun had dropped behind the granite shoulder on the town's edge when the Ministry man appeared, the colonel just behind him. 'We have to go back to Asmara now,' he said. 'The driver's waiting in the Land Cruiser.'

'What about the visit to the trenches?' Alex asked him. 'You told us we were going to Menekusetyo.'

'Get into your vehicle right now,' he ordered flatly. 'This is a directive from the military. We must leave this sector at once.'

On the road we passed another battalion being rushed in convoy to the front. More troops were gathered by the roadside at Adi Keyh, saying farewell to family and climbing onto transport. Children danced through the crowd, holding up torn fragments of an Ethiopian MIG that had been downed by the missile battery on the hill above the town. Our Foreign Affairs Ministry minder still wanted to hurry us away, and Alex concurred; if we got back to Asmara in time he could file before the BBC's deadline and the World Service would at last be able to run a balancing report from the Eritrean side of the war. It was becoming dark, and on the road north we passed through towns and villages where shop lights glowed on bunting stretched across the street. The people, caught up in the mood of Liberation Day, cheered us on as heroes; our mud-smeared vehicle marked us as having come from the front. I kept my head well down.

Alex got his story out that evening – Zalambessa was in Eritrean hands; Ethiopian claims to have captured it were false – and the news was carried by other journalists in their reports. Many combined this hard information with material from a Ministry of Foreign Affairs press release that described enemy attacks utterly crushed on the central front, ' . . . with Ethiopia suffering the biggest losses in a day since it resumed its war of aggression two weeks ago'. Later, at the American Bar, Eritrean friends from various government ministries stopped by to congratulate Alex on what they evidently felt had been a clear propaganda victory for their country in the international information war. He thanked them wryly.

The BBC's early broadcast the next morning carried an

almost mirror-image report from their front-line correspondent with the enemy army: Zalambessa was now in Ethiopian possession, having fallen to an assault the previous night just hours after we'd been there. Eritrean news was claiming that their own forces had withdrawn 'strategically' to 'prepared positions' – which we assumed must be the trench line we'd crossed at Serha on the edge of the plateau – but we soon heard that things were much more serious: Sen'afe had been overrun and its patriotic populace were now in flight northwards, along with those who'd been living in the adjacent refugee camps. The new front line ran somewhere along the wide valley where we'd seen the Eritrean helicopters the morning before. Adi Keyh was in range of Ethiopian shells. It seemed that the cause that I had so recently embraced was heading for defeat.

⊕

Everyone was going to the war. Outside Asmara's sports clubs and colleges, mothers and sisters stood amongst the piled shoulder bags of their seventeen-year-old boys, saying goodbye. Lines of buses rolled through the city on the way to the depots. The newspapers were exploring new heights of rhetoric: 'In May 1998 we came to learn that the pounding and insatiable heart of the Ethiopian Empire, the beast we swore we had tamed, was camouflaged and mute but still sinister and shrill,' declaimed the English language *Eritrea Profile*. 'In an unparalleled act of ingratitude, the TPLF has put a dagger on Eritrea's back. Unfortunately for the attackers, the tip of the dagger broke before it reached the spinal cord. The spinal cord is the will of the Eritrean people. Tempered with adversity and steeled with an iron determination, no one, least of all a Woyani, that despicable [*sic*] of God's creatures, can trifle with Eritrea's will, Eritrea's spinal cord.'

Asmara was a fretful mesh of rumours, obsessive and exhausting. I missed the lucid simplicity of surgical work. We decided to head for Mendefera, the town at which the next Ethiopian assault was being directed. To the west they threatened it along the road they'd captured at the beginning of their offensive; southward, Ethiopian infantry had advanced to below the town of Adi Quala on the escarpment; and their success on the central front put their tanks on a road that approached Mendefera from the east. My Health Ministry credentials would give me access to the town's hospital, but getting through the checkpoints on the road presented a problem. Guy and I set off from Asmara in our beat-up Niva and managed to get through the first barrier beside the airport. Later we got sandwiched in a convoy of ammunition lorries, and I knew we would be turned back at the next roadblock. Then salvation came; in the form of an ambulance, its blue light flashing, skimming down the side of the truck-line. Guy pulled out and stuck close behind it. Alerted by the siren, the checkpoints raised their barriers and waved the other vehicles off the road so that we could pass straight through. In the villages people scattered from our path. We didn't stop until we reached the courtyard of Mendefera hospital.

The doctors here were on standby to evacuate if the town should be attacked. Adi Quala, sixteen miles to the south, was already being cleared, its civilian population joining the relocated occupants of the border refugee camps in a new collection centre on the Asmara road. Mendefera town had that jangled feeling of imminent upset, with streams of trucks pulling soldiers from the front to the west – where the defences seemed to be holding – and moving them eastwards to counter the new threat. Mud-camouflaged buses were running a shuttle, heading south to Adi Quala with troops and returning with displaced townspeople, who were dumped on the roadside at the edge of town. Women walked along the main street with babies on their backs; children dragged bags and baskets filled with the artefacts of their uprooted lives.

In anticipation of being evacuated, the hospital's surgeon – trained in Germany and experienced in trauma work – had been transporting post-operative cases north to Asmara as soon as they were stable enough to be moved. A long, metal-framed tent was set up in the hospital grounds as a dressing station for the less severely wounded: men with gunshot and fragmentation injuries to their limbs, who did not require immediate surgery. Among the assistants there I found Tsehai; called back to active duty as a medic after the Agraa refugee camp, where we'd met her some weeks before, had ceased to exist. I asked her about the fate of each of the people we had met there: the gregarious teacher, the administrator, the old men of the camp militia with their worn weapons. 'Displaced, in a new camp somewhere, I don't know.' Tsehai twisted a length of gauze expertly through a hole in the shoulder of a wincing fighter. 'This is my job now. Someone else will be looking after those people.'

Most of the wounded came from Adi Quala. The town stood on the edge of the escarpment, overlooking the Mereb Valley that formed the border. As long as the town held out it formed a southward salient, splitting the Ethiopian forces trying to close on Mendefera. The enemy were unleashing a storm of shells on Adi Quala and the road behind it. Most of the Eritrean army casualties had not occurred in the front line, but were the result of this plunging barrage; a truck or two of reinforcements hit on the way to Adi Quala could mean twenty dead and as many injured flooding into the Mendefera hospital. The Ethiopian bombardment proved to be the prelude to a great infantry attack, with human waves of soldiers hurling themselves up the slopes of the towering escarpment. The ensuing Eritrean casualties kept me occupied at the hospital for two days. Then Guy and I got to see that front as well.

On the plateau behind Adi Quala the carcasses of donkeys, killed by shell-fire, bloated in the fields. We were taken to Adi Keshi, the pretty village we had seen high on the ridge when we'd been at the Agraa refugee camp before the offensive started. The avenue of ancient trees that had enclosed the glinting roof of the church had been felled to widen the track for tanks. The basalt blocks of the village walls were tumbled by shells, and the black bedrock smashed to glassy flakes where they had struck. Familiar debris – bloodied uniforms, unwound dressings, single sandals – showed that some of the projectiles had hit their targets. Eritrean soldiers were gathered in the euphorbia groves along the edge of the escarpment, keeping watch over the plains below from where the attack had come. The ground around their feet was densely metalled with expended shell-cases from their assault rifles and machine-guns. The wind gusting up the slope brought an unmistakable stench that caught at the back of the throat.

The Ethiopian 23rd and 28th divisions had tried a frontal attack up the face of the ridge. The commander of the sector pointed out some low hills jutting from the plain a couple of miles away, where the enemy were now entrenched. Then he led us down a winding goat-track towards the valley to show us his victory. About three hundred feet below the summit we came across the first body. It lay on its side, arms outstretched as though beseeching a last embrace. A head-shot had spilt black and purple brains over the rocks. The next lay some yards farther on, prone as though dived into the ground; and then a group of three around a broken RPG launcher. The dead were Oromo; members of one of Ethiopia's ethnic groups with a history of revolt against whoever ruled in Addis. The TPLF – as well as mortgaging the coffee crop of the Oromia highlands to pay for jets and tanks – were also using the war to decimate their internal enemies.

Forty corpses were tumbled across the stony terrace. According to the commander, three thousand more lay scattered on the slopes below, where they had been killed as they climbed, but the area was under enemy shell-fire and too dangerous to approach. The men wore camouflage uniforms of similar pattern to the Eritrean soldiers. Their equipment was the same durable Eastern Bloc issue, and on their feet they wore plastic sandals – Congos – just like the victorious fighters on lookout from the ridge above. The earth was littered with trash: bits of paper, letters, wallets, broken biscuits, sections of machine-gun belt. Most of the bodies appeared to have been shot in the head – some had also been burned by blasts, or had the flesh shredded from their chests – but they all still looked like men, and we covered our mouths to try to stem the smell.

⊕

Later, I saw images of those enemy dead – and countless others – endlessly repeated on Eritrean television for the raising of morale. As the war news got worse, the body count grew on the filler programmes that cycled again and again between the official communiqués. Between long-lens shots of running figures obscured by explosions and tracer rounds arcing across shadowed valleys, the camera tracked with lascivious slowness along lines of Ethiopian corpses. Soon each edit sequence was familiar: the upraised, mummified hand, the thigh cradling a face whose features were slipping with decay. In village squares across Eritrea, in bars and restaurants, everyone watched. It seemed inevitable that this parade of carnage must brutalize those who saw it and I wondered if the Eritrean people had forgotten that the dead lay on both sides, for they exclaimed and clapped as the government spokesman reported massive new enemy losses, and described each withdrawal of their own forces as a strategic prelude to eventual victory.

A million civilians were now reported to be on the move, displaced from the central and western borders by the Ethiopian advance. Those who came from the central sector ended up at the refugee centre at Dbarwa. We passed through it one afternoon, on our way back to Asmara for provisions. The displaced were camped among the ruins of an earlier war; old Italian army barracks, bombed by the British in 1941. New slit trenches had been dug in case of Ethiopian air-raids, and running children used them for a game, jumping back and forth across them with deranged hyperactivity. Adults milled about, forming brief groups that mobbed the food sacks and then flung themselves off in pursuit of something else – blankets or a sheet of plastic to keep off the approaching rains – with a restless despair that was transmitted to each batch of new arrivals stepping off buses at the edge of the stony field.

That evening in Asmara we met with the journalists at the usual bar, to catch up on the latest developments before returning the next morning to Mendefera. The Organization of African Unity had arranged peace talks which were due to begin in Algiers, but no one expected the fighting to stop. The news from the fronts obsessed everyone; even the beggars and glad-handers stopping at our table to bum cigarettes could speak of nothing else. Groups of white-helmeted military police patrolled the streets on the lookout for draft-evaders, or deserters that had slipped through the line of 'battle-police' stationed behind the trenches. The Ethiopian government, certain of victory, had announced that it would fight while negotiating and negotiate while fighting. It chose the next morning, at the same moment as the talks were starting, to prove that it meant what it said.

We had swung onto Martyr's Avenue to reach the Mendefera road when above the Niva's rattle came a scream of military jets overhead, and a rolling crackle of explosions. Black smoke rose above the rooftops from the direction of the airport. Drivers stopped their vehicles and stood in the roadway, staring; others began U-turns in every direction, and cyclists weaved crazily between the swerving cars. From somewhere behind us, in the growing traffic jam, ambulance sirens wailed. Motorcycle police were throwing roadblocks across the road ahead, turning back all vehicles. I was sure that the Mendefera road would soon be shut – at the first sign of a reverse, the response of the authorities was to restrict foreigners from leaving the capital – so as Guy drove, I leaned out of the widow, brandishing my stethoscope.

We were directed straight through the barriers. A couple of pick-up trucks roared towards us from the direction of the airforce base. Their windscreens were punched through by bomb fragments and the backs were piled with wounded whose blood streamed down beneath the tailgate. Near the entrance to the military side of the airport – where the column of smoke rose – we were brought to a halt. An officer approached our vehicle. 'We have everything under control in here, doctor,' he said, 'thanks for offering your help.' I expected him to turn us back but he waved the Niva onward towards the Mendefera road. Over his shoulder an Eritrean MIG screamed skywards in almost vertical take-off, its after-burners flaring in pursuit of the raiders. High to the north an arriving cargo-plane – a rare aid flight, dissuaded now from landing by the bomb-attack – was swinging back to return to Khartoum. Our isolation was complete.

Dust hung over the desert as we approached Mendefera, where another Ethiopian air-strike had just missed the nearby radar station. The sustained enemy pressure on three sides of the town induced a claustrophobic closeness. Television sets were on all day, issuing communiqués and denunciatory speeches against Ethiopian imperialism. From the night-time distance came subsonic thuds, felt rather than heard, of bombardment along the eastern road. Shots were fired up the street in a sudden black-out; red flares drifted over the roofs.

At dawn I was woken by a sharp tapping noise and then the sound of glass shattering in the next room. It transpired that the rising sun, bouncing off the hotel's bathroom windows, turned them into mirrors that attracted the big black carrion-crows to peck at their own reflections. A soldier told me that the birds used their powerful beaks to crack through the skulls of the unburied Ethiopian dead.

The hotel stood on the road leading southwards. A stream of exhausted women and children limped along it, discharged by the destructive energy of the battle-zone. The beautiful sister of the hotel-owner fed them tea and bread where they collapsed on the verge; then they shouldered their burdens and walked on. Senior pupils from the Mendefera boarding school were piled into buses and convoyed off for military service through waving crowds. And all the time at the hospital we received new casualties from the front – sometimes a trickle, sometimes a flood – men lying still in the agony of abdominal wounds, or gasping for breath through blood-choked lungs.

✪

Then, about a week later, the Addis government declared that its objectives – recovery of its sovereign territory and the destruction of Eritrea's army as a military threat – had been gained, and the war was over. BBC World Service reporters described the Ethiopian withdrawal from the south-west province: Barentu town was back in Eritrean hands, and they hadn't even had to fight for it. The reaction among Eritreans was initial disbelief, and then a fierce indignation. They claimed that the Ethiopians – who were finally complying with the terms of the Organization of African Unity peace talks – were in reality turning tail and running in the face of an Eritrean counterattack. The Eritrean government went so far as to announce victory, saying that the Ethiopian pull-back was due to the defeats inflicted on them on the central front. We decided to return again to the capital where more objective news might be available.

Asmara churned with the usual contradictory rumours: the Ethiopians were regrouping for a huge assault on Adi Quala; Eritrea was organizing a massive counter-offensive just before the rains, due in a week's time. State television continued its military theatricals – marching columns of fighters silhouetted against sunset skies – but now the images had the poignancy of a lost prowess, and people I spoke to had started to express the unthinkable: that their government of superannuated guerrilla leaders should go. Human and economic wastage in this war – both antagonists were among the world's ten poorest countries – had been enormous. Perhaps a hundred thousand had been killed and wounded on both sides, but the real figure was impossible to assess the Ethiopians didn't seem to bother keeping count, while Eritrean policy was that the families of their dead would not be informed until well after hostilities were over.

There remained the battalions of Eritrean wounded who would need reconstructive surgery and long-term rehabilitation. Armed with a letter from the Ministry of Health, I visited Asmara's main Halibet Hospital. The young medical director – 'he was not even a fighter', someone in the Ministry had sniffed deprecatingly – showed me around his well organized operation. The beds were full of casualties transferred here for complex surgery that had not been available at the sort of district hospitals where I'd been working. I recognized a couple of the men from the wards at Keren and Mendefera. One had been hit in the neck by a bullet that had passed through the jugular vein and carotid artery, creating an abnormal communication – a fistula – between the vessels. This high-pressure bypass hummed audibly when one stood close; a pulsating mass of clot in the wound that might rupture, fatally, at any moment. Another man had had his lower jaw sheared away by shrapnel, leaving his tongue writhing pinkly in a raw pit on the front of his neck. Unable to swallow, he oozed saliva steadily into a wad of dressings.

The demand was now for specialist operating skills, but it was reassuring to be reminded that our basic trauma surgery at the Keren and Mendefera hospitals – under treatment conditions only a step removed from the front line – had been worthwhile. I was drinking with some journalists in the capital's slatternly Diana Bar when I was greeted by a young man whose eyelid drooped in a permanent half-wink. There was a dressing on his forehead. 'Doctor!' he exclaimed, embracing me like a fighter. 'Remember me at Keren hospital? Shot in chest?' After a moment I did: he'd come in with multiple wounds and I had put a thoracic drain between his ribs. He told me he was due for surgery soon to have a shell-splinter removed from his head. I was delighted that he was still alive.

The journalists were delighted too, for a different reason: there was something about this encounter that chimed with their view of the sort of resolution required for a good story. They ordered up another round of fake White Horse whisky to drink the man's health, and he and his comrades pulled up chairs and joined us. For a brief time a rapport bloomed between the media cynics and the Eritrean fighters, as they traded perspectives on this shared war. The conversation echoed around me: suddenly I was back in the heat of the operating room, working forearm-deep in the belly of a wounded man and feeling his blood soak through the surgical gown above the rubber cuff of my glove. It was among the world's wounded that I had found the essence of humanity, without disguise; an exile, I had found a home in the suffering of bodies. The survival of this patient seemed like an extraordinary gift, a validation of my entire existence. Opposite me the young soldier raised his glass, his damaged eyelid twitching.

With the end of the fighting it was now possible to leave Eritrea: an aircraft would be flying out the following morning to Jeddah, from where we'd be able to connect to Cairo and thence to the world. The original reason for my visit to the country – Berhane's wedding – felt an extraordinary age ago; my jumbled recollection of the festivities had become subsumed into the chaos of the war. Earlier that evening I'd called Ariam to ask what news she had heard from her husband. 'None,' she had said. 'Not a single word since he left for the front.' Her voice was perfectly steady, and I remembered that she had been a soldier too. 'Yesterday I moved back to the home of my parents,' said Ariam. 'When Berhane returns we will see about the future.'

⊕

The aircraft gathered speed, flashing by a pair of MIG fighters refuelling beside the runway. Beyond the tail-section of a long-wrecked Russian transport plane we left the ground and climbed steeply, banking eastwards. Hard sunlight washed over the mountain ranges that stepped downwards towards the coast. We had to stay overnight in Cairo, and as I sat the next morning beside the airport hotel's swimming pool, drinking coffee, I was seized by an eviscerating sense of loss. I missed that all-pervading atmosphere of involvement that the war had brought. For a time I'd been so intensely part of it; a member of a society that had reacted like a single organism to each particle of news, each rumour from the front. Now I felt orphaned by war's withdrawal, and oddly lost outside its irreconcilable dichotomy: the ability to bring out the finest in people, and to debase.

Almost every Eritrean I'd come to know – refugees, soldiers, doctors and nurses; the casualties who'd passed through my care; even the unbending officials – were like Berhane and Ariam: people who did what they were asked and never questioned the strategy of their leaders or whether they were being used, or used up, in a worthwhile way. Few asked these things in Eritrea; there was no cynicism. The war was there and it was for all to serve according to their abilities. Only for a tiny minority did that path lie in trying to get away: I'd met just a very few Eritreans who thought enough of life to refuse to be cannon-fodder, and who had asked me for medical advice on ways to avoid the army. And though at times I'd despaired of the national self-righteousness – that impenetrable conviction of rectitude that would brook no discussion – the Eritreans were fine people, and if the war carried on I feared that they would eventually be ground down and degraded, that the clever ones would flee and the best would die.

After my return, it took months to assemble some sort of understanding of what I'd been through there. Missing elements continued to materialize, like the delayed arrival of a shell long after the sound of the gun. One came in the form of a small white envelope with an Asmara postmark, addressed to me in a handwriting I didn't recognize. Ariam's name was on the back. Immediately I expected the worst – why hadn't Berhane written himself? – and put it aside, unable to face the possible burden of bad news. A few days later an airmail letter arrived bearing Berhane's distinctive scrawl, and I opened them both and read that he had just returned to Asmara from Tesenay in the far west, where he and his unit had been in action near the Sudan border following the Barentu retreat. 'I am very well,' he wrote, 'except your longing and missing you. Dear my friend, I realized you have worried about me. You have been having bad news. But the situation is not like that.'

Epilogue

For the present, I work underground. Not in a reeking bunker with shit on the stairs, but in the profound, air-conditioned calm of a medical practice in the centre of London's financial quarter. The suite of consulting rooms lies several levels below the street. The floors above, and the deep green carpets, muffle all sound. Sometimes a human voice leaks through the partition that separates my office from an adjoining one: the voice of a colleague, in consultation or consolation. There is no daylight, only the flat white of neon. There have been times when a shelter like this would have been an ideal treatment area, while artillery thumped above. Instead it has the hush of an isolation ward.

I am acquiring some clinical experience for a qualification in the specialist field of occupational medicine – an interest that began when I saw those first cases of industrial mercury poisoning – and my text-books lie open on my desk while I await the arrival of my next patient. From this subterranean room I can feel, through the surrounding earth, the thud of construction work as foundations are sunk nearby for another banking headquarters. Now and then there is a sudden change in air pressure as the ventilation system kicks on, like the barometric shock-waves of a far off barrage.

I'm accustomed by now to dealing with the victims of war and crisis; swept away by forces they cannot escape, or crushed by the realization of their own helplessness. But in this new conflict – perhaps the strangest I have seen – my patients are under an attack far more insidious: from the very elements of the lives they have constructed for themselves. These brokers, bankers and traders are hard-working, productive individuals trying to survive in a ruthless environment. They are driven relentlessly by the pressure to succeed, and are laid low by the diseases of success: heart attacks, ulcers, anxiety attacks, addiction. When the financial tides go against them they suffer the terrors of failure; the sleep disorders, depression, impotence and alcoholism. In advance or in retreat the threats are endless. Some will eventually crack under the strain.

I am asked to assess a man whose incandescent performance on the futures floor over the past few months has been rewarded with massive bonuses and growing responsibility. Deferred to by all, his eccentric behaviour has been taken as clear evidence of his genius. Sometimes after work he's done crazy things in the stockbrokers' bars, but this has only added to his aura of omnipotence. Recently, though, unease has spread among senior management after clients began to complain about this paragon's increasingly weird business decisions. Challenged, the man attempted to describe the complex, personal formula he used for anticipating market movements. When he revealed the subliminal signals he has been receiving from sell-by dates on soft-drink cans, he was sent to me.

'It's all coded, doctor,' he explains, pacing the room with his overcoat half-shed. 'You just have to listen for the clues. A month ago I was in Paris when I realized that the people there weren't really speaking French. They were talking in code, in a made-up language that I wasn't supposed to understand. I tried to act as though I hadn't noticed, but eventually one of them went too far. As he passed me in the street he said something about my dealing record. That's privileged information: confidential. I demanded to know how he'd got it. There was a lot of shouting and the police came and tried to arrest me. That's how they keep you quiet if you find out what's going on.'

It is not difficult to make a diagnosis – the man is suffering from acute schizophrenia – but I wonder at the sort of environment he works in where no one has apparently found anything odd about his paranoid delusions. I arrange for him to receive psychiatric care. Then I try to explain the situation to his line manager.

'What do you mean, a psychiatrist?' she demands. 'This guy isn't crazy. In fact he's one of the best traders we've got.'

'At the moment he is clinically ill,' I explain. 'He needs treatment. But in all likelihood he'll recover fully. He seems to have been quite well adjusted until he was exposed to levels of stress that he couldn't deal with. It happens to soldiers in combat: some become psychotic, but recover quickly when they are taken out of the front line.'

'What do you mean, "front line"?' she counters. 'He's just a futures trader. No matter how good he was at his job, we can't take him back if he can't work under stress.'

In the 1930s the cutting edge of medical research lay in the hunt for new hormones. The discoverer of insulin received a Nobel prize, as did the scientist who'd first worked out how the thyroid was controlled. All over the world, researchers were subjecting laboratory rats to unpleasant stimuli designed to evoke the secretion and 'capture' of new hormones. Professor Hans Selye, working in Canada, noticed a consistent experimental finding among his rodents. Whatever the type of discomfort – noise, pain, cold or immobilization – the same pathological picture appeared. The lymphatic system, necessary for fighting infection, became shrunken. The adrenal glands enlarged, pumping adrenalin into the circulation, and the stomach shed its protective mucosa and became a mass of raw erosions. The organism could survive for a while, trying to adapt to the new demands it had to face, but if the stress was maintained it would eventually succumb.

'Stress illness' became a subject of strategic importance during the Second World War. In the winter of 1942, doctors among the German forces trapped in Stalingrad reported soldiers dying suddenly, without having been wounded or suffering from any diagnosable illness. A senior army pathologist named Girgensohn was flown specially into the besieged enclave to investigate the phenomenon. With formidable efficiency he managed, under constant shellfire, to perform autopsies on the bodies of fifty men who had died of no obvious cause; precious fuel was used to thaw out the cadavers so that they could be dissected. In half he found signs of starvation. The rest of the deaths he attributed – polishing his theory during the seven years he spent subsequently in a Russian prison camp – to metabolic exhaustion, caused by inexorable physical and psychological pressure.

Now, the existence of stress-related illness – even in circumstances markedly less extreme – is well accepted, though not really any better understood. I meet its casualties, sent by their company personnel departments with obliquely worded letters suggesting that they are no longer functioning according to the needs of the organization. Perhaps these people are off with illness too often. They might be hyperactive, with difficulty in concentrating on their work. Some have developed stomach ulcers. Sometimes the letters carry a suggestion of betrayal: here is an employee, they imply, who has let us down; perhaps you could furnish us with the means to fire him. In such cases the responsibility of the clinician is oddly skewed. The consultation is being carried out for the corporate client, the Company. But compassion, and the contract of care, exist between the doctor and his patient. Issues are sometimes far more complex than 'Human Resources' comprehend.

A man is referred to me because he has been too relaxed. In the afternoons, when the markets enter their closing frenzy, he has been observed sitting at his desk apparently lost in reverie. As I talk to him he seems somnolent, almost drugged. He tells me about a series of incidental symptoms: backache, neck stiffness, headaches. He admits to being tired, but blames it on the hours he spends commuting to and from the office. He cannot accept that the quality of his work has deteriorated, or that the institution to which he has given his commitment is preparing to scrap him. Finally, the man denies drinking too much, his bluff faltering only when faced with the laboratory confirmation of alcoholic liver damage.

How could he have reached this abject stage, after negotiating every step toward success? With financial foresight he'd married a colleague, another high-flyer, and their combined incomes had made it possible to buy a wonderful home; to start a model family. Yet he has found no fulfilment. He hardly sees his young children except when he is exhausted. He is too tired to do any exercise. No longer hungry, he eats great, artery-clogging business lunches. His weight has increased, with his cholesterol level climbing steadily through the danger zone. I remind him of his fitness level at a previous health check just three years before, when – slim and ambitious – he'd played football, jogged and swam. He offers a wry explanation for his plight.

'Success brings guilt,' he explains. 'I never thought it would happen, but when I was promoted out of the shark pool to executive level the money became easier to earn, and there's so much of it. It just flows in, but without the anxiety of earning it. I owe my company for making me what I am, and now I worry that I'm no longer doing the best I can for it. So I try to compensate. Someone has to wine and dine the clients, and I've taken that on. I've tried to become the company's ace corporate entertainer.'

I carry out pre-employment medicals on those at the beginning of the process: the new recruits, ardent to enter the fray. Feeling like a doctor on an army medical board, I examine them – eye tests, urine tests, blood tests, physicals – knowing how these young bodies will thicken with age and the attrition of stress. Those who make it onto the trading floors will live in an environment of uncertainty. Isolated behind a desk, hemmed in by computer screens, communicating in ciphers down a neck-cradled telephone, they will seldom see daylight. Their meals are bolted sandwiches, their reactions geared to the overhead news-screens carrying the market fluctuations. The traders work on commission: the better they perform, the greater the money, prestige and power. But behind every achiever, gnawing at his heels, gallops his nemesis: another climber – sharper, hungrier, more ruthless – waiting to usurp him. And over each corporate structure hangs the scythe of the merger, the faceless disdain of remote chief executives who can cancel a company and dissolve its workforce in a switch of contracts.

One of my patients is undergoing a comprehensive health assessment – a privilege offered by employers to productive staff – that includes a cardiac stress test. In the laboratory, beside banks of recording equipment, he pedals a specialized exercise bike furiously at the wall. Webs of electrocardiograph wires trail from electrodes stuck across his chest and a mouthpiece muzzles him, measuring concentrations of oxygen and carbon dioxide in the air he forces in and out. He blinks sweat from his eyes as he tracks the lines on the cardiac monitor; not so much in concern at his own fitness, but as to how it might compare with that of his colleagues.

'I know that Max Guano from the dealing room was in here earlier,' he pants as he is released from the apparatus.

'How long did he go on the bike? How soon did he reach maximum heart rate?'

Hoping – in a sympathetic way – to invoke a little insight and avoid violating confidentiality, I tell him that his question reminds me of the joke about two walkers faced by a voracious cheetah. One abandons himself to terror. The other hastily dons a pair of running shoes.

'Are you crazy?' screams the first man. 'You can't outrun a cheetah.'

'I don't have to,' says the other. 'I just have to outrun you.'

My patient, though still trying to catch his breath, laughs generously. I can see he's humouring me: someone who has chosen the unfashionable career of making people better, rather than making money. By the standards he uses to judge himself and his colleagues – market performance, affluence, consumption and style – I am a complete loser. Within their system the pressure to win is high. I recall one man's response when, after a similar exercise test, I'd said that I would refer him to a cardiac specialist: his electrocardiograph recording suggested that he might be at risk of a heart attack.

'You don't have to tell my company, do you, doctor?' was his first concern. 'They'll take me off the dealing floor if they know.'

No levity had occurred to me on that occasion: how can one raise a laugh out of someone who finds failure more frightening than death?

But even for those who make it to the top – who are rewarded with success – there is no protection. My patients include company directors, the ones that make the choices that make others sweat. Their decisions affect thousands of people, millions of pounds. Their reach is worldwide: 'global' is the term that they prefer. Some are powerful enough to influence the policies of governments. A percentage of them earn salaries that, with share options and bonuses, exceed the entire annual health budgets of some of the ragged countries in which I've worked. Money has made these men visible, given them form. Their corporate empires are based on the trading of stocks whose value bears no relation to the concrete assets – plant, products and order books – of the companies that issue them. But dealing in abstract wealth, how do these men define themselves? If money begets power, what does phantom money produce? The lavish lifestyle so wondrously acquired can become a source of doubt. The country house, the children's private schools, the ponies and the all-accessories four-wheel-drive vehicle become increasingly unreal. The stage is set for a disaster, a Great Depression.

Sitting opposite me is a powerful man. He is the director of an international investment banking group, and everything – from his firm, close-shaven cheeks to his conservatively stylish suit – indicates success. He makes decisions involving millions; he undoubtedly earns his salary and his limousine. But his assurance has abruptly cracked.

'A ghost?'

He nods, doggedly confused.

'I was asleep at my girlfriend's flat. Something woke me. I opened my eyes and I could see clearly, although it was dark. A figure stood at the foot of the bed, looking at me.' He shakes his head sharply, as though trying to jog the image from his mind. 'I tried to wake my girlfriend but a weight pressed me to the bed, so great that I couldn't move a finger. The duvet felt as if it was made of lead.'

He runs his hands over his pinstriped knees. 'I know that room is pitch dark when the lights are off. I shouldn't have been able to see a thing, but I could see its eyes. I couldn't move, and I knew that I was going to die. It was my death looking at me.'

'It must have been very frightening,' I say, 'but there is a logical explanation. What you've just given me is a classic description of a phenomenon called sleep paralysis, right down to the fear and the inability to move.'

He dismisses my suggestion. 'A psychiatrist tried to tell me that, but he doesn't know what I saw. Neither do you. It was my death.'

He explains that his relationship with his mistress has ended, his marriage has collapsed. He has been to counsellors, to mediums, to crystal healers, even to a Catholic priest. All, he feels, have tried to fashion his experience to fit their own realities.

Outwardly he still resembles the essential City stormer, the sort that sweats through regular sessions with his personal trainer to keep his stomach tight and his cholesterol level manageable. But the experience has forced a great rift in the beliefs that formed him. Now that he has seen the certainty of his death, nothing else has any truth. The great desires – possessions, accolades, power – that once motivated him are withered away. All he can do is what he has always done: to play the global markets. He does so with a nerveless fascination, watching himself make decisions about millions without any longer seeing the point of it. I feel a great compassion for the man. I wonder how much longer he can continue.

I talk about life, about motivation and hope, but to no avail. The man's desolation is as complete as that of a conscript who has stepped on a landmine and now stares endlessly at his stumps. I realize that, tucked away in a sidestreet near the Bank of England, I am seeing the same pathology, the same shock of dislocation that I have encountered on other battlefields. All the figures I have for him – the blood results, the cardiograph, the very wires of his life – are meaningless. He sits beside my desk, distracted, like a man with another appointment to keep.

'There is no rush,' I tell him. 'Some try to avoid their deaths, others go out to find it. All will reach it at the same time.'

'What do you know about it?' he asks, perhaps forgetting my profession. 'What do you know about death?'